The Passion of Montgomery Clift

The publisher gratefully acknowledges the generous
support of the Humanities Endowment Fund of
the University of California Press Foundation. The publisher
gratefully acknowledges the generous contribution
to this book provided by Dartmouth College.

The Passion of Montgomery Clift

Amy Lawrence

UNIVERSITY OF CALIFORNIA PRESS

BERKELEY   LOS ANGELES   LONDON

University of California Press, one of the most distinguished university presses in the United States, enriches
lives around the world by advancing scholarship in the
humanities, social sciences, and natural sciences. Its
activities are supported by the UC Press Foundation
and by philanthropic contributions from individuals
and institutions. For more information, visit
www.ucpress.edu.

University of California Press
Berkeley and Los Angeles, California

University of California Press, Ltd.
London, England

Library of Congress Cataloging-in-Publication Data
Lawrence, Amy.
    The passion of Montgomery Clift / Amy Lawrence.
        p.   cm.
    Includes bibliographical references and index.
    ISBN 978-0-520-26046-7 (cloth : alk. paper)
    ISBN 978-0-520-26047-4 (pbk. : alk. paper)
    1. Clift, Montgomery—Criticism and interpretation.
2. Motion picture actors and actresses—United States—
Public opinion.   3. Motion pictures—Social aspects.
4. Popular culture—United States.   I. Title.
PN2287.C545L39   2010
791.4302'8092—dc22   2009019423

Manufactured in the United States of America

19 18 17 16 15 14 13 12 11 10
10 9 8 7 6 5 4 3 2 1

This book is printed on Cascades Enviro 100, a 100%
post consumer waste, recycled, de-inked fiber. FSC
recycled certified and processed chlorine free. It is acid free,
Ecologo certified, and manufactured by BioGas energy.

CONTENTS

ILLUSTRATIONS

Color plates follow page 150.

ACKNOWLEDGMENTS

I would like to thank everyone who helped in the preparation and completion of this book. Those who read multiple versions and gave me much-needed encouragement and criticism include Terry Lawrence, Al LaValley, Mary Desjardins, Steve Cohan, Michael DeAngelis, Mother Dolores Hart, my editor at the University of California Press, Mary Francis, and the anonymous readers whose contribution is especially appreciated. I would also like to thank the librarians and archivists who provided their invaluable assistance, especially Barbara Hall at the Margaret Herrick Library at the Academy of Motion Picture Arts and Sciences, the staff at the Billy Rose Theatre Collection at the New York Public Library for the Performing Arts, and the staff at the USC Warner Bros. Archive. I would also like to thank my colleagues at Dartmouth College for their moral support and the administration for its financial support.

This book is dedicated to my mother, Nancy J. Lawrence, and to Carrie Kirshman (who should have been in the first one).

FIGURE 1. Montgomery Clift in a 1948 *Life* photo shoot. Bob Landry, Time &
Life Pictures, Getty Images.

Introduction

ALTHOUGH FANS ARE OFTEN said to "worship" or "idolize" stars, Montgomery Clift sparks reactions so extreme that his fans describe him in terms approaching religious ecstasy. Trying to articulate decades later how deeply moved they were when they first encountered the actor in films such as *Red River* (1948), *The Heiress* (1949), *A Place in the Sun* (1951), and *From Here to Eternity* (1953), Clift's fans struggle to express the indescribable. According to one, Clift had a "face of almost impenetrable beauty."[1] For another, "His beauty was so sensual and at the same time so vulnerable it was almost blinding."[2] Clift biographer Patricia Bosworth states, "He was so gorgeous you could hardly look at him."[3] Rapt in their memory of a vision, fans-turned-authors recall their response to the actor's image as if it were a physical force. According to Elizabeth Taylor, the first time she saw Clift, her heart stopped.[4] But beauty alone cannot account for how deeply moved fans were—and are—when contemplating images of Clift. For them, Clift's physical beauty expresses something deeper than mere aesthetic grace. Karl Malden said simply, "He had the face of a saint."[5]

Since his screen debut in 1948, Clift has appealed to a wide range of audiences. Among the disparate groups who have made up Clift's fan base during the past six decades are heterosexual men in the postwar years who admired the stoic soldier of *From Here to Eternity* or the cowboy who stands up to John Wayne in *Red River;* teenage female fans who sighed for the vulnerable, doomed romantic in *A Place in the Sun* or *The Heiress* in the early 1950s; gay men who have redefined Clift's image since the 1970s, identifying the erotic potential of the idealistic young heroes of *The Search* (1948) and *I Confess* (1953), or enjoying the double entendres in *Suddenly, Last Summer* (1959).

Among these various audiences, two competing myths about Montgomery Clift dominate. In the first, he is a rebel icon. A young idealist indifferent to fame and hostile to the ways of Hollywood, a zealot in his unwavering dedication to acting, Clift emerges full-blown as the best actor of his generation only to be cut down by a near-fatal car accident that leaves him a shattered wreck hopelessly addicted to alcohol and painkillers. The second myth presents Clift as the epitome of a gay man persecuted by a homophobic society. Repeatedly cast in his later years as a target of social and professional persecution (in *The Young Lions* [1958], *Judgment at Nuremberg* [1961], *Freud* [1962], pop songs, and multiple biographies), Clift the tragic victim is reconfigured as a specifically gay martyr, his career a commentary on a closeted era.

Each story is part of a larger narrative we might call "paradise lost," a neat division of "before" and "after," with Eden located in the years between 1948 and 1954. The accident in 1956 marks the moment of irreversible loss.[6] Both narratives grant Clift an active role in fashioning the first part of his career—spearheading a new style of acting, resisting the status quo, fighting to maintain his independence and the right to a private life—while confirming F. Scott Fitzgerald's declaration that there are no second acts in American lives.

Despite different audiences' varying investments in formulating Clift's legacy, there is a striking consistency when it comes to the elements cited as essential to Clift's appeal: his beauty (particularly his face), his devotion to acting, and the way he suffered both physically (especially as the result of the accident) and mentally (the pressure he is assumed to have been under because he was gay). Clift's suffering can be fictional (part of his performances) or biographical (what we think we know about the actor's life). Either way, it is central to the various narratives that purport to explain the actor's effect on his fans.

Exceptional beauty, prolonged suffering, and enviable success followed by tragic loss are not unique to Clift's star persona. Other pop-culture figures from the same era occupy similar territory. Clift's costars Marilyn Monroe and Judy Garland have the same iconic status, the same reputation for charisma and self-destruction, the same demons of insecurity and addiction, the same early deaths. All three suffered at the hands of a callous film industry and a voracious and often hostile press. The propensity to canonize stars after their deaths is also not limited to Clift. The 1950s alone offer a long list of the posthumously exalted: James Dean, dead almost as soon as he was famous; Elvis Presley, whose epoch-making success was followed by a long decline and tawdry death; Rock Hudson, forced his entire career to evade exposure as a gay man only to be outed by death—the list goes on. As recent works indicate (*American Monroe* by S. Paige Baty; *James Dean Transfigured* by Claudia Springer; *Elvis Culture: Fans, Faith, and Image* by Erika Doss), the sainted star is a phenomenon produced by fans provoked by unexpected loss.[7] Death changes everything. The scales fall away and suddenly we *see*.

What is unique about Clift is not only that his canonization preceded his martyrdom but also that the aptness of religious discourse in describing the Clift phenomenon was acknowledged from the beginning, and not by fans alone. The studios that promoted him; the directors who cast him; the popular press that built, questioned, and reconstructed his public image; and even the actor himself repeatedly resorted to this specialized vocabulary to describe the effect he produced. As an actor, Clift was well aware of how he was seen; he was also a canny observer of the position stars occupied in American life. After consulting with members of a religious order prior to filming *I Confess,* Clift noted, "Their passion for saints is like ours for movie stars."[8]

A SCENE AND A PHRASE

The idea for this book was sparked by a scene from *I Confess.* It was not the first time I had seen the film. I had been thinking about the ways fans use films in their lives, remembering them in fragments or coming across them by chance, out of chronological order, and regardless of their original context. It occurred to me one day that certain unresolved questions about Clift's character in *I Confess* (such as why he decides to become a priest when he returns from World War II) could be answered in part by other Clift characters (especially Steve in *The Search*). Watching *I Confess* again (a film I never liked), I was impressed by the direction (as usual), struck by Clift's effortless grace (as usual), frustrated by the plot (ditto), when suddenly—out of nowhere—everything changed.

But how to explain that moment—or my own amazement at the sheer audacity of it? Looking back, it was a simple matter: Clift read a line in a way I did not expect, shifting the scene to a different level. Then he did it again—transforming the scene once more, this time with a single word.

That one brief moment made me want to see everything he had ever done, and read (or reread) anything about him I could get my hands on.

I had been a fan of Clift's before. Twice, in fact. When I was a child, *Raintree County* (1957) and *Suddenly, Last Summer* were particular favorites, as I recall. As a young adult, I replaced these with *The Heiress, From Here to Eternity,* the telephone scene in *The Misfits* (1961), and Clift's supporting turn in *Judgment at Nuremberg* (1961). Being a fan is a condition that, once experienced and internalized, can lie dormant for years. This is how most of us function. The active phase of fandom takes energy and time. In active pursuit, a fan has to see all the films, read all the books, and be absorbed by the topic night and day. This phase can end abruptly (seeing *Lonelyhearts* [1959] as a teenager put a sudden end to my desire to see all of Clift's films). But mostly the active phase peters out as existing materials are exhausted.

Revisiting works that have been written about Clift, I was struck with great force by one quotation—Karl Malden's description, cited above, of Clift (his *I Confess* costar) as having "the face of a saint." The more I thought about that phrase, the more complex it became, opening up issues of representation, of the actor as both object and artist, and of the disjunction between ethereal imagery and earthly biography. Although some aspects of it were at odds with my own experience (stressing the beauty of Clift's face at the expense of his acting and his voice—both central to that transformative scene in *I Confess*), Malden's observation was the first of many examples I was to encounter of people resorting to religious metaphors when struggling to describe the effect Clift had on them.

The use of terms such as *adoration* or *awe* in relation to stars is usually dismissed as embarrassing excess, the hyperbole of hysterical fans/fanatics. The very persistence of these terms, however, suggests that religious discourse offers fans a unique way to express an important aspect of their experience. Scholars of star studies and fan culture have long acknowledged the religious strain in fandom. In her book *James Dean Transfigured,* Claudia Springer notes that references to rebel figures like Dean, Clift, and Brando are often "imbued with sentiments held in common with religious devotion; mythification, exaltation, ritual, worship."[9] In *Star Gazing,* Jackie Stacey divides one chapter into sections labeled "Devotion," "Adoration," "Worship," and "Transcendence."[10] Through her correspondence with female fans, Stacey finds that "the feelings of love and adoration towards stars are often represented through the discourse of religious worship," or what she calls "the language of religious love."[11] While Stacey does not attempt to explain the source or function of religious language in fan response, out of loyalty to her correspondents she does not dismiss it either. In *Heavenly Bodies* (the title itself an appropriation, however ironic, of sacred language), Richard Dyer describes how critics in the past have indulged in "distancing, denying, [and] denigrating" the "quality of emotional intensity" they recognize in fans.[12] Stacey, on the other hand, explains that she has included discussions of adoration and worship in her study of fans' identification with stars because these categories "are forms of spectator/star relations which recurred in accounts of Hollywood cinema of this time and they seemed to me to be representing something rarely considered."[13]

As we will see, the use of religious terminology is not something restricted to a specific period or a particular group of fans. A supple and flexible instrument, religious language is easily adapted to cover a range of circumstances. If the first part of Clift's career finds the actor described in beatific terms ("the face of a saint"), the films of the second half have spurred fans to imagine him in a more complicated array of religious configurations. Saint Sebastian haunts *Suddenly, Last Summer;* coworkers on *The Young Lions* compared the actor (unfavorably) to Jesus Christ. In films such as *Judgment at Nuremberg* and *The Misfits,* scenes of physical and mental anguish establish him as an icon of suffering. Short stories, novels, plays, and even songs have been written about Clift as vision, Clift as acolyte, Clift as martyr. These new works in turn feed back into the mythic figure of Montgomery Clift.

While the reaction testified to by fans sounds comparable to what others might call "a religious experience," it is important to bear in mind that these same fans are acutely aware that Clift is an actor playing a role. In fact, Clift's status as an actor is central to the narratives that have been created to explain the star's appeal. What I am arguing is not that fans believe that Clift himself is a saint or even that the characters he plays are saints, but this: that seeing Clift on-screen moves people in ways they describe as deeply positive, producing feelings of intense pleasure and empathy, and a sense of connection that they remember with gratitude, often for the rest of their lives.[14] What fans are searching for when they resort to religious terms is a way to express what otherwise would be inexpressible—the ineffable experience of being moved beyond words. The name "Montgomery Clift" thus collapses into a single term what fans recognize to be multiple layers of representation.

Few fans know all there is to know about their favorite actor, nor do they need to. What each person means by "Montgomery Clift" is different and idiosyncratic. My reading of Clift is not meant to be definitive or superior to the responses of other fans. One of the things I do want to stress, however, is that "Montgomery Clift" is never solely or exclusively the product of fan desire. Understanding Clift's active, conscious participation in his own career as an actor challenges and complicates the myths that would reduce him to victim or elevate him to sainthood. It also allows us to reevaluate the second half of Clift's career—a period too easily jettisoned by proponents of the tragic myth. In the eight films Clift made after the accident, we find some of the actor's best performances (as well as some of his worst).

At the same time, it is important to distinguish the actor's work (consciously performed by an individual in a specific historical and industrial context) from the star's persona, an image in constant flux as it migrates across films, magazine stories, biographies, documentaries, publicity and promotion, and homages from the late 1940s to the present. Star images can be explored from a variety of angles using an array of methodologies. In *Masked Men*, Steve Cohan focuses on the historical reception and production of Clift's image, detailing the way the actor was portrayed in fan magazines of the period.[15] Other works focus on fans (Dyer on gay male responses to Judy Garland, Stacey on British women and classic Hollywood female stars), mixing contemporaneous accounts with the recollections of fans.

My aim is to address the Clift that constantly evolves as fresh elements are added and others drop away. New works—critical, historical, fictional—continue to insert Clift into contexts that could not have been foreseen during the actor's lifetime, while once widely known elements of the actor's life or image are forgotten by the public at large. Even the reading of such seemingly fixed texts as the actor's films changes over time as they are taken up by new audiences, recycled for new media, presented in fragments, or revisited years later by audience members who have themselves changed. However, because Clift's films are the texts that fans, scholars, and critics share as common reference points, this book is structured around them. They will, for the most part, be discussed in chronological order. This approach will help to highlight the differences between the performer's experience (creating work within a specific historical moment) and what audiences have done ever since with works created by, for, and about him.

Beginning with *The Search* and *Red River*, we see the transporting effect the beautiful young actor had on those seeing him for the first time, whether that encounter happened in 1948 or 2008. (Noël Alumit's 2001 novel, *Letters to Montgomery Clift*, illustrates how Clift continues to be discovered by new generations of fans. In the face of accusations of escapism, fetishism, and idolatry, the novel's child-hero demonstrates the positive value of all these features of fandom.) In *The Search* and *Red River,* Clift is a revelation. In the former, he introduces a new style of acting; in the latter, he helps reinvent the western by introducing a new style of masculinity. The somewhat misleading image of Clift as a rebel has its roots in this film, in which Clift's character is simultaneously mutineer and loyalist. *Red River* is also Clift's first flirtation with gay and bisexual imagery.

When Clift's young female fans respond strongly to the actor as a romantic (heterosexual) ideal in his next three films, they are simultaneously hailed and rejected as models of emotional excess as their ecstatic response mimics extremes of religious experience. The climaxes of *The Heiress* (1949), *The Big Lift* (1950), and *A Place in the Sun* (1951) present the "absolute gift" that cinephilia offers—the opportunity for viewer and star to merge in scenes of ecstatic suffering.[16] As an actor, Clift recognizes and attempts to complicate audience reaction to these morally complex characters by developing a radically interiorized acting style.

In Hitchcock's *I Confess* (1953), Clift's introverted acting style becomes a limitation in a story whose main character has already been silenced. Clift plays a priest who cannot clear himself of a murder charge without violating the confidentiality of the confessional. The phrase "the face of a saint" comes full circle as we confront the way acting (language, voice, intelligence, humor, wit) is contrasted directly with mute, static images of the face. This raises two questions: Can "sacred subjects" be represented photographically? and What are the limits (if any) of a close-up of Clift?

As Prewitt in *From Here to Eternity* (1953), Clift plays another character who is stoic in the face of persecution, a rebel who is nevertheless a man of faith adhering to a moral code. While this film cemented Clift's appeal, it came out at a time when questions about the actor's private life were beginning to appear with increasing frequency in fan and scandal magazines. Accounts of Clift's drinking and homosexuality, promulgated in stories told by former friends such as Kevin McCarthy and Truman Capote, establish the precariousness of Clift's position in a scandal-obsessed period. This context makes it all the more intriguing that Clift chose (and was chosen for) the film adaptation of James Jones's best seller, a novel in which homosexuality is the subject of an extensive subplot involving Prewitt and his friend Maggio.

When a disfiguring car accident made Clift's body an object of speculation for fans and critics, biography threatened to override the actor's work as the defining element of his star image. His choices as an actor began to be dismissed as the uncontrollable expressiveness of his injured body. In the four films made immediately after the accident—*Raintree County* (1957), *The Young Lions* (1958), *Lonelyhearts* (1959), and *Wild River* (1960)—Clift's body becomes a signifier of irreversible loss. Attempts to cast him as a young romantic only underscore the chasm between actor and role. The question of Clift's political views arises in relation to the involvement in these films of controversial figures from the McCarthy era, including directors Edward Dmytryk and Elia Kazan. By the end of the decade, in *The Misfits* (1961) and *Judgment at Nuremberg* (1961), Clift had found ways to use his postaccident appearance so that it supported his work as an actor instead of overshadowing it. By comparing Clift in these films with his earlier work, we can see how the actor continued to shape each performance with great care despite increasing difficulties on the set.

Cast as a doctor in *Suddenly, Last Summer* (1959) and *Freud* (1962), Clift no longer has to engage in a heterosexual masquerade, as the issue of each character's sexuality is displaced in favor of his professionalism. Although *Suddenly, Last Summer* has been adopted recently by queer theorists as a key text from the late 1950s, the various readings of the film illuminate the problematic status the actor holds in gay culture. Like Saint Sebastian, Clift is simultaneously desired as an erotic object and rejected as an image of masochism and martyrdom. Accounts of the production of *Freud* establish the real-world consequences Clift faced when working with a homophobic director, as John Huston tried to sabotage the actor by encouraging hostility toward him on the set, rewriting scenes on short notice and publicly blaming Clift for production delays.

The final chapter of this study explores the work Clift did (and did not do) in the last years of his life. The actor's association with religious roles becomes overt as extensive correspondence reveals the efforts made to secure Clift a role in George Stevens's *The Greatest Story Ever Told*. This account also underscores how unemployable the actor had become. On the other hand, Clift's little-known vocal work, especially his performance as Tom in a 1964 audio recording of *The Glass Menagerie,* demonstrates the endurance of his skills as an actor. A comparison of this and his performance of the same role on radio thirteen years earlier provides evidence of how the actor—as an actor—improved with age. In *The Defector* (1966), on the other hand, acting cannot overcome the signs of physical decline.

Since Clift's death, new works continue the debate over how the actor should be seen. Songs by R.E.M. and the Clash take opposing stances, the former ("Monty Got a Raw Deal") worshipping at the feet of the crucified

Clift while the latter ("The Right Profile") excoriates him as a self-loathing has-been. While Kenneth Anger's *Hollywood Babylon* holds up the actor to ridicule by exposing his most personal secrets, *Terminal Station* (the 1983 reconstruction of Vittorio De Sica's *The Indiscretion of an American Wife,* which had been released in a truncated version in 1954) proves yet again Clift's ability to transcend suffering through acting.

Late in Clift's life, during a four-year period of involuntary unemployment, a magazine story paid ritual tribute to the actor. In the opinions of three of his former directors, Clift was "one of the finest actors in the world," "one of the finest, if not the finest actor I ever worked with," and "one of the three or four greatest actors extant."[17] The author attributes the actor's reputation to his legendary work ethic (Clift's "fantastic dedication to the art of acting") and quasi-mystical standards ("only those who give with all their souls win Clift's admiration"). Because it is some years after the accident, however, the article spends equal time elaborating on what it calls his "torment," comparing the actor to an "injured bird," "terrified" and "impossible to comfort."[18] Only Clift's friend, actress-comedienne Nancy Walker, considers it possible that Clift has improved with age. "When I first met him I thought he was the most beautiful man I'd ever seen," Walker states.[19] Observing how much he has changed, she declares, "He is more beautiful now than he ever was. God, isn't it marvelous?"

FIGURE 2. Clift in a photo shoot for the "Stars of Tomorrow" segment in *Motion Picture* (December 1948): 33.

ONE

The Face of a Saint

FROM THE BEGINNING, Montgomery Clift was hailed as exceptional. In December 1948, *Life* magazine featured an earnest Clift on its cover over the title "New Male Movie Stars." While the other candidates for stardom (including Richard Widmark, Ricardo Montalban, Louis Jourdan, Peter Lawford, and Farley Granger) were presented as a group, Clift had already been singled out.[1] "Clift, 28, heads the list of new male movie discoveries," *Life* proclaimed.[2] This pronouncement was widely seconded at the time and would be reiterated for decades. One critic, comparing him with contemporaries Marlon Brando and James Dean fifty years later, asserted that Clift was "the purest, and least mannered of these actors, perhaps the most sensitive, certainly the most poetic. He was also remarkably beautiful."[3] Spencer Tracy put it more bluntly: "He makes most of today's young players look like bums."[4]

One distinct advantage Clift had over the other newcomers in December 1948 was the recent release of his first two films, *The Search* and *Red River*. The first appeared in March, the second in September. As with much of Clift's legend, the question of which film should be considered his first is subject to debate. Although *The Search* was the first to appear in theaters, *Red River* was the first film Clift made, having been produced two years earlier and its release delayed.

Choosing to begin with one film over the other has important consequences, not least raising the question of whether we give precedence to the actor's experience or to that of the viewer. The linear chronology of the actor's life and career is relatively simple; the reception of his work is more complex. How fans think of an actor may vary depending on which film they see first. Once the actor and the audience fall out of sync (after the star's death, for instance), new audiences and new fans can discover the actor through any one of his films, regardless of its original date of release. By situating *The Search* and *Red River* as the main contenders for Clift's "first film," I do not mean to privilege Clift's original fans over those who came later. Each fan's discovery of Clift is fundamentally similar in terms of affect and the process that follows. These two films, however, hold in tension various poles of Clift's persona repeatedly cited by fans: among them his startling beauty, his reputation as an actor, his resistance to the studio-propelled star system, and his ability to convey a sense of effortless naturalism—the impression that here is an ordinary person, unself-consciously being himself. By comparing the degree of influence Clift had on each production, his performances within the films, and the (continuing) reception of each, we can see how both films may serve as exemplars of the initial encounter between actor and fan.

The impact of Clift's performance in *The Search* is unmistakable. Fashion photographer and portraitist Richard Avedon remembered the first time he saw the film: "The minute Monty came on the screen I cried." Trying to account for this reaction, Avedon (himself familiar with the ways beauty can be produced) offered possible reasons—"because he was so realistic and honest and I was deeply touched"—and then settled on acting. "He seems to be creating a new kind of acting—almost documentary in approach. It has the style of reportage."[5] Figures in news reports or documentaries, however, seldom produce this kind of intense, instantaneous effect. If Clift's performance was, by definition, not quite documentary, it nevertheless seemed to be a new kind of acting.

In fact, Clift had a long theatrical past. Hollywood had seen him coming for years. Clift had begun his career as a child model. After one amateur production, he made his professional debut as an actor at the age of fourteen. He entered the theatrical world playing children, then moved on to become a "stage juvenile," the category set aside for young men who could play "the son," a friend of the son, the boy next door, and so on. Considered a potential child star, he was offered the lead in the film *The Adventures of Tom Sawyer* in 1938. He turned it down and continued to work in the theater for another eight years. His time spent onstage would be roughly equal to the span of his film career.

Clift's theatrical roots are frequently misrepresented or misunderstood.

Although he was well established long before he began visiting The Actors Studio in the late 1940s, Clift is more likely to be labeled a Method actor than a former child performer or Broadway juvenile. Despite protestations to the contrary (by Clift as well as his biographers), the identification of Clift as a Method actor lingers for several reasons.[6] The actors associated with the Method all made their film debuts after the end of the war (Clift in 1948, Brando in 1949, Dean in 1955). Their appearance coincided with breakthrough works by playwrights such as Tennessee Williams and Arthur Miller, members of a generation whose style and subject matter announced a new American theater fundamentally different from what had come before. The Method defined itself in opposition to an earlier, supposedly more artificial performance tradition; its proponents were depicted as rebels whose idealism was incompatible with standard Hollywood practice, especially in terms of promotion and publicity. "Explicitly founded in 1947 to inculcate respect for the actor as an artist," The Actors Studio promoted itself (and its variations on Stanislavskian theories of acting and actor training) as the most "serious" branch of American theater, producing focused, proselytizing adherents, members of the vanguard, the leaders of tomorrow.[7]

Unlike Brando and Dean, with whom he is most often compared, Clift synthesized the multiple and radically different approaches to acting that coexisted in the United States in the 1930s and 1940s.[8] On one hand, he was the product of a relatively informal apprenticeship system where the secrets of the trade were handed down from one generation to the next. Within this tradition an actor picked up whatever he could while on the job, learning theater history via anecdotes, and technical training from observation as much as from direct instruction. Between 1935 and 1945, Clift had the opportunity to learn from legends. Over the course of fourteen plays, Clift costarred with actors who had been stars before the turn of the century (Dame May Whitty, Alla Nazimova) and those whose names evoked earlier times (Cornelia Otis Skinner) as well as some of the biggest names in the theater of the day (Tallulah Bankhead, Fredric March). He also worked with performers who would eventually be best known for their film work, including Edmund Gwenn, Sydney Greenstreet, Celeste Holm, Martha Scott, and Kevin McCarthy. Clift appeared in plays written by Moss Hart, Robert Sherwood, Lillian Hellman, Tennessee Williams, and Thornton Wilder (he played George to Martha Scott's Emily in the original production of *Our Town*), and worked with directors Thomas Mitchell, John Cromwell, Elia Kazan, and Jed Harris.

One of the most intriguing influences on Clift stemmed from his work with Alfred Lunt and Lynn Fontanne. Though remembered primarily as a married couple who appeared in drawing-room comedies (Noël Coward's *Design for Living,* in particular), Lunt and Fontanne were recognized in their day as the personification of what might be called a polished realism that included the use of overlapping dialogue and an emphasis on subtext. Subtext came from the actors; it did not exist on the page. Thus, a play's fullest meaning could be established only in performance. To convey the way emotional momentum overwhelms words, the Lunts concentrated on perfecting techniques that could reliably produce such effects. This style of acting is considered "technical" because the actor focuses on the physical performance of a statement or action, rehearsed as rigorously as an acrobatic act in order to ensure the timing.[9] While such external acting supposedly creates predictable effects regardless of the actor's feelings, the result can seem as spontaneous as the more intuitive, allegedly less premeditated style associated with later schools of acting such as the Method.

It was not until the late 1940s (when Clift began dividing his time between New York and Hollywood) that he started attending Bobby Lewis's classes at The Actors Studio. Nevertheless, according to Patricia Bosworth, it was Lunt to whom Clift "invariably" gave "credit for his development as an actor. 'Alfred taught me how to select,'" Clift reported. "'Acting is an accumulation of subtle details. And the details of Alfred Lunt's performances were like the observations of a great novelist—like Samuel Butler or Marcel Proust.'"[10] Despite this background, Clift is still so routinely linked to Method acting that the idea of Clift studying Alfred Lunt's technique is as disconcerting as it would be to hear that Robert De Niro learned everything he knew from watching David Niven. Although the two kinds of training proposed different routes for the actor to pursue, both systems of preparation led to the same end. In Clift's case, technique was perfected to such an extent that it could pass for none at all.

The careful application of makeup, for instance, was one of the skills Clift had mastered to the point that it was nearly undetectable even in the ultranaturalist context of a neorealist film. Theatrical-style makeup had long been thought inappropriate for cinema's medium shots and close-ups, but its use was debated in the theater as well. In the American naturalist acting style of the thirties, makeup could be controversial, the matter weighed as if it were a moral issue. For some, makeup was a kind of cheating. A *real* actor, it was felt, could produce external effects from the intensity of his internal beliefs. In his star-making role as a killer on death row in the play *The Longest Mile* at the end of the twenties, Spencer Tracy is said to have "acted" unshaven, having chosen to forgo any assistance from spirit gum, pencils, or creams. (Tracy, long held up as a model of American naturalist acting, was also bothered by the feminine connotations of wearing makeup. He felt that no profession in which you painted your face could be truly manly.) An actor who worked with Clift in the theater, however, recounted that "Monty always looked . . . so natural I thought maybe he didn't use any makeup. One night before a performance he let me watch him make up. It was extraordinary. It took a good half hour. . . . He worked like a painter. He explained as he went along why he was highlighting and shadowing. He had learned it all from Alfred Lunt. I tried it later but it didn't look the same on me."[11]

For contemporary audiences, Clift's craftsmanship was invisible. Director Fred Zinnemann frequently told the story of a viewer coming up to him after a screening of *The Search* and asking, "Who's that soldier you got to act?"[12] For an actor with more than a dozen years of theatrical experience to be mistaken for a nonprofessional, a "real person," would have been the ultimate compliment in both Method and neorealist terms. Turning to the film itself, we can see the results of Clift's efforts to appear transparent and natural.

THE SEARCH

In *The Search,* Clift plays "Steve" Stevenson, an American soldier in Germany after World War II, waiting to be shipped home. One day he finds a child living wild in the rubble-filled streets. He brings the boy home and gives him basic medical treatment, food, and shelter. As they become friends, he begins teaching the boy English and promises to adopt him and take him to America, not knowing that the boy's mother is alive and searching for him.

In describing *The Search* as a Clift film, I am already distorting it through a lens of fandom. The film as a whole is the story of the boy (Ivan Jandl). Clift does not appear until more than half an hour into the film. The first part of *The Search* is a semidocumentary about displaced persons and the bureaucracies set in place after the war to reunite families. Wholeheartedly embracing neorealist aesthetics, the film was shot on location in Europe and focuses on a child (as did many key neorealist films, such as *Shoeshine, Bicycle Thieves, Germany Year Zero,* sections of *Paisan,* and *Rome, Open City*). In this case, the boy has been separated from his mother and is virtually mute, cut off from memories and language. Brought to a relocation center with other children, he escapes and hides in the ruins of a bombed-out city. Unfortunately, this section of the film is off-putting because of its dated style and the simplification of political issues that, to this day, refuse to be simplified. (Once rescued, the war orphans are sent to sunny British Palestine, where a bright future awaits.) Fortunately, the rest of the film abandons geopolitics for a finely detailed, small-scale domestic melodrama and succeeds beautifully.

When he first spots the boy, wearing rags and with bloody bare feet, Steve is slouching in his Jeep, one knee up past his elbow as he munches on a sandwich. Realizing he is being watched, he turns directly to the boy and offers him the sandwich, chewing as he talks. The boy hesitates to come forward, so Steve turns away. He lays the sandwich on the ground and drives away, only to make a U-turn and come back. The boy runs, but Steve jumps out of his Jeep before it has even stopped. Chasing the boy, Clift flails his arms and makes a show of breathing heavily. He finally catches the boy and sits him down in the Jeep, Steve's neat uniform now disheveled. When they arrive at Steve's quarters, Steve carries the boy, struggling and kicking, under one arm, then passes him around his back as he takes him indoors and kicks the door shut behind him. Having managed to secure the boy in the living room, Steve and his friend Fischer (Wendell Corey) attend to the boy's blistered feet. At one point, Steve tries to take a hard line, but when Fischer spots the number tattooed on the boy's arm, they realize he has been in Auschwitz and their manner softens.

The lack of a shared language and the fact that Clift/Steve is interacting with a child allow for a great deal of pantomime. Trying to convince the boy that he is free to come and go, Steve says, "Look," holding his finger up for attention. "See this door? It's not locked. See?" He opens and closes it, walking in and out. "Look. So long," he waves, going out. Returning, he says, "See?" In the next scene, sitting at a table and trying to teach the boy to say "no," Steve points his finger up, shakes his head slowly, and raises his voice. Enunciating carefully, he leans forward and asks, "Would you be good enough to say the word *no?*" He pauses and leans back. "Just no. No. No, no, no, no!" he repeats loudly, leaning forward and making a synchronized chopping movement with his hand. He pauses and raises his eyebrows and says "No?" with a rising inflection. "Okay, forget it." He walks away from the table, talking to himself in three short, almost mumbled sentences: "Thank you for your patience. You've been most—kind. I think I'll get drunk." Doing a take after taking a sip (hiking up his shoulders and sticking his tongue out to suggest the alcohol's kick), he puts the glass down

FIGURE 3. Clift (Steve) and Wendell Corey (Fischer) in *The Search,* 1948.

and says to the boy, "Here, have a drink," and collapses in a chair, his legs out stiff in front of him. The boy sniffs the glass and says, "No." Clift sits bolt upright in his chair in a take that could be seen from the third balcony. Asking again and receiving the same answer, he expresses his delight, patting the boy on the shoulder, picking him up in the air, setting him down, clapping his hands, and spreading his arms out wide.

The quick alternation of mumbled "private" speech and broad physical playing creates a sense of range within the scene and establishes Clift's ability to play comedy. The next scene, when Steve and Fischer receive a letter from the relocation office telling them that the boy's mother is presumed dead, gives the first glimpse of Clift's subtler dramatic style. Reading the letter aloud to Fischer but keeping his voice quiet because the boy is in the room, he reads, "All the other mothers are dead." Brief pause. "They were gassed." As he reads this line, he lowers the letter to his waist and says it without looking at the paper. The boy, now called Jim, calls out to Steve from offscreen, and Clift quietly says, "Yeah," and crosses in front of Fischer, his hands in his pockets. The camera follows to create a two-shot of him and the boy. He leans over Jim, one hand resting on the table, the other on the back of the boy's chair. He pats him on the head and calls him "lad." With his head bent down and most of his face in shadow, Clift's posture and soft voice communicate a newfound tenderness. Called back by Fischer, Steve decides to take the boy to America, raising his voice when his friend points out the difficulties he will encounter. Going back to the boy at the table, Steve ignores Fischer until he leaves, then pats Jim on the cheek and says, very quietly, "Take it easy, kid. It's okay." Because his face is turned away from the camera when he says this and it is said so quietly, Clift implies that Steve is calming himself as much as the boy, who does not seem agitated.

The increasing closeness of the pair is communicated mostly through physical proximity and touching. When Fischer's family comes to visit, Steve gets Jim ready for dinner, bringing him new shoes and draping a tie around his neck. As Jim, preoccupied by the concept of "mother," stands next to Steve, Steve helps him on with his jacket, briefly resting a hand on Jim's shoulder. Stopping on the stair landing, Steve buttons up Jim's coat and then guides him into the dining room, this time with both hands proudly and protectively on the boy's shoulders. When Jim runs away to look for his mother, he and Steve are reunited on a hillside. Starting to run, Jim hesitates, then rushes to Steve and cries in his arms. Clift plays the scene smiling, with his head bent well forward over the boy's, mussing Jim's hair. "Don't say anything. I know."

Sitting by the river, Steve has to tell Jim that his mother is dead. Clift is coiled up, his arms around his knees and his back to the camera so that we can see only the top half of his face when he looks toward the boy on his right. With an unusual lightness, smiling at times, and with an occasional embarrassed laugh, he says, "Jimmy . . . I've gotta tell you—huh. It's best that you know. . . . Your mother is dead."

> JIM: Then I can't find my mother ever?
> STEVE: No.
> JIM: And my mother won't ever come back?
> STEVE: No, dear, she won't.

The first word of Clift's last line here, "No," is said in a low voice, shortly and without embellishment. The effect is firm and unequivocal. The rest of the line is more interesting. When he says, "she won't," Clift's voice wavers on *won't*, as if he is about to say it with a rising inflection, then stops. This creates the impression that he might be about to ask a question or is preparing for a question. The word *dear* ("No, dear, she won't") raises issues that I will address later.

When the first biographies of Clift were published in the late 1970s, the authors went to great pains to give Clift credit for the success of this scene, praising his skill in working with children. Patricia Bosworth writes at length about Clift sitting with young Ivan Jandl, going over their lines and establishing a comfortable rapport. ("Monty always had a special affinity for children, and he worked with Ivan slowly, patiently cueing on his lines until the cameras began to roll.")[13] A former child actor himself (or at least a young adolescent), Clift was secure enough in his technique not to be intimidated by the unpredictability of young costars and welcomed the chance to ad-lib as the occasion warranted. Bosworth and Robert La-Guardia both stress a second point—that Clift rewrote this scene extensively to create the illusion of spontaneity and ad-libbing. They also mention the arguments this provoked with the producer (the father of one of the screenwriters) and the ironic fact that the film was later awarded an Oscar for best screenplay.[14]

By inserting behind-the-scenes accounts about the production into their readings of the scene, Clift's biographers position Clift as a fighter, a serious actor with high standards, willing to do whatever it takes to make a film better. While later stories about Clift's actions on the set portray his working process as problematic (e.g., an insular, isolated star holding up production because of his insecurities and ill health), descriptions of the making of *The Search*—and its ultimate success as a film—validate Clift on this occasion. Above all, these stories reiterate that Clift's performance is not "natural" but the product of hard work—creative, conscious labor.[15]

Clift's work on *The Search* began well before he appeared in front of the camera. Developing his ideas about the character he was to play, the actor wrote extensively to director Fred Zinnemann. In a letter dated June 25, 1947 (a month and a half before his starting date of August 10), Clift discusses how he sees the part, establishing at the outset his attitude toward playing saints.

> Now—the film [meaning the script]: I like it very much. Very much indeed. I look forward to what I shall read next.
> The part: I'm perfectly happy with its size. A part built up might tend to deviate from the truth and then how should I play it? My being starred does not necessitate a bigger part in my mind. It is certainly the story of the mother and boy and I think it would be dangerous for your sakes to alter this.

There is one place in the film that does disturb me. . . . After Stevenson makes up his mind to stay and help the boy. I get the feeling of a kind of outward nobility. Somehow this spontaneous nobility is not very interesting. If one goes ahead and does whatever presents itself from day to day—this can be noble but only in retrospect. It's the "volunteering" to stay and help that I object to in Stevenson. . . .

He should long to get home, but—he's brought this kid on himself (he obviously likes him) and when his friend points out he's the only one who can help the boy—he stays—protesting—but still he stays.

Does this give some idea of what I mean? I don't want Steve to anticipate the help he is going to be to the boy—. If he does what he should do *reluctantly*—it widens the scope of the part—allows whole avenues of humour. This would be a great delight to act. If Stevenson teaches the boy English because he should—then finds himself intrigued against his will (oh, ther *[sic]* personal vanity of a good pupil!) well—this would be a fine relationship.

Mostly the end result would be to get away from doing "good" things for "good" reasons—which in a man is not very intriguing.[16]

This lively letter not only gives a glimpse of how engaged and enthusiastic Clift was, it demonstrates the conscientiousness with which he approached his work. Consider his detailed reasoning in favor of complexity over goodness. Bosworth quotes a later interview in which Clift recalls, "As the script originally was written, I was a boy scout type spreading nobility and virtue all over the lot."[17] According to Clift, saintliness is not interesting; as an actor, he wants something more. Resisting simplistic depictions of nobility, Clift conceives Stevenson's "goodness" as being, above all, pragmatic. The short-term help he offers the boy (food, medical care) develops into longer-term commitments of shelter, clothing, and education, which in turn grow into concern for the child's emotional well-being and ultimately the soldier's own attachment to the boy. Stevenson's compassion deepens and grows, but it is not motivated by abstract principles.

Clift's biographers also stress the self-effacing character of Clift's interventions. Contradicting the stereotype of actors as egotistical narcissists, Clift argues *against* increasing the size of the part (though he does want star billing). In rewriting his scenes in *The Search,* Clift shortened or eliminated much of his own dialogue. Bosworth recounts that when Clift proudly showed his heavily revised version of the script to his brother Brooks, what struck Brooks most was the brevity of the speeches.[18] Other scripts annotated by Clift show the same willingness to cut his own lines.

Clift might have been admirably lacking in vanity when it came to his character, but as a professional fully aware of his commercial value, he did not hesitate to press for the best accommodations, star billing, and pay. An active participant in his own career, Clift not only collaborated on artistic matters such as the interpretation of the character and rewriting the script; on this occasion he also negotiated his salary. In a series of wires to Zinnemann and the film's production company, Clift balances his artistic goals, financial considerations, and determination to appear in an independent, non-Hollywood film. First, he asks for $50,000 for three months' work. The production company says no. A counteroffer suggests cutting the schedule in half, to only four to five weeks' work. Clift agrees to cut his salary in half and offers to work for seven weeks, but adds a request for 5 percent of the world gross and approval of the treatment.[19] The company agrees to 5 percent of the gross, but offers only $15,000 in salary in return for a five-week schedule.[20] While the salary is dramatically less than Clift asked for, it is still the most the company has agreed to. The producers withhold approval of the treatment and mention repeatedly that because the film is in a neorealist vein there should be no star billing. Finally director Zinnemann intervenes, agreeing to Clift's request for $25,000, setting the schedule at six weeks, and declaring that star billing will be acceptable.

In *The Search* Clift establishes his image as a natural. Sui generis, transparent, Montgomery Clift is a figure of endless promise, seemingly inseparable in manner, tone, and moral character from the character he plays. It is no surprise, then, that *The Search* sparked many fans' love for the star. Writer Christopher Isherwood recorded in his journal in 1948 that he had just "seen and fallen for Montgomery Clift in *The Search*."[21] In this film more than in any other, seeing Clift and loving Clift are the same thing.

CINEPHILIA

Film theorists have long tried to define the intense emotional, intellectual, and physical pleasure people have experienced while watching films. But what is this experience? Where do we locate the spark that ignites such passion for imaginary figures engaged in fictional activities? How is it that a spectator can be moved with such immediacy upon encountering a multilayered representation such as an image of an actor acting? Sometimes the source of a viewer's passion is said to be the film itself, giving rise to the most minute textual analysis; at other times actors whose careers span many films appear to be the charismatic provocateurs of heart-stopping fascination. Some fan studies have argued that viewers alone can tell us why they feel so passionately at certain moments in certain films. Yet when asked, the viewer is often at a loss when it comes to identifying the parameters of his or her own experience. How to describe this pleasure, this sense of being deeply moved, when indescribability seems to be one of its central effects?[22]

In a 1921 essay French critic Jean Epstein gestures toward this phenomenon, labeling as *photogénie* the unique genius, spirit, or essence of the moving photographic image that excites his keenest response. But it is hard to pin down what it is about the quality of the cinematic moment that makes it *photogénie* and that produces such a powerful effect on the spectator. "One runs into a brick wall trying to define it," Epstein declares, figuratively throwing up his hands.[23] For Epstein, true *photogénie* is "something that escape[s] rationalised, critical theoretical discourse."[24]

Decades later, Paul Willemen reopened the question of *photogénie* in an attempt to define cinephilia.[25] The latter—a passionate, almost addictive love of cinema—may be said to develop as a consequence of an encounter with *photogénie,* but such a formulation merely grounds one vaguely defined term in another. Both cinephilia and *photogénie* are terms that attempt to account for the sense of something ineffable in the encounter with cinema even as they evince the same resistance to definition. Repeatedly, Willemen finds that these terms have been defined negatively. Like *photogénie,* cinephilia as a term "doesn't do anything other than designate something which resists, which escapes existing networks of critical discourse and theoretical frameworks."[26]

"Something" that escapes, "something" that resists, "something, some element" that evokes what it is not: Epstein and Willemen are each convinced that there is a precise, unmistakable "something" that provokes the filmgoer's most fervent response. But the very use of the word *something* proclaims their failure to name it. Willemen refuses to accept that that something cannot be more accurately defined: "The point is not that photogénie is indefinable: it is rather that the impressionists [who coined the term] decreed it to be so and then deployed an elaborate metaphoric discourse full of lyrical digressions and highly charged literary imagery in order to trace obsessively the contours of the absence which that discourse is designed to designate and contain. This is why every attempted definition must be accompanied by a denial of its adequacy."[27]

Willemen relocates the phenomenon. Instead of being a quality the viewer discovers "in" the film, *photogénie,* like cinephilia, is a relation between viewer and screen. Because the audience member actively invests a text with his or her own imagination, points of reference, and desires, the most intense pleasures of cinema take place not on the screen but in the mind of the viewer. "Photogénie, then, refers to the unspeakable within the relation of looking and operates through the activation of a fantasy in the viewer which he or she refuses to verbalise."[28]

Willemen's palpable frustration is fueled by his suspicion that the true definition of photogénie is being purposely hidden. While he does not question that it is possible to describe the "unspeakable in the relation of looking," the viewer's willful refusal suggests that to do so might be simply too embarrassing. Once fantasy is activated in the viewer, touching on his or her private desires, it would be too revealing to say what that fantasy was. But the viewer is not the only one who cannot or will not say.

Willemen himself does not provide a description of the unnamable something that underlies cinephilia. At times it seems as if he is afraid of what he might find—that "the unspeakable within the relation of looking" may be in fact something far worse than lyrical digression or metaphor. If the true meaning of photogénie lies somewhere along the trail of denial and evasion, it might be helpful to examine what Willemen himself finds unspeakable, the potential meanings he raises only to deny.

A possible key to defining photogénie, the magical foundation of cinephilia, is raised and discarded in a single sentence: "As a cinephile," Willemen writes, "I could readily fetishise that it's all about actors."[29] This backhanded dismissal acknowledges the attraction actors have held for cinephiles without fully explaining why this attraction would be inadequate as a source of their cinephilia. While it will be important later to discuss fetishism as an issue in itself, the question here is simply: Why not? What would be wrong with a love of cinema being all about actors?

Time and again Willemen dodges the appeal of looking at actors on film. When he describes Epstein's essays on cinema as "the first major attempt to theorise a relationship to the screen," he rhetorically displaces a central facet of photogénie that Epstein has no problem identifying by name. In fact, the original theorists of photogénie are much more precise in describing what moves them than Willemen gives them credit for. "I will never find the way to say how much I love American close-ups," Epstein writes. "Point blank. A head suddenly appears on screen and drama, now face to face, seems to address me personally and swells with an extraordinary intensity. I am hypnotized." Close-ups are essential: "The close-up, the keystone of the cinema, is the maximum expression of this photogénie of movement."[30]

But it is not the close-up as a technique that moves Epstein so profoundly. In the first place, *photogénie* is never still. At one point, Epstein defines *photogénie* as "cadenced movement."[31] Therefore, the profound effect of *photogénie* cannot be reproduced by looking at a publicity still or a poster. Second, the content of the film close-up is crucial. As Willemen acknowledges, Epstein found the "something that escaped rationalized, critical theoretical discourse" "in faces as they were reproduced on the screen." (*Photogénie* remained unpredictable, though, being found in "some faces, not others.")[32] For Epstein it is personified by Sessue Hayakawa, "the tranced tragedian," who "sweeps the scenario aside. . . . He crosses a room quite naturally, his torso held at a slight angle. He hands his gloves to a servant. Opens a door. Then, having gone out, closes it. Photogénie, pure photogénie."[33]

Epstein may stop short of defining *photogénie,* but he is fluency itself when describing a shot of an actor. Confronted with a close-up, Epstein is so close to the face he is lost in it—its suddenness, its personal nature, the unexpected intensity and intimacy produced by sheer size, along with the dizzying loss of perspective and critical distance. The actor's face is all-encompassing. It blocks out everything—genre, plot, narrative structure—and becomes the drama. "For ten seconds, my whole mind gravitates round a smile."[34] "The tragedy is anatomical. The décor of the fifth act is this corner of a cheek torn by a smile. . . . 1000 meters of intrigue converge in a muscular denouement [that] satisfies me more than the rest of the film. Muscular preambles ripple beneath the skin. Shadows shift, tremble, hesitate. . . . A breeze of emotion underlines the mouth with clouds. . . . Seismic shocks begin. Capillary wrinkles try to split the fault. . . . The lip is laced with tics like a theater curtain. Everything is movement, imbalance, crisis. Crack. The mouth gives way, like a ripe fruit splitting open."[35] The effect on the viewer can be described only in cosmic terms and mixed metaphors. "The eye sees nothing but a face like a great sun," Epstein exults. "Hayakawa aims his incandescent mask like a revolver."[36] From this kind of adoration it is but a step to religious awe.

It was French film theorists in the twenties who originally postulated that "the camera . . . turned certain actors into 'astral bodies'" (what we call stars); the film actor—a figure made of light—became literally "heavenly" in both the astronomical and the religious meanings.[37] Among this group, it is Epstein who reaches the pinnacle of rapture in his encounter with the face of a star. Only religious language will do: "If I stretch out my arm I touch you. . . . Never before has a face turned to mine in that way. Ever closer it presses against me, and I follow it face to face. [There isn't even] air between us."[38] "I consume it," Epstein proclaims. "It is in me like a sacrament."[39]

This is the kind of language that scares people. Popular culture is suddenly exposed as a cunning secular disguise for Religion, that notorious opiate of the masses, seducing weak-minded fans who are unable or unwilling to break the chains of their voluntary stupefaction in Plato's cave.

Fans of Clift may find themselves on occasion rapt in contemplation of his beauty, yet they are also keenly aware of the fact that he is acting. Instead of breaking the spell, however, this awareness of an actor's performance can itself trigger the fan's awestruck response. According to Mary Ann Doane, "at its most basic," cinephilia "is a love that is attached to the detail, the moment, the trace, the gesture." This experience is "most readily localizable in relation to acting," with "a gesture, a body position, a facial expression, or an uncontrolled utterance that somehow escapes scripting."[40]

The most telling exchange in Willemen's essay "Cinephilia" (which is constructed as a dialogue) occurs when Noel King, Willemen's interlocutor, seizes on a detail and in the process not only reveals his own cinephilia but also situates it firmly in relation to stars. When Willemen mentions Brando's use of a glove as a prop in *On the Waterfront* (1954), King jumps in with what is by far his longest interjection in the article. Every bit as excited about Brando as Epstein was about Hayakawa, King demonstrates the need to own each moment through detailed description: he describes the actor's gestures, compares them to the script, cites comments made afterward by the actor and the director, compares this "ad-libbed" use of a prop with other moments in the film when ad-libbing could have happened but didn't (thus reinforcing the uniqueness of the earlier example). It is as if he can't stop talking. It is a classic fan moment.

Yet despite assiduous attempts by theorists, scholars, and academics to distance themselves from such irrational, emotional excess, the use of religious language persists. Consider Epstein: "The close-up is the soul of cinema."[41] "The close-up transfigures man."[42] "The spirit is visible" on-screen, a fact that endows actors with an "almost godlike importance."[43] Epstein quotes a contemporary ("M. Jean Choux, the film critic of the newspaper *La Suisse*") to underscore this point. "How close-ups deify[!] Oh, these faces of men and women displayed so harshly on screen. . . . An extraordinary import is emitted from these close-ups. In them, the soul is separated in the same way one separates radium." Choux even envisions members of the film audience as if they were pilgrims at Lourdes: "a thousand immobile heads whose gazes are aimed at and monopolized and haunted by a single enormous face."[44]

Willemen dubs the adoption of religious terms to define cinema's effect "the discourse of revelation."[45] The word King uses is *epiphany:* a transcendent moment "in which something (a gesture, a voice), some element within the representational system, evokes a sense of its own 'beyond.'"[46] Criticism itself comes to serve as proof and by-product of an epiphanic event. "It is the function of the cinephile to identify an epiphanic moment,"[47] "to find formulations to convey something about the intensity of that spark"[48] — though what constitutes such a moment (besides its effect) remains unspecified. Willemen agrees that those who experience cinema through these special heightened moments are more likely to write about their cinematic experience than those who do not. It has "something to do with bearing witness" (again, religious terms are called in), "the need to proclaim what has been experienced, to draw attention to what has been seen." He adds, "There is always something proselytising about cinephiliac writing, a barely contained impatience with those who have eyes but do not see."[49]

As early as the fifth century, Saint Augustine identified the urge fans felt to persuade others to see what they see in their favorite actors. "For in the theatres, dens of iniquity though they be, if a man is fond of a particular actor, and enjoys his art as a great or even as the very greatest good, he is fond of all who join with him in admiration of his favourite. . . . The more fervent he is in his admiration, the more he works in every way he can to secure new admirers for him, and the more anxious he becomes to show him to others."[50]

Centuries later, fans still try to entice nonbelievers. Some even go so far as to produce new texts as testaments to their devotion. Actively engaged with the star image, fan productions stand as monuments to the fan's own experience, and contribute to and extend the star's existence as a mythic figure. One work in particular illustrates the way Clift functions as a living presence in the lives of his fans, and can serve as a primer on the development and phases of fandom in general. It starts with *The Search.*

LETTERS TO MONTGOMERY CLIFT

Noël Alumit's *Letters to Montgomery Clift* (2002) takes the form of an epistolary novel built entirely on a fan's imaginary relationship with Montgomery Clift. The image of Clift (the characters he portrays as well as the person portrayed in biographies) becomes a daily source of emotional support for a troubled boy negotiating adolescence.[51] Torn from his family in the Philippines when his father is arrested for political dissent in the 1970s, the novel's main character is separated from his mother and sent to live with relatives in Los Angeles. There he finds himself an outsider in terms of language, nationality, family, and sexual orientation. Even his name changes as he moves from Filipino relatives to Anglo foster families. Sometimes he is called Bong, sometimes Bob. As he struggles to understand his family's legacy of political persecution, he envisions Clift as both patron saint and guardian angel, a young soldier who literally glows, bestowing smiles of limitless understanding, goodness, and love.

The character's first encounter with Clift seems to happen by pure chance. "I turned on the television, watched the late night movie. When the commercials ended, a voice from the TV said, 'And now we return to *The Search* starring Montgomery Clift.'" The uncannily specific parallels between the plot and Bong's life lend that first glimpse of the star the ominous power of fate.[52] "In the movie, in *The Search*, Monty Clift plays a soldier. He finds and cares for a small boy whose mother was taken away by bad people. He takes the boy home. He gives him candy. He buys him shoes. He teaches him English. He keeps him safe. He guards him till his mama comes" (4–5).

From the beginning fandom is shown to be a learned experience, with fan practice mimicking religious ritual. When the novel starts, Bong is being raised by his bitter, resentful aunt. But while Auntie Yuna insults and abuses her nephew, she also trains him in a set of practices that apply equally well to the worshipper and the film fan. For instance, she creates shrines and writes letters: "She wrote letters to God and dead relatives. She put them next to a burning candle by the Jesus Christ cross on her shelf. 'The spirits will read them,' she said. 'It's better than praying because prayers just go from your head into thin air. . . . Letters are solid proof to the saints, to our ancestors that what I was praying just don't disappear'" (4).

Having become a fan, the boy looks for a way to express his gratitude to Clift. Fans experience the star's performance on a deeply personal level, therefore it seems logical to reciprocate—to tell the star personally, as an individual, the effect his or her work has had. To say thank you. Again, Bong learns this practice from Auntie Yuna, who harbors expectations of communication and reciprocity and considers letters to God and the saints a legally enforceable form of prayer. Although fans understand that actual communication is unlikely (always being dubious whether the star personally reads letters lumped into the category "fan mail"), nevertheless, the need to write persists. Formality gives way to familiarity as fan and star are soon on a first-name basis. Nicknames are allowed. Death is no barrier. Bong begins to write fan letters to Clift even though it is the 1970s and he knows that Clift is already dead.

> Dear Monty,
> I saw *From Here to Eternity* last night. You were wonderful. (74)

In exchange for such acts of devotion, the fan/worshipper is promised regular access to deep emotions. One of Bong's first letters to Clift is about his *aunt's* feelings as a fan.

> dear mr. montgomery clift . . .
> I LOVED MONGOMERY CLIP she said. this is a good sign because i do not think auntie yuna loves very much. . . . I CRIED WHEN HE DIED she said. I CRIED WHEN I READ 1950S SCREEN IDOL MONGOMERY CLIP DIED. I WAS A GIRL. BACK IN THE PHILIPPINES. IN 1966. HE WAS DEAD AT 45. HEART TROUBLE she remembered reading. (3)

Bong's aunt doesn't only show the boy how to enact fandom, she demonstrates the confusion of performance and person that exemplifies the fan's relation to an actor. "From Here to Eternity was a difficult movie to watch," Bong writes Clift. "You get beat up in that movie. You played a soldier and your fellow soldiers beat you up. I hated seeing you in such pain" (74).

As with all fans, Alumit's character identifies himself according to his favorite films. He has seen *The Search* "15 times." For him, the film establishes Clift's status as benevolent father figure. ("Will Mama come back?" "No, dear, she won't.") His second favorite film (which he has seen eleven times) is *From Here to Eternity*, in which Clift plays another young soldier. Other favorites are films that allow Clift to sidestep issues of sexuality as he redefines his relationships with the most beautiful female stars of the decade. Doomed romance with Elizabeth Taylor (*A Place in the Sun*, a film Bong has seen nine times) gives way to "best-friend" status with Marilyn Monroe (*The Misfits*, eight times).

The emphasis on repetition calls to mind Barbara Klinger's observations on the effects and purposes of repeated viewings of the same film. At first, she argues, repetition affords the fan a sense of "comfort and mastery." But even though we are watching the same film, "successive encounters . . . result in a different experience" of the text.[53] As Bong finds when he first sees *The Search*, the "interplay between film narrative and the viewer's past . . .

ignites a chain of autobiographical associations, deeply affecting the process of comprehension." "Repeated encounters with the same films over time" (seeing *The Search* fifteen times) "amplify [these] associative possibilities."[54]

Having mastered the films they consider key, fans must broaden their horizons as repetition risks deadening the films' original impact through overexposure. In addition to his favorites, Bong tries to see every film Clift ever made. Kind words are bestowed on *Indiscretion of an American Wife, The Heiress, The Young Lions, Lonelyhearts,* and *Suddenly, Last Summer,* but several of Clift's other films are notable by their absence (e.g., another young man in uniform in *The Big Lift,* the ideal father/husband/best friend in *Raintree County*). Bong's devotion is circumscribed by external factors. Growing up watching television in Los Angeles in the 1970s, he is dependent on programming decisions made by others. Some films cannot figure into the boy's fantasies because they are not in circulation (though even then, it is hard to account for the absence of *Red River*).[55] When his latest foster family acquires a VCR in the early eighties, the first film his best friend, Cousin Amada, tapes for him is *Freud*.[56]

Once he has seen all the films he can, Bong moves on to written materials, especially books and fan magazines. Because the novel is initially set in the 1970s, Bong cannot rent or own videos or DVDs, search Web sites, or purchase memorabilia on eBay.[57] Books, however, are ownable, thus qualifying as fetish objects. "I bought a book. It cost over ten dollars, which is a lot of money for a kid. I bought it because it was about Monty. His face was on the cover" (23). Every detail of the fetish object matters—and the uses to which it can be put. "I kept *The Films of Montgomery Clift* under my pillow when I slept. . . . I kissed the book, a yellow book with Monty's exquisite face on top. Monty dressed in a suit, his warm eyes staring straight at me. Two creases were on his forehead and his hair was combed back, a sheen atop his head. Even though paper was what I felt on my lips, I kissed the book anyway" (23).

In *Object Lessons: How to Do Things with Fetishism,* E. L. McCallum acknowledges the resistance fetishism provokes in those not caught up in its thrall: "The fixation on the fetish is generally viewed as a pathological repetition compulsion, bound up in the return to the thing which gives satisfaction and cutting the fetishist off from relation to others." In her reappraisal of fetishism, McCallum argues that the fetish can serve the fetishist in a variety of positive ways. For instance, the fan/fetishist uses repeated encounters with the object as an opportunity to construct meaning and a sense of self. "By building the fetish relation, the fetish subject creates herself; by situating herself among others through the fetish object the subject interprets herself in a world, and can share her interpretation with others."[58]

When Bong practices being like Montgomery Clift (incorporating sayings, gestures, styles, and attitudes he has observed in films and photographs), he is enacting the process of repetition, interpretation, and performance through which, according to McCallum, we constantly reshape and reassert our identities.[59] Bong's recognition and acceptance of his own sexual identity is also achieved via his identification with Clift. Reading the first serious biographies of Clift as they become available in the late 1970s, he focuses on their revelations about Clift's personal life: "I breezed through *Monty* by Robert LaGuardia. . . . LaGuardia's book was more personal, Bosworth's book was more factual. Both agree on one thing: Montgomery Clift was attracted to men. I found relief in knowing that" (84). Armed with published accounts of Clift's sexuality, Bong finds (imaginary) support in accepting his own developing sexuality. Around this time, he writes, he masturbates to the sounds of lovers in another apartment, "imagining *him*."[60]

Rather than close himself off in a fantasy world, Bong tries to use his knowledge of Clift to build relationships with others.[61] Carefully, he begins to share his admiration for Clift with people he is close to. Like the teenage girls in *The World of Henry Orient* (1964), Bong and his cousin Amada use information garnered from the biographies to make a pilgrimage to places associated with Clift: the Upper East Side of Manhattan where he lived, the cemetery where he is buried.[62] "I walked the streets of New York knowing he was there," Bong reports, projecting his fantasy-ideal onto the world (101).

As he considers making his fandom public, Bong weighs the possibility of building a community based on admiration for Montgomery Clift. He declares, "I wanted to start my own club, a fan club." The first requirement for forming a club (as any child knows) is deciding on a name. (An actual Clift fan club in the 1950s called itself the Cliftonettes.) Bong calls his "The I-Love-Montgomery-Clift-Because-He-Understands-Me-Like-No-Other Club. Membership: one." Having chosen a name, he needs a set of rules. "Club Member Requirements: An intense yearning to worship a dead matinee star because he provides comfort, because he provides hope. Club Dues: Be willing to give part of your soul. Club Activities: Watch Monty movies no matter what hour his movies come on. If it means staying up till three in the morning to catch him on the late, late-night movie, that's what it means" (104).

Bong's club reflects his mixed feelings about whether to avow his devotion publicly or keep it private. His club rules jumble the external aspects of fandom (the appreciation of texts, overcoming obstacles, etc.) and its most profoundly private part—imagined reciprocity, in which the fan's relation to the image is refashioned as a relationship with the star. The fan's expertise about the actor is inverted; instead of "I know everything about him," the situation becomes "he understands me." Bong's club has a membership of one because he is afraid to express to others the intensity of his feelings. When he eventually tells his best friend, his attempt to share backfires.

What Bong's friend and fellow fan Amada does not know is that Bong has been hallucinating Clift's presence in his daily life. "My first vision. I was behind a tree when I saw someone. The sun was in my face. All I could see was the outline of a tall man, slender. He stood straight with shoulders arched back like he was at attention. A military cap was on his head tilted to the side. It was Monty dressed in his soldier's uniform from *The Search*" (20).

As the crises in Bong's life come to a head (he realizes that the relatives he lives with in Los Angeles have been supporters of the Marcos government— the regime that kidnapped, tortured, and possibly killed one or both of his parents), Bong's identification with Clift leads him to self-destructive behavior. Where earlier it was sufficient to simply comb his hair to resemble Clift's (75), now Bong crashes his motorcycle in imitation of Clift's car accident, leaving his face scarred.[63] Bong's hallucinations intensify as he is committed to an asylum.

> I'd sit by the window of my room entranced in my world with Monty. We didn't speak, but sat together. He wore an outfit from *From Here to Eternity:* slacks and a Hawaiian shirt. . . .
>
> Monty took me places without ever having to leave my room. . . . I'd find myself with Monty in the California desert, dry and barren. We'd find a shade in a cluster of cactus trees, shaped like deformed hands. He wore a cowboy hat, jeans, and a plaid shirt. He'd pull out a cigarette and the smell of tobacco drifted past my nose, a taunting smell. The drumming hooves of horses could be heard nearby. [*The Misfits*]
>
> Sometimes we were at a cotillion. We were dressed in tuxedos with shiny black shoes: golden cufflinks held our sleeves together. He'd serve me punch and we'd sit quietly in an ivy-embraced gazebo. [*The Heiress*] (178)

As Bong finds pleasure, comfort, and imaginary companionship fantasizing about Clift, he becomes less and less connected to the world around him. "I would willingly go with Monty. Hours, days, weeks seemed to pass.

When I returned, I'd find liquid food crusted dry around my mouth or dripping onto my shirt. I don't remember eating or being fed" (178).

Bong's psychotic episodes reinforce the fear that once fans begin using fantasies of a star to flee a bad situation they risk becoming stuck, trapped in their imaginations, cut off from others. Despite his hospitalization, Bong resists any attempt to pathologize his attachment to Clift. "Brainwasher, or Dr. Butterworth [his psychiatrist], thought I was psychotic; he thought I wasn't in touch with reality. . . . I told him the drugs didn't work because there was nothing wrong with me. . . . 'Montgomery Clift tells me things, makes things happen. He makes me feel good. Is there anything wrong with that?'" (172).

The hostile male psychiatrist labels Bong "dependent" and suggests, "We need to break you of this habit." Bong shifts the argument away from a medical discourse by describing his star worship in religious terms. (Remember, club dues require a willingness to give part of your soul.) "I wouldn't be here if I said I believed in Christ, would I? If I told you I believed in Jesus, and He works in my life, and I pray to Him, I would be considered a good Christian person. Whether it's Jesus or Monty, they're symbols people turn to in times of crisis. I can pray to whoever I want, believe in whoever I want" (172–73). The doctor disagrees. "Your religion is a 1950s movie star. There is something absurd about that." According to medical science, apparently "Jesus and Montgomery Clift are two different things" (172–73).

The addition of religious devotion compounds the potential negative effects of fetishism. The urge to annihilate the self by being absorbed in an intense imaginary relationship with an idealized Other finds an echo in Amy Hollywood's discussion of the writings of medieval mystic Margaret Ebner (1291–1351). A German nun in the Dominican order, Ebner wrote about her visions and sensory transports in a work titled *Revelations*. Aspects of her experience bear a striking resemblance to Bong's experience as a film fan. Like Bong, Ebner had books and images she could cherish in private. "I possessed a little book in which there was a picture of the Lord on the cross. . . . When I wanted to sleep, I took the picture of the Crucified Lord in the little book and laid it under my face."[64] Ebner's identification with the object of her devotion, however, is on a scale that is, fortunately, beyond what most fans could imagine. As with Bong's psychotic phase, Ebner's mental images are vivid to the point of hallucination. "It was as if I were really in the presence of my Beloved," Ebner writes, "as if I had seen his suffering with my own eyes and as if it were all happening before me at this very moment."[65] Ebner, however, does not remain a mere spectator of suffering, watching from the outside. "I felt an inner pain in my hands as if they were stretched out, torn and broken through. . . . In my head I felt a wondrous pain . . . that seemed so excruciating to me that I began to tremble. . . . I perceived the same painful brokenness in all my members, especially on both sides and on my back, arms, and legs, so that it seemed to me I was in the last throes and that all this suffering would continue until death."[66]

Fans seldom go this far. Recovering from his most destructive fantasies, Bong finds a way to justify the intermingling of religion and fandom in terms of cultural tradition. "The West has an accepted form of religion or spirituality. Praying to ancestors is not one of them. . . . I come from a part of the world where the dead are revered and prayed to. A dead uncle or aunt is just as precious as a saint or some other form of deity" (173). But religious institutions in Alumit's novel are not noticeably more receptive to Clift-worship than psychiatry had been. Culturally Catholic, Bong hears a sermon in church on the sin of "praying to False Idols." "I thought about you, Monty," he writes. "There's nothing false about you" (75).

Idolatry is a matter of misreading, reacting to a sign as if it were the thing itself. In this sense, idolatry is different from fetishism. The fetishist is aware that the signifier is a signifier—in the case of film, an image of an actor acting. Idolatrous reading, on the other hand, stops at the signifier instead of proceeding through it toward what is signified. Idolaters fail to understand that a sign is never complete in itself but points elsewhere. Contemporary theologians point out that "idolatry is . . . an epistemological error"—"the symbol always points to something beyond itself. Not recognizing this is idolatry."[67] The idolater's mistake consists of settling for an inadequate sign rather than looking past it to the infinite. In theological terms, such "literalism deprives God of his ultimacy."[68]

Catholic religious art is founded on representations of human bodies (forbidden in Judaism and Islam, and treated with extreme caution by Protestant Christians).[69] The church's concern with images sprang from its theological insistence on the centrality of the body, the need to communicate the flesh-and-blood aspects of Christ. For the church, Jesus Christ was not an invisible, purely spiritual deity but a human being, living a human life and dying a fully human death that prepared the way for the resurrection—a resurrection not just of the soul but of the body as well. In the first centuries of the church, Saint Theodore the Studite proclaimed iconoclasts, those who would eliminate human images, "Christological heretics, since they deny an essential element of Christ's human nature, namely, that it can be represented graphically. This amounts to a denial of its reality and material quality."[70]

But even those within a strictly Catholic tradition could take the position that God is beyond representation. A church father expressed this position as early as the fourth century when he wrote, "Do not paint pictures of Christ; he humbled himself enough by becoming man."[71] The strictest Protestant arguments forbid depictions not only of the Divine but of any person. In the 1750s, British poet and religious monomaniac Christopher Smart warned against the deleterious effects of portraiture, as "something in the spirit may be taken off by painters."

> For Painting is a species of idolatry, tho' not so gross as statuary.
> For it is not good to look with earning upon any dead work.
> For by so doing something is lost in the spirit & given from life
>   to death.[72]

Bong's idolatry does not consist of seeing Clift as a god; he is quite clear that Clift should be situated within the continuum of ancestors and saints. In the hierarchy of figures represented in religious art, saints are the non-divine exemplars, models of human behavior who are still subject to fallibility, representations of whom would presumably provide examples for the faithful without the presumption of replacing the Ultimate with a mere collection of signs.

Recovered from his illness, Bong outgrows the more obvious displays of fandom. Having seen the films, read the books, and created his own narratives, he has integrated "Clift" so completely into his life that the references become increasingly subtle, so much so that they barely register in his consciousness and are not flagged in his letters. Hitchcock's *I Confess,* for example, is never mentioned by name, but Bong's sympathetic female psychiatrist is a big Hitchcock fan (Hitchcock's *Spellbound* is about a female psychiatrist) and the love of Bong's adult life is named Logan—the priest Clift plays in the film.

In some ways, Alumit's depiction of star worship may be too linear, too obviously functional. Fandom comes across as, essentially, a phase of adolescent development. In his study of religious feeling, William James recognizes that acute religious experiences often occur during adolescence, but he suggests that we resist the urge to reduce religious feeling to a phase.[73] Nor can it be reduced to a psychological phenomenon in which being a fan helps one through a tough patch, and then all is well (fandom as therapy).[74]

Nevertheless, in the process of writing his novel, in effect building his own monument to Montgomery Clift, Noël Alumit testifies to the value an actor can have for a fan. He also confronts the three major transgressions of which fans are accused: escapism, fetishism, and idolatry. By delineating the way these processes enable the boy to survive traumatic circumstances, the author makes a case for their personal, political, and practical value.

Escapism, like *political correctness,* is a term that disallows the very thing it names, silencing debate. Unlike the pursuit of pleasure or the entertainment of desire, escapism is defined negatively as the avoidance of the important for the frivolous. Alumit makes it clear that fandom is not simple escapism. Bong's devotion to Clift does not *prevent* him from pursuing the political, historical truth about his family and eventually finding his mother. In fact, by identifying with a supportive model of masculinity, he gains a sense of alliance as well as a prop that helps him resist his duplicitous uncle and oppose, vicariously, a corrupt political regime and its legacy.

Despite his encounters with the darker aspects of fetishism, Alumit's character is more in line with McCallum's rehabilitation of the term. "Foremost among fetishism's virtues," McCallum tells us, is that it transforms suffering into "satisfaction."[75] By providing a structure "to *work through* loss rather than avoid it," the fetish makes it possible for the fetishist to "experience [loss] without being overwhelmed by it."[76] Bong's losses are heavy: his parents, his country, his culture and sense of home. It is through the sustaining vision of Montgomery Clift that Bong finds the strength to seek out his mother, face the history of his country, reconcile himself to his life in the United States, and ultimately create a new home.

In terms of idolatry, we can simply say this: if being a fan is comparable to religious devotion, and if religion is the opiate of the masses, then *Letters to Montgomery Clift* reminds us that opiates, strategically administered, can be lifesavers.

ANOTHER BEGINNING

For many viewers in 1948, *Red River* provided the same sense of revelation others experienced seeing *The Search.* In a memoir written in the early 1970s, Caryl Rivers re-creates the impact movies had on her as a teenager in the late forties. In a chapter titled "The Dream People," she describes how she and her friends "instantly, inexplicably, simultaneously" fell in love with particular male stars. "Foremost among them was Montgomery Clift. . . . All the girls in the eighth grade fell in love with Montgomery Clift. . . . I think every girl who saw him in the quiet dark of a movie theater of a Saturday afternoon fell in love with Montgomery Clift."[77] Such a response, its religious dimension implied by the incantatory repetition of the actor's name, was not limited to girls. Like Rivers, film historian David Thomson first saw Clift in *Red River* and, like Rivers, he remembers it vividly decades later, describing his attitude about Clift as "beyond adoration."[78]

Rivers cites Clift's beauty in this film as the immediate cause of enchantment: his face, his eyes, "the straight, perfect blade of a nose that should have been the work of some sculptor the equal of Michelangelo." Clift's appeal depended less on overt sexuality than idealized romance; consequently Rivers emphasizes delicacy over testosterone. "His face had the fragile perfection of a fragile porcelain vase," "his dark eyes like the deep water of a cavern pool holding the promise of worlds of tenderness." The young teen found the idea of actual sex "pretty revolting." By contrast, "love" with Clift would consist of "long, languorous sighs," Rivers imagines, "and he wouldn't think of putting his hand on my thigh."[79]

At the same time that she acknowledges Clift's impact on her generation, Rivers wonders how someone who was "no more than a flat shadow on an asbestos screen became the repository of all the dreams of all our summer nights, a tabernacle for all our unfulfilled wishes."[80] What Rivers describes— tabernacles, repositories—are empty vessels waiting to be filled by the fantasies of viewers. Clift, of course, was more than that, but in his first films, his lack of history was part of what made him available for these idealized projections. Without a public image or widely known body of work, Clift was just an image, beautiful but without depth, a blank screen, a shadow.

The myth of Clift-as-vision, "love at first sight," cannot be maintained for long.[81] The first time we see Clift in *Red River,* his unfamiliar beauty has already been contextualized by virtue of its insertion within a film that is both a western and part of the postwar era. As the film goes on, Clift's looks will serve a variety of functions as the plot and Clift's character work through a specific set of historical, social, and generic contradictions.

RED RIVER

As in *The Search,* Clift's character enters the film late and without fanfare. A prologue introduces Tom Dunson (John Wayne) and his fiancée, who is soon killed by Indians. Coming upon a survivor of the massacre, Dunson takes the young boy, Matthew Garth, under his wing. Years pass (we are told in a title card) as Dunson builds his cattle herd. Having fought in the recent Civil War, Matt (now played by Clift) returns to Dunson's ranch.

In this first scene it takes a long time for Matt to say anything. As Dunson announces plans for an upcoming cattle drive, Matt stays in the background. With one foot resting on a rock, his hands on his knee, Clift holds an unusually relaxed pose long enough for us to register its sinuous line. Matt eventually suggests a different route for the drive but allows himself to be overruled by Dunson. Even though Clift plays Matt as voluntarily submissive in this scene, the way he pauses before stepping forward to take part in the scene makes it clear that he might not always be.

Matthew Garth's function is to open up to question long-held assumptions. Clift begins to do so in a subtle and indirect way. Instead of openly confronting Wayne's character, Clift establishes Matt's contrariness by becoming the anti-Wayne—swaying when Wayne is solidly planted, centering his posture on his hips where Wayne calls attention to his chest, soft-spoken and precise where Wayne is loud and preemptory. Clift's decision never directly to challenge the established star was said to have sealed director Howard Hawks's belief that Clift could hold his own with Wayne on-screen.[82]

As a genre, the western presents the West as the proving ground of American history (Manifest Destiny, "the winning of the West," "the last frontier") and American (especially male) identity. *Red River* questions each of these tenets in its focus on Dunson and Garth. Dunson is depicted less as a pioneer and more as a land-grabbing outlaw, murderer, thief, and cattle rustler. Early in the film he shoots three Mexican men who have valid title to the land he has appropriated for his ranch; later he casually absorbs other ranchers' cattle into his herd. As a consequence, the Production Code office found the script "thoroughly unacceptable."[83] Although the borderline legality of Dunson's violence was toned down (with the killings staged to suggest self-defense—barely), the suggestion of criminality is not erased. With John Wayne as the embodiment of such now-dubious values, Clift is called upon to present Matt as a new kind of American, one with a different perspective, a different style of leadership, and a different kind of masculinity.

Presented with an opportunity to establish his manliness early in the film, Clift/Matt undermines the entire project by adopting a decidedly playful demeanor. In the double-entendre–filled gunplay between Matt and Cherry (John Ireland), two good-looking young men compliment each other's prowess with a pistol. What is so remarkable about this scene is the casualness with which the performers engage the gay subtext. (The release of *Brokeback Mountain* in 2005 occasioned frequent references to this scene.) Smiling, physically at ease, eyes sparkling, neither actor can keep his eyes off the other, and no one attempts to repress any subversive alternate readings. No gruff machismo arises as a defense against being "misunderstood." It is as if the actors are free to say outrageous things because they know that the legacy of "a John Wayne western" makes them unassailable. How far can they push it? The crowning twist is when Wayne himself is brought into their subtextual sexual play. When Cherry praises Matt, Matt says pointedly, "Leave room for a third."

CHERRY: Who?

MATT: Dunson.

CHERRY: Is he that good?

MATT: He taught me.

The fearlessness with which the actors flirt with the possibility of alternative sexualities is attractive and liberating. Clift and Ireland not only decouple manliness from heterosexuality, they make it look easy—even to the point of implicating Wayne. More than anything else, it may be Clift's fundamental lack of seriousness about such weighty matters that accounts for the backlash against the actor that repeatedly crops up in stories about the making of the film. While Clift's biographers insist that he became a "real cowboy" (one calls him "a crackerjack cowpoke"),[84] other critics gleefully recount Clift's "failings" on the set—he couldn't ride, couldn't throw a punch, and needed stuntmen ("real" men) to disguise his shortcomings.[85] Although stuntmen famously substituted for Wayne in dangerous action scenes (the legendary Yakima Canutt in *Stagecoach* [1939], for example), the urge to depict the Broadway actor as an emasculated eastern sophisticate and the established Hollywood actor as "the real thing" (a genuine "man of the West," a real American who just plays "himself") suggests how unsettling the destabilization of this particular icon could be.

The possibilities of a sexual relationship between Matt and Dunson might seem circumscribed by Wayne's right-wing reputation (hence Cherry's presence in the scene with Matt), but the script does not preclude such a reading, nor do the performers. In scene after scene, Matt and Dunson's relationship is established by the way they relate to each other wordlessly, with their bodies, gestures, posture. They display a profound, unspoken ease in each other's presence. Despite their contradictory personae, it is not hard to see Wayne, "a beefy six-foot-three, and Clift a willowy five-foot-ten" (as Garry Wills describes them), as a couple.[86] But while the body language tells us one thing, the plot pursues a different agenda, setting out to break up the male couple, disrupt their intimacy, insert a heterosexual option (arguably the least persuasive part of the film), and recuperate the Dunson-Matt relationship by reestablishing it along traditional patriarchal-filial lines.

Positioning itself as "a new kind of western," *Red River* acknowledges its debt to the past as it stages the transition from one generation to the next, endorsing (for the most part) the new generation's methods, style, and values.[87] In its focus on generational change, *Red River* is responding to its historical moment as part of the immediate postwar era. Much of what is at stake in *Red River* (produced in 1946) is made visible when we see the film as a hybrid of the western and the war film. As a crypto-war film, *Red River* is so radical that its critique of authority could be represented only in disguise. Understood this way, the subversiveness of Clift's performance becomes even clearer. It would be a full decade after the end of the war before another filmmaker would risk producing a film that openly advocated mutiny.[88] What seems revolutionary in war-film terms, however, can simultaneously serve a conservative function by establishing strict limits on male social and sexual relationships. Looking at the film in some detail, we can trace the interweaving of love and mutiny, the western and the war film, as played out in the relationship between Dunson and Matt, Wayne and Clift.

Intimacy between Matt and Dunson is expressed in classic manly war-film manner—with cigarettes. Matt rolls one, lights up, and then either hands it to Dunson (when they are mounted side by side, watching over the cattle) or makes no objection when Dunson walks up and takes it from him (the scene in the saloon in which Dunson signs up men for the cattle drive). In their first scene together, Matt gives Dunson a rolled cigarette, then lights it for him. Dunson cups Matt's hands as he lights up, then grabs Matt's wrist, noticing that he is wearing a bracelet Dunson gave him when Matt was a boy. Even though he has been gone for more than a year, Matt still wears the symbol of fealty. This first scene between them in the film establishes the dynamics of the characters' relationship (domineering and submissive) as the actors find ways to express in physical terms the gesture's emotional weight. The bigger, older man takes it for granted that he can physically take hold of the younger man, who yields quite contentedly as the characters maintain eye contact—a long moment in which the audience can read the fact that they have a past.

Despite his apparent passivity, Matt is not a pushover. At all times he has a mind of his own, but in scene after scene he *chooses* to be submissive. In an early scene, Matt differs with Dunson over "appropriating" other ranchers' cattle. Every time a steer does not have the Red River brand, Matt says, "Let him go" or "Turn him loose." Dunson rides up and orders everything rebranded with *his* mark. Matt pauses, then reiterates the boss's orders with full vocal authority. He does not crumble, though. When Dunson dares him to challenge the decision, Matt holds his own, saying, "You're gonna wind up branding every rump in the state of Texas except mine." Dunson turns to another man and says, "Hand me that iron." When we cut to Matt's reaction, Dunson says, "You don't think I'd do it, do you?" Matt half-laughs, "No, I don't." The way Clift delivers the line suggests that Matt isn't all that sure. The line does not require consonants that close the mouth, like *m* or *b* or *p*, so Clift can do something he often does—speak with his mouth half open, using his lower lip against his exposed upper teeth to enunciate. Here it produces an effect of uncertainty.

The branding line is not only of a piece with Matt's double entendres with Cherry; the entire scene is in direct violation of a peculiarly precise taboo. From its earliest incarnations, the Production Code specifically forbade branding of any kind, including the branding of cattle.[89] In the late-twenties list of "Don'ts and Be Carefuls," branding is number fifteen, and the 1930 Production Code includes it under the heading "Repellent Subjects."[90] This prohibition was probably due to the sensational 1915 hit *The Cheat,* in which a society woman is branded on the shoulder by a depraved would-be lover (played by Sessue Hayakawa). It would be hard to imagine *Red River,* a film about a major cattle drive, without a cattle-branding scene, but the threatened branding of Clift's character brings an unexpected sexual charge to the relationship of Dunson and Matt—one introduced this time by Dunson. The shock of imagining John Wayne imagining marring the surface of Clift's beautiful body is not entirely put to rest by Matt's optimistic laugh.[91] (Dunson *does* mark Matt at the end, scarring his cheek in their final showdown; Matt smiles broadly as he bears the wound.) In this scene, though, Dunson backs down because Matt's independence is valuable. As in a war film, a good subordinate should be intelligent and show initiative. In his first scene, Matt not only proposes an alternative route but has a map already prepared. Nevertheless, a subordinate accepts that his superior officer makes the final decision. All Matt's skills and judgment at this point are channeled into this supporting role.

When Dunson signs up men for the cattle drive, the familiar outlines of the war film begin to emerge. As Wayne and others had done in countless

FIGURE 4. Lobby card for *Red River,* 1948: Noah Beery Jr. (Buster), Clift (Matt), and Walter Brennan (Groot).

recent war films, Dunson addresses the men before him as soldiers—or, to be precise, as veterans. "Most of you men have come back to Texas from war. You came back to nothin'." In the film he is referring to economic problems in the cattle business, but the sentiment applies just as easily to the postwar economic outlook, an effect that would have been stronger when the film was shot in 1946. The scene is played as a call for volunteers. No one is drafted for this mission, and there will be "no hard feelings" for anyone who opts out. As in the military, the only real sin would be desertion. "Every man who signs on for this drive agrees to finish it," Dunson tells them. "There'll be no quittin' along the way. Not by me and not by you." The general will be there, side by side with his men.

But while Dunson often strides through scenes, undeterred by anyone or anything, it is Matt who is shown as being on an equal level with the men, part of the group. Ever the good lieutenant, Matt is a conduit from the men to their commanding officer because he is more in tune with their needs, smoothing the edges when an order seems harsh. Soon, however, even Matt begins to question Dunson's methods.

After a man has unwittingly provoked a stampede, Dunson announces his intention to whip him. Refusing to be punished in this humiliating way, the man pulls a gun and prepares for a showdown with Dunson. Matt shoots him, but instead of trying to protect Dunson, it turns out he wanted to protect the man *from* Dunson. Having wounded the man, Matt turns on Dunson, saying tensely, "You'd have shot him right between the eyes." Dunson responds, "Sure as you're standing there." In contrast to Dunson's hardness, Matt comforts the man he shot, inviting him to "take along an extra horse" so that he can get home all right. The man in turn thanks Matt— the man who shot him—for saving his life.

The next time Matt disagrees with Dunson, three men have been killed. Confronting Dunson, Matt insists, "You didn't have to do that back there." Dunson mounts a pallid defense: "You think I'm responsible for that?" Matt turns Dunson's earlier retort back on him: "Just as sure as you're sitting there." The rift between them grows as tensions mount.

The mutiny comes the next day, when two men who had abandoned the drive are delivered to Dunson for justice. In a hieratic composition, Dunson is seated in the middle of the shot, one wounded leg spread out toward the right where the cook Groot (Walter Brennan) kneels and tends to it, the other knee pointing toward Matt who stands in profile on the left of the screen, leaning back with his arms crossed. As Cherry is hailed approaching from a distance with the two men, Matt looks quickly to Dunson; Dunson, a half-empty bottle in his hand, checks Matt's reaction; Matt, looking into the distance, slowly takes an unlit cigarette out of his mouth.

Remaining seated, a wounded Dunson asserts his power over the captured men while calling attention to his physically disadvantaged position. "Get down off them horses. I don't favor lookin' up to the likes of you." As they dismount, the prisoners are framed by Dunson on the left and Matt standing on the right, with Cherry on his horse, blocking any exit from the rear. Labeling them deserters and "common thieves," Dunson is interrupted by one of the men: "The law might see it different." Dunson drowns him out: "I'm the law." As the man reasserts his commitment to the mission and the team, finishing with a Capraesque appeal to the common good ("This herd doesn't belong to you. It belongs to every poor hopin' and prayin' cattleman in the whole state"), Matt, his back to us, moves away from Dunson to stand among the men. In contrast to the mounting agitation around him, John Wayne underplays as Dunson, asking the prisoner, "You finished?" A defeated voice says, "Yeah." It is Matt the film cuts to as the condemned man says, "Now you can get your Bible and read over us after you shoot us" (Dunson's customary course of action). In a close-up, Wayne/Dunson tilts his head languidly and pauses for a moment. "I'm gonna hang ya."

As we see the men's reaction, a low voice offscreen delivers a drawn-out, almost moaning "No." Cut to Matt, who for the first time directly contradicts Dunson in front of the men: "No, you're not." Dunson, squinting into the sun, is shocked and slow to react. Matt repeats, "You're not gonna hang them." Dunson shifts the bottle in his hand. "Who'll stop me?" For the third time, Matt defies him. "I will."

Although Matt seems to have triumphed, assuming leadership and instituting a more democratic style of command, the scene continues, the camera lingering on Dunson as if unwilling to let him go. Reinscribing the tyrant as a man in pain, dispossessed, frustrated, helpless, and exposed, the film refuses to posit the mutiny as a solution. Instead, the rift between Dunson and Matt becomes the new crisis that must be resolved, the break between the two an unacceptable loss that threatens to undermine whatever progress each man might make alone.

THE LIEUTENANT'S COMMAND

Unlike the unyielding Dunson, Matt shares his doubts and fears with others. One of the first things he says (and repeats in several scenes thereafter) is "I don't know." Matt and Groot ponder what might happen when Dunson catches up with them. Matt makes it clear he was a reluctant mutineer. "It all happened so fast. I hadn't—started out—I couldn't let him hang Teeler and Laredo." Groot asks, "You ain't sorry ya done it?" and Matt answers, "I dunno." Holding his chin in his hand, with his hat off and hair hanging over his forehead, he looks unusually boyish. "He was wrong," Matt asserts, loud and clear; but then he sighs, rubbing his face. "I hope I'm right."

Unlike Dunson, Matt admits when he is afraid and shares his feelings with others. When they are afraid, he comforts them. The night after the revolt, everyone is edgy. One man, thrashing in his sleep, calls for a gun. Matt rushes over and wakes him. He smiles gently, half-kneeling beside the man, and says, "You were having a nightmare. You all right?"

Matt's leadership style is opposed to Dunson's in scene after scene. When the men find a cow killed by arrows, Matt is surrounded by people looking to him to make a decision. His first choice is to consult others, but when he receives contradictory advice, he looks ahead and starts giving orders. Matt's attitude about his team is highlighted again one day when a cowboy rides up and excitedly tells everyone that a wagon train is nearby, carrying women and coffee. Unlike Dunson, who refused to praise the men and tried to keep them too exhausted to rebel, Matt decides to give them some rest and recreation. This style of leadership not only proves thoughtful but also has practical benefits. The next day Groot points out the motivational effect when he observes, "I ain't never seen such a bunch of men—everybody wants to ride point."

There is only one occasion when Matt does not spend time justifying his decision. When they come across Indians attacking the wagon train, Matt takes it for granted that the men will follow him and fight. As they charge ahead, Matt is simultaneously the commanding officer and one of the men.[92]

The film loses its power the way many war films do when women are introduced. In confirmation of *Red River*'s war-film roots, I would argue that it is no coincidence that some of the film's censorship problems were the same as the ones that were to arise with *From Here to Eternity*. A memo from the Breen office to Hawks states, "The indication that the various girls are nothing more or less than prostitutes is entirely unacceptable, as well as the many lines of dialogue by the men indicating their sex desires for these women."[93]

By this point, not only has Matt been cut off from Dunson, but as soon as Millay (Joanne Dru) is introduced, Cherry virtually disappears from the film. Clift's performance does little to smooth over Matt's nearly schizophrenic behavior in his scenes with Millay: using Hawksian tough talk when cutting an arrow out of her shoulder, being unusually passive when she seeks him out in the fog, and appearing unusually absorbed in her sensual presence (the fur on her collar, the texture of her hair) when she surprises him in his hotel room in Abilene. (Needless to say, the Breen office declared the "illicit sex affair between Mathew and Millay" out of the question "since it [was] not treated with the proper compensating moral values.")[94] Paradoxically, Millay's visit to the hotel firmly returns Matt to his place among the men, this time by virtue of his having established his commitment to heterosexuality.

When Matt emerges from his hotel after a night with Millay, Clift plays the "morning after" as a timeless moment, familiar to any audience, applicable to any soldier in any war film. The scene is a single long take. Matt saunters out of the hotel, nodding "Mornin'" to the men outside as he descends the stairs. He strolls up to one of the men and gestures for a cigarette. Behind him, Millay comes out onto the porch to stand by Groot. The men look at her. Matt, lighting the cigarette, half-turns his head as if aware of something behind him. He listens for a second, then figures it out. Shaking out the match, he turns casually back to the man on his right and smiles broadly. Clift's whole body unwinds. His chest rises and broadens, and he leads with his hips as he swaggers toward the fence in the foreground. Although Matt's night with Millay signals his heterosexuality, the scene emphasizes the homosocial as Matt cements his closeness with the men by becoming one of the guys.

As a film about a mutiny, *Red River* could end either way—with the death of the rebel (restoring order) or of the tyrant (validating revolt). But director Hawks throws in a curve that allows him to have it both ways. The previously "inevitable" clash between Dunson and Matt is deftly sidestepped when the plot is reconfigured in terms of sexual politics. Once Millay has been established as the heterosexual option, positioned equidistant between Dunson and Matt (she, too, could go either way, propositioning both men in quick succession), the love between Matt and Dunson can flourish once again, the possibility of homosexual love having been (supposedly) eliminated.

Now Matt's exaggerated display of total submission can be openly embraced as filial. When Matt refuses to fight back, even to the point of allowing Dunson to shoot him, the character's mutiny is reconfigured as a greater loyalty. Matt usurped Dunson's power not for the men's sake, as it seemed, but ultimately for Dunson's sake. By remotivating the troops and delivering the herd, Matt has delivered Dunson from the burdens of leadership. Matt has made it possible for Dunson to remain a hero by stepping in before Dunson could irredeemably destroy what he had built. When Millay literally comes between the two men at the end, shouting at them to stop fighting and realize that they love each other, Dunson and Matt suddenly recognize that they *can* express their love within this new formulation of familial devotion. By showing Dunson that he has been both worthy partner and heir, Matt enables Dunson to share and eventually cede leadership to the next generation. The last shot is of the new brand—the Dunson *D,* the two lines of the Red River, and an *M* for Matt. Dunson retains the patrilineal name and the power to erase Matt's last name (Garth) now that Matt's name and filial status have been realigned under the sign of Dunson.

In *Red River,* Clift helps revitalize a genre by introducing a new kind of leader and a new kind of man. Strong but sensitive, democratic and egalitarian, he has new ideas and new methods, his ways of relating to the men he commands at odds with the strict hierarchies of earlier generations. His willingness to endure suffering bespeaks heroism and integrity more than masochism. Through persistence, conviction, and sheer stubbornness, Clift's Matt stands toe-to-toe with John Wayne, insisting that Wayne and the western genre give way and revise their traditional definitions of manliness to accommodate Clift.

HE'S A REBEL

Red River serves as a template for Clift's image as both rebel and heir apparent. In a movie star–nostalgia book of the early 1970s, David Shipman summarizes the three main facets of Montgomery Clift's star image: "He attracted attention partly because he was a fine actor, partly because he was very handsome, and partly because he refused to conform." Nonconformity was expressed not so much by Clift's acting as by the way he handled his career. Shipman describes Clift's attitude about the film industry as a series of renunciations. "He did not choose to work unless he felt like it, he did not choose to be tied by long-term contracts, he did not go to premieres, did not indulge in fake romances, did not marry."[95]

If, strictly speaking, only a few of these statements are true, all of them are essential to the legend. Clift did attend the premieres of his own films (whether posing with Taylor at the opening of *The Heiress* or crawling up the aisle, drunk, at *Judgment at Nuremberg*).[96] He posed for publicity stills, sat for interviews, and, after the release of *Red River,* signed a three-picture deal with Paramount.[97] Publicity stills from *Red River* and the flood of material that appeared before the release of his first Paramount film, *The Heiress,* contradict the image of someone refusing to cooperate with the Hollywood publicity machine.[98] In fact, by actively participating in publicity and promotion, Clift tried to exercise some control over how he was seen outside of his performances and selection of roles.

The desire to depict Clift as a nonconformist rebelling against the system seems to be more important to Clift's fans than it was for Clift himself. When he begins to shape his image in earnest, Clift's attempts at self-definition already stress a counternarrative to the rebel image proffered by studios and fan magazines. An acute observer of his persona-under-construction, Clift attempted to steer the conversation away from whether he was rebellious and focus attention on acting. "I am neither a young rebel nor an old rebel, nor a tired rebel but quite simply an actor who tries to do his job with the maximum of conviction and sincerity."[99]

In October 1949, after the release of *The Search, Red River,* and *The Heiress,*

Modern Screen featured an article titled "My Own Story by Montgomery Clift" (with "as told to George Scullin" in very small print beneath the heading). In this allegedly first-person essay, Clift repositions his supposed rejection of the Hollywood status quo as a dedication to acting. He begins by distancing himself from his public image. "This fabulous business going on today—'Montgomery Clift, the brightest comet ever to burst into the firmament of Hollywood stars'—has me dazed, but not confused. I still know who I am. Now all I have to do is find out who the Montgomery Clift is that they are all talking about."[100]

It is a commonplace for stories such as this to proclaim that previous accounts have been unreliable and this one is the real thing. This assertion is underscored by the redundant title ("My Own Story"), the claim that the actor wrote the article himself, and the use of first person. Clift promptly takes advantage of his authorial prerogative to divide himself in two: "Just to keep you from getting me and that celluloid Montgomery Clift confused, I'll tell you who *I* am straight. You will get *his* story from other sources, so let him struggle with his own publicity." This false image, Clift writes, "must be quite a fellow. Bobby-soxers' idol, the middle-aged matrons' Romeo, the man's man, and the actor's actor. Also something of a heel, I've heard tell."[101] Rejecting these labels, he realigns himself with "serious" acting (i.e., the kind associated with the theater). "Seriousness" is something that needs to be fought for. "I am supposed to be difficult to deal with now because I want a contract that allows me to approve my scripts and have the rest of the time to return to the stage, or just wander off by myself. That, to my mind, is not being difficult."[102]

What others mistake for arrogance, ingratitude, or uncooperativeness is resituated by Clift as dedication to craft. Clift attributes his idealism to a series of theatrical heroes (Lunt, Thornton Wilder, Lillian Hellman, Tennessee Williams), all of whom maintained a consistent or exclusive connection with the theater. "Working with people like that," he concludes, "watching the way they carefully preserved their right to progress along their own paths to their own objectives—can you wonder that a would-be actor like myself would fight shy of a seven-year contract that would cost me the rights to the very things which they had taught me were the most valuable?"[103] Artistic goals should always take precedence over material success, he avers. At one point in his theatrical career, he writes, "I plunged into four flops in a row and ended up the season applying for unemployment insurance. . . . That was the low ebb. And though I hadn't made any money, those four flops had made me richer in acting experience than my previous four years."[104]

Despite a certain dubiousness regarding stars' actual authorship of these kinds of essays in fan magazines (not to mention the parenthetical credit to Scullin), I find that the literary voice in the article closely resembles that found in Clift's private letters. There too, Clift's opinion of his own work is exemplified by uncompromising standards and constant self-criticism. Writing to a friend, Clift stated that a man must be "a judge of himself."[105] This "would-be" actor appraised his film work cautiously, evaluating the films he had made so far from a critical distance. "Specifically—I am embarrassed by myself in *Red River* and proud of *The Search*. That's important. I could wish it were not so but there it is."[106]

The trope of Clift as someone outside of himself,

FIGURE 5. "Clift Sees Self," *Life* (December 6, 1948). Photographed by J. R. Eyerman, who supposedly used infrared lighting while Clift watched a screening of *The Heiress*. Time & Life Pictures, Getty Images.

CLIFT SEES SELF

Montgomery Clift, who rose to stardom with *The Search* and *Red River*, shares with his colleagues on the previous pages an intent concern for his craft. Photographer J. R. Eyerman set up infrared lighting equipment to catch Clift's face in the dark as he looked at sequences from his new picture *The Heiress*; the result (*below*) gives a good impression of the easy and expressive charm that has made him popular.

CLIFT WATCHES intently as he is shown playing a dashing and conscienceless fortune hunter making love to an heiress (played by Olivia de Havilland).

AS MOVIE PROCEEDS Clift registers mild interest, frank amusement, concern and finally uncertainty while he watches first rough version of the picture.

watching, recurs throughout his career. The same December 1948 issue of *Life* that showcased Clift literalizes the concept of actor-as-audience in a special layout titled "Clift Sees Self." Already described as a serious actor who "shares with his colleagues on the previous pages an intent *[sic]* concern for his craft," Clift is shown over the course of five photographs covering his eyes and squirming in his seat as he watches a rough cut of his next film, *The Heiress*. *Life* reads the actor's reactions as if they were a performance: "Clift registers mild interest, frank amusement, concern and finally uncertainty while he watches first rough version of the picture *[sic]*."[107]

In this series of images we are presented with the multiple positions Clift occupied: as producer of a performance, object of the gaze, and spectator. As an actor on-screen he has selected and performed gestures and line readings in order to produce effects for audiences to read. In the process he has made himself into an object, a text to be studied. As an audience member, possessor of the critical gaze, he is in a position comparable to that of any audience member. At the same time, he is in a unique position to evaluate the distance between what he intended and what he achieved.

There is another layer of meanings that can be inferred from these photographs: Because Clift is an actor on-screen, he has become fair game in public. His reactions to himself, when he is presumably alone and in the dark, are sought out and put on display. At the same time, because he is an actor and this photo layout is publicity, we do not know whether to read his gestures and facial expressions as genuine (internal emotional states unconsciously producing visible physical symptoms) or a performance. Above all, Clift is declared to be seeing not his performance but himself—a collapsing of distinctions between performer and performance that assumes that when an actor appears on-screen, he cannot help but expose the truth of his inner being.

Publicity like this encourages audiences to believe that they too can see Clift's inner self. The tendency to interpret actors' work as a reflection of their essence has long been recognized as characteristic of the star system. Clift's choice of roles, acting style, and popular beliefs about Method acting at the time (that the performance came from within, based on the personal memories and feelings of the actor) made it even more likely that, as we shall see, Clift's performances would be read as the deepest expression of his true self.

TWO

The Bobby-Soxers' Idol

FROM THE FIRST IT WAS assumed that Montgomery Clift was a star with a special appeal for women, especially bobby-soxers—enthusiastic teenage fans who made themselves a cultural force (and important potential market) in the mid-forties. Fan magazines promoted Clift relentlessly to this audience with articles designed around story lines and photographs the editors assumed girls would respond to. The main theme was romance.

Promoting his soon-to-be-released *The Heiress, Movie Stars Parade* in November 1948 warns potential female fans to "Watch Your Heart!" Once infatuated, the fan is invited to proceed through the stages of an imaginary relationship, using the magazine as her guide. The June 1949 *Photoplay* promises the inside scoop on "What It's Like to Date Monty Clift." In October, *Modern Screen* proves itself invaluable by arranging for actual fans—real girls just like you and me—to go to the movies with Monty. A photograph that spans a page and a half shows Clift sitting in a theater surrounded by young women—eleven college fashion editors (complete with hats and white gloves) chaperoned by two older ladies and a gentleman. "At a special screening of *The Heiress*," the caption informs us, "these college fashion editors compare the real Montgomery Clift with his celluloid version."[1] The eager young women twist in their seats to get a look at Clift, who, of course, welcomes the attention of strangers. The smiling actor, we are told, "relaxes under their scrutiny."

Glamour photos offer the reader glimpses of Clift not available from his films. Vivid color portraits of the alternately bright-eyed or brooding ac-

FIGURE 6. Lobby card for *The Heiress,* 1949: Olivia de Havilland (Catherine) and Clift (Morris).

tor (ubiquitous cigarette in hand) appeared in the pages of magazines long before Clift starred in his first color film (*Raintree County,* in 1957).[2] Rarely reproduced, these photographs contradict the assumption (conveyed by his best-known films as well as the images reproduced in biographies) that the images of Clift cherished by contemporary fans were exclusively black and white. These full-page images (see, e.g., plate 2), unmarred by text, are not only suitable for framing but designed for it.

The fan magazines that provided such keepsakes reassured the female fan that she need not be embarrassed by the supposedly irrational nature of her devotion to a screen idol; her feelings, in fact, were endorsed by actual movie stars.[3] Before the release of *A Place in the Sun, Modern Screen* (May 1950) presented a two-page story credited to Shelley Winters, who reveals that she too is "Mad about Monty." Beneath a giant floating head of Clift, a tiny Shelley strikes a showgirl pose, showing off her figure. On the cover of this issue the title of a Lizabeth Scott advice column is placed directly over the magazine's title: "For Girls Only" expresses *Modern Screen's* philosophy in a nutshell. Two months later (July 1950) *Movie Stars Parade* compliments the female fan on her single-minded zeal, proclaiming proudly that the love of fans is neither frivolous nor shallow; a full-page color close-up of Clift accompanies the story, whose title trumpets the sentiments of the female fan/reader—"Forever Monty." The title could also be read as a pledge from Clift to the reader, the signature at the end of a letter, as befits the fan's classic fantasy of reciprocity.

Although the dream of meeting, dating, and eternally loving Montgomery Clift continues to be available to those who have become fans since Clift's death, to men as well as women (as *Letters to Montgomery Clift* shows), historically Clift's appeal was assumed to be age- and gender-specific, as well as heterosexual. Still, there was something "different" about Clift. According to one source, "The platonic rapture [the bobby-soxers] felt on seeing him was unlike anything a Hollywood male lead had previously inspired."[4]

FEAR OF FANDOM

As Ackbar Abbas has noted, "When fascination is involved in cultural and political theory, it is more often disparaged as a state of illusion and passivity, characterized by the loss or suspension of critical faculties."[5] The intensity of the attachment female fans felt for Clift provoked a backlash typical of the long-established disdain "social critics, psychologists and journalists" had had for fans since the 1920s.[6] As Samantha Barbas describes in *Movie Crazy*, "Women and girls, in particular" were thought to be uniquely prone to "mass hysteria."[7] As film fans, women's emotional attachment to stars first came to be seen as "a pressing national crisis" when they "screamed, swooned, and wept hysterically" at Rudolf Valentino's funeral in 1926.[8] The bobby-soxer was merely the latest female figure to be caricatured in this way.[9] Labeled "aggressive and violent, unintelligent and unrealistic, simple-minded and immature, and at the very least, naïve," the bobby-soxer combined all the negative qualities with which fans had been tagged—childishness, hysteria, gullibility, even mental deficiency.[10] A 1950 article referred to them as "Our Drooling Movie Fans"; another called them "filmorons."[11] Although bobby-soxers had been pegged as "a promising new consumer base" for the film industry, their public displays of emotion were unnerving to forces of social order. When thirty thousand bobby-soxers "rioted" in anticipation of a Frank Sinatra concert at the Paramount Theater in 1944, the police commissioner of New York declared, "We can't tolerate young people making a public display of losing their emotions."[12] In response to a 1947 instance of this "new fandom menace," *The New York Times* "urged fan clubs to keep their 'half-neurotic, half-idiotic hero worship' at home."[13]

Over-the-top reactions to Clift were not restricted to impressionable teenagers. Describing the young Montgomery Clift, Loretta Young gushed, "His face was so gorgeous and so romantic, and everything he did, if you just looked at him, oh, you just died!"[14] (By the time Clift made his film debut[s] in 1948, Young had been a star for eighteen years.) Young's description highlights the sheer physical impact seeing Clift on-screen could have. It may be an experience beyond words, yet it demands to be described in minutest detail. The effect of the experience, however, can be so intense it impedes the speaker's control of body, language, and reason.

Words gush forth as the speaker experiences an irresistible urge to communicate under the pressure of intense emotion. Grammar breaks down, sentences are left incomplete as the speaker blurts out incoherent fragments (his face was so gorgeous and so romantic—and everything he did—if you just looked at him—oh—). The attempt, even compulsion, to try to put the overwhelming experience into words is marked by repeated beginnings (everything he did—if you just looked at him—). Words and phrases are simultaneously exaggerated and imprecise—gorgeous, romantic, the face of a saint—always inadequate. Ultimately, the attempt is abandoned as words fail. What might begin with an ejaculation ("Oh! Wow!") inevitably ends with an announcement of failure ("I can't describe it") or a limit state ("you just died"). Compelled to speak but doomed to fail, fans often strike people as embarrassing, embarrassed, inarticulate, foolish, childish. Nevertheless, their repeated attempts exemplify the depth of their need to describe the indescribable.

The fan's diminishing mastery over language is matched by an increase in the involuntary expressiveness of the body. Those who, in effect, find their bodies speaking for them are subject to being labeled hysterical, their pleasure pathologized. To quote Stephen Heath on the female hysteric: "Hers is a body in trouble with language."[15] Linda Williams, on the other hand, points out that involuntary physical responses are the hallmark of certain genres (e.g., laughing out loud during a comedy or screaming at a horror film).[16] An intellectual event (such as understanding a joke) evokes an immediate physical effect. Looking at Montgomery Clift, for instance, can make his fans gasp, bite their lips, hold their breath, and of course laugh out loud (see his "star entrance" in *A Place in the Sun*). What causes such an effect can be explained, but not the intensity with which it is experienced. Intellectual awareness does not fully account for and cannot itself produce the physical effect. The physical sensation incorporates but also seems to bypass consciousness. It is the intensification of emotion (a combination of physical and intellectual processes) occurring at such moments that can lead to the loss of distinctions between pleasure and pain, the mental and the physical, reason and emotion, knowing and feeling, defined as ecstasy.

"An overpowering emotion or exaltation; A state of sudden, intense feeling; Rapturous delight; The frenzy of poetic inspiration; Mental transport or rapture from the contemplation of divine things," ecstasy is experienced, expressed, and described in terms that are simultaneously (and inseparably) intellectual *and* physical, language-based and in excess of language (an excess that might in earlier times have been designated as spiritual or metaphysical).[17] In an ecstatic state, one is hyperaware of the body and simultaneously outside it, beyond physical sensation. Flooded with intense, contradictory stimuli, those in the throes of ecstasy struggle to express something that can be expressed only by a form of thinking or understanding that attempts to intertwine language and the real, affect and reason.

D. N. Rodowick attempts to relocate the spectator's ecstatic experience to an aesthetic/secular realm in what Jean-François Lyotard calls the "sublime": "Suspended in hesitation and agitation between pleasure and pain, joy and anxiety, exaltation and depression. . . . the spectator suffers an intensification of her or his conceptional or emotional capacity."[18] For William James, however, it is this very aspect of intense emotionality that defines religious experience. In *The Varieties of Religious Experience,* written in 1902, James argues that what most people mean by "religion" or "religious experience" is above all "a higher kind of emotion," one that "redeems and revivifies an interior world which otherwise would be an empty waste."[19] "If religion is to mean anything definite," he asserts, "we ought to take it as meaning this added dimension of emotion."[20] The bobby-soxer's allegiance to her object of devotion—in the face of criticism, ridicule, and being called childish—proves the emotional depth of the initial experience. As Freud says, "Infantile feelings are far more intense and inexhaustibly deep than are those of adults; only religious ecstasy can bring back that intensity."[21] The assumption that bobby-soxers' reactions to stars were the manifestation of misplaced religious feeling was recognized at the time. In the autumn of 1947, a writer for *Today's Woman* advised fans to "strengthen their religious commitments [in order] to curb the spiritual hunger."[22]

Despite the fan magazines' romantic fictions and the censure of social pundits, young women who were fans of Clift at end of the 1940s were a diverse group who inevitably resisted simple categorization. Nancy J. Lawrence, my mother, has been a Clift fan since she was a teenager. She was fifteen—the perfect bobby-soxer age—when *A Place in the Sun* was released. Her "fan practice," as it were, does not follow the path laid out by either Alumit in *Letters to Montgomery Clift* or the fan magazines. She has not seen every film Clift ever made, nor does she intend to. For example (and most surprisingly), she did not see *A Place in the Sun,* Clift's most deliriously romantic film, and refuses to see it to this day. Asked why, she explains that it is *because* she is a fan. "I can't bear to see him with a sad ending like *A Place in the Sun.* I don't like to see him suffer."[23] But asked what she liked about Clift at the time, she focuses exclusively on his sensitivity. "He seemed so fragile. It brought out the mother in me. . . . It was as if he needed someone to take care of him." She demurs, "I might be the only one who felt that way," but as with most fans, what seem to be private feelings are in fact widely shared. Only a handful of Clift's films stand out for her fifty years later. "The only movie I really remember seeing him in was *The Heiress.*" *Red River* evokes Clift's capacity for suffering and unorthodox masculinity: "I remember the way John Wayne picked on him. He was just not your natural-born cowboy." She laughs when she recalls seeing bits of *Raintree County* on television in the sixties. "It was really kind of a dumb movie, wasn't it? I'd really like to see that sometime. Never did see the end." She remembers *From Here to Eternity* as a Burt Lancaster–Frank Sinatra movie ("Was he in that?"). Then why does she feel so strongly? "It's interesting, when you think how little I remember him from, that I'm so attached to him." When pressed, she can only say, "I just had a real bonding with Montgomery Clift. Some people you really don't care as much. Look at James Mason in *A Star Is Born.* He goes off into the lake there and I really wasn't upset about it."[24]

Although this fan attributes her bonding with Clift to personal idiosyncrasy, many of Clift's fans cite the actor's sensitivity and vulnerability as the root of their attraction, rather than the actor's beauty or (imaginary) romantic potential. Sensitivity is an internal quality, the ability to empathize with others, imagine their fears and find ways to put them at ease. In Clift's early films *(The Search, Red River, The Heiress,* and *The Big Lift),* the character's sensitivity is demonstrated in scenes in which he is gentle, soft-spoken, and able to laugh at himself, admit his own fears, and soothe others. In certain contexts, such qualities are not valued. In the presence of aggressive, domineering figures like John Wayne, Clift's characters are in danger of being ridiculed, shunned, or physically attacked. The combination of sensitivity to others and vulnerability in a hostile world creates privileged moments in which fans are invited to imagine merging with the character on an emotional, empathetic level—to share his pain, read his mind, and know exactly how he feels.

Clift's attempts to define himself as a humble acolyte, pursuing acting as both craft and vocation, succeeded because the conception he put forward coincided with what the fans were looking for and what fan magazines offered—access to the star's inner life. By acknowledging the part acting played in Clift's life, fans could feel that when they saw him act, they were seeing the "real" Clift.

In his exploration of contemporary reactions to Clift, Steve Cohan shows how fan magazines of the period used the same terms to describe Clift in performance that they used to describe Clift the person: intensity, integrity, interiority. Cohan traces the way these terms become the circular validation of the actor that in turn sanctions the devotion of his fans. "Every new role submerges him further in the performance as a result of his intensity, which the fan discourse appreciates as proof of his integrity."[25] "Integrity" in turn was seen as the key to his inner life, to the thing he cared about most—acting. Submerged in performance, Clift allegedly revealed not only the character but his own deepest feelings—his fervent devotion to acting. When playing a part, fans felt, Clift was most authentically himself. "For Clift the qualities of integrity and intensity make 'acting' and 'being himself' equivalent terms."[26] Publicity of this kind helped establish acting as deeply meaningful to Clift, so that in watching him act, fans could feel they were being invited to share something meaningful to *him*. This simultaneously provided fans with an explanation for their intense response to the performer and confirmed their own sensitivity and intuition.

Having established acting as his calling, in his next films Clift foregrounds performance in a way that seems in direct contradiction to the qualities for which he was celebrated. According to Cohan, "transparency confirms the actor's fusion with whatever persona he adapts for a film role."[27] In *The Heiress, The Big Lift,* and *A Place in the Sun,* however, Clift underscores the extent to which his characters are aware that they are playing a role. Questionable in their integrity and identity, these characters are fundamentally self-conscious. Marked by doubleness, Clift's characters in these films are morally ambiguous; their actions questionable, even criminal; and their motives obscure, sometimes even to themselves.

As a lover, a Montgomery Clift character is often a man with a secret. In *The Heiress* and *A Place in the Sun,* Clift plays a young man performing a role, managing his effects. Conscious of his own beauty, Clift's Morris Townsend enters the world of *The Heiress* in full expectation of being loved. The character's kindness when he meets the awkward, shy Catherine (Olivia de Havilland) would endear him to any audience. He is gentle, playful, relaxed. The qualities Clift brings to the role emphasize the character's sensitivity to Catherine's feelings and make it hard for the audience to dislike or distrust him. The story of *The Heiress,* however, turns on the characters' (and the audience's) ability to gauge Morris's motives. What is the distance between Morris's pleasing surface and his true feelings? How do we quantify the balance between sincerity and pretense that constitutes charm?

When Catherine is introduced to Morris at a dance, he enters the scene as a voice-off, stepping into the image only when invited. Catherine's confidante and main source of emotional support, her aunt Lavinia (Miriam Hopkins), pointedly leaves them alone together. Morris politely asks, "May I?" and takes her place. As Catherine and Morris sit side by side in a medium shot, we are invited to consider them as a couple. De Havilland keeps her head down and shoulders hunched to give the impression of pained shyness. Heavy eyebrows, dark complexion makeup, and a low hairline define her, in Hollywood terms, as an old maid. Morris, on the other hand, fairly glows with youth. Although Clift was only four years younger than de Havilland (twenty-nine to her thirty-three), the age disparity seems much greater. In this shot, our first chance to look closely at him, Clift deploys his beauty with complete confidence and nonchalance. Later in the film when Catherine gushes, "Oh, Father, don't you think he is the *most beautiful* man you've ever seen?" it is not an exaggeration. But how can we (or Catherine) tell whether he genuinely likes her or is merely being polite?

Sitting beside Catherine at the dance, Morris asks her to add him to her dance card. As she writes, trying to hide the fact that the page is blank, he leans over playfully and says "Two *r*'s in Morris." Taking a breath, he launches into an elaborate compliment: "Miss Sloper, I consider you do me a great honor. You see, I'm rather choosy, too." He shows her his empty dance card. By putting them on the same level, he puts her at ease. Gently mimicking her clumsiness, he makes a show of trying to untwist the string holding the pencil to his dance card despite his bulky white gloves. He says her name repeatedly as he writes it down four times. When they finally begin to dance, he patiently teaches her to follow. When Morris offers to bring her some punch, Catherine assumes this is his excuse to get away. She resigns herself to dancing with an ungainly older man, only to see Morris returning with two glasses. Freed by her partner's sudden indisposition, she tries to apologize, but Morris takes a severe tone. Straightening his posture, pulling at a cuff, and beginning to remove his right glove, he responds coldly that she *should* be sorry. "Had the gentlemen kept his health I should have invited him out with sabers." He smiles at the end, to let her know he is joking about being cross.

Little performances like these establish that Morris is consciously playing a role, but it is an open secret, one he shares with Catherine. What she and we do not know is whether he is merely fulfilling a social role, behaving like a gentleman, or toying with Catherine, leading her on. Each character in the film, confronted with this dazzling polished surface, must decide whether any of Morris's purported feelings are genuine.

Clift is especially charming when his character is called on literally to perform. Visiting "Miss Catherine" at her home, Morris sits at the piano and offers to play a French song. Failing to convince Catherine to sit beside him, he calls attention to his seeming incompetence as a wooer by calling out to her, "Can you hear me 'way over there?" Accompanying himself on the piano, he begins to sing in a serviceable, modest voice. When he makes a mistake, Clift/Morris does a self-deprecating take—presenting the character as someone who is not afraid to look foolish or to laugh at his own expense. By showing Catherine his chagrin at his inadequacy, he makes it a source of shared amusement. He clears his throat and starts again, reciting a translation of the lyrics from their simple high-school French. "The joys of love last a short time. The pains of love last all your life." It is faintly ridiculous, but considering that the character knows that and that the childlike Catherine drinks in every word, who could resist?

Despite Clift's image as a matinee idol, straight romantic roles, especially those set in the nineteenth century, do not particularly suit him. Around this time, partly as promotion for *The Heiress,* Clift played Heathcliff in a radio version of *Wuthering Heights.*[28] He has seldom seemed as emotionally uninvolved as he sounds when called upon to pour out lines like these: "Cathy. Oh, Cathy my darling. Where are you? Oh, come back to me once more, oh my heart's darling! Hear me this time, Cathy, my own." His costar adopts an English accent; Clift doesn't bother. The emotional violence of Heathcliff (who is described by the announcer as "handsomely sinister with his dark heart and Gypsy eye") seems completely foreign to Clift. The combination of sadism and sexual heat that comes so easily to Olivier in the 1936 Wyler film, or to an actor like James Mason in the 1940s, will never be part of Clift's repertoire. By choosing instead to imbue Morris with a sense of humor, Clift saves the character from this kind of romantic excess.

What Clift cannot do, though, is mesh fully with the film's style. Writing to a friend, Clift declares his performance in *The Heiress* "mediocre"— "too glib, too modern, and in too much contrast" to those of his costars Ralph Richardson and Olivia de Havilland.[29] De Havilland's career up to this point was exclusively based in Hollywood, while Ralph Richardson's involved Shakespearean training and years in British theater.[30] Because Clift's unique blend of Broadway and Method situates him as an outsider like Morris, his discordant style can be rehabilitated in terms of character. If the actor seems out of his depth at times, an argument could be made for that being exactly as it should be. Morris is a pampered boy, most comfortable surrounded by older women like Aunt Lavinia who are eager to make him their pet. He does not have it in him to become hardened like Catherine, who famously proclaims later in the film that, when it comes to cruelty, she has been "taught by masters."

One scene with Catherine's coldly disapproving father, Dr. Sloper, emphasizes Morris/Clift's attempt to stand up to a master. When the imperious Dr. Sloper implies that Morris is a fortune hunter with a conspicuous lack of career prospects, Morris asserts that he has no debts and, like a gentleman, has been living quite correctly "on the remnants of my property." The haughty formulation is spoken with a hint of the mid-Atlantic accent prized in the American theater in the pre–World War II era. Combined with a stiffening of the backbone and defensive toss of the chin, Clift's performance here might be a glimpse of his theatrical legacy.

At one point early in his career, Clift went through a phase in which people thought he was consciously imitating Alfred Lunt, his mentor, teacher, and director, especially in vocal terms: sudden variations in volume, unexpected pauses, and unpredictable pacing. It should come as no surprise, then, that on finding himself in a film adapted from the recent Broadway hit *Washington Square,* Clift would call on mannerisms from his own theatrical past. Nevertheless, the fact that Clift/Morris resorts to this old-fashioned, traditional style when confronted by Richardson's Sloper only underscores Morris's insecurity. Although Sloper's keen, unflattering assessment of Morris will prove true, director William Wyler maintains a balance in this scene between truth and hope. By arranging for Richardson to be taller than

Clift in almost every shot in the scene, Wyler shifts our sympathy to Morris by reinscribing the vulnerability that female fans of the day prized about Clift.

Nevertheless, according to LaGuardia, throughout the shoot director Wyler struggled with Clift's inescapably "modern" quality—a problem the actor himself recognized.[31] Some of this effect is due to factors that are usually outside the actor's control in a large-budget studio film—in this case costume, hair, and makeup. There is something zoot-suitish about the padded shoulders of Morris's jackets and the swooping wave of his hair, that seems fatally fashionable for 1949.[32] In one shot, after he has proposed to Catherine, urging her to be true "no matter what comes," Clift/Morris sports eyeliner, lip liner, and a copious amount of Brylcreem in his hair. Near the end of the film, however, there is a scene in which Clift's performance seems so irreconcilable with the period that it confirms Wyler's intuition. Having abandoned Catherine when he thought she would be disinherited, Morris returns years later and tries to win her back. Left alone for a moment, thinking Catherine has welcomed him, he strolls around the grand house he was once so fond of. At one point, Clift puts his hands in his pockets and shifts his weight onto one leg in a way that seems markedly informal and thus at odds with the period. Although there are not many characters to compare him to, no one else in the film stands this way. With fake sideburns and a cheesy mustache designed to make him look older (an "aging" affect that is no more convincing than the white paint in John Wayne's hair in *Red River*), Clift's youth betrays him.[33] Where Morris is more out of his depth with Catherine than ever (something the audience now knows), in this final scene Clift is barely in the same film.

The "truth" about Morris (that he was after Catherine's money all along) is never definitively established in the film—at least not by Clift. When Morris fails to arrive at the appointed time on the night Catherine thinks they will elope, she and the audience are left to deduce that it was Dr. Sloper's threat to disinherit her that determined Morris's absence. When Morris returns some years later, knowing that Dr. Sloper has died and Catherine has inherited everything, Clift does not play the character as either a lip-smacking would-be seducer or as an exposed con artist. Never actively evil, Morris seems simply shallow, thoughtless, even childlike in his desire to be taken care of. In the end, he is as gullible as Catherine used to be; he believes everything she says.

The film ends when Morris returns to elope with Catherine at last and finds himself locked out of her house. He pounds on the door, begging to be let in. De Havilland and the film collude against him as she turns her back to the door. Morris is still imploring her as the shot fades to black. What is most striking about Clift's performance here is that his character is in such an emotional state he is reduced to grunting, having lost the ability to articulate words. In Clift's hands, even an unsympathetic character's suffering can be moving.

Scenes of suffering are especially likely to evoke an intense emotional response from the audience. Paramount was "deluged with mail from young girls in shock" that any woman could turn her back on Clift.[34] Asked fifty years later to explain what she liked about Clift, former bobby-soxer Nancy Lawrence focuses exclusively on his sensitivity to pain. "He was so vulnerable! Just reeking of vulnerability. Just suffering so."[35] Epstein gestures toward the voluptuousness of these fantasies of empathy when he describes his ideal close-up as an image of agony: "Pain is within reach. . . . I can count the eyelashes of this suffering. I would be able to taste the tears."[36] The end of *The Heiress* provides the briefest glimpse of a person pushed past the breaking point, but, as Clift's fans attest, it is a potent one.

THE BIG LIFT

Although *The Heiress* was commercially and critically successful, Clift's next film, *The Big Lift,* failed to excite much interest, even from his fans. Overshadowed by the films that preceded and followed it, *The Big Lift* has never been the subject of the kind of intense emotional engagement evoked by *The Heiress* and *A Place in the Sun*.[37] Even though all three films are romances that end in sorrow, in this film Clift foregrounds a lightness of touch and refusal of pathos that preclude the depths of audience identification invited by the other films' sense of the tragic. It is precisely Clift's playfulness in this part that makes it possible to see the choices he makes as an actor and to appreciate his use of detail and control of tone. It also establishes the film as a valuable contrast to the more successful, darker films, where story and cinematic elements contribute so powerfully to the reception of the actor's performance.

At first blush, *The Big Lift* seems to be a rehash of Clift's earlier roles. Between 1948 and 1954, Clift played soldiers or veterans in five of his eight films. As a group, Clift's soldiers are unusually blessed. Unscarred physically or emotionally (we never see them in combat), they face the future undaunted. Bright-eyed and gleaming, they are not heroes but average Joes marked by a special grace. In the immediate postwar years, they hold pure promise—above all for an audience eager to welcome home such fine young men. (Despite his repeated enlistments on film, Clift was ineligible for military service because of chronic illness. Classified 4F in May 1942 after a severe case of amoebic dysentery that required an extended stay at a clinic, Clift was troubled by acute, recurring colitis for the rest of his life.)[38] Shot on location in occupied Germany (as *The Search* had been three years earlier), *The Big Lift* marked a return of a kind for Clift, who had undergone changes of his own in the interim. This time he not only received star billing and pay, he also commandeered a captain's house. Rank has its privileges, and a star outranks a captain.

The film begins, as *The Search* does, as a documentary. A title card proclaims, "This picture was made in occupied Germany. All scenes were photographed in the exact locale associated with the story." As we watch actual newsreel footage, a male voice-over fills in the basic details of the Soviet blockade of Berlin and the western Allies' decision to begin airlifting supplies to the civilian population. Suddenly, we see the familiar title card for MovieTone News and footage of a line of bathing beauties. Hoots and hollers erupt as an audience of soldiers is revealed watching the newsreel we have been seeing.

Unlike Steve in *The Search,* Sergeant Danny MacCullough in the first half of the film is mainly concerned with securing female company. His first comment on hearing that the company is shipping out is that he is going to miss his date. Once they arrive in Germany, he plans to break the monotony of constant missions as soon as he meets a woman. Wherever he is, whoever he is (soldier, mechanic, or man on the make), Danny's restlessness is signaled by the way Clift wears his uniform.[39] When we first see him he is ready for his date, pressed and proper, his tie tucked, his hat (officially, a "garrison cap") neatly folded. On the plane to Germany, he wakes with his shirt unbuttoned and his hair mussed. On the ground he grabs a black leather jacket and gloves (and drops one) as he reports for training. He seems most at home in his mechanic's jumper and baseball cap, doing airplane maintenance, tossing ropes, standing on the wing, and singing rude songs about the Navy.

His uniform, in all its variations, is not a problem. As he changes from scene to scene, we see that the army offers him an unexpected range of options, the chance to play different roles and fulfill several functions. The first indication that his uniform might not be sufficient to his desire comes when his plane lands in Berlin and the crew is held up on the tarmac, watching a color guard perform an elaborate routine. When the men on the plane realize they are the ones being celebrated (they are bringing in the hundred thousandth delivery of the airlift), they become nervous and self-conscious. In a long tracking shot, the three men march forward, with Danny on the right. He has a smudge of grease on his forehead and hurriedly wipes his hands on his pants. Noticing that his jacket is hanging open, he struggles to zip it up but fails. Kowalski (Paul Douglas), his older foil, strolls outside the honor guard, telling Danny, "Don't bother, you look simply lovely." The man next to Danny barks, "Fix your hat." Danny pulls down the brim with both hands while the camera frames the two of them marching. Nervously staring straight ahead, Danny says to the officer, "I feel just as though you and I were getting married, Lieutenant."

The gay innuendo is neutralized by a heterosexual punch line. Waiting to be introduced and given a token of the local women's gratitude, Danny expects to meet an old lady. He half-turns to his buddies and almost smiles (which has the same effect as rolling his eyes or raising his eyebrows, though he does neither). When imposing-sounding "Frau Burkhardt" turns out to be a youngish blonde (Cornell Borchers), Danny's face goes blank as his eyes explore her face, hair to chin. Asking for her phone number, he comically reveals a pencil and pad, already in hand. Telling her that his only hope of getting to see her again would be if his plane caught fire, he jokes that he might be tempted to start the fire himself. Walking away, he pivots on a stiff leg to reveal a cigarette lighter cupped in his hands down below his belt. This sly shared joke gives way to open exuberance when he tosses the gift she has given him—an attaché case—into the air with both hands while walking away.

Most of the comedy in the film comes from similar performances of self-consciousness shared with others. A reporter stops Danny after the ceremony to ask if he will be the subject of a story on how the flour delivered by the airlift is transformed into bread in Berlin. Danny declines in a polite "aw-shucks" way: "I've read some of those 'pale blue yonder' stories." When he realizes it means a day in Berlin with Frederica Burkhardt, he agrees. He and the reporter both understand the rules. The reporter tells him, "You know the Air Force doesn't mind a little publicity now and then." Danny jumps in, shaking the man's hand enthusiastically, "They don't? I didn't know that." Each performs a fake sincerity that signals their recognition of puffery and institutional foibles. Mocking the gap between official representation and a serviceman's actual experience is a well-established gag among the troops. On the flight to Berlin, Danny plays reporter for the other men in the cabin while the actual reporter watches. "Tell me, Ser-

FIGURE 7. Lobby card for *The Big Lift*, 1950: Clift (Danny) with Cornell Borchers (Frederica).

geant," Danny asks the pilot, "do you find this life exciting?" Then, staring into the copilot's eyes, he muses, "You Air Force men are certainly interesting to listen to. Aren't they amusing, Mr. O'Malley?" When he attempts to answer a serious question about whether the airlift gives him a sense of accomplishment, the other fliers salute and hum "three cheers for the red white and blue," undercutting his clichés with patriotic hyperbole. Clift ducks his head, scrunches his hat, and purses his lips to show that Danny gets the message.

The savvy of the "average GI" does not run deep enough to amount to cynicism. Complaints rarely rise above grousing, obstacles are seldom more than an inconvenience. Unlike in *Red River,* no one opposes orders, and no one questions leadership or its goals. This probably has a good deal to do with the declaration on the film's second title card, which announces, "With the exception of Montgomery Clift and Paul Douglas, all military personnel appearing in this film are actual members of the U.S. Armed Forces on duty in Germany." The closing credits are a tracking shot along a line of men standing at attention, identified by name, rank, and branch of service. The last shot is also significant when it comes to the film's attitude about the military—another title card thanks the U.S. Armed Forces "without whose cooperation this film could not have been produced." Not only is the military omnipresent, the presence of so many nonprofessionals constitutes an acting challenge that is more an issue of neorealism than Method.

At the same time that he is signaling self-consciousness, not as an actor but as a character who is playing the all-American "hometown boy" for the press, Clift must also fit in seamlessly with a cast of nonprofessionals. Clift has to seem as versed in (and unself-conscious about) handling aviation technology as the actual pilots and engineers without putting them in the shade when it comes to line readings. The scenes where he plays one of the boys, for instance, showcase Clift's ability to erase himself. On Danny's first trip to Templehof, the landing strip precariously surrounded by tall buildings in the heart of Berlin, Clift sits on the floor of the plane between the pilot and the navigator. As one recites a checklist, Danny performs each task and repeats the order aloud. The ability to disappear is a basic theatrical skill Clift would have learned on the stage; a supporting actor has to know how to be present while letting the other actors dominate the scene. The comic takes (wincing at how close the plane is to the buildings) are given to Douglas.

Once the setting shifts to Berlin, most of Clift's scenes are with fellow professionals as the documentary style recedes and the fictional story takes over. Where *The Search* feels neatly divided in half, *The Big Lift* tries to integrate its political denazification arguments with fictional relationships between characters. Paradoxically, this makes the overtly political aspects of the film even more obtrusive. In place of the rapid-fire recounting of events surrounding the airlift that characterizes the opening scenes, the film's second act delivers potted lectures on how democracy is superior to fascism and how fascism had its roots in a "father complex." These "debates" substitute for character development as Danny's grumpy friend Sergeant Kowalski browbeats his German girlfriend, Gerta. When she introduces herself as "Gair-ta," Kowalski booms, "Gertie's good enough." Unlike Kowalski, who trumpets his disdain for the local population, Danny soon finds himself literally walking in someone else's shoes.

Entering Berlin, Danny is not prepared for the extent of the destruction. In the cab on the way to meet Frederica, he tests his German, dramatically rolling his *r*'s when he reads the address "Bar-ba-rrossa Strasse." Stopping amid a landscape of bombed-out buildings, he insists they are in the wrong place until he sees Frederica shoveling rubble with a female work crew. His voice drops as he admits that the cabdriver is right. Being humbled by the suffering of others prompts him to drop any pretense of knowing Germany. Although the switch from performance to sincerity leaves Danny vulnerable, it serves as a sign of his humanity and distinguishes him from Kowalski's know-it-all xenophobia.

Danny's détente with German civilians begins with an act of kindness that leads directly to another change of clothing. Seeing a workman dive for a discarded cigarette butt, Danny offers him a fresh cigarette and another for his friend. When the friend, hanging posters, bends down to receive the gift, he spills white paste all over Danny, ruining his uniform. Washing up at Frederica's apartment house, he emerges in a robe borrowed from a congenial fellow, Herr Stieber (O. E. Hasse), who spies for the Russians. When Frederica cannot collect Danny's uniform from the cleaner (who has been arrested), she and Danny have to cross the city to find the proprietor. Having lent Danny his robe, Stieber now offers his clothes.[40]

Danny objects, but the next shot shows a man on the street, his back turned, as pedestrians pass by heading for the subway entrance. As he turns around, we see it is Danny in a black cap, a black overcoat, gray suit, and black shirt. The clothes are baggy but not comically so. They can be read two ways: as clothes that no longer fit someone who has been without food, or as fashionably hip, oversized in a zoot-suit, late-forties way, like the plaid jacket George buys himself in *A Place in the Sun* or the supersize padded shoulders of the jacket Clift wears in a publicity still for *The Heiress*. Hungry and hip, Danny/Clift looks like a jazz musician.

Danny's masquerade is played for comedy at first. He uses paper to cover the holes in Stieber's shoes, rides in the subway where Berliners are harassed by the Russians, and runs for a tram that is so crowded he has to hold Frederica close. They rehearse the way things are now versus what would have been permissible in the old days. At a nightclub, he practices his German, working on using the familiar form of address, and drinks arm in arm with her in a way that leads to a kiss.

The most charming but least expected moment in the film is when the MPs arrive at the club and Danny, who could be court-martialed for being out of uniform, hides by pretending to be the fourth member of the trio on the bandstand. Singing "Chattanooga Choo Choo," Montgomery Clift is very funny.[41] He has never appeared looser on film. He bounces up and down inside his oversize clothes, a parody of an amateur. Oblivious to the careful harmonies of the pros, he bravely belts out the lines he knows. When the singers switch to German for the second verse, Danny is stuck. As the

FIGURE 8. Lobby card for *The Big Lift:* Clift, Borchers, and O. E. Hasse (Stieber).

MPs canvassing the crowd come closer to the stage, Danny begins to ad-lib train sounds—"chuh, chuh, chuh"—and even pretends to pull a rope for a steam whistle while providing a falsetto "beep!" Trying to be invisible, he keeps his eyes on the floor or gazes at the ceiling, chugging around in a circle in his train pantomime so that his back is turned just as the MPs pass.

Unfortunately, *The Big Lift*'s best moments are side by side with the worst. At the club he also sits through some heavy-handed civics lessons courtesy of the blustery Kowalski and his German mistress: "But what *is* democracy?"

Danny's impersonation of a Berliner begins to darken as it becomes clear that others have more serious things to hide. Kowalski follows a German out of the club. Confronting him, Kowalski accuses him of being a prison-camp guard who had beaten Kowalski every day to teach him German. (Part of Kowalski's antagonism toward this man is the German treatment of Poles. In a few lines of dialogue cut from the VHS tape version that is commercially available, Kowalski tells Danny that Frederica's father, whom she described as a brave anti-fascist, actually informed on his wife [her mother], who was a Pole.)[42] As Kowalski begins assaulting his former tormentor,

Danny and the women hurry to stop him. When shouting fails and Danny can't pull Kowalski away, he hits him. At just this moment he is seen by the MPs, who mistake him for a German civilian assaulting an American soldier.

Danny and Frederica run into the Russian sector, where they are caught by the Russians when they try to slip back to the Western side. While Russian and British soldiers argue over precisely where a line on the ground separating the two sectors used to be, a huge crowd gathers, and the couple nonchalantly slips away. There is one disturbing moment, though. Frederica argues their case, but when the British ask about Danny, she identifies him as her husband who was wounded in the throat. In response, Clift produces a strangled gurgle as we pick out a large horizontal scar on the right side of his throat. This scar was visible earlier, in the scene where the two search for the cleaner, but it had no meaning then. An accidental physiological detail of the actor's body (the result of childhood surgery), the scar contributes an unexpected weight to this scene.[43]

After an impromptu party at Frederica's, Danny tries to hurry everyone out, presumably so that they can be alone together. In the next scene, however, he is sound asleep when she accidentally or intentionally wakes him up. As they kiss, framed in the window, backlit by airlift planes taking off directly at them, Danny has changed places. He can now see the airlift from the perspective of those on the ground.

Arriving at the base the next morning, he no longer fits—or rather his old worldview does not fit him. His uniform has shrunk dramatically. This gives Kowalski another shot at a sissy joke. Knowing it's coming, Danny cocks his head back and displays his misshapen outfit. "Like the new look?" he asks. Kowalski responds, "Just adorable." Danny's time in Berlin has made a man of him; he has outgrown his old self and is not the boy he used to be, but is it real growth, or is he being reshaped/misshapen by a manipulative woman—infantilized, cut down to size?

Earlier, when he first met Frederica in Berlin, Danny spotted something out of place about her. "You've got an English accent. Where did you get it?" he asks with exaggerated diction, as if attempting an accent himself. When Danny thinks she is not who she seems, he makes a game out of it. Kowalski sees it as deceit. He shows Danny proof that Frederica has lied about her past. When Danny confronts her, she admits everything, and he walks away. On his journey through town, though, he sees how the people of Berlin are suffering. He shrugs off an Artful Dodger type (an overdressed, cocky kid, cigarette hanging from his lip) who tries to sell him something. He reacts in a close-up to homeless children living on their own in a dark-

FIGURE 9. Lobby card for *The Big Lift:* Clift and Borchers in the rubble.

ened concrete space. He stares at an old lady pushing a cart, wearing rags tied around one foot instead of a shoe. Exhausted by the misery that surrounds him, Danny sits outside a restaurant until two workers bring out the garbage. Before they can set the bins down, people rush forward, fighting to snatch what they can. Ashamed, Danny returns to Frederica sitting on a pile of rubble. Without saying a word, he bows his head and takes off his hat. He sits next to her, accepting that he has no right to judge what people have done to survive.

The character of Frederica is ambiguous until the end of the film, which accounts for two inserts that seem stunningly awkward at first. Strolling through a park littered with statues commemorating military victories, Danny remarks that the shattered stones are "not so victorious now." A sudden cut, punctuated with melodramatic music, accentuates the glowering look she gives him in response. After they have made plans to marry, there is another glimpse of her dastardly shiftiness. After kissing her lingeringly at a fence, Danny leaps into a Jeep to return to work. Suddenly we see her smirk at his retreating figure, again with the music. Again, he does not see what we see.

The truth about Frederica's deceitfulness is finally revealed when Herr Stieber intercepts a letter in which she outlines her plan to marry Danny, get to America, and then leave him for a German boyfriend who lives in St. Louis. When Danny arrives at the courthouse for the wedding, Clift underplays. At first we are not sure whether he knows. As Kowalski and Gerta look on, Danny shows Frederica the letter, and turns and leaves without a word. (*The Search* also cuts away abruptly from Clift's character at a moment that might otherwise provide an emotional climax. In *The Search*, Steve is told that Jim's mother has been found. Clift, in a two-shot with his back to the camera, turns his head to look over his shoulder, a surprised expression on his face. As mother and child find each other, the film ends. The emotional consequences for Steve are left unrepresented.) When Danny walks away from the courthouse, Gerta runs after him to assure him that not all German civilians are deceptive. He takes the information in stride (nodding, making no comment), and the next time we see him he is heading home.

Back on the base, Danny crosses the tarmac with his hands in his pockets and head down. He brightens only when he hears Kowalski speaking German to a cleaning crew—something he had refused to do earlier. Kowalski has decided to stay in Germany for a while; he admits he might have been wrong about Gerta and the others, adding, "If we never made mistakes, we'd be second lieutenants."

The Big Lift and *The Search* end in the same place. Young soldiers stuck in a postcombat military, without fixed plans, become involved with a German citizen as a lark. Moved by pity and compassion, they become emotionally involved. Lacking definite plans but possessing an inherent optimism, they are open, willing to commit for the future. When the long-awaited chance to return to the United States arrives, it is transformed into a crisis. Each character's emotional connections have been formed here in Europe, not at home. He will have to break those bonds in order to return. He may be hurt, but both films assure us that it is all for the best. We do not know exactly what will happen to Danny or Steve, but we are reassured that while returning veterans may be sad, they are also wiser, good people emotionally enriched by their experiences abroad, ready for that shiny new American life.

A PLACE IN THE SUN

Like Morris Townsend but to a much greater degree, George Eastman in *A Place in the Sun* is in a precarious position. A social outsider, he is keenly aware of being under observation. Afraid of making a mistake, he constantly watches himself, policing his actions. Clift's George Eastman is someone whose true feelings are so deeply submerged he is a mystery even to himself. *The Heiress* and *A Place in the Sun* are two of Clift's most popular films, and each features him as the romantic lead. But, as he did with Steve in *The Search* and Danny in *The Big Lift,* Clift deemphasizes ideal qualities in favor of complexity and nuance. He also intensifies the characters' enigmatic qualities, often at the risk of becoming opaque. In *A Place in the Sun,* George's self-consciousness is just the starting point for what will be one of Clift's most intensely internalized performances.

The title sequence contains the essence of Clift's performance as George Eastman. In this extraordinary shot, Clift also receives his first out-and-out star entrance in a film. Introduced as a figure with his back to us, Clift's character is hidden in plain sight. Hitchhiking on the side of a highway, suitcase in hand, he backs toward the camera. Suspense builds, questions form, as the audience is forced to wait until the last credit fades. Finally, climactically, the actor turns to face the camera and we see Clift in a medium shot, his half-zipped leather jacket revealing a clean white T-shirt. As if this breathtaking image were insufficient, the camera moves in for an enormous close-up—and Clift smiles. If beauty alone were enough to spark the devotion of millions, this shot would do it. At first this close-up resonates with Epstein's description of a close-up of Hayakawa as a shameless invitation to wallow in the beauty of the actor before the character has been established. Clift and director George Stevens are more subtle than that. When Clift smiles, it is not an open, unguarded expression. He keeps his lips together, the smile starting as a smear on just one side of his face. The wrinkles around his eyes, a presumed by-product of his smile, make his expression seem slightly questioning. He squints into the sun so that even at this distance we cannot quite see his eyes.

This is the key to his performance—either his back is turned or his face is lost in shadow as we wait for those few transformative moments when he will face the camera, open, happy, bathed in light. Even then, as shot/reverse shot is introduced in this opening scene and we see the giant bathing beauty on the billboard he is staring at, we are left with the puzzle Clift's character struggles with—whether what he most desires is the woman, a life of leisure, or both. At this point, Angela Vickers (Elizabeth Taylor)—soon to be his ideal—interrupts his reverie by blasting her car's horn as she whizzes by. His absorption in the image broken, he turns to find someone willing to give him a ride. But the ride waiting for him is not the one he hoped for. The debutante in the convertible has passed; in her place he finds a dilapidated truck stuffed with chickens and an old mattress. George hesitates, but when (through a dissolve) he arrives at his destination, he is smiling and chatting amiably with his benefactor.

A poor relation, George has come to his wealthy uncle's factory to ask for a job. Hesitantly presenting a card at the front gate, the unprepossessing young man finds he has unexpected cachet and is taken straight to the boss's office. Escorted to the inner sanctum, George is allowed to use the phone and sit at the big desk. Surrounded by luxury (wood paneling, oil paintings, books, an ornate desk with two phones and two lamps), he looks small and out of place as he twirls in the big leather chair. As in *The Heiress,* Clift takes pains to problematize the character's likability. In this scene, where Clift is some distance from the camera and we cannot quite decipher his expression, we are not sure if the character is innocently eager or cunning and calculating.

Like an actor, George works hard to manage his appearance. Invited to visit his uncle's home, George's first stop is a shop window where the young man in leather and jeans gazes up at a tailor's dummy holding a sign that says "Tweeds $35." The two mannequins in the window are supposed to reflect George and his cousin Earl, whose resemblance to each other is supposed to accentuate the differences in their upbringing and class status. Although the film works hard to establish a resemblance, the little-known actor who plays Earl (Keefe Brasselle) falls short in the face of Clift's exceptionalism, being relegated, if unintentionally, to the role of pretender—something that directly contradicts the narrative, which has George in that role, with Earl as the unreachable star (see plate 3).

Entering his uncle's palatial home in his new suit, George is out of place, a visual lightweight compared to the other men in their dark evening clothes. After an awkward introduction to the rest of the family, he sits on the edge of a large wing chair, his elbows on his thighs, legs apart with his hands folded between them. Everything about George communicates that he is alert and tense, self-conscious at all times about how he is being perceived. Not quite sitting up straight but not slouching either, Clift strains forward while holding himself tightly in place. Throughout a halting conversation with his aunt, George never separates his hands, gesturing with his fingers, even raising his feet, but clutching his hands together the whole time. When the conversation runs dry, Clift/George shifts his weight and leans awkwardly on the arm of the chair, staring at the floor, waiting to be spoken to.

Then Angela Vickers enters. When George was admitted to the house, he waited for the butler to introduce him before he began his long walk toward his future. The strikingly beautiful Angela lets herself in and waltzes through the foyer, plunging into the conversation, sure of being welcome. From her distinctive car horn to her constant chatter, Angela establishes her lively presence on the sound track, one directly at odds with George's cautious reserve and the reticence of his working-class girlfriend, Alice. Seeing Angela close up (a soft-focus shot that wipes out any sense of space as it jettisons the sharply focused shots-in-depth that preceded her), George is struck dumb. Everyone in the room gravitates to Angela as George steps away toward the far edge of the frame. Gazing at her, he is shown alone and silent, outside the vivacious crowd we hear off-screen.

The next day at work, George's cousin Earl takes him on a tour of the plant. Given a job in the packing department, otherwise staffed exclusively by women, George meets Alice (Shelley Winters). On the shop floor, everyone has posters on the brain. Huge displays featuring reclining women in bathing suits line the upper walls, hanging over the characters' heads like thought balloons or the relentless repetition of capitalist advertising. Each shot of Alice and George calls attention to the distance between the workers and these carefree bathing beauties. The women who work here do not resemble the company's models. Alice is the only one who comes close, but it is clear that circumstances are against her. Her shapeless apron and smock make her look more like the older women than like Angela. Compared to the casually windswept hair of the swimsuit models, her curls are too tight, almost priggish, while the lighting emphasizes her pouty expression and pasty skin, and the low camera angle gives her a double chin.

The relationship between Alice and George, forbidden by company policy, takes place in darkness and silence. Frustrated one night with his attempts at self-improvement (the memo he is trying to write has half its words crossed out or misspelled; a book titled *High School Self-Taught* is prominently featured nearby) and preoccupied with Angela Vickers (her family's name written in lights outside his window), George grabs his tweed jacket and goes out. In a darkened movie theater, he finds himself sitting near Alice. When he moves closer, she says, "Small world." A young seaman next to her, who at first seems to be her date, glances toward her with a hostile look and says, "That's what you think." The hapless Alice can't even get picked up by a sailor.

Walking home, George lays one hand lightly on Alice's shoulder, his gesture clearly a well-rehearsed imitation of sangfroid. Although George is presumably pursuing his own desires, the relationship with Alice routinely reduces both of them to shadows of themselves. Stopping in front of Alice's boardinghouse, he steps right through a hedge to kiss her, diving into darkness. "I've been wanting to do that for so long," he breathes, their faces visible only as two-dimensional silhouettes. As he leads her toward the house, they pass behind the heavy shadows of tree limbs, where they embrace again.

As their relationship progresses, the darkness deepens. Caught by the police necking in an old convertible, they end up in Alice's room, wrapped in impenetrable night. There are areas of light around them, but they are completely engulfed. Even as the camera moves in closer, eventually veering toward an illuminated radio playing dance music, we are unable to make out the characters except for a murmured word or two. When George leaves the next morning, his back is to us and we do not see his face.

George's scenes with Angela, by contrast, are lit for maximum glamour, culminating in the series of extreme close-ups for which the film is famous. They officially meet at another party at his uncle's. As he arrives alone, a high-angle long shot separates him from the couples around him. Throughout the long take, groups form and exit the room, eventually leaving George back where he started, alone and casting a glance over his shoulder at where the party used to be.

When Angela encounters George this time, he is in his element—alone. Like Catherine Sloper (but in a twentieth-century idiom), Angela's first response to "the most beautiful man you've ever seen" is "Wow." To deflect the fact that she might be awestruck by his beauty, the direction of her gaze in this shot suggests that what has truly impressed her is George's prowess with a pool cue (he has just sunk a three-rail shot while holding the cue behind his back). As Angela closes in, weaving her way toward him in a spellbindingly circuitous route, she ponders what it means for him to be alone. Is he "being dramatic" (is this an act?), or is he "being exclusive"? These possibilities situate him in social terms—either trying to impress others or to set himself apart. With a third possibility, "being blue," Angela begins to imagine his thoughts, suggesting that she might know how he feels because she has felt the same way. Venturing sadness as possible common ground, she enacts the fan's privileging of suffering as an opportunity to merge with the star. Angela's pursuit of George also gives the fan the thrill of identifying with Elizabeth Taylor. Beautiful, confident, wearing fabulously fashionable clothes, Angela does not hesitate to act on her desires (which are also ours). It is through her that we can imagine pursuing the enigmatic George/Clift.

In the scene where they declare their love for each other, Angela reads

FIGURE 10. Publicity still for *A Place in the Sun,* 1951: Elizabeth Taylor (Angela) and Clift (George).

him the way a member of the audience would, interpreting his emotional inaccessibility as a sign of depth. "You seem so strange. So deep and far away. As though you were holding something back." This time she receives an answer. "I am," he tells her. "I love you. I've loved you since the first moment I saw you. I guess maybe I even picked you before I saw you." Angela does not notice that her importance diminishes with each sentence— George's declaration of love slips from having her as its object, to her appearance, to the mere idea of her.

As Cohan has pointed out, except for the first declaration of love, it is Angela who makes all the moves in their relationship.[44] A passive object of spectacle, Clift's George invites women to desire him without scaring them off. Compared to a character like Brando's Stanley Kowalski in *A Streetcar Named Desire* (1951), whose brutal animal appetite obliterates the women he desires, Clift/George offers those who desire him a position from which to act. Like the audience, George is thrilled to identify with Angela, to become the mirror that reflects her class-based confidence, her decisiveness, and her active desire. Whisking him out of the crowded ballroom, Angela divulges her feelings in private. Proposing they meet secretly, she suggests, "I'll pick you up outside the factory. You'll be my pickup." (When she does stop by later in the film, she honks her car horn rather than come up to the door, like the fifties stereotype of a self-absorbed teenage Romeo.) Angela knows that George has been trained to obey, having observed his telephone conversation with his mother (a call he was pressured into by his uncle). Angela brazenly interrupts by blurting, "Hi, Mama," into the phone and letting a flustered George handle the fallout—"Mom, I just met her! . . . Yes, Mama. I will, Mama.") Later, as they melt into each other in a series of unforgettable close-ups, she assumes the kind of authority she knows he responds to. "Tell Mama. Tell Mama all."

In the close-ups that follow, Taylor and Clift enact the ecstatic state of merging with the Other, depicting the loss of boundaries that characterizes the fan's relationship with the image of the star. Abandoning the dissolves that characterized the first half of the film, Stevens uses simple cuts to suture the audience into this moment, making the close-ups so large that each actor's face exceeds the frame's ability to contain it. Over-the-shoulder shots partially obstruct our view of the stars' faces so that we have to struggle to see. At the same time we are too close *not* to see. The dialogue continues over every cut—even several cuts in a row—until we lose track of where one shot ends and another begins. This sequence epitomizes spectatorial ecstasy.[45]

This celebrated sequence exemplifies Edgar Morin's description of the kiss in cinema in general. In *The Stars,* he argues that the kiss "is the triumphant symbol of the role of the face and the soul in twentieth century love. . . . It is the profound expression of a complex love which eroticizes the soul and mystifies the body. . . . It thus symbolizes a communication or symbiosis of souls."[46]

As Jean Epstein points out, close-ups offer the filmgoer the best opportunity to meld with the star in fantasy and therefore provide the most profound experience of transcendence. This is "the absolute gift" the viewer receives, he argues, to be addressed at such an intensely intimate level ("never before has a face turned to mine in that way") and to be asked to share the star's emotions from so close there isn't even "air between us."[47] As the difference between Self and Other collapses ("It is in me like a sacrament"), other binary distinctions dissolve as well. Gender differences dissolve as cross-gender identifications are accomplished effortlessly, without regard for the viewer's biological form or sexual orientation.[48]

At the same time, this sequence may contain a warning to fans (who might be too blissed out to notice) about the danger of losing oneself in a fantasy of any kind, religious or secular. The confusion of identity played out in this sequence can at times seem more suffocating than ecstatic as George, like a worshipper or a fan, is swallowed up in the idealized, supersize image before him. If George is a fan, then Angela is the star; a face on a billboard, a name in lights, she is Elizabeth Taylor as she kisses him and the screen goes black. Called two of the most beautiful people in film history on the basis of this scene, the two stars strongly resemble each other.[49] Not knowing where one ends and the other begins presents desire as a closed circuit, with each character drowning in the self-referentiality of narcissism.

Despite the brilliance of the close-up sequence featuring Taylor and Clift, it is the scenes where George is alone that give the audience seemingly unmediated access to the character and his thoughts. They are also a lesson in acting. No longer signaling his self-consciousness about appearance through clothing, Clift/George turns inward. In these scenes Clift has to find a way to reveal the character without speaking, with his face in shadow or his back to the camera.[50] (Playing highly emotional moments with his back to the audience is something Alfred Lunt was known for.)[51] It also elicits (and requires) an intense imaginary investment on the part of the viewer. When a fan thinks, "He needs me," it is true. The actor needs the audience to complete the moment. If we do not fill in what the character is thinking or feeling, no one else will.

The most famous example of Clift's internalized acting occurs when he first thinks about murdering Alice. Returning from a failed attempt to secure an abortion for Alice, George enters his room as a silhouette, lit from the hallway behind him. He closes the door and pauses in darkness for a long moment. Turning on a light, he finds himself faced with a calendar. He tears it off the wall, puts it on the table, and circles a date. At this point, the scene begins the first of a series of long takes. We dissolve from the date to a medium shot of George staring down at the table. As he stands, breathing, caught between the (now) open door on the left and the name "Vickers" flashing in lights outside the window on the right, we hear a radio announcer warning about the dangers of summer fun. As he says the word "fatalities," we cut to a high-angle close-up of George, his head bent forward, his face bathed in shadow. Under his brow, though, we can see his eyes, wide open and alert. When the announcer mentions the number of people "drowned," George drops his gaze. After a moment, he inhales and begins to turn screen right, then sinks back, his eyes again in shadow. Finally, when the announcer urges, "so be careful," George pulls himself away, turning his back to us when he moves to close the door (again).

There is a quick cut (almost imperceptible) as George turns toward us, his face again in shadow, the left side of the screen dark and the right in soft focus. As the music on the radio blends into the film's score, Clift stands in this close shot for a full thirty-six seconds, more than two-thirds of it without voice-over. Breathing, his mouth slightly open, his eyes dart back and forth as the music grows in tempo and volume, evoking a train. Finally, there is a cut to a medium shot of his back as George instantly turns and dives onto his bed, burying his head under the pillow. His brief moment of blocking the sound of his thoughts out of his head is interrupted by the sound of Angela's car horn as she pulls up outside.

The idea of murder now becomes associated with this structure— George hiding (his back to the camera) intercut with an inscrutable close-up. At the lake, when Angela tells George that people have drowned there, Stevens frames the shot from behind so that we see the lake and the mountains in the distance, with Angela centered in the foreground. As the "train" music begins, we cut to a close-up of George and what we might call his guilty listening. Although his face is well lit, it is partly obscured by his shoulder. When the sound of a loon breaks the spell later in the scene, Angela exits the shot, and Stevens re-creates the scene's first shot so that it is now George's back framed by the lake. In one of the most haunting images in the film, this shot slowly begins to dissolve to Alice hesitantly walking across her front yard, waist-deep in the superimposed waters of the lake. This unusually slow dissolve takes fourteen seconds and evokes Pre-Raphaelite John Everett Millais's *Ophelia,* a painting featured prominently in George's furnished room.

When Alice interrupts George's idyllic vacation with Angela's family at the lake, the question of George's true character will soon be answered. (As in the earlier scene when he spoke to his mother, George takes the phone to the bar and tries to speak quietly to Alice as Angela waits nearby, keeping a keen eye out.)[52] As he did in *The Heiress,* Clift in *A Place in the Sun* manages to maintain an essential ambiguity. In *The Heiress* there is no clincher shot to establish once and for all that Morris's courting of Catherine is entirely pecuniary (unlike, say, the jarring inserts of Frederica in *The Big Lift*). He is spoiled and callow, but then he is young. In *A Place in the Sun,* George's head may be filled with thoughts of murder, he may be tempted, but his actions are ambiguous. He is truly manipulative only when he takes Alice to be married at City Hall and finds the offices closed for La-

FIGURE 11. Frame grab from *A Place in the Sun:* Clift/George thinking about murder.

bor Day and the door locked. Alice stumbles away in terror but George, left alone in the shot, seems quite cheerful. As he follows Alice in a tracking shot, George for once can't stop talking, proposing they take a trip to the lake and have a picnic. When he catches up with her, they exit the shot, the camera staying behind, studying a cavernous, empty courtroom as we hear him say, "Let's try and make the best of it, huh?" As the shot dissolves, the doorway to the courtroom continues to frame George and Alice as they drive through the woods to the lake.

In the boat, George seems to have a change of heart. After what seems like hours of rowing, Alice encourages him to relax and there is a moment of rapprochement. "Al, I'm sorry that I've been . . . so nasty to you. I will make it up to you. I'll stick by ya." Facing her directly, with the apologetic posture of a little boy (shoulders hunched inward, arms between his legs), Clift signals complete sincerity. But when Alice starts to reassure George about their future together, he turns away, bringing up an arm and a knee to close himself off from her. He leans into darkness, his hand covering his mouth as if he is afraid of what she might see in his face. When Alice mentions that they may have to scrimp and save, but that she isn't "afraid of being poor," he cuts her off with an abrupt "Stop it." "Whatsa matter?" she asks in a whiny tone. "Just—stop it!" He stabs his right hand out toward her, then puts his fist to his mouth to block the violence he may inadvertently express, physically or verbally. As she continues to needle him in her aggressively pathetic way ("maybe you wished I was dead"), he again cuts her off, loudly denying his manifest guilt. "No, I didn't," he insists, standing and retreating as far from her as possible in the boat, with a mumbled "Leave me alone." When she stands awkwardly in an attempt to come toward him, he commands, "Stay where you are," but it is too late, and as they both stand, the boat tips and they fall into the water.

The staging makes Alice and her unpleasantly exaggerated emotions responsible for the accident. When George is arrested for her murder and accused of having struck her with an oar, we know it is untrue. The accusation of premeditation, however, raises room for doubt. Trying to work it out with a priest in his cell before his execution, George himself seems genuinely unsure how to define his guilt. He is certain he wanted her dead and certain he took no overt action to cause her death. Whether he made an effort to save her or simply let her drown is the question. After George and Alice fall into the water, there is a sudden cut to an extreme long shot of the small boat, then a dissolve to the same shot the next morning, only now the surface of the lake is calm. When we dissolve to George climbing out of the water—falling, exhausted, breathing heavily—he is again in darkness. Climbing directly into the camera lens, he blots out the image, bringing the darkness with him.

While *A Place in the Sun* elicits sympathy for George, substituting an amorphous moral guilt for overt criminality, Clift does not romanticize the character. (He even fought to have Betsy Drake play Alice because he felt that she would be more sympathetic than Shelley Winters—a change that would tilt the balance of sympathy even farther away from George.) Ultimately, the film argues, George's main failing consists of not knowing himself. Until he knows what he wanted, he cannot comprehend the true nature of what he did (or failed to do). Accepting his guilt before the execution, George seems more vague than enlightened when he says, "I know something now I didn't know before. I'm guilty of a lot of things— most of what they say about me." The whole sequence on death row creates a feeling of dazed dreaminess, of an inability to come to terms with what is happening. As he walks to his execution, George walks into a visual fog—a memory visualized by the extreme close-up of Angela rendered

in slow motion and superimposed over him. Uplifting as a vision, begu
ing as a screen star, empty as a billboard, the giant blurred image leads hi.
to oblivion.

In *The Heiress, The Big Lift,* and *A Place in the Sun,* Clift's association with
saintliness is primarily a by-product of his offscreen image: the young actor-
zealot devoted to a higher calling, the acolyte humbling himself in service
to his art. Our awareness of the actor *as an actor* reinforces our awareness
of the depths of his vocation even when he is simply inviting us in to play.
In the first two films, Clift flirts with the audience, sharing his characters'
self-consciousness and their awareness of their own comic failings when
called upon to perform. In *A Place in the Sun,* on the other hand, the actor bets heavily on an interiorized style to convey the character's fundamental
inability to come to terms with his own actions and desires. Clift's next film,
I Confess, utilizes this same uncommunicative exterior but with different
results. A composite of characters from Clift's earlier films, Father Logan
is a man with a secret. Simultaneously an idealistic former soldier and a former lover, a potential murderer and a potential saint, he finds himself under constant surveillance, watched by others as closely as he is watched by
us. In the process, Clift's performance in *I Confess* raises questions about
the limits of his acting style and the relation of representation to interiority, and of acting to sainthood.

FIGURE 12. Publicity still for *I Confess,* 1953: Alfred Hitchcock and Clift reading the script.

THREE

Actor as Saint

A PRIEST IS BEING QUESTIONED by the police about a recent murder. His vows forbid him to reveal what he knows, even as he comes to be suspected of the crime himself. Up to this point, Father Logan (Montgomery Clift) has been a model of discretion, carefully concealing matters he chooses to keep private. Interrogated by someone as determined as he is, Logan is pressed harder than ever before to divulge at last what lies behind his studiedly impassive surface.

Detective Larue (Karl Malden) tries to catch Logan out regarding his whereabouts the night of the murder. Using misdirection, Larue opens the conversation by casually reminiscing about his own days as a choirboy. Logan merely nods, establishing that he is too serious and perhaps too smart to be taken in by small talk. Larue tries flattery, pointing out that Logan was a war hero. Logan shrugs. "I survived," he replies, establishing his humility as well as his credentials as a man of few words, a "man of action." Playing cat and mouse, Larue apologizes disingenuously at one point for confusing Logan. "With a murder one has to jump from one detail to another. Forgive me. Perhaps I jumped too suddenly for you." In a striking low-angle shot, lit for innocence, Clift/Logan opens his eyes wide, establishing that he is open-faced, candid, and not trying to be cunning. "Well, it seems I don't follow as fast as you jump."

Like Larue, Logan can be precise in a scholarly way, meeting a direct challenge with a carefully parsed argument. (In this he is reminiscent of a later cinematic saint, *A Man for All Seasons*' Sir Thomas More, patron saint of lawyers.) Larue calls attention to the coincidence of a priest seen leaving the victim's house at the time of the murder and Logan's arriving there the next morning and asks, "What have you to say?" Logan, in a closer shot, responds carefully. "A man of intelligence would not be led to believe anything on so little evidence." Clift raises his eyes and smiles, batting his eyelashes to underscore the character's guilelessness. This may be what Hoskyns has in mind when he says, "Monty produces his usual quizzical, hesitant innocence."[1] Dropping the pretense of the hypothetical, Larue asks Logan point-blank, "Where were you at eleven o'clock, Father?" At this point, Clift's performance takes a sudden, unexpected turn. Sunk in his chair, Logan draws a ragged breath, looks to the left, and answers, "I was walking." An upward inflection at the end of the sentence leaves it sounding unfinished, hanging in the air. "Alone?" Larue asks. "No," Logan answers.

As read by Clift, the line "I was walking" nearly floats, insubstantial and barely under vocal control. Saying "No," Clift holds onto the *n* for a moment, as if sampling the word before he commits. In addition to the unexpected intonation (Clift pitches his voice high, then slides downward in a kind of glissando), there is a sudden restriction in volume as he almost swallows his answer. The effect is one of indecisiveness, to say the least; in character terms, it is hardly a resounding assertion of innocence. Considered as performance, though, this moment has a remarkable effect.

Until now, Logan has made constant eye contact with Larue. But when Logan is asked where he was on that night, Clift delivers almost a parody of suspicious behavior. Literally shifty-eyed, he moves his eyes from side to side, looking down to avoid eye contact. Visually and vocally, Clift has abandoned the enigmatic reserve of earlier scenes and suddenly become hyperlegible. Not only does this performance contradict Logan's earlier placidity, the actorliness of it abruptly changes the audience's field of expectations. The telegraphing of performance as such adds layer upon layer to the character (he is telling the truth *and* hiding something, he knows how incriminating this sounds and starts to realize where it might lead); the line reading also displays the actor's facility, his wit in resorting to a completely unexpected melodramatic tradition of pantomime, his sheer nerve.

This astonishing moment is followed by two scenes in which the actor's expressiveness is shut down, his participation restricted to mute, static close-ups. Back at the church, Logan is hounded by the murderer, who is fearful that Logan will talk. Logan turns on him suddenly, and the killer recoils, afraid. But Clift's face in the close-up is blank. Pacing the city streets in the next scene, Logan is in torment, knowing that—despite his innocence—

FIGURE 13A–B. Frame grabs from *I Confess:* Clift (Father Logan) guileless and guilty.

if he turns himself in he will be arrested, put on trial, and publicly humiliated. Returning to the church, the site and cause of his dilemma, he gazes up at the altar. At this point, the film cuts to what the script refers to as a "BIG HEAD CLOSE-UP." What has Logan decided? Is he moved by religious feeling or trapped by it? Clift's face remains expressionless, ambiguous, indecipherable.

This is the crux of *I Confess*. Every aspect of the character and the plot would seem to mesh beautifully with Clift's acting style: balancing simplicity, sincerity, interiority, and integrity under intense pressure as the stakes increase at every turn. Torn between saving his reputation—even his life—and maintaining his vows as a priest, Father Logan is trapped, unable to speak out. Clift, too, is constrained, locked in mute close-ups as he plays a character forbidden to express himself. The close-ups that represent Father Logan's enforced silence in *I Confess* are a limit point of acting, the place where we confront the question, Are we engrossed by Clift's performance as an actor or enraptured by the face of a saint?

SACRED SUBJECTS

If the attraction to Clift were truly a "cult of the face," then a close-up—any close-up—would suffice.[2] But the face in cinema, regardless of how beautiful, is never only a face. From Epstein's meditation on Hayakawa to Roland Barthes's on Garbo, classical film theorists have found close-ups of the face to be the privileged site where viewers feel they have encountered the performer's soul.[3] Richard Dyer identifies Bela Balazs's discussion of close-ups as "giv[ing] expression to a widely held view, namely that the close-up reveals the unmediated personality of the individual."[4] Balazs goes further than that, however; he posits the equivalence of the face and the soul. In the close-up, Balazs argues, "the solitary human soul can find a tongue more candid and uninhibited than in any spoken soliloquy, for it speaks instinctively, subconsciously. The languages of the face cannot be suppressed or controlled."[5]

The idea that the face provides direct access to the soul is problematized first by the issue of acting. Balazs's position that the soul speaks "instinctively" through the close-up directly contradicts Barry King's definition of "'good' acting," which involves "the concept of intentionality," including the actor's "conscious mastery . . . over verbal, gestural and postural behavior."[6] Through training, repetition, and rehearsal, the actor can summon these skills "at will in relation to consciously formulated expressive purpose."[7] According to Balazs, on the other hand, the moral character of the performer would supersede his or her performance (i.e., management of effects).

The second problem with Balazs's position centers on the issue of representation. As Mary Ann Doane points out, cinephilia may be the result of "a relation between spectator and image, but it is the photographic base which acts as the condition of possibility for such a relation."[8] Any visual representation of a saint substitutes coded signs to signify spiritual qualities, mystical visions, and other kinds of unrepresentable events. The indexicality of photography, however, fundamentally alters the viewer's relation to the image. Soon after photography was introduced people began to question how—and whether—religious figures could be represented in this medium. Even someone as rare as an officially certified saint—beatified, canonized—presents problems in relation to photography.

Under canon law, a photograph of a living saint is a logical impossibility. Sainthood is always retroactive—one must have been dead long enough for postmortem miracles to have occurred and been verified. No one can be designated a saint in life, only recognized as *having been* one. To claim otherwise would be presumptuous and premature (before its time). Pictures of Saint Bernadette exemplify this irresolvable displacement in time. In images taken of Bernadette Soubirous in 1863, we have photographs not of a saint, but of a woman who would eventually be recognized as having been a saint. In fact, the church objected to photographs of Bernadette being offered to the public, as they could not vouch for her or for the authenticity of her claims to have been visited by the Virgin Mary. (It was only when it was decided that the proceeds could be used to construct a church in honor of Mary at Lourdes that the church agreed to oversee the production and marketing of photographs of Bernadette.)

Even more curious than the history of their production is what we see in the photographs themselves. Images taken by L. Samson in 1863 show the saint reenacting the moment of her vision. Self-consciously adopting a pose familiar from the iconography of religious paintings, Bernadette *performs* "saintliness." She kneels. Her eyes gaze upward. Her clothes are the costume of a "simple peasant." The pose makes the *signs* of saintliness visible; Bernadette Soubirous, meanwhile, remains resoundingly ordinary. If there is any transcendence going on, it happened elsewhere, in another time and another place.

If these photos were not identified as being of a popularly known, officially sanctioned saint, would we even try to see anything beyond these staged signs? Language names the image and guides our reading of what we see. Simply by virtue of having a title, the visual work is inserted into a narrative. The saintliness of Bernadette is invested in the image from outside the text; it is historical/hagiographic information added by the viewer.

These early photographs of Bernadette also underscore the importance of working with good collaborators. Although the photographer's dated aesthetic threatens to overwhelm her, Bernadette manages to separate herself from it by her very awkwardness. While there is no doubt that Montgomery Clift is a better actor than Saint Bernadette was, it is entirely to her credit that she is not at ease posing; it can be read as a sign of authenticity.

This brings us to the second question raised by photographs purporting to be images of saints. If the person being photographed is not a saint but merely someone posing as one, how does the fact that that person is acting—not present as him- or herself—affect our reading of the image?

In the 1860s, English photographer Julia Margaret Cameron created numerous religious images. As painters had done for centuries, she posed anonymous models as mythic figures—angels, saints, Jesus, Mary, and Joseph. The problem her work reveals is that with photography we can clearly see that someone is posing. The photographer's models are too prosaic, too "real." Cameron's posed photographs insist on the discrepancy between the indexical presence of the model and the exalted referent. There are two possible results: the ordinary is proposed as transcendent but never quite makes it, or the ordinary becomes exalted in *preference* to the failed fiction.

Partly what we are dealing with in Cameron's work is the relation between image and word. The images do not live up to their titles. The artifice is tacky (cheap scenery, thrown-together costumes, halos scratched into the prints); the roles are never fully inhabited. Cameron's models stubbornly remain people playing dress-up in the back garden. But in the process of failing to become one with the role of Mary or Joseph, these ordinary people come to seem transcendent in themselves, in their aspiration, in their yearning to believe, in the collaborative effort of photographer and model to reach something beyond them both. As in disavowal, we know the models will inevitably fall short while we hold on to the possibility "yet maybe after all. . . ." Transcendence, if anywhere, is found in everyone.[9] As George Bernanos and Robert Bresson would have it, "All is grace."

But there is danger in such profligate grace. Art historian Carol Mavor argues that Cameron's images "verge on sacrilege." "As much indebted to portraiture as to religion," her photographs are "a tribute both to the Virgin and Mary Hillier."[10] Cameron described Hillier (a "little maid of my own from early girlhood") as "one of the most beautiful and constant of my models. . . . The very unusual attributes of her character and complexion of her mind, if I may so call it . . . are the wonder of those whose life is blended with ours."[11] In other words, who needs Mary (the Virgin Mother) when we can gaze at Mary (Pre-Raphaelite housemaid)?

The irreducible doubleness that requires these images to be read simultaneously as portraits of Hillier and fantasies of Mary calls for a complex response. Cameron's saints are vividly human as religious figures (Mavor calls them "fallen Madonnas," "*altered* images of Mother, scratched with sexuality and printed with flesh") and touchingly fallible as people who inevitably fall short of a spiritual ideal.[12]

Cameron's models try very hard to appear blissful or transcendent, but what we see again and again is the labor of posing, how wearing it is. One of Cameron's nieces remembers what it felt like posing as a "sacred subject" between 1864 and 1865: "Pressed into the service of the camera, our roles were no less than those of two Angels of the Nativity, and to sustain them we were scantily clad and each had a pair of heavy swan wings fastened to her narrow shoulders, while Aunt Julia, with ungentle hand, touzled [sic] our hair to get rid of its prim nursery look. No wonder those old photographs of us, leaning over imaginary ramparts of heaven, look anxious and wistful. This was how we felt."[13] Ironically, while Cameron's figures yearn to be persuasive and the photographer made her models work long hours to achieve what they could, as the photograph of Saint Bernadette shows, real saints don't try half as hard.

Unlike Bernadette, who is a saint regardless of the success or failure of representation, or Julia Cameron's nieces and employees, who are not saints regardless of the pretext of any given artwork, Montgomery Clift occupies a more complicated position because of his status as a professional actor—in other words, the co-creator of his image. He is not merely an object dressed up and posed by others (no matter what some promotional stills may suggest). Nor is he simply standing before the camera, revealing his true, inner moral state. His image is an image *performed* by him. He is simultaneously the model and the artist-laborer who produces the signs by which the model can be read.

In defending the religious use of images of the divine, John of Damascus reassured the faithful in the early centuries of the church that "honour paid to an image passes on to its prototype; he who worships an image worships the reality of Him who is painted in it."[14] Even though artists used human models, the holy figure invoked by being *named* is the true subject, with artist and models mere mediators between the viewer and thoughts of the sublime.[15] The question of who exactly is represented when model and artist are one and the same and when that person is involved in a masquerade is complicated exponentially by photography.

The debate over photography's relation to the sanctified reaches its peak when confronted with the issue of self-portraiture. For centuries painters had used themselves as models in works openly referred to as *Self-Portrait as. . . .* Such a title announces its multivalent purpose: to demonstrate the artist's skill by balancing the realist requirements of portraiture with the evocation of a historic or mythical figure. In Albrecht Dürer's *Self-Portrait as Saint Sebastian,* for example, the artist not only cited the martyred saint (to whom we shall return later), but also displayed his skill in representing the human figure by depicting himself nude.

At the end of the nineteenth century, American photographer Frederick Holland Day made a number of photographs in which he reenacted Jesus's crucifixion, with himself in the starring role. Day did not take what he called his "sacred subjects" lightly. As his biographer Estelle Jussim relates, to achieve the proper appearance, Day "starved himself for months and let his hair grow while keeping himself in seclusion. When he climbed on the cross, he was an emaciated, tortured symbol of suffering, his ribs protruding like those of a Gothic grotesque."[16] "On a hot July day in 1898," while "the actors playing Mary and Joseph were suffocating in the authentic costumes obtained from Egypt . . . the half-naked Day writhed under his crown of thorns."[17] The result was a "small, beautifully executed Study for the Crucifixion, which had been Boston's first view of frontal male nudity" (heavily shadowed in the pictorialist manner); several stiff, less-impressive panoramas of Christ on the cross with attendants below; and the remarkable series of close-ups Day placed in a specially designed gilded frame and titled *The Last Seven Words.*[18]

The shock of a nude Christ (decried in Boston as "blasphemy, or worse") may have been an important part of the visceral response to Day's photographs, but nudity only exaggerates the fundamental question of photography's unstable position between "reality" and "art."[19] In a photographic self-portrait, the artist was thought to be not simply posing but presenting *himself* as a holy figure. That was a different beast entirely. A London critic declared Day "guilty of the most flagrant offence against good taste that has ever come under our notice."[20] Another pronounced the photographs "repulsive" on the grounds that "we are looking at the image of *a man made up to be photographed.*"[21] Despite his attempt to disappear into his role, Day-as-model is too present. As the critic cited above averred, "In looking at a photograph you cannot forget that it is a representation of something which existed when it was taken."[22] The unique individuality of the model is so pronounced that it overshadows the holy personage he or she purports to represent. For turn-of-the-century critics, the indexicality of photography made sacred subjects impossible.

"The crowning objection," an opponent excoriating Holland Day proclaimed, "lies in the fact that he himself poses before the camera as . . . the Divine Founder of Christianity!"[23] In other words, who does he think he is? In a photographic medium, the image of one person posing as another is not just a matter of appearances but one of dueling biographies. In this case, the biography of the artist threatens to overwhelm that of the saint. It is no longer simply, Who does he think he is? but, Who do others think he is? That is less a matter of indexicality than of publicity—something actors know too well.

As with movie stars, Day's personal life inevitably became part of a public persona that was used to measure his work. A British newspaper at the turn of the century "reported some of Day's renowned eccentricities, such as smoking a water pipe and wearing Turkish robes."[24] *Eccentric* clearly functions as code for "homosexual," as do other terms used to describe Day and his work, including *charm, dreamy fascination, delicacy, refinement,* and *subtlety.*[25] The late 1890s was not an auspicious time to be perceived as a gay artist, especially in view of the worldwide scandal surrounding the trial of Oscar Wilde. In the midst of this atmosphere of homophobic hysteria, it is little wonder that Day's work should correspond to "the fin-de-siècle mood [that] identified the artist with the suffering Jesus."[26]

Some contemporary supporters tried to direct attention away from Day the person by creating Day-as-actor. This enabled them to compare his work with photographs of the Oberammergau Passion play, first published around this time. (A film version, produced by Eden-Musée, appeared in 1898.)[27] Controversies about Oberammergau aside, citing the production would be one way to establish an accepted tradition of people presenting themselves in the role of Jesus. Photographing them doing so would be analogous to photographing anyone adopting the same persona: "In both cases a living person is used as the model," a contemporary supporter of Day argued. In terms of social hierarchy, however, such references were not likely to provide much of a boost. As Jussim notes, "It was hardly in the interests of pictorial photography to compare representations by actors with an attempt to create high art."[28]

In his monumental work *The Antitheatrical Prejudice,* Jonas Barish traces contempt for actors from antiquity to the present day. In 200 C.E., for instance, the Roman writer Tertullian declared that "actors deserve to be hated by all right-thinking people."[29] Two hundred years later Saint Augustine, who understood the pleasure to be had watching a favorite actor, nevertheless decried the excesses of fandom, laying the "degeneracy" that led to the fall of Rome at the feet of fans. "Those who took refuge in Carthage following Alaric's sack of Rome," he proclaims, "were daily in the theatres, indulging the craze of partisan support for favourite actors."[30] Finding similar disparaging remarks in the work of everyone from Plato to Nietzsche, Barish concludes that the "prejudice" against actors (and their fans) has "a nearly universal dimension."[31] "The fact that the disapproval" of actors has persisted "through so many transformations of culture, so many dislocations of time and place, suggests a permanent kernel of distrust waiting to be activated."[32]

Centuries later, actors are still either overvalued or despised—often both at the same time.[33] Because they are keenly aware of how they appear to others, they are assumed to be vain. Because they expose themselves to physical and emotional scrutiny, they are called exhibitionists.[34] Because they are persuasive in asserting beliefs they do not hold, they are accused of insincerity (*Imitation of Life* [1959]: "Oh, Mama, stop acting"). Because they desire applause and can fake passion for strangers, they are assumed to be promiscuous. Because they play many parts, they are assumed to lack a core personality (a television pundit describing a murder suspect: "He's a sociopath. He's an actor"). Because they are not who they pretend to be, they can be only hypocrites and frauds. Because they seem fearless and thus enviable, they are idolized and resented. (As one source points out, "Malicious gossip attaches most vigorously to actors" who are "conspicuously successful.")[35]

Negative attitudes about actors are rooted in the philosophical and religious assumptions that make up Western history. What begins with Plato's antimimetic arguments reappears later under the guise of theological proscription. According to Matthew Wikander, for "antitheatricalists and moralists . . . everything worthwhile lies outside the arena of representation, and moral responsibility inheres in attacking representations as false."[36] This position makes the conflict between acting and religious belief particularly acute. Protestant reformers, for example, damned both priests and actors by equating them—each accused of hypocrisy ("merely feign-ing sentiments [they do] not feel"), dressing up, performing piety, placing themselves apart from the congregation or audience, seemingly elevated above the common person while being in no way more worthy.[37] From this perspective, "good acting is like bad religion," with actorliness the antithe-sis of saintliness.[38] Actors (especially one like Clift who works in a "natu-ralist" style) are thus put in an impossible position, their job requiring them to stage "the inner self"—which is "by definition unplayable."[39]

Historically, actors have been attacked not only for what they did on-stage but for who they were offstage. Actors were held to be highly suspect as people. A writer in the seventeenth century asked, Who could trust "the man who can turn easily in every direction" and who is so morally mobile he is "prepared to assume any shape?"[40] Required to transform themselves from one play to the next, actors sacrificed the "simplicity . . . purity, [and] stability" claimed to be necessary for a balanced life since Plato.[41] If they played many roles (or one role too well) they either became alienated from their true selves (in Rousseau's view) or, worse, lacked a self to begin with (in Diderot's).[42] Thus corrupted by their profession, actors were said to suffer from "poor moral health."[43] Although he recognizes that the social distaste for actors is mostly due to historical circumstance, Diderot admits he "finds them repellent . . . in their offstage lives." He lists their failings at length: "ostentatious, dissipated, wasteful, self-interested," actors are "isolated" and "vagabond" with "few morals, no friends."[44] According to such antitheatrical sentiment, actors are seen as "somehow maimed, incomplete people."[45] For Diderot, "even their greatest practitioners . . . are little better than clever puppets."[46]

And what if it becomes impossible to distinguish between the actor on-stage and off?[47] Seventeenth-century observers worried that "with enough repetitions of a role [the actor] might be thought in danger of absorbing its qualities permanently into his own nature."[48] This was an especial risk for those who played villains. (As Barish points out, actors who played he-roes were rarely credited with becoming better people in the process.) There is one instance, though—perhaps the only one in the history of Western theater—in which acting was promoted as producing a positive *spiritual* effect *for the actor*. In a French play called *Le véritable Saint Genest* (1645), an actor "undergoes a conversion" while playing a saint in a play within the play, and is martyred as a result. "He has been singled out for favor pre-cisely *because* he is a brilliant actor," Barish argues. "The theatre has fitted him for martyrdom."[49]

In *I Confess* Clift is called on to make perceptible and legible the inner psychological and spiritual state of a character who has dedicated himself, body and soul, to obeying the command to remain silent about what he has learned in confession. This law of silence is not only a verbal prohibition: the priest should communicate nothing of what he knows through either word or deed, by look or gesture. Consequently, both actor and character are operating under extreme constraints. Like the pseudo–Saint Genest, Clift has been singled out for this impossible role precisely because he is a brilliant actor. Father Logan has also been selected (as we shall see, perversely) for the honor of performing his priestly office even to the point of martyrdom. Initially, the results are similar, as actor and priest are greeted with impatience and dissatisfaction. Throughout the film, questions about the character echo those about the actor, regarding the relation of outward appearance to interior spirituality; the relation of seeming to being in religious and theatrical discourse; in terms of the external pressures brought to bear on Logan and Clift; and in the creation of Clift/Logan as erotic object.

In *I Confess,* will we find at last what—if anything—lies behind "the face of a saint"?

I CONFESS

The plot of *I Confess* hinges on the main character's refusal to speak. Arrested and put on trial for his life, his best defense is a meager "I can't say." Every major character in the film tries to provoke a response from Father Logan, only to be exasperated by his silence. Critics have been equally frustrated, seldom discussing the film except to express a fundamental dissatisfaction. The most generous, Robin Wood, declares the film to be "earnest, distinguished, very interesting, and on the whole a failure."[50]

Because the character's motivation is as opaque to the audience as it is to the other characters in the film, the central mystery around which the film is constructed remains unresolved. The implied answer to the question of why he will not speak even to save his own life is simply "because he is a priest." This response, however, raises more questions than it answers. Why does it mean so much to Logan to be a priest? Why did he become a priest in the first place? How does he feel about the situation in which he finds himself?

Reactions to Clift in *I Confess* have been mixed. Donald Spoto calls Clift's performance "unconvincing because it lacks any real depth or sense of anguish"; "Clift's method acting comes across as merely wooden."[51] A reviewer in a contemporary trade paper thought just the opposite: "Montgomery Clift has seldom equaled his Father Michael, a man who, though his patience is tried, never once wavers from his priestly vow to keep the confessional inviolate. It is an eager, smooth and convincing portrayal."[52] Decades later, Peter Bogdanovich concurs: "I think without Clift the picture would be tremendously depleted."[53] A critic who is a priest, Father Neil Hurley, asserts that Clift "elevates the creaky plot immensely." Hurley applauds Clift's ability to convey the "priestliness" of the priest, an achievement he attributes to "a brooding mien, a distant look, and a mystical sense of sacerdotal solemnity." But even Hurley recognizes that Clift's "remarkably interiorized" performance ("more than Hitchcock expected or really wanted") risked making the character unreadable.[54]

From the opening scene, I Confess dwells in the ambiguity of appearances. The film opens on a dark night in a European-looking town. Signs clutter the empty streets, giving contradictory directions. Hitchcock strolls past. An arrow points toward an open window. The camera moves through it into a room where a dead body lies, a beaded curtain swaying in a doorway indicating that someone has just left. The camera continues to pan right until we are outside again, where we see a man hurriedly walking away. As he walks down a rain-soaked cobblestone street, we see by his cassock that he is a priest. Harshly backlit, he seems to be struggling with the buttons around his neck. When he turns in to an alley (in a dramatically lit shot), he quickly removes his cassock to reveal a suit underneath.[55]

Despite some objections, Hitchcock insisted that I Confess had to be shot on location in Quebec City.[56] As he repeatedly told the press, it was the only city in North America where priests still wore cassocks as their daily attire.[57] What he did not mention was that a cassock makes an excellent disguise. The cassock as a uniform publicly announces one's identity as a member of the church while suppressing the identity of the individual wearer. As such, it serves as an all-purpose distraction, a kind of sleight-of-hand that draws our attention away from the truth.

In I Confess, the first priest we see takes off what he wears and instantly becomes someone else. As the man who was a priest walks up the stairs into a church, he is seen by Father Logan, an insider looking out. Absentmindedly standing at the window, Logan is in the process of taking off his cassock too until he sees the man entering the church. At this point we know that Logan is a priest because he dresses like one. But we also know how easily clothing can be discarded.

Logan enters the church and addresses the void: "Who's there?" He is answered by silence and darkness. He turns back to fetch a candle, and then walks down the central aisle until he comes upon Otto Keller (O. E. Hasse), praying. As Logan walks toward Otto, the scene is almost too easy to read. Logan strides forth, the bringer of light, while Otto hides, on his knees in the dark. When Deborah Kerr, who worked with Clift on *From Here to Eternity*, described Clift it was in terms reminiscent of this scene with the candle: "Such intellectual purity, Monty's. His mind is so clean and uncluttered—like a very pure flame inside him."[58] A reporter observing the production on location in Quebec described Clift as "quiet, thoughtful, intelligent, and obviously deadly serious about the art of acting," and praised him in sartorial terms: He "is a credit to the cassock he is wearing."[59]

Logan stands over an Otto obscured by shadow. He is sympathetic but confused. He asks simple questions. He is brief, clear, open. Otto babbles, rushing from topic to topic, his speeches incoherent, filled with obscure references and subtext as he tries to explain himself while concealing everything. Finally Otto stands, face-to-face with Logan for the first time, and half-states, half-demands, "I want to make a confession." This is the turning point. Otto is not making a request but contracting an obligation. Logan *submits* without another word. Even before he is bound by the seal of the confessional, he has been silenced by Otto. Otto takes control, and Logan acts as is required by his duty as a priest.

Confession is a highly codified ritual that takes place in a space specially designed for the acts the confessional contains and produces. Room-size like a camera obscura, the confessional is an apparatus designed to organize relations of hearing. It increases the focus on hearing by minimizing visual stimuli and restricting physical motion in semidarkness (like cinema). It also controls the directionality of sound and endows specific sounds with meaning. The priest sits in the center compartment and hears from one penitent at a time, the one on his left or the one to his right. Which one is determined by the priest opening a small window into one of the compartments by means of a sliding door. This motion is audible so that the occupants all know by aural cues when they should listen, speak, or remain silent. Such an architectural device serves the purpose of what Jonathan Sterne calls "mediate auscultation," or the use by trained specialists of a mechanical device or apparatus for listening.[60] The device shows users *how* to listen and suggests what they should listen for. Institutional values determine which sounds have meaning and which are designated "meaningless." (For example, a doctor with a stethoscope would listen to the resonance of a voice within a chest and ignore the words being said; a priest would hear the words and dismiss the cough.)

In *The History of Sexuality,* Foucault describes the power relations underlying confession as a religious practice.[61] In *I Confess,* however, Otto completely upends the traditional power dynamic between priest and penitent, exposing an unforeseen weakness in the priest's position. In the confessional, Logan's ability to maneuver—like Clift's performance—is dramatically restricted. From the first, what he can say has been predetermined. "When was your last confession?" When Otto does not answer, Logan presses the issue: "Can you say approximately?" Ironically, the mundane quality of this routine not only satisfies the demands of the church, it also creates suspense. We know what Otto has done. The delay in his saying it only increases our eagerness to see how Logan will react. With a cut to an extreme close-up of Otto's mouth, the previous two-shot is divided into separate close-ups. The confession we have been made to wait for finally happens as Otto blurts out, "I killed Mr. Villette." Cut to Logan, alone, with the shadow of a cross on his forehead, symbolically marking him both as a priest and a bearer of the cross. There is a long pause.

This is the kernel out of which the film develops: Otto's mouth to Logan's ear, with Logan silenced as a result. Otto's confession demands a response, but confession as a religious practice forbids a response. As with all suspense-film heroes, Logan is placed in an impossible position, which can (and will) only get worse. The film's suspense will be built on how—or whether—he gets out of this position or is destroyed by it. Eventually Logan says all he can say: "Go on," and the scene dissolves to Otto completing his confession to his wife, Alma.

The first time we see Logan after the confession is the next morning after Mass, when he is about to remove his vestments (also marked by a cross). When Logan arrives back at the rectory, he wears the same style of cassock worn by the other priests: Father Millais, the senior priest, who speaks in a convoluted, insinuating, Jesuitical style; and Father Benoit, the naive young priest, who seems to have no work to perform though he is always either coming or going. Logan is placed between the poles of canny older priest and idealistic youth. He is supposedly neither cynical nor naive.

Even before he comes to be suspected of the crime, Logan's appearance is routinely monitored by others. During the breakfast scene, we find he has also become the object of a series of looks. As Thomas Leitch points out, Logan is constantly subjected to suspicious gazes.[62] The other charac-

FIGURE 14. Lobby card from *I Confess:* Gilles Pelletier (Father Benoit), Dolly Haas (Alma Keller), Clift, and Charles André (Father Millais).

ters watch him, trying to reconcile what they see with what they assume based on his clothes and job. The morning after hearing Otto's confession, Clift's Logan seems pleasant, unruffled, inscrutable. As she serves the coffee, the housekeeper (Otto's wife, Alma, played by Dolly Haas) scrutinizes Logan's bland surface, trying to find some visible sign of what he knows. With a traveling point-of-view shot, we see him through her eyes: he is blank.

Managing appearances, both Logan and Otto go to Villette's the day after the confession because they are expected. Not only do they continue to do their jobs, they intend to be seen doing their jobs. Both also have secret motives. Logan had an appointment with Villette, so here he is. He cannot let what he has learned in confidence change his behavior. Otto, who has come to "discover" the body and call the police, sees Logan arrive and arrange to speak with the police later. As Larue, the police detective, questions Otto, Hitchcock frames him in an extreme close-up. A giant eye, staring past Otto's head, Larue sees Logan meet a woman across the street and begins to wonder. Logan, it seems, has another reason to be there, one that remains secret. When he meets the woman, he quickly steers her away. She says something cryptic ("We're free"), raising the question, Free from what? or *for* what? The introduction of Ruth (Anne Baxter) multiplies the opportunities for guilt associated with the title as it raises questions about the main character.

Suspense requires the suggestion that Logan has his own secrets; the Production Code required that a priest be above suspicion.[63] Consequently, the film imposes a silence beyond that governing the rules of confession. There follows a series of scenes in which Logan refuses to divulge not only what he knows, but also who he is. This leaves the other characters as frustrated and dissatisfied in their encounters with him as spectators and critics have been with the film.

Dissatisfaction

When Otto returns to the rectory after speaking to the police, he finds Logan standing on a ladder, painting a wall. Otto makes himself the center of attention, announcing to Father Millais that Villette is dead. "I discovered the body. I called the police." As he relates the news, Otto cannot take his eyes off Logan. He waits for a response, a reaction. But every potential reaction shot presents the same thing—Logan with his back turned, not responding. Clift's performance as an actor at this moment is remarkably subtle and suggestive. Do we see Logan pause, or is he just being careful with the paint? (Clift's friend Jack Larson recalls this scene as an example of Clift's work process. "The first time that I ever saw him working on something [was] on *I Confess*. He was working out how to paint a room."[64] This was also the first time they met. Clift was in a cassock, Larson dressed as a sailor.)

As soon as Otto enters the room and sees Logan, he begins taking off his jacket and unbuttoning his sleeves, presumably preparing to help Logan paint. But once Father Millais has exited, Otto rushes to Logan.

> OTTO: Father, I must speak to you. I know what you must think of me. But I can't give myself up, I can't. They would hang me. Hasn't God forgiven me, thanks to you? But the police never would.
>
> LOGAN: I don't know what you're talking about.
>
> OTTO: But it was *I* who confessed to you. It was *my* confession. I want you to speak to me about it.

As Otto pleads for guidance, Logan responds, "There *is* nothing I can add to what I've already said." Throwing up his hands, Clift tries to make this line as sympathetic as possible, but Logan is still not giving Otto the advice, or attention, he wants.

Technically, Logan is adhering to a rule regarding confession that is less known than the law of silence. Not only are priests forbidden to tell others what they have heard in confession, they are not supposed to mention it to the penitent afterward or show any signs of knowledge outside the confessional. Otto understands things differently. For Otto, the confession has initiated a relationship, an extremely close one based on sharing the deepest confidences. Logan, however, refuses to let that relationship develop any further. Otto reads Logan's refusal to engage as resistance and presses him. "Aren't you young? Haven't you ever been afraid? You are so good. It's easy for you to be good." Climbing the other side of the ladder, constantly looking up at Logan on his pedestal, the unlovely, unlovable Otto begins to reach out to touch his idol—"Have you no pity for me?"—only to be interrupted by Alma, calling his name. The scene ends in uncomfortable silence, Alma positioned between the two men, the obstacle in the middle of a triangle.

The other person who presses Logan for an emotional revelation is Ruth, the woman he met outside Villette's. She and Logan meet on the ferry to confer (or rather, she summons him and he complies). Like Otto, Ruth attempts to deepen her relationship with Father Logan (whom she calls by his first name, Michael) by confessing something. She has loved him for years, despite her marriage. "I love you, Michael. I've always been in love with you. I know it's wrong." She assumes he also has been living a lie and only threw himself into the priesthood out of disappointment over losing her. When, on the contrary, he reaffirms that he chose to be a priest, she refuses to believe it. As is typical of her character, Ruth becomes convinced his life revolves around her and begins speaking for him:

> RUTH: You're in love with me. You've always been in love with me. You haven't changed.
>
> LOGAN: Ruth, I've changed. You've changed, too.
>
> RUTH: You want me to pretend then.
>
> LOGAN: No, I don't want you to pretend. But—R-Ruth. Do you understand? I *chose* to be what I am. I *believe* in what I am.

Logan tries to explain that he is concerned for her ("I want you to see things as they are and not—not go on . . . hurting yourself"), but Ruth shudders at his gentle but unambiguous rejection. Even though Logan has diplomatically avoided saying outright that he does not love her (and, even worse, that she has been deluding herself), she reacts with embarrassment and fury. "Don't pity me. I—I shan't trouble you again."

Again, Logan's resistance to letting a professional relationship develop into a personal one is experienced as rejection, and those who have failed to draw him closer turn against him. In an earlier version of the script Ruth does more than withdraw. After telling him, "I shan't bother you again," she adds a bitter dismissal, "I don't care what happens to you now." The script makes her hostility even more explicit when she hears from her long-suffering husband that Logan has become a suspect. "I hope he's in trouble—terrible trouble," she responds.[65]

Ruth's frustration with Logan was mirrored by Anne Baxter's discomfort in working with Clift. While other actresses were routinely complimentary when it came to working with him, Baxter complained that when she and Clift performed this scene on the boat, she wasn't "getting anything" back from him (which might have been the point). In the scene on the ferry, she relates, "I was to look longingly at him while baring my soul. To do that, I needed something, some response from him. But there was nothing, just a blank and distant gaze."[66]

With both Otto and Ruth, Logan has a ready answer for his inability to respond in kind. One critic spells it out: "Michael cannot reciprocate because of his priestly vows."[67] Unless we know Logan's inner convictions, his vocation, his vows can be seen as an entirely external constraint. They might also be an excuse. Nevertheless, external constraints are real and, in the film, plentiful.

Not only do Alma, Otto, and Father Millais keep an eye on Logan at the rectory, but he is also being watched by the police. When he goes to meet Ruth on the ferry, we see a squad car pull out from the curb to follow him. There is even a comic moment when police and church surveillance become interchangeable. On the ferry, Logan tells Ruth, "You shouldn't be seen talking to me. There are probably police all over the boat." Hitchcock cuts to three possible sets of undercover agents: a father with a child, a man with a newspaper, and two Franciscan friars. (The last couple must be Hitchcock's addition, as the Franciscans do not appear in any version of the script.)

The third character who becomes progressively more frustrated in his dealings with Logan is Detective Larue. The disarming resurgence of nineteenth-century Delsartean pantomime discussed above sets up the scene's climax: Logan's proclamation of ineffectualness.[68] Earlier, when Larue tried to find out the identity of the woman he saw with Logan at Villette's, Logan took refuge in privilege (without identifying it as such).

FIGURE 15. Clift and Anne Baxter (Ruth) on the set of *I Confess*.

His priestly prerogative, however, is phrased as personal choice, even personal insufficiency: "I wish I could discuss it, but I can't." He stresses that the woman has nothing to do with the murder: "You'll have to take my word for it." Larue responds, "I respect your word, but I need your help." In a striking low-angle close-up, Logan asserts, "I'm unable to help"—again depicting his refusal as weakness. Frustrated when Logan refuses to say with whom he was walking, Larue asks, "Father, don't you want to help me?" Logan answers weakly, "I've done my best." "But you refuse to answer my questions," Larue insists. Breaking out of the mise-en-scène of previous shots where Larue impinged on his space, Logan is shown from an intense low angle. As an actor, Clift writhes within the frame as Logan struggles to speak despite all the things that restrain him. "I'm sorry. I know . . . I—I—I—It isn't possible for me to answer them."

Logan's maintenance of professional boundaries prevents emotional contact with others, leaving them dissatisfied and frustrated. Three times running, in scenes with Otto, Ruth, and Larue, Logan cannot articulate *why* he is who he is. He can't speak. He can't act. The only thing he makes absolutely clear is that he can't help. Logan's interiority and seeming passivity drive the characters around him to extremes. Otto frames him for murder. Larue wants to arrest him. Ruth is furious on the ferry and decides to "help" Michael by going to the police to give him an alibi. Ruth's self-sacrificing gesture (in addition to humiliating her husband) provides the motive the police have been looking for and seals Logan's fate.

Interestingly, like Baxter, Karl Malden complained about his personal frustration with Clift the actor in ways that paralleled the interaction between their characters. In his memoirs, Malden says he felt shut out by Clift. After having had wonderful rehearsals, he thought that Clift ignored him during the scene, conferring instead with his friend and drama coach Mira Rostova, who stayed on the set during shooting. Like Baxter, Malden sounds excluded, jealous, and hurt.

Logan's refusal to connect, to comply with emotional demands, is exemplified by his silence, his holding himself aloof. Because Logan keeps everything inside, interiority becomes the film's model of spirituality. This privileging of religious practices that are cloistered and private over public expressions of faith that take place in communal settings is entirely in sync with the "aura of withdrawal and introversion" typical of Clift's acting style.[69] It also fits in well with Hitchcock's preference for conveying information through editing and mise-en-scène instead of dialogue and avoids the censors' sensitivity regarding psychological explanations (as we will see). But the assumption that spirituality is a private, internal struggle as opposed to a matter of social activism or community relationships has serious theological implications. In this way, *I Confess* reflects a key film from the period whose main character, production methods, and representation of spiritual practice are surprisingly similar.

Robert Bresson's *The Diary of a Country Priest* (1950) also faces the challenge of how to represent an internalized spirituality while focusing on a character who is socially isolated. Both films are emotionally distant texts, built around characters who struggle with their inability to communicate or to respond in any satisfactory way to expressions of dissatisfaction from those they are trying to help. We have seen how Logan's inability to explain his refusal to communicate results in his deepest beliefs being obscured or unexpressed. The title character in *The Diary of a Country Priest* finds himself in a similar position. One critic links the French priest's suffering directly to his internalized spiritual life. "In that film, we have a deeply interiorized curé so attuned to divine inspiration that the sins of the parishioners and townspeople weigh heavily on him."[70] Unable to share his experience with others, he suffers in silence. For the most part, he lives in silence. The other characters dislike these saintly heroes precisely because they are saintly. "People don't hate you for your simplicity," the French priest is told. "They defend themselves against it. It burns them." "You're *so* good," Otto murmurs to Logan. "It's easy for you to be good."

Both films exemplify the postwar interest in neorealism through their use of location shooting, an ascetic style, and an aesthetic that privileges "nonprofessional" acting. Critics have compared the two leading actors in terms of style and looks, one stating outright that "Clift's countenance and bearing resemble those of the cleric in the moving Robert Bresson film."[71] The two actors, however, were very different in terms of training: Claude Laydu, who starred in *The Diary of a Country Priest,* was an amateur whereas Clift was good enough to be mistaken for one. Even with their different backgrounds, Laydu and Clift were not very different when it came to preparation. Like Clift, who spent a week in a monastery in Quebec the summer before shooting began on *I Confess,* Laydu spent "time fasting and meditating in Normandy before filming started."[72] One author finds such activities "superficially akin to the tricks and techniques of Stanislavsky or the Actors' Studio," echoing a distrust of acting that surely resonated with Bresson and Hitchcock.[73]

In their films, Bresson and Hitchcock look for ways to make their characters actor-proof. Bresson does this by casting nonprofessionals. "The thing that matters is not what they show me but what they hide from me and, above all, what they do not suspect is in them," Bresson said.[74] In this formulation, actors are not in control of the effects they have; the image produced uses them but its production is beyond them, despite them. To circumvent "tricks" such as acting, the director may not even tell the performer who the character is supposed to be. It is said that "Claude Laydu did not realize until he had watched the final version of the film that he had been playing a saint."[75] Hitchcock, by contrast, attempts to bypass (or supersede) the acting of an established star by relying on editing. Time and again in *I Confess* we cut to a close-up of Clift/Logan at a moment when he finds himself unable to speak, compelled *not* to communicate. *Diary* also privileges silent close-ups of the main character as Bresson, like Hitchcock, supplants acting with editing and expressive mise-en-scène. In these silent close-ups, the characters are struck speechless as the audience struggles to imagine the priests' pain at being unable to express their inner feelings. Too much suppression of the character's thoughts and emotions, though, risks leaving audiences frustrated and dissatisfied.

The elevation of "nonacting" reinforces both films' definitions of the spiritual. When it is said that Bresson "rigorously eliminates the psychological and the social alike, to centre everything on the spiritual drama,"[76] two things are assumed: that actors provide psychological depth to characters, and that they must be stopped from doing so because in these films spirituality is neither psychological nor social. Because the spiritual is indescribable for Bresson and Hitchcock, it is also unrepresentable. In Bresson's film in particular, Christian spirituality ("oneness with Christ") cannot be represented because it "achieve[s] its apotheosis only through absence . . . as renunciation, that is to say, rather than as plenitude."[77]

While absence can serve as a signifier of spirituality as an emptying out, Bresson provides the audience with a sense of psychological insight that is excluded from *I Confess*. Nearly every scene in *The Diary of a Country Priest* has a similar structure: we see (and hear) words being written in a diary, then we see an image that often proves to be the first half of a point-of-view shot, then we see a close-up of the main character, looking, followed by a quick fade to black or a dissolve. The meaning is in the structure, not the performance. The character sees (what we see), he reacts (silent close-up), blackness allows him (and us) a moment to digest what he has seen, and then he writes down his thoughts (the diary shots). His reaction is implicit, not enacted; it is also displaced. It is not until after the pause of the fade to black, a moment of absence, of total darkness, that "meaning" becomes expressible. Meaning is formed in the ellipsis; its expression is delayed until we fade in on the diary where the character writes it out, translating his thoughts into image, word, and sound. The use of voice-over reinforces the impact of seeing the words the priest writes in his journal. Seeing the words being written presents us not only with word-as-literature but also with writing as a process, as a source of visual design, and as an example of movement—all of this (sound, literature, cinema) contributing an abundance of material for the audience to use in deciphering the main character's internal state. Hitchcock's film is less accommodating.

If spiritual experience is internal, inexpressible, or an emptiness waiting to be filled by God, the only external proof of spirituality would be the disturbance it creates. Logan causes pain *because* he is good. Logan will not be bad (break his vows or violate postconfession protocol), and being good isn't helping—it is making things worse. In *The Diary of a Country Priest,* the priest may be a saint who dies absorbed in a vision of grace, but he is isolated and distrusted. It is typical of Bresson that grace is bestowed inexplicably on people who are difficult and not very likable and who seem to be going about it the wrong way; but in the end, he implies, there are many paths to God, and who can explain? As for Hitchcock's priest, does the interiorized, inaccessible spirituality of Logan signify that he is also a saint? We do know that he is a priest. But is that an internal necessity or a performance? Is he genuinely devout or has he found himself trapped playing a part?

Flashback

He didn't know he could never love me enough.

RUTH

The most important question about Logan, finally, concerns his vocation—what it means to him to be a priest and why he became one in the first place. A flashback provides the perfect opportunity to explain Logan's motives, giving us access to his inner life. But while the flashback promises to reveal all, we find the issue of vocation constantly displaced by the question of (and fear of) sexuality.

Logan arrives at police headquarters where Ruth; her husband, Pierre; Larue; and the district attorney have already gathered. Ruth is about to tell all. She possesses the secret of where Logan was (and whom he was with) the night Villette was killed. Sex is in the air. Ruth reveals that she was being blackmailed by Villette over her relationship with Logan. Are Logan and Ruth having a sexual relationship? Have they had one in the past? Reveling in being the center of attention, Ruth takes the long way around to answer these questions. She begins with the distant past, when she and Michael were in love.

The first part of the flashback is Robin Wood's famous example of Hitchcock being "too sophisticated for the sophisticated."[78] Ruth's voice-over, the overtly "romantic" music (which is simultaneously a little creepy), and the delirious, off-balance, low-angle shot show us Ruth's view of herself while revealing her account to be highly subjective and potentially unreliable. She floats down the stairs in slow motion and soft focus, alighting in Michael's waiting arms. They kiss. They are, she tells us, very much in love. The impression of romantic bliss continues as they embrace under paper lanterns at a dance that evening, but doubts quickly arise. Michael is in uniform, and when the dance is interrupted by an officer making an announcement, Ruth tells us, instead of clinging to her when war threatened, Michael enlisted the first chance he got. "I hated him for that. I was selfish even then."

She complains about his correspondence. "His letters were long at first. Always serious. I didn't want serious letters." Dejected, she looks at the gray, rainy street below as two anonymous figures in cassocks walk by. As the letters dry up, Ruth marries. Nevertheless, she is eagerly waiting at the dock when Michael returns from the war. At this point in the flashback, discrepancies increase between Ruth's narration and what we see. She throws herself into Michael's arms, but we can see that he is quite surprised to see her and he does not reciprocate her passion. Later that day, on a picnic, he talks to her (though because Ruth is narrating in the present, we cannot hear him). In voice-over she tells us, "Michael talked and talked. He told me all the thoughts that had come to him during the war. I didn't want to hear about the war." She grabs him and kisses him (to stop him talking). When she's done, he looks a little curious, and continues his monologue as if he had not been interrupted.

It begins to rain. They try to enter a house, but it is locked. They run to a gazebo and take refuge there. Ruth is soaked. Michael gives her his jacket. They sit on a bench, look at each other, and smile. The next morning she awakes, fully dressed and covered by his jacket. She has evidently slept on a narrow ledge. She looks around for Michael (emphasizing that he is not beside her). A cut finds him smiling broadly at her from the far side of the gazebo with a table between them.

What happened during the night in the summerhouse is rendered ambiguous enough that audiences could imagine the possibility of sex while the filmmakers maintained its deniability. (This vagueness turned out to be sufficient for the censors and useful, later, for the plot.) The ellipsis that makes ambiguity possible is created by a cut to gray blankness and a slow pan right that finds a close-up of Ruth in the present day at the police station. After a noticeable pause she says, "It stopped raining in the morn-

ACTOR AS SAINT   107

ing." Baxter signals this line's highly significant indirectness by saying it with particular dramatic emphasis, casting her eyes down at the ending. The line brings to mind two things: one a precept, the other a literary reference. In Dante's *Inferno*, we learn that the studious Paolo and Francesca have succumbed to temptation from a similarly opaque line: "We read no more that day." When time is purposely left unaccounted for, the conclusion to be drawn is presumably self-evident. This assumption is also illustrated by the classic warning to priests to avoid being unchaperoned when counseling women: *Solus cum sola non cogita bientur orare Pater Noster* (A man and woman alone together do not think of reciting the Our Father).

While he might not have known she was married that day in the summerhouse, the night Villette was killed, Logan, as a priest, should have known better than to spend any time with Ruth alone—if only for appearances' sake. The assumption that a man and a woman alone have opened the door to scandal (public speculation about sexual activity) is precisely what gives rise to Villette's blackmail. It will also prove significant during the trial. While no one can prove improper conduct, it cannot be disproved either. In the flashback, Ruth tells us that Villette owned the summerhouse. Seeing Michael there and assuming he was with a woman, Villette "made some remark," prompting Michael to knock him down. When Ruth steps forward, Villette greets her as "*Madame* Grandfort," prompting Michael to look at her with a perplexed expression. She explains to her listeners: "I hadn't told him I was married." Villette, seeing Ruth at Michael's ordination five years later, begins to blackmail her. She goes to Michael for help the night of the murder and agrees to meet him outside Villette's house the next morning. Hearing he is dead, she says, "We're free."

The flashback is usually discussed in terms of what it reveals about Ruth's subjective perception of the past, but it is constructed through frequent returns to the present. By cutting back and forth from the sexually available young soldier to the priest in his cassock, the film raises the issue of the *priest's* sexuality. The distance in time is erased by the proximity of one image to the other as Father Logan in the present is shown to be as much the object of Ruth's sexual desire as was Michael in the past.

The close-ups of Logan listening to Ruth introduce a new perspective, one that undercuts her self-dramatizing romanticism. When she begins with the highly sentimentalized account of their love ("Have you ever been young, Inspector?"), we cut to Clift/Logan resting his head on his fist in a near-comic display of embarrassment or boredom. When Ruth heavy-handedly skips over their night in the summerhouse, the camera zip-pans to a close-up of Michael. His hand delicately frames his face, fingers on brow and cheek, his eyes cast down. He is a picture of concentration—but a picture that can be read more than one way. On the one hand, Logan assumes a pose as if he is listening to a confession—Ruth's confession of her adulterous desire, the years of being blackmailed and of keeping secrets from her husband. At the same time, though, he may be biting his tongue, refraining from correcting her by introducing his own version of what happened.

When Ruth finishes her tale, satisfied, Logan thanks her because she has confessed *her* guilt for his sake. At the same time, she is also putting on a show. As it did for Otto, confession gives Ruth the chance to get Logan's undivided attention while showing off her masochistic devotion at the same time, as if to say, "I will undergo public humiliation for you." The confession also demonstrates her power, showing him that she can hold the attention of all these men, and that he owes her. Given her mixed motives, it is not surprising that the alibi Ruth provides ("I was with him at the time") in fact sounds like another accusation of impropriety, or that her "help" results in clinching Larue's case against Logan. By implying that Logan was so heartbroken about her marriage that he renounced the world and proving that he could be provoked to violence for her sake, she implies he might also have killed for her (and for himself).

Another way to read the close-ups of Logan in this scene is as proof that he has once again been silenced. Hearing Ruth's account of *his* past, his motives, his character, he is displaced from his own story. Aware of her exaggerations, he cannot (or will not) publicly contradict her. The close-ups isolate Logan from the other people in the scene, his silence intensifying his suffering by intensifying his isolation. Yet again his silence increases his inaccessibility to the characters and to the audience.

Because the flashback covers the period when Logan discovered his vocation and became a priest, it is the sequence that comes closest to explaining what being a priest means to him. The film's lack of an explanation for Logan's strict adherence to his priestly duties leads to speculation, some of it negative. Hitchcock critics Claude Chabrol and Eric Rohmer criticize Logan for pride when he remains silent while standing trial and accuse him of wanting to be a martyr. "His sin, if sin there is, is not that he has been a man before becoming a man of God, but, on the contrary, to have given way to the intimidation, the blackmail, of wanting to redeem by heroic and paradoxical conduct what need no longer be redeemed: to give way to the temptation of martyrdom."[79] As Barish points out, martyrdom can be suspect because it is fundamentally theatrical: "To court martyrdom was to claim a starring part on the stage of history, to become a 'visible saint,' the-atricalizing one's sanctity by revealing it triumphantly before the Supreme Gaze."[80]

When the lack of concrete information about Logan's motives fails to satisfy viewers, some are moved to invent a backstory to explain the otherwise inaccessible interior life of the main character. In his book *Soul in Suspense*, Father Hurley explains Michael's decision to become a priest. "A priest . . . replaces his dead brother (a World War II victim) as a seminarian. The spiritual motivation is never developed; the reason is internal and sentimental."[81] (This story appears nowhere in the film or in the different drafts of the script of *I Confess*.)[82] Interestingly, while Hurley accounts for—even creates—Logan's vocation, it is nevertheless based on motives Hurley disapproves of. Evidently even a nonexemplary motive is more tolerable than none at all.

It may be pure coincidence, but the fictional brother Hurley creates for Logan actually has some connection to the play on which the film was based. While there is usually a cursory mention that the film is based on a play, no one who has written about *I Confess* discusses it. A close examination of the play provides some insight into how representations of priests (including their vocations, their duty to the church, and the sexuality of the clergy) change in different times and places.

Nos deux consciences (Our Two Consciences) premiered in Paris on November 15, 1902. Paul Anthelme (the nom de plume of Paul Bourde) wrote the play as a vehicle for the famous French actor Constant Coquelin, to whom it is dedicated.[83] An English translation of the play by Paulette d'Arvil, dated February 1948, was available when Louis Verneuil gave Hitchcock the first treatment for the project. In the play, there is more than enough information on the priest's reasons for joining the church. You could even call it an excess of backstory. Nevertheless, we do hear directly from the priest his own account of his background, the true nature of his relationship with the woman in question, and why he became a priest.

Confronted by his bishop with rumors of impropriety, the main character, referred to as the curé, explains that his family worked for aristocrats when he was a child. His older brother had an affair with the daughter of the house. When the young lovers were separated by their families, the brother committed suicide and their father died of a broken heart. Having seen how dangerous and messy romantic love could be, the character decided to become a priest. Years later, he finds himself at a parish where the woman his brother loved now lives with her husband and children. It turns out that after she and the brother were separated, she had a child. She asks the priest to take money to the people raising the baby. He agrees, meeting the woman in discreet locations on a regular basis and then disappearing for a couple of days. This pattern continues until the sickly child dies. The man who is eventually murdered was blackmailing the woman and sending threatening notes to the priest regarding his private meetings with this wealthy woman of the parish.

The abundance of information about the priest's past in the play is progressively reduced as the script is developed until it is merely that Michael had an affair with a woman before he was ordained.[84] The character in this case is accused not of breaking his vows but of having had sex with someone before entering the seminary—or, as Chabrol and Rohmer put it, of having "been a man before becoming a man of God." The assumption that the priest should be not only celibate but also virginal is expressed (cryptically, of course) by Father Millais when a police officer comes to the rectory to escort Logan to his interview with Larue. Taking the painting of the walls as the pretext for his parable, Millais asserts to Logan, "I believe that this room has given this gentleman from the Police Department the idea that we hide grime with paint. But it is not so. . . . We have made certain that the walls underneath are spotless." All the church's candidates for ordination have been thoroughly examined to make sure they are pure. Their cassocks are not camouflage or a disguise but an official certification of what lies within.

But, as Millais asked earlier, can there be paint with no smell? All that scrubbing to make sure the walls are spotless implies that there was something that needed to be scrubbed off. Sin precedes absolution; thus, absolution presupposes sin. If cleansing indicates a stain, then it becomes necessary to hide traces of cleaning. Father Millais protests too much. He wants no smell from paint that covers no grime. A possibility that remains unstated at this time is that cleanliness itself might provoke the urge to stain. (A 1995 Canadian film called *Le confessional* [Robert Lepage], set in Quebec City, alternates the present day with the autumn of 1952, when *I Confess* was being shot. A figure in the present tries to cover up the past and give his parents' house new life by repeatedly painting a wall, but the stains left by old family pictures keep coming through. In this telling, which is harsh on both the church and Hitchcock, the grime cannot be covered, and things smell to high heaven.)

Of all the treatments (three), early screenplays (three), outlines, and numerous revisions of the final script that were produced between 1947 and

1952, only one gives Logan a stated motive for becoming a priest.[85] In George Tabori's July 19, 1952, revised draft, Logan tells Ruth about the war while they are on the ferry. "You fly a plane and you're lonely. You start diving, pushing a button. Somewhere below, a village blows up. This is the worst kind of hatred. You either go mad, or come to a point when you find you can't stop short of loving everyone." As Ruth says in the film, "The war *had* changed him." This account of *how* it changed him was cut and not replaced.[86]

If the play and the film refuse to provide Logan's reasons for choosing the church, another set of texts might help. Clift played many soldiers, including one who shared the postwar dislocation and guilt expressed by Logan the bombardier.[87] In his last theatrical role before going to Hollywood to begin work on *Red River,* Clift played a Canadian Air Force pilot in Tennessee Williams's and Donald Windham's *You Touched Me!* (September 1945).[88] In the first act, Clift's character, Hadrian, confronts acquaintances in an English country house. "When I walked back into this place this morning my blood ran cold with amazement. . . . I've been a bomber pilot. I've bombed Berlin. And Hamburg and Bremen, Cologne and Ludwigshaven. I've flown over cities and watched those cities blow up like boxes of matches. Then flown back over the channel, as calm as Matilda crosses to take a tea cup." Hadrian has no doubts about the weight of his actions. "I know what I've committed—atrocities! . . . Whoever does it, whatever reason you give—it's still an atrocity when you blow up a city! And it leaves you feeling—maybe not guilty, but—somehow a little—*responsible* for—things!"[89] The denunciation of aerial bombardment as an atrocity is absolute and unqualified; matters become muddled only when the veteran attempts to fix his own part in relation to the act. The speech loses momentum as the character's last sentence breaks into fragments and equivocation: "maybe not guilty," "somehow a little," "responsible" perhaps, but only for anticlimactic "things." When veterans in the immediate postwar period cannot reconcile the justification of the war on the one hand and the scale of damage done on the other, the question of personal guilt will not go away.

You Touched Me! resonates with a handful of later works involving Clift and Tennessee Williams. The domineering aunt ("Sit up straight, don't hunch!") and Matilda, a dreamy girl who "has the delicate, almost transparent quality of glass" are clearly forerunners of Amanda Wingfield and daughter Laura in *The Glass Menagerie.*[90] The heroic struggle of heterosexual masculine vitality against the stifling world of women ("not [their] predatory maternity but aggressive sterility") proclaims the play's status as an adaptation of a D. H. Lawrence short story.[91] Yet another idealistic ex-soldier in the Clift canon, Hadrian recalls Steve in *The Search,* Danny in *The Big Lift,* and Logan in *I Confess.* Contemplating the immediate post-war period, each character looks around to see where he is and what he has done, and ponders how to move forward. "Everything's slipped back to normal," says Matilda, smiling. Hadrian interrupts, "'Back to normal' was not quite all we dreamed of." Hadrian wants change. "Or are you convinced it's going to stay like it was except for there being the finest new bunch of ruins for tourists to visit since Pompeii?"[92]

Clift's films played an important role in familiarizing audiences with the ruins of postwar Europe: driving a Jeep through bombed-out Munich in *The Search,* courting a German woman who sorts rubble at a bombed site in Berlin in *The Big Lift.*[93] In Williams and Windham's play, heterosexual romance culminating in marriage is figured as the most direct way to effect change and embrace the future (as it is in Lawrence, where overweening masculinity crushes lesbian desire). But marriage repeatedly fails to provide a solution to the question, What next? (One character asks another about Hadrian, "You don't suppose he's taken the vow of celibacy, do you?") Treachery on an international scale puts an end to the marriage plot in *The Big Lift;* the reemergence of the mother permanently divides soldier and boy in *The Search.* In *I Confess,* any possibility of marriage is precluded by Logan's decision to become a priest. But where Father Logan, Danny, and Steve are close-lipped about their war experience, Hadrian alone has the chance to express his bewilderment and find closure. "I didn't know I had all that on my chest. I feel better."[94] The others are left to find their own paths back.

In *I Confess,* there is no one Logan can talk to about his predicament. In the play, on the other hand, as soon as the priest realizes that he could be arrested, he turns to the church for help. He talks to his bishop:

> I would like to do my duty, but I fear I don't have the strength. . . . I have often meditated on the life of the martyrs, I try to be inspired by their faith . . . but I cannot expect these superhuman virtues of myself. . . . I am a feeble creature, well-intentioned, but mediocre; I don't think my soul is strong enough for such a serious test. My mother's despair, the public contempt I'd have to endure, prison, perhaps the scaffold. Oh my God, my God. I beg you, monsignor. Isn't there any possible way for me to escape these terrors?[95]

This speech allows the audience to hear the priest's doubts, emotions, and second thoughts. Instead of behaving "like a man of overweening pride" tempted by martyrdom (as Chabrol and Rohmer describe Logan), this priest explicitly does not want to be a martyr. Weak, afraid, he is desperate to avoid the public humiliation of a trial. His resistance to the burden placed on him by his vocation is clearest when he asks the question that defines his position: "Am I absolutely forced to stay silent?" When the bishop tells him he is ("The secret of the confession is inviolable, without exception"), the priest continues to argue. "But no one could have foreseen a case of such vileness, such diabolical machinations, as that of which I find myself a victim." Again, he asks the central question on which the plot hinges. "Is it possible that it is permitted for a criminal to thus use the sacrament of penance to make his calculations succeed?"[96]

Another film that focuses on the spiritual crises of priests, made a year before *I Confess,* has a scene that addresses a similar question: Does the law of silence apply when the so-called penitent is not only insincere but cynically manipulative? In Douglas Sirk's *The First Legion* (1951), a priest (Charles Boyer) hears a scandalous confession: the local doctor (Lyle Bettiger) has perpetrated a hoax and allowed everyone to believe it was a miracle. The doctor, a former seminarian and confirmed skeptic, begins his confession by informing the priest that this is not a confession in religious terms. When the priest proposes they make the truth public, the doctor refuses and insists that the priest cannot reveal the information because of the (presumably retroactive) seal of the confessional. With pure Gallic contempt, Boyer dismisses this childish attempt to parry theology with a Jesuit who is also a lawyer. Without sincere contrition (regret, sorrow) and repentance (the desire to atone and live a better life), there can be no sacrament, no absolution. Absolution cannot be given by accident, and it is not negotiated. The dogma standoff is side-stepped when Boyer volunteers not to reveal what he has heard, leaving the matter to the doctor's conscience. (Although there is no indication that Clift saw either *The First Legion* or *The Diary of a Country Priest,* it is clear that Clift *did* have other films in mind when preparing for the role. A friend at a monastery warned him, "I'll never forgive you if you come out looking like Bing Crosby.")[97]

In the film's theatrical source, the sinner's impenitence—along with his premeditated exploitation of the rules of confession—is raised as a possible disqualification of the confession *as* confession. But this argument is quickly dismissed. The bishop tells him, "My son, this man will answer for his conduct before the sovereign judge, but your duty will not be changed." He does assure the priest, however, that he will be rewarded in heaven, and the priest gives in. "My father, you have enlightened, consoled and fortified me. If God wants my life as testament of my faith, I hope that I will be able to give it."[98]

This conversation (longer and more involved than the excerpts reproduced here) shows exactly how much the film chooses to leave unsaid. This exchange not only provides an opportunity for the church to explain its position, it also clarifies the character's attitude about his situation and his vocation. The priest is permitted to speak (to the proper ecclesiastical authorities); the law of silence is not muting. He does not take the obligation to remain silent to the extreme of not telling anyone (which could bring up the issue of pride). He talks to someone about his dilemma and tries to find a way out. In the play, there is also comfort for the priest in his knowing that the church knows he is innocent and can appreciate the sacrifice he is making. In the film, the priest is out in the cold and no one knows the truth about the murder except us, the real killer, and his wife.

Pursued

As Otto removes faded flowers from the altar, Logan walks the length of the church, quickly, purposefully, coming face-to-face with Otto but passing him at the last minute without giving a sign of having seen him. Otto begins to follow Logan, who turns on him. "I'm going to be arrested, Keller." In the entire film, this is the only thing Logan will ever say that can be read as an emotional response at finding himself in this situation. (It was a line Hitchcock kept despite its having been singled out as a violation by the Catholic Church.)

In the film, all the priest's doubts and fears are displaced onto Otto. And all the talking. When Logan says he is going to be arrested, Otto hurries after him: "You? Why would they arrest you, Father? You're trying to frighten me perhaps. You think by telling me that I will give myself up. You think I'm easily frightened after what I have done?" As Logan marches down a long hall into the rectory, he is shadowed at each step by the real murderer, who badgers him with nagging questions about Logan's integrity, courage, and devotion to his vows (i.e., his ability to remain silent under pressure). "So what are you going to do when they arrest you? Perhaps you will point your finger at me. Perhaps you will say it's Keller. That's what you will do, is it? You are a coward after all. You are frightened. Maybe they will hang you instead of me and that frightens you. Perhaps you will tell them. You can't tell them as long as you are a priest. Can you?" Logan cannot defend himself from the words. Like Claudius murdering King Hamlet, Otto pours poison into Logan's ear, and Logan cannot keep it out. Once he has opened himself up to hear Otto's original confession, he can no longer shut out this unwanted intimacy. The confession has broken out of the confessional and pursues him.

When Otto talks to Logan outside the confessional, there is a breakdown of boundaries, not only physically, but in terms of power. Within the confessional there is formality, ritual. Logan asks prescribed questions; Otto answers. When Otto addresses Logan publicly, he breaks that formality and in doing so, changes the power dynamic. The penitent now has power over the priest. He silences Logan, asking questions Logan cannot answer. Otto, on the other hand, can't stop talking, redefining Logan in terms that apply equally to himself. He displaces his fears onto Logan: you're frightened, you're a coward after all, you're afraid they will hang you, you'll talk, you can't talk. It is a conversation in which Otto plays both parts.

Otto's monologue stresses how alike they are, at least in Otto's mind. Father Millais also sees them as a team. The first time he speaks to Logan, it concerns Keller, as Millais asks what "they" are doing about the painting. The implication of Otto's speech is "Inside, you are like me. Your worst traits are about to be exposed and become apparent to everyone." Otto could be seen as the dark side of Logan, perched on Logan's shoulder like a conscience-demon. On the other hand, the close tracking shot of Logan and Otto invites a comparison of them as opposites. Clift/Logan is young and handsome, looking straight ahead as he strides forward. Otto—shorter, older, not handsome—trots after Logan, watching him closely from behind. Logan is in black with his white collar, while Otto wears white with a dark tie. Clutching his flowers, Otto looks like a bride about to be jilted— though with Logan in a cassock, it is Otto who wears the pants.

Although it is not in his best interests legally, Otto cannot resist pushing Logan to the breaking point. Fear coupled with his newfound power gives Otto's relentless needling the undertow of a sadistic thrill. The erotic component of confession permeates every scene between Otto and Logan. As with Ruth's self-exposure during the flashback scene, Otto opens up his hidden, innermost self to Logan. They share the secret of Otto's guilt. Once he has accepted Otto's confidences, Logan finds himself surrounded, cornered, invaded by Otto's unending speech.

When Hitchcock talked about casting Clift, his reasoning evokes this shot more than any other moment in the film. Hitchcock said of Clift, "He looked like the Angel of Death was walking beside him."[99] In *I Confess,* the person walking beside Clift is O. E. Hasse as Otto. But Hitchcock was not necessarily referring only to this film. In *A Place in the Sun,* the film that consolidated Clift's status as the most popular young male actor of his day, there is a tracking shot strongly reminiscent of this one in *I Confess.* At the very end of *A Place in the Sun,* Clift's character, George Eastman, walks down a long hallway on his way to his execution. The camera tracks back, keeping him in a constant, moving close shot.

While this scene showed Hitchcock that Clift was willing to play characters who died and that his fans would not rebel, the moment that cements the connection between the two films is the startling use of a jump cut at the heart of both of these shots. It is a jarring moment in each film, and seemingly unnecessary. In *A Place in the Sun,* we cut from a medium shot of Clift walking toward the camera to a closer shot. In *I Confess,* as Otto and Logan turn a corner (right after Otto says, "You think I'm easily frightened after what I have done?"), there is a jump cut that repeats a moment of their turn so that they seem to take a step together, in sync in a time out of joint. The cut is a stutter in the rhythm of their walking, but its syncopation adds a kinetic boost, a jolt of the unexpected that heightens the stakes.

If Hitchcock borrowed the jump cut from *A Place in the Sun,* even more important was what he found in *The Big Lift.* It wasn't just Clift; it was chemistry.

Despite the fact that *Red River, The Search, The Heiress,* and *A Place in the Sun* were all bigger commercial and critical successes for Clift, George Seaton's *The Big Lift* is the film Hitchcock cited fifteen years later as pivotal to his decision to cast Clift in *I Confess.* One of Clift's biographers suggests that "Hitchcock was especially sensitive to the sexual ambiguity of Clift and of O. E. Hasse, with whom Monty had worked in *The Big Lift.*"[100] In their first scene together in the earlier film, both men exude an immensely likable ease and familiarity. Hasse plays a pragmatic double agent who openly tells the American that he is a spy for the Russians—and for the Americans, too. Because he is so open about his two-sidedness, the character seems almost guileless. Unlike the tense, overeager Otto, Hasse's character here is funny and seductive, Clift's receptive and comfortable. Keeping up a steady stream of patter, entertaining his accidental guest, Hasse constantly moves around the room while Clift reclines in a chair, wrapped in a robe (that he has borrowed from Hasse's character), being entertained.

FIGURE 16. Lobby card for *The Big Lift (Two Corridors East):* Hasse and Clift.

As Hasse talks, making jokes, struggling with English, he continually reaches out to touch Clift—first on the wrist, then on the knee. . . . It is a charming—and uncensorable—seduction scene.

When Otto tells Logan he is trapped ("You can't tell them as long as you are a priest"), Logan turns on him. Otto steps back, frightened speechless by what he sees. But what is he reacting to? We might read anger or frustration into Logan's face in the close-up. It is dangerous to allow others to define your feelings and infuriating when they tell you how you feel. While Logan carefully avoided directly contradicting Ruth when she told him on the ferry, "You love me. You've always loved me," there is more at stake when Otto tells Logan that he is a coward who is about to be arrested and possibly hanged—and then reminds him that he is a priest. Nevertheless, the close-up of Logan fails to account fully for the alarm it has allegedly produced. Neither angry nor sardonic, his face a blank, Logan turns and abruptly leaves the rectory.

About to be arrested, Logan decides to go for a walk.

If a character will not talk, he must be read. As an actor, Clift must express his character's ordeal through his body. Physicalizing emotional crises, Hitchcock creates scene after scene of Clift's character walking. In the first minutes of the film we see three men walking: Hitchcock, Otto, Logan—each a commentary on the others. When Clift spent time at a monastery in Quebec before filming began, part of his research focused on how to walk in a cassock. He described what he observed to a friend: "Priests walk in a special way because they wear robes or habits. . . . When they walk they push the material forward with their hands."[101] For François Truffaut, the way Logan walks, his constant "forward motion," "shapes the whole film. It also concretizes the concept of his integrity."[102] Whereas one critic finds Clift's priest "morally immobile," physically he is almost compulsively mobile.[103]

Chabrol and Rohmer suggest that Logan's physical journey, his dogged progress from place to place, *is* the story: when he leaves the rectory the morning after the confession, when he is seen pacing outside the dead man's apartment, pursued through hallways by the frightened killer, walking the streets before he's arrested, walking down the winding staircase after the unsatisfactory conclusion of the trial, and walking toward a loaded gun at the climax. But it is not the walking alone. These scenes are often capped by Hitchcock's other stylistic signature in the film: the static close-up. The alternation of movement and close-up, freedom and containment, is the heart of Hitchcock's approach to the story and of his conflict with Clift. As the rest of this scene shows, editing trumps acting.

Having left the rectory, Logan hurries determinedly through the city. In a sequence that constructs meaning from editing, we see Logan arrive at locations that bear symbolic significance and seem to comment on his position. He crosses a busy street where a policeman directing traffic seems to be pointing directly at him. In a self-reflexive bit, he stops outside a movie theater and sees a lobby card for the film *The Enforcer*. It features a man in handcuffs, held between two policemen. In the reverse shot, Logan reels. Wiping sweat off his face, he moves on. In a store window he sees a suit of clothes on sale, draped on a headless mannequin.

More difficult to read than the first two encounters, this last segment is one of the more daring elements in the film. The first encounter with the policeman shows that Logan is worried about being a wanted man, the second that he is afraid of being publicly humiliated, arrested, paraded in handcuffs. The shot/reverse shot of Logan looking at the clothes, on the other hand, tells us not about his feelings but about his plans. The only way we know he is thinking about trying to escape is that he contemplates changing his clothes. (This echoes the scene early in *A Place in the Sun* when George buys a new suit before he goes to meet his uncle's family.)

The issue of clothing, as we have seen, is central to any character's identity, to actorliness and the issue of religious hypocrisy. Logan may be kept silent by force of circumstance, but the constraints on him are made explicit by what he wears. When Otto demands that Father Logan hear his confession, Logan stops before entering the confessional, kisses a stole, and places it around his neck. Like the cassock, the stole establishes his identity as a priest, in this case constraining his speech by marking his entrance into a formal, ritualized state for the sacrament of confession. On the other hand, in the first half of the film, Logan is out of his cassock rather frequently.[104] When Logan is not wearing his cassock, others find him more approachable, more vulnerable. The closest Otto gets to him physically is when Logan is in khaki while on the ladder painting. When Ruth telephones to arrange the meeting on the ferry, Logan (presumably having been about to go to bed) comes downstairs wearing a white shirt without his ecclesiastical collar. These are the two characters who want a nonpriestly response from him. His casual clothes are a sign of his past, but also a constant reminder of who he was before he was a priest and who he might be again. If being a priest means dressing like one, then by abandoning the clothes he could just as easily *not* be a priest. Escaping from his clothes would mean escaping from the church *and* the police.

Intercut with this sequence of Logan's reactions to what he sees are scenes of the police stopping priests all over Quebec City. A humorous touch, these shots suggest that all priests look alike. Wearing a cassock makes them unrecognizable as individuals. For the moment, there is safety in the anonymity of the cassock.

In the final script, when Logan looks at the headless dummy in the store window, his own face was supposed to appear superimposed or reflected exactly where the mannequin's head would be. This does not happen in the film. When Logan envisions an alternative identity for himself it is as half a man, headless, anonymous, faceless.

Discussing another Hitchcock film on the sufferings of an "innocent man wrongly accused," Robin Wood describes the ordeal experienced by the main character in *The Wrong Man* (1957). Like Logan, that character can be seen as "passive, gentle, slightly ineffectual, lacking any strong identity." Hell for this character is "the total anonymity with which he is threatened." The experience of having others define him and speak for him, of having his own words go unheard, culminates in an institutionalized "stripping away of identity" when he is arrested and booked.[105] Like the character in *The Diary of a Country Priest*, Logan's passivity can be seen as a voluntary emptying-out—of desire and doubt—a surrendering to God. But when he looks at the store window, Logan confronts a hollow form as a possible image of himself.

Is Logan hollow? Do his clothes cover an inner emptiness? We know he has nothing to hide. Ruth tells her husband, with exhausted regret, "He hasn't *done* anything." Maybe there is nothing behind the clothes because the clothes are all he is. Logan needs a uniform to hold him together—and ritual and architecture and surveillance.[106] Before he was held together by his priest's uniform he was in the army. As Ruth says, he joined up the first chance he got.

In order to know what Logan is thinking and feeling at this moment, we need to know what is happening inside a character defined as someone who refuses to tell. In this case, the ambiguity of the scene undermines the shot/reverse shot effect Hitchcock relies on. (This may be another scene influenced by *The Big Lift,* where Danny goes for a walk after having a tiff with Frederica and sees the suffering of Berliners. The point of that scene is relatively plain, the character's reactions and change of heart clearly telegraphed. In *I Confess,* however, the result is very different.)

Based on this particular series of shots, critics have found it difficult to agree on what the character Father Logan is feeling. Chabrol and Rohmer believe they can describe Logan's inner experience as he reels outside the movie theater: "Father Michael experiences a sort of vertigo in recognizing his feelings of guilt." I speculate that when he looks in the store window, he is thinking about buying a suit as he tries to escape. We could just as easily suspect that he stares at the headless dummy because, being in French Canada, he is afraid of the guillotine.

Passing beneath a statue that states (too) clearly the intolerable weight of the cross he carries, Logan ends up back at the gates of the church. (Wood declares that the so-called "'impressive' use of church architecture is an external substitute, uneasily offered, for any effective realization of the priest's dilemma.")[107] As Logan collapses against a stone wall, the camera moves in, presumably to capture the anguish on his face, but he quickly covers his face with his hands. We do not see his face until he has composed himself. Inside the church, we see a low-angle shot of the domed apse and its towering altarpiece. Logan looks up. The meaning of the close-up is established not by acting but by the shot's position in a sequence. Back at the police station, Detective Larue is on the phone. Supervising the search for the fugitive cleric, he looks up and sees what he was waiting for—Logan standing in the doorway. Without a word (of course), Logan turns himself in.

FIGURE 17. *I Confess:* Hitchcock (far left) on location in Quebec with Clift (upper left).

The trial finally provides the opportunity for Logan to speak for himself. His answer: "I can't say." Asked about his relationship with Ruth during the events alluded to in the flashback, he says, "We were good friends" and "I saw nothing wrong with being caught in a storm." The opacity of these remarks makes them irritatingly uninformative, a trait shared with his comments on the priesthood. Asked what being a priest means to him—a key point raised by the flashback—he replies in another uninformative, negative formulation: "I never saw the priesthood as a place to hide." Logan's resistance to openly proclaiming his beliefs reduces his testimony to a series of careful qualifications and dissemblings. He cannot describe what being a priest means to him because it is not describable; he cannot define it because he is absorbed within it. In a way, it is too obvious, with no inside or outside. As he said on the ferry, "I believe in what I am"; "I chose to be what I am."

In regard to his relationship with Ruth, we can only assume that his "simplicity" ("we were good friends") suggests openness, innocence, nothing to

FIGURE 18. Publicity still for *I Confess:* Logan on trial.

hide. The repeated answer that there was "nothing wrong with being caught in a storm" dodges the question of whether he and Ruth slept together. By referring exclusively to the past, the period in the flashback, and not to the night of the murder, Logan never addresses directly insinuations about his more recent meetings with Ruth.

Although Clift has no lines once Logan is off the stand, the actor took his reaction shots as seriously as his lines. In his copy of the script, he wrote instructions to himself about how to react on the page opposite the stage directions. When testimony against Logan is given, Clift writes, "Feeling shame."[108] As the judge sums up the case, Clift writes, "Concentrate."[109] When the verdict is announced he writes simply, "Sigh."[110]

The trial itself is played out as a series of looks. The person whose gaze is confined, not surprisingly, is Michael Logan. He cannot look at Otto or Alma in the gallery during his testimony because it could indicate his privileged knowledge. (According to Production Code files, it "could be an indirect violation of the Sacramental Seal of Secrecy.")[111] Instead, it is Otto and Alma in particular who serve as models for the film's viewers. They are the audience at a spectacle. But they also have a personal connection to the star. As each stares, rapt in his or her personal reverie, Otto is especially fascinated. His desire has propelled the film to this point. He set the plot in motion, chose the costumes and props, cast the main characters, and, when the trial begins, gets to sit back and watch. What does he hope to see? Watching Logan testify, Otto has the rare treat of seeing himself played by Montgomery Clift. When Logan plays Otto's part—friendless, accused, on trial—he plays it heroically. Stalwart, admirable, desired by others (Ruth), he openly proclaims he has nothing to be guilty of. For Otto, it is a vicarious thrill, all danger averted as he watches himself get away with murder while Logan suffers in his place, trapped and on public display.

Otto also directly exercises power over Logan by testifying against him. Amazed that it works so easily, he capitalizes on the unexpected coincidence that the victim was blackmailing someone close to Logan. Keller puts Logan in Keller's position when he testifies that Logan was extremely upset in the church. He attributes his own weakness to Logan. Having asked Logan earlier, "Weren't you ever afraid?" Otto sees to it that he will be. But he also gives himself Logan's strengths. When he testifies about comforting the frightened Logan, Otto gets to be the hero, witness and kindly support to a troubled friend. He gets to be superior to Logan. Even better, he gets to *be* Logan.

If the trial is about Logan being made a spectacle of, the fulcrum of a series of looks, the most important spectator after Otto is his wife, Alma. Sitting beside Otto, figuratively standing by her man, Alma watches Logan, too, but she watches differently. Like the film audience, she knows that Logan is innocent, imagines what that must be like for him, and suffers on his behalf. But why does she watch so closely? To see if he will crack, implicate her husband, save himself? Studying Logan's face, Clift's face, what does she—or we—hope to see?

For much of the film Alma seems mousy and browbeaten, with a hunched posture and soft, quavery voice. Ultimately, she proves stronger than we would expect. As the script was being developed, the character of Alma was quite different from the one we encounter in the film. In fact, of all the characters, she underwent the most extreme transformation. In the play *Nos deux consciences,* the title refers to the wife *and* the priest. Both are bound by vows, he to the priesthood, she to support her husband. Secondary victims of the same man, the priest and the wife understand each other's position. (There is even a suggestion of an underlying sexual attraction between them.) In the play, the murderer never confesses to the priest, his wife does (she feels guilty about having the money her husband stole). Nevertheless, the priest cannot identify the real killer without using knowledge gained in confession. In his argument with the bishop, the priest points this out, wondering if "he didn't send his wife here yesterday night in order to bind me to him by the secret of the confessional."[112]

In the first treatment by Alfred and Alma Hitchcock, it is the wife who is truly guilty. A harridan who bullies the husband into killing, she is driven by greed and thrilled by money. As Otto's character is built up over several drafts of the script, Alma's power is reduced. In Tabori's August 9, 1952, script, she is a sex slave to her husband, a masochist enthralled by a fascist in polished boots. When Otto tells her about the killing, "suddenly, with tremendous sexual passion, she goes to him, embraces him   kisses him, his face, his ears, his neck."[113] By the time the film is made, Alma has become Otto's pawn. Weak, fearful, dominated, less overtly sexual, she functions as Otto's excuse for committing murder, his opportunity to speak to Logan in the first place. Before the confession he tells Logan, "You saw that my wife and I were not common servants. . . . It was my wife, working so hard. It breaks my heart."

In addition to being tremulous, German actress Dolly Haas plays the character as simple, glowing, ultimately honest and good, delicate but stalwart. With the casting of the doe-faced Haas, Alma has become a sympathetic victim with sympathetic eyes, watching.[114]

Alma's role complements Ruth's. Where Ruth "never loved" her husband Pierre and wants to be unfaithful with Logan, Alma is faithful to Otto, or at least submissive and obedient. While Ruth meets Logan behind her husband's back, Alma watches Logan at breakfast the next morning for her husband's sake. As a society hostess, Ruth wears fancy off-the-shoulder gowns and large diamond bracelets, drives a convertible, and has fashionably permed hair. Alma is plain, wearing the same nondescript cook-housemaid clothes most of the time, with a plain apron. Although she wears no jewelry and has her hair pulled back in a simple bun, she has an inner glow.

Ruth and Pierre rarely face each other, their backs turned to each other while one speaks to the air. Their relationship is formal and correct, bitter and cold. By comparison, the single most beautiful shot in the film (one that has nothing to do with Clift or Logan) consists of Alma leaning out of a window to talk to Otto. It is the morning after the murder and she despairs that Otto will be caught. "What is it, Alma?" he asks. "You're going to the police?" she asks fearfully. "What is today, Alma?" he asks, rhetorically. "Isn't it the day I tend to Mister Villette's garden?" "But he's dead," she insists. Otto is unmoved. "I always work in Mister Villette's garden on Wednesdays. Today is Wednesday, Alma." Like James Cagney when he steps outside and pauses to close his eyes, having just been released from prison at the end of *Each Dawn I Die* (1938), or Clift turning his face up to the sun while standing in the archway of a Spanish-style bungalow in a series of late-forties publicity stills, Alma's face receives sunshine like a benediction. Of all the exteriors shot on location for *I Confess,* there is something about the quality of the light in this shot—the first instance of daylight in the film—that makes it not just beautiful but moving.

Although she yearns for her husband and helps him hide the cassock and the gun in order to frame Logan, as Alma watches Logan testify, she begins to feel torn. The change comes when Otto and Alma sit side by side, watching the same trial but having different experiences. Otto is excited, fascinated, Alma empathetic. She suffers for Logan when she sees him attacked in court. By the end of the trial, Ruth has become content with her husband and renewed her commitment to her marriage, presumably never to pursue Logan again. Alma breaks with her husband, literally turning on him, and does so in favor of Logan.

Scandal is the result of an excess of reading, when we substitute what we "know" (common sense) for the limited amount we actually do know. As the jury deliberates, what they take as "known" is surprising. Donald Spoto says that, with Quebec being "strong in the traditions of French Catholicism, the people there would be outraged by the disclosure that one of their priests at one time had an affair."[115] Nonsense. Spoto fails to recognize how deep French anticlericalism can be. For the French, lustful clerics come with the landscape. A hallmark of the Enlightenment, accusations of clerical sexual impropriety are taken for granted in the play written half a century before the film. It is the Americans (as imagined and represented by the members of the Breen Office and the Legion of Decency) who would be shocked.

FIGURE 19. Lobby card for *I Confess:* Clift and Haas.

Priests just don't do such things—it's a scandal even to think it and Lo gan in particular is "good." Too good.

Although Hitchcock was eager to tell potential critics that he was never planning to show a priest as a murderer, it was always essential that the characters in the film would believe the priest to be a murderer. Imagine the thrill for a good English Catholic like Hitchcock, educated by Jesuits, to present a situation in which everyone was openly contemptuous of a priest. In *I Confess* Hitchcock gets to have it both ways—the endless salacious speculation and the unshakable defense that he was "innocent all along."

The French Canadian jurors (local performers, not Hollywood imports) are cynical and blasé. The foreman summarizes their position by taking it for granted that Logan and Ruth were lovers and that it must have been an ongoing affair. "Of course it wasn't just the one time." The (assumed) adultery is not titillating to the jury. They take it in stride. The murder is the issue. In fact, that voicing of the assumption of a long-term relationship is pretty much all we see of the deliberations. The verdict is announced in court.

The verdict is similar to the coroner's finding in Hitchcock's *Vertigo* (1958) five years later. Like Scottie, Logan is found not guilty but not innocent either. The jury finds insufficient evidence connecting him to the murder. Logan barely has time to exhale when the judge interrupts to declare his dissatisfaction with the jury's decision. Logan is free, but only technically. The judge and the crowd think he has gotten away with murder.

Alternative Endings

The verdict is where the film veers away from all previous source material. In every version prior to the final film, Logan is convicted and sentenced to death. In the earliest treatment by Alfred and Alma Hitchcock, he is executed. Little surprise that, as with the script's other potentially controversial moments, this raised strong objections from multiple sources.

In addition to finding the story "corny, unoriginal and quite unbelievable," Lee Wright of Simon and Schuster asserted, "Most important of all, I think, is that the present ending is really quite immoral, and I must confess that I was shocked. I think the story should be written so that the priest is saved." The objection was not so much in favor of a happy ending as it was theological. The publisher suspected that Logan was being set up to be seen as more than a martyr. "The attempt to make a parallel between the death of the priest and the death of Christ is just not either good or right."[116]

Despite such passionate distaste, the ending proposed by the Hitchcocks has a distinct cinematic flare. The priest is in the death house. A crowd has gathered outside the prison. A guard comes out and puts up a notice announcing that the execution has taken place. It is over. In what sounds like a classic Hitchcock touch, one by one those outside the prison drop to their knees in prayer until one person is left standing—the killer.

> There is a wild expression on his face. He starts to scream, "He was innocent! He was innocent! God have mercy on me!" He rushes through the awakening crowd to the prison gates. He hammers on them with both fists, crying out, "I did it! I did it! Take me—I did it!" as the scene
> FADES OUT.[117]

Although it was written in March 1948, the treatment's proposal for the final scene is strongly reminiscent of the end of *The Heiress*.

The September 3, 1947, treatment of *I Confess* by Louis Verneuil is perhaps even more shocking. "Dressed in a convict's stripes," the priest announces that "he is going to die for Mel" (the name of the killer in this version).[118] The killer visits the priest in his cell the night before his execution and offers to confess to the police. The priest forbids it, saying it would be "monstrous" for him as a priest to use knowledge gained in confession to pressure a would-be penitent. It would be a kind of moral blackmail. He even dissuades the killer from going to confession in the church in order to ensure that no undue pressure has been brought to bear and that any penitence is genuine.

When the killer leaves, unable to avoid future guilt by saving the priest's life and prevented from saving his own soul by going to confession, the priest's friend, a doctor, visits his cell. They continue a discussion they were having about faith. The priest declares he has won the argument. "I was right when I told you that only religion offers a man the opportunity to sacrifice himself beyond all limits. Like Jesus Christ, God has chosen me, granted me the grace to die for the redemption of my fellow creatures. In my most ambitious dreams I never hoped for such glory."[119]

I should say not. This speech, and the motive it reveals, has several obvious problems. First, there is the suggestion that the priest is going to the electric chair to win an argument. Second, and even more notably, not only does the character *want* to be a martyr, he wants to be crucified. His reasoning, baldly stated, is presumptuous to the point of blasphemy: "God chose me to die for your sins."

The priest gets his messianic wish, but Verneuil is not Hitchcock. His ending lacks the visual punch (as well as the acting opportunities) available in the earlier treatment. In this version the killer meekly turns himself in to the doctor-friend after the execution, and the film ends with a close-up of a plaque with the following dedication: "Fr. George Townsend / (1903–1947) / Martyr to his Faith / He Died for the Redemption of his Fellow-men."

These inventions are not exclusively Verneuil's fault. The jail-cell visit from the killer, the doctor-friend who stays with the priest for his final hours, and the argument about faith are all in the original play. A so-called "well-made" play from the turn of the century, *Nos deux consciences* ends with a melodramatic flourish. Afraid to go to the police to clear the priest but stricken with remorse, the killer commits suicide moments before the execution. His wife, now freed from her vows of wifely submission, rushes to the prison to save the day. Is she too late? The priest has already been led away. She demands the execution be stopped. The guards relent, leave the stage, the suspense is unbearable, until—*ta da!* The priest is returned to his cell, alive, and graciously accepts the apologies of one and all. (There is a nice final gesture when the priest declines to celebrate his deliverance on the grounds that a man has not only died but also condemned himself forever by committing the mortal sin of suicide.)

Could any of these endings have worked in the final film? If an "innocent man wrongly accused" should actually die, it would be an insult to the justice system (albeit Canadian). If a priest were to die for the faith without the church being aware of his sacrifice, it would make the church look uninformed, out of touch with its best members. More important, the audience would never have stood for it. Clift's character could be executed in *A Place in the Sun* without provoking outrage because there is the constant possibility that he is guilty—if not of murder, at least of evil intent.

Trying to imagine it, the sheer, fabulous outrageousness of Logan being executed, I find the major question that comes to my mind is, What would he wear? To indulge this fiction momentarily, let us visualize alternative endings with different costumes. Since none of these versions, Hitchcock's, Verneuil's, and Anthelme's, shows us the actual execution—keeping it offstage and offscreen—the method is left unspecified. The electric chair, the guillotine, the gallows. Let's say he hangs. If Logan appears on the scaffold in prison garb (the "convict's stripes" noted by Verneuil), it would suggest his final humiliation. His cassock has been taken from him—a cruel irony to lose his identity as a priest at the very moment he is giving his life for the priesthood. It might even suggest that, having been convicted of murder (and suspected of adultery), he has been defrocked, that the church has abandoned him at the moment of his greatest sacrifice. On the other hand, if he were to be hanged wearing a cassock . . . now, *that* would be visually dramatic.

In the film, he is not executed. He is not even convicted. All the issues raised by the first two-thirds of the film must be resolved in another way.

Sex Sells Saints

Besides Otto, Ruth, Larue, the judge and jury, and the mob, there was one more group that was dissatisfied with Father Logan—the studio's marketing department. Commercially, it was very inconvenient for Logan to be a priest. As a consequence, the film's advertising hides the fact whenever possible. Although *Going My Way* (1944) and *The Bells of St. Mary's* (1945) had been major hits a few years earlier, *I Confess* lacked the heartwarming qualities of those films. Promotional material for *I Confess* emphasizes suspense over religion, with strong doses of sexual tension and sexual violence thrown in. One ad trumpets, "A Love-Shame she couldn't Admit! / A Kill-threat he couldn't escape! / Relentless Hitchcock Excitement!" The script for the trailer describes the film this way: "Electrifying Drama with the Brand of Alfred Hitchcock Burned into Every Scene."[120]

In order to direct attention away from the film's religious context, production stills frequently show Clift wearing civilian clothes or an army uniform (see plate 4). A publicity still (staged for the ad campaign) features Logan and his former fiancée, Ruth, standing side by side in a courtroom. Ruth wears her customary suit and Logan a suit and tie. (In the film Logan always wears his cassock in court.) The French poster *(La loi du silence)* features an overheated painting of Clift wearing a brown sports jacket as he passionately kisses Ruth (a vivid interpretation of the first part of the flashback sequence).

A more startling change occurs in relation to Logan's neckwear. A small Spanish-language ad *(Yo confieso)* features Clift's head bobbing in midair, cut off at the neck, presumably so that no clerical collar can be seen (plate 5). The most amazing example of anticlerical (or nonclerical) intervention can be seen in a lobby card that reproduces a shot from the film. Logan and Ruth are on the ferry (plate 6). Because he is leaning against the railing of the ship we can see him only from the waist up. Although he is clearly wearing a cassock in the film, in the advertising his collar has been painted over and the cassock colored blue so that it looks as if he is wearing a Nehru jacket at least fifteen years before they came into fashion. (The use of color is itself misleading. The phrase "Filmed in Canada's colorful Quebec" on all the lobby cards implies that the film is in color.)

Clift biographer Barney Hoskyns refers to Logan as "this beautiful priest torn between the spiritual and the sensual," but it is not apparent in the film that sensuality constitutes a serious temptation.[121] If Logan is torn between the sensual and the spiritual, it is only advertising people who think so.[122] Consequently, they supplement the character's (real) spiritual struggle with a manufactured sensuality more in keeping with the film's suspense genre.

The original American poster also misrepresents the film as it emphasizes sex and erases the religious setting (plate 7). The central image shows Clift (in a dark jacket) with his hand over Anne Baxter's mouth. He holds her head back and embraces her threateningly. On the right side is the slogan "If you knew what he knew what would you do?" Together, the image and the question suggest that the man might be driven to murder the woman as the result of some secret knowledge—either he knows something about her, or he has found out that she knows something about him. The scene depicted may in fact be the crime that must be kept secret.

An "action scene" (completely fictitious) is included on the far side of the poster in the bottom right corner. In a drawing of a street scene at night, a man in black holds a gun while another man runs away. The man in black

FIGURE 20. Poster for *La loi du silence,* the French release of *I Confess.*

may be wearing a cassock (a gun-toting priest) but the image is cut off at his waist and a lamppost divides him in half, covering the place where one could differentiate a cassock from the tail of a jacket. The true killer appears on these rain-soaked, cobblestone streets in the film's opening, but no one chases him with a gun—least of all Father Logan.

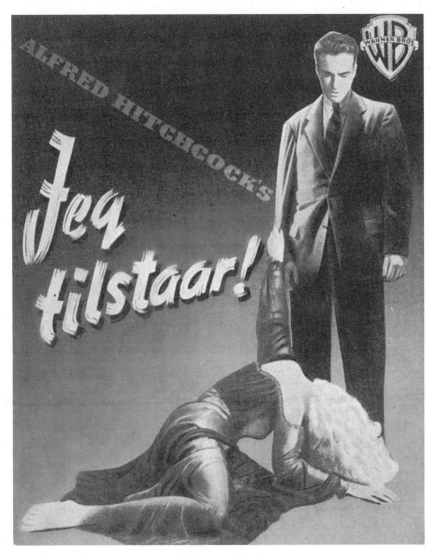

FIGURE 21. Danish program for *Jeg tilstaar! (I Confess)*.

In most of the advertising, the question of to whom the "I" in the title refers is deliberately left ambiguous. Where does the guilt lie? Depending on the design, it could alight on anyone. A Mexican lobby card (featuring the wonderful title *Mi secreto me condena,* "My Secret Condemns Me") has a film still of Ruth speaking on the phone in her bedroom while her oblivious husband is seen far in the background, implying that she has the secret that needs to be confessed. On the side of the card is a drawing in classic "hard-boiled" style, presumably of Clift (in a dark suit) with a blonde straight out of Mickey Spillane. She throws herself (or has been thrown) at his feet, her long hair trailing on the ground, her legs visible through her black negligee as she clutches at his arm, begging for forgiveness or for mercy ("I confess"). This attempt to insert some hot-blooded sex and violence is singled out for the film's Danish publicity (*Jeg tilstaar!*). Not only does the stylized cover art reappear (this time as the featured image) but subsidiary publicity stills of Clift kissing Baxter are also included as a (false) promise of what is to come. Only a German poster features the film's actual killer in proximity with the title (perhaps because he is played by a German actor).

The advertising for *I Confess* creates an imaginary parallel text in which established modes of promotion and Clift's persona as shaped by his previous roles substitute for what is actually in the film. Ironically, the film *does* offer the kind of dangerous sexual relationship indicated in the ads, but it is subject to a silencing as profound as any surrounding the film's production, marketing, or reception. Potential viewers looking for a "Love-Shame" the protagonist "couldn't admit" or "A Kill-threat he couldn't escape" need look no further. And the "Electrifying . . . Brand of Alfred Hitchcock" *is* "Burned into Every Scene."

A Little Shame, A Little Violence

No matter how hard the Production Code office fought any expression of sexuality on Logan's part, Hitchcock arranged for the priest to be the object of desire. But in place of the heterosexual romance the publicity people hoped for, Hitchcock inserted a "perverse," obsessive desire. The most taboo desire, of course, is not Ruth's adulterous lust for a priest, but Otto's treacherous, persistent demand that Logan be his "friend." To chart this desire, the film shifts in its final scenes from Logan's travails to Otto's desire.

Otto has propelled the narrative of *I Confess* from first scene to last, but he is at cross-purposes with himself. He admires Logan yet despises his supposed virtues. "You're *so* good. It's easy for you to be good." He looks up to Logan—literally in the scene on the ladder—but also wants to bring the priest down to his level. When Otto's life and freedom depend on keeping Logan quiet, he pursues him through the rectory, pushing him to break. Imagining that Logan has broken his vow finally allows Otto to see them as equals.

After the trial, when Alma begins to tell the police who the real killer is, Otto shoots her and several others as he attempts to flee, pursued by the police through the Château Frontenac. Cornered, Otto moves toward a window to evaluate his chance at escape. Hearing Logan outside in the hallway with the police, Otto turns back, choosing to berate Logan rather than save his own life. Assuming Logan has told the police everything, Otto relishes the opportunity to point out his hero's feet of clay. "My only friend—Father Logan. How kindly he hears my confession and then—a little shame, a little violence—that's all it takes to make him talk. It was too much for you, huh? You are a coward like all other people, aren't you? A hypocrite like all the rest." Still bound by the law of the confessional, Logan has no choice but to suffer the abuse in silence. Why does Otto want to destroy Logan even if it means his own ruin?

Brett Farmer describes the queer subtext weaving through the term Otto uses again and again—*father*. If we replace *father* in the oedipal sense with *father* in the clerical sense, Otto illustrates an argument psychoanalyst Francis Pasche makes about gay male desire: "The gay male subject initially recognizes and engages the father through a negative oedipal scenario of 'passive desire.' . . . This desire is subsequently recast as an unconscious wish to displace and undo the father's position of phallic privilege."[123]

Otto, like Pasche's gay subject, is compelled "to correct, remake, thwart, parody, and finally destroy" the father. In the process, "the father is reduced to the level of a sex object." Robbed of his symbolic claims to status, Logan has been shamed, hissed, mobbed. Turned into pure spectacle at the trial, Logan/Clift in Farmer's words is "repositioned as a site of receptivity for the gay subject's desires."[124] At the trial, Otto can look all he wants, savoring the display of Logan's shame and enforced passivity.

At one point, the film was supposed to end with a chase scene across rooftops, the kind of suspense-filled action scene found in such Hitchcock films as *Blackmail* (1929) and the first version of *The Man Who Knew Too Much* (1934). Eventually it was decided that the film would end in a ballroom, with a climactic showdown involving Otto, Logan, and the police.[125]

The theatrical setting of this final scene associates Otto with another Hitchcock character, the elegantly androgynous Handel Fane, played by Esme Percy in Hitchcock's *Murder!* (1930).[126] Fane and Otto are both abject characters, outsiders, one a "half-caste," the other a German refugee, "a man without a home." Both fall short of their ideals of beauty: Otto unattractive, pudgy, with bad skin; Fane unprepossessing, especially when compared to the svelte actress Diana Baring and the aristocratic actor-manager Sir John (Herbert Marshall). Each man dresses up in the course of the film, disguised as either the person he wants or as the one he wants to be. Chabrol and Rohmer put it well: "Each being has need of the mirror of somebody else's conscience; but in this universe . . . [each] sees in that mirror only his own deformed and exposed image. The suspicion he directs against his counterpart turns back like a boomerang and overwhelms him with shame."[127]

Each man wants to be the person he frames, yet each hates that person because that person is, *effortlessly*, everything he cannot be: young, pretty, and good. Fane has two ideals. As a female impersonator, he mimics Diana when he wears drag, and echoes Sir John's elegance when he wears a suit to audition for him. Otto wants to be as good as Father Logan and as handsome as a young Montgomery Clift. The ideal quality of the desired one destabilizes each man's identity, bringing home to him his own inadequacy and the hopelessness of his longing. Needing to be their ideals, they also need to destroy them if they are to have any hope of continuing to exist. But destroying the people they want to become is just another form of self-annihilation.

Otto Keller and Handel Fane each arrange to die in a theatrical setting. Fane stages his death during a performance at the circus, just as Otto provokes the police into shooting him fatally as he leans against a stage. In each case the police are witnesses, but each man is really playing to an audience of one, Fane to Sir John, the famous actor-playwright who could have given Fane the role of a lifetime, and Otto to Logan.

At the end of the film, Otto finally gets what he wants. Logan leaves the safety of his position in the hallway, where he was shielded by the police, steps into the open, and deliberately crosses the room, closing the distance between himself and Otto. At last, Otto and Logan are on the same level, the space between them wide open. Logan has been moved out of the formality of the confessional into an unmediated (or at least less physically separate) space that allows, in fact demands, a personal response. He cannot be separated from the penitent anymore.

Throughout the film, Otto and Logan have been separated by physical obstacles. In the confessional at the beginning, there is a grille in the wall separating the two men. When the scene dissolves to Otto completing his confession to Alma, there is a bed frame between them. In the painting scene a ladder stands between Otto and the priest; during the trial Logan is behind railings, boxed in visually and structurally by his job and his position in relation to church and state. In the first confession scene, the confessional, what would be termed in the Middle Ages a closet, can now be seen as two closets side by side, in the modern sense. Each man is in the closet; they have privacy from the world but are physically separated from each other.

Another barrier that must be eliminated is Alma, who has been as much an obstacle as the grille. When Otto physically reaches out as if he would touch Logan during the painting scene, Alma comes between them visually and verbally. When Logan's reaction to Otto's confession proves unsatisfactory, Otto completes that confession to Alma, establishing her as his second choice, a substitute for Logan. Now Logan is put in Alma's position. As he approaches Otto in the ballroom, Logan is sure Otto will not shoot him. "Why will I not shoot," Otto asks. "Because you called me 'Otto?' Alma used to call me Otto." By putting Logan in Alma's place, Otto makes Logan his soul (*alma* in Spanish). "Where is my Alma?" Otto asks (Where is my soul?). When Logan tells Otto that Alma is dead, Otto instantly replies, "You killed her. It is your fault." Otto needs Logan to take the guilt, but not only in the course of clerical duty. In this sense, Otto and Logan, more than Otto and Alma, form the kind of couple Jacques Rivette identified as being at "the heart of all Hitchcock's films"—those couples "obsessed by guilt" who "live through the same experience" and "manage to make the sin hesitate between two souls until it is abolished by the irremediable confusion of their destinies."[128]

Even though he is trapped, Otto cannot resist pointing out how he and Logan have become interchangeable: "I am as alone as you are." Logan replies, "I'm not alone," but Otto argues, "Oh, yes. You are. To kill you now would be a favor to you. You have no friends. What has happened to your friends, huh, Father? They mob you. They call at you." (Lesley Brill misunderstands Hasse's accent and, interestingly, transcribes Otto's line as not "they mob you" but "they martyr you.")[129] "It would be better if you were as guilty as I," Otto continues. "Then they would shoot you, quickly." Raising his gun to point it at Logan, Otto is shot by the police. As he falls, he cries out, "Father, help me!"

I Confess starts with a confession that is never completed. The entire narrative unfolds as we wait for Logan's response. As Otto falls wounded into Logan's arms, the sacrament of confession is finally brought to a close with Logan reciting the words of absolution in Latin, *ego te absolvo in Nomine* — (I absolve you in the Name of —). The word left unsaid is *Patri*, "Father."

All the barriers between Otto and Logan are gone. If the confession begins early in the film and ends in the last shot, what has been accomplished between is exactly the disappearance of those barriers, making it possible for Logan and Otto finally to share physical and emotional space. Dying in Logan's arms, Otto has achieved what he wanted, but what about Logan? According to the shooting script, after supporting "Keller's prone figure in his arms," "Michael leans close to [Otto], then straightens up until his head fills the picture in a BIG HEAD CLOSEUP. His expression is serene."[130] This is not what we see in the film.

Although he holds Otto in the final close-up, Logan keeps his head down, his face lost in shadow in classic Cliftian fashion. When we do glimpse Logan's eyes, they are filled with tears. Logan's openness to others causes him pain, while the role that mandates that openness denies him true communion with others. People he should have helped (including Otto and Alma) are dead. Like the main character in *The Diary of a Country Priest*, Logan "is perpetually taking on a responsibility not his own, and in the very act of doing so, being returned to his own solitude."[131]

I Confess ends with a tight close shot of one man lovingly holding another in his arms, and the censors couldn't touch it. Just as he did with Mrs. Danvers in *Rebecca* (1940), Hitchcock gets away with it under their very noses. In his next film Clift has another chance to hold a man in his arms (though again on the condition that the man is dying). It would also give him one of his best opportunities to play a character persecuted and martyred for standing by his beliefs and whose essential condition is solitude.

It is difficult for *I Confess* to be genuinely moving on a religious or a psychological level because of its reticence on essential issues. The film silences the main character more obsessively than the narrative conceit requires. The script suppresses any discussion or recognition that there might be struggle with (and within) a vocation. The acting interiorizes the main character's emotional and spiritual life to such an extent the audience cannot form a firm sense of the nature of that life. The director bypasses nonverbal expressions of inner life (psychologically expressive acting) in favor of shot/reverse shot patterns that leave the characters' motives ambiguous at best.

If we are to find a saint at the heart of *I Confess*, we will have to look at qualities the actor brings with him. In describing Clift's contribution to the film, Peter Bogdanovich lists a few: "It's the extraordinary depth of feeling that you get from Clift's face, from his movements, from his seriousness, from his sobriety, from his romanticism, that makes the part as powerful as it is."[132] Perhaps these qualities are what Father Hurley was alluding to when he said that "Clift's presence" in *I Confess* was "paying a never-ending dividend" that Hitchcock could not have foreseen.[133]

These laudatory sentiments were written decades after the film appeared; it was the mixed contemporary responses that worried Clift. His friend Jack

Larson recalled that Clift "was very disappointed in the reviews. . . . I remember one review. It was a critic he admired in England that he was very upset about because he rather disregarded Monty in *I Confess* by saying 'Montgomery Clift gives his performance of the priest in his familiar bottled-up acting style,' and it offended Monty very much and disturbed him very much."[134] The review is actually from the American *Look* magazine, and the critic finds positive things to say about Clift as well, granting that Clift "plays the role effectively in his familiar bottled-up style."[135] Many actors are inclined to remember bad reviews more sharply than good ones, but as bad reviews go, this one is far from devastating. Evidently, though, something about it disturbed Clift so much that his friend remembered both the occasion and the phrase vividly half a century later. "He accepted all my compliments about *I Confess* with great happiness," Larson adds, but he still "complained about how he was being perceived by the critics. They were, like, 'on to him.'"[136]

FIGURE 22. Publicity still for *From Here to Eternity*, 1953.

FOUR

Facing Persecution

WHEN THE FIRST serious biographies of Clift appeared in the late seventies, they were promoted as exposés, positing homosexuality as the key that explained Clift's life. Robert LaGuardia's *Monty: A Biography of Montgomery Clift* was the first, published in 1977. Despite LaGuardia's sensitivity about "outing" people (he explains in a preface that he uses pseudonyms "for Monty's male lovers" in order to avoid "possible social embarrassment to them"), the publisher did not hesitate to foreground Clift's sexuality. "Women—and men—couldn't resist him," proclaims a blurb on the paperback.[1] Patricia Bosworth's *Montgomery Clift: A Biography* followed soon after (1978), endorsed by a parade of Clift's coworkers and fellow celebrities. Elia Kazan promises unparalleled access: "Here it is—the real thing—inside Montgomery Clift."[2] Garson Kanin hints at sensational subject matter: "Those of us who knew him are given revelatory material—often shocking." Both books depict Clift's life as "tragic" and fix on sexuality as the cause of his self-destructiveness. The jacket of Bosworth's book labels him "a man maddened by his homosexuality." LaGuardia's promos are no less extreme: "In the end, drugs, alcohol, and his own conflicting sexual desires consumed him." "Finally," LaGuardia's publishers assure us, "*Monty* captures the truth of a tragic life."[3]

Despite the sensationalism with which these books were promoted, both biographies are fair, sympathetic, and responsibly researched. If, in the end, Bosworth's book has the edge as the definitive biography, LaGuardia's is more in tune with issues pertaining to gay life in New York in the 1950s and 1960s.[4]

141

Nevertheless, it would be fair to say that together these two works changed Clift's image forever. Today, if someone knows "Montgomery Clift," it is as a gay actor.

Because this conviction only became widespread a decade after Clift's death, it might seem revisionist to consider Clift and his performances through the prism of homosexuality, a modern perspective imposed on texts. A glance at contemporary responses to Clift, however, shows that homosexuality was always part of Clift's persona (to the extent that it could be named or signaled in the 1950s): rumored in fan magazines, part of Clift's own concern about how his performances were perceived, and, most significant, implicit as a gay subtext in the roles themselves.

An important caveat: if we take it as given that Clift was gay (and that, too, is subject to debate), we should not assume that this has a necessary, constant, or legible effect on his work as an actor. Biography does not trump labor. Clift's personal life did not dictate how he performed his roles, nor should it dictate how we read his performances. Understood this way, there is no such thing as a "gay actor"; there are only actors (actors being people who present themselves as someone other than who they are, someone different from themselves). In terms of reading the films, knowledge of or references to Clift's personal life open the possibility of a "queer" reading of a Clift character but do not privilege it. Lastly, it is important to keep in mind Clift's awareness of this as a career issue and his management of his image in relation to social expectations and those of the film industry. The professional (and personal) consequences should he have failed to control his own image are not debatable. While some have accused Clift of being in the closet, for an actor in the 1950s, it would be more accurate to describe him as keeping a lid on a situation that could explode in his face at any time.

RUMORS OF THE ARTIST'S BIOGRAPHY

Fan magazines of the day are littered with sexually suggestive headlines regarding Clift's personal life—something not, in itself, unusual. But read through a modern filter—following the outing of Clift by LaGuardia, Bosworth, and their sources—such headlines come across as a barely disguised warning to a public figure to stay in line. In 1949, in conjunction with Clift's first big buildup prior to the release of *The Heiress,* fan magazines featured the kind of introductory stories typical for most new stars.

Motion Picture announces, "A New Star Is Born" (with a picture of Clift in bed). Any references to sexuality, however, remain firmly entrenched within a romantic heterosexual discourse. The August 1949 *Movieland* promises readers the inside scoop on "Making Love the Clift Way." In 1951 the same publication offers the more provocative "Two Loves Has Monty." Both stories, however, use the actor's name as shorthand to discuss the characters he was playing in upcoming films. "Making Love" is accompanied by a series of five stills leading up to a kiss in *The Heiress,* and Monty's "Two Loves" are the characters played by Elizabeth Taylor and Shelley Winters in *A Place in the Sun.*

Moving beyond the love life of Clift's screen characters, the May 1954 *Photoplay* delivers "Montgomery Clift's Tragic Love Story," a tale of heartbreak in which Clift and "a girl whom we will call Mary" realize they must part. "Affection was not enough for a long-time partnership," *Photoplay* declares.[5] Stories like this, which even the magazine admits "could have walked right out of the pages of some of the world's most romantic fiction," are a response to whisperings about Clift, labeled a "recluse" and "the oddity" elsewhere in the article.[6] As early as February 1949, *Modern Screen,* for example, began figuring Clift's personal life as a question, asking, "Is It True What They Say about Monty?" followed three years later by the more combative rhetorical query "Who Is Monty Kidding?" The June 1953 *Screen Life* informs readers, "He's Travelin' Light." Light in the loafers? Throughout the early 1950s, ambiguous but suggestive stories such as *Motion Picture*'s "The Lurid Love Life of Montgomery Clift" or *Movieland*'s "How Embarrassed Can You Get?" (over a photo of Clift sleeping on a park bench) could be countered by testimonials such as "The Monty Clift I Know" by Elizabeth Taylor in *Screenland* (May 1950).[7] But as Clift's career continued and stories about stars became more pointed with the advent of the scandal magazines, *Screenland* (November 1956) ran the following headline (over another cover featuring Elizabeth Taylor): "Monty Clift: Woman Hater or Free Soul?" Bypassing indecisiveness in favor of active misogyny, the headline implies that Clift's indifference to women could be a sign of something deeper.

Screen Album, in particular, was eager to insinuate that Clift's many longterm friendships with women were unreliable indicators of a standard heterosexuality. Their August–October 1954 edition features a story on Clift's longtime friend Libby Holman, ungallantly titled "The Girl Friend Isn't Exactly Girlish." Holman's role in Clift's life puzzled many onlookers. An "older woman," she was read as a mother figure as well as (or instead of) a lover. A 1957 issue of *Hollywood Romance* states outright, "Montgomery Clift Searched for a Wife . . . and Found a Mother." Clift continues to be paired with Elizabeth Taylor in the media's imaginary, here in a photograph from the set of *Raintree County* with Clift sitting on Taylor's lap ("Tell Mama all") and in the coupling of their stories. The headline about him is matched with one about her: "Elizabeth Taylor Searched for a Lover . . . and Found a Father." Although the latter is presented as understandable, the alleged choice to be a mama's boy is defined as sick. As it says on the cover, "What Drove Liz to Mike Todd [Sent] Monty to the Psychiatrist's Couch."

A 1955 special issue of *Screen Album* on "Young Stars and Their Loves" reports a recent sighting of Clift and Holman. The wording is blunt: "She's too old for him, but they do have fun together. They had fun last winter at Mont Tremblant in Canada, where they went skiing. Montgomery came home with a case of the gout (according to Dorothy Kilgallen) and/or a strained tendon (Walter Winchell), but whatever the ailment, it landed him up in Roosevelt Hospital. Since he's a boy who likes his privacy, he used a false name."[8]

This is not the last time Clift's body will be placed in the midst of speculations about his health and sexuality. As this quotation implies, the "boy who likes his privacy" finds ways to keep professional gossips guessing, though the effort lands him in the hospital. But "whatever the ailment," his unnamed malady requires him to disguise or erase his very identity. Secrecy is a recurring motif, the desire for privacy a joke, as we are told parenthetically, "(Clift's secret phone number is so secret he hardly tells it to himself)."

The new complication, *Screen Album* hurries to report, is the introduction of a third party. (The story is titled "The Triangle Got Lopsided Because . . ."). "When last seen, in fact, Libby was being escorted not only by Montgomery, but also by Roddy McDowall. Libby had one lad on each arm, and the trio appeared blissful." Ménage à trois or camouflage? Whose friend was whose? And which one was the beard? "You want to know what's with Montgomery's love life?" *Screen Album* asks. "So do we, pal, so do we."

Although an answer to the indirectly but persistently posed question of Clift's sexuality is implied in stories like these, it was more fruitful for fifties gossip columnists to maintain Clift's sexuality as an enigma than it was to discover "the truth." By keeping it a mystery, the fan and scandal magazines could provide the "answer" repeatedly, selling story after story, year after year, each promising—this time—to reveal what had remained hidden. (This tactic also shielded them from lawsuits.) After Clift's death, bi-ographers could be more direct in naming homosexuality, as their pub-lishers trumpeted the revelations in appropriately breathless terms (using slogans along the lines of "At last it can be told!" or, as Kazan wrote, "The real thing"). Nevertheless, the true complexity of Clift's emotional and sex-ual life is not recoverable. He tended to compartmentalize the people in his life so that even those who thought themselves close friends were not aware of the full range of his acquaintances, or the nature of his relation-ships with others.[9] While calling him bisexual (as brother Brooks Clift in-sists in Bosworth's book) can be read as a last-ditch attempt to sidestep homosexuality full stop, still it might not be possible to limit Clift to one identity.

Identifying Clift exclusively as "a" homosexual disregards the serious and often long-lasting relationships he had with older women such as Libby Holman, Myrna Loy, Mrs. Walter Huston, and others. Although these re-lationships do not conform to traditional stereotypes of heterosexual ro-mance or even heterosexual desire, it would be presumptuous to dismiss them as mere masquerade. Clift himself seems to have been protective of these relationships, especially the one with Holman. It is rumored that he turned down the lead in *Sunset Boulevard* because the story of the younger man involved with an unstable older woman could be seen as unflattering and unkind to Libby Holman (and himself) if read as biographical.[10] (A play written at the end of the 1950s, *Single Man at the Party*, was also said to be based on Clift and Holman. It also features a beautiful young man involved with a heavy-drinking older woman, and even though the young man is gay, he comes to recognize that his relationship with her is the most important in his life.)[11]

What is more interesting than imagining Clift's personal life—and more demonstrable—is the effect rumors of homosexuality had on his work. Sur-rounded by increasingly hostile press, aware of the consequences should he be involved in scandal, Clift knew that the wrong word, a suspicious ges-ture, even something as inconsequential as a rumor could destroy his ca-reer. Considering the stakes, it is not surprising that Clift would demon-strate self-consciousness about how he might be read, beginning with his very first film. LaGuardia reports, "He was concerned about how he used his hands; he would ask friends on numerous occasions if he was using them in an effeminate way."[12] All actors scrutinize their every gesture in terms of how it will be read by others; only some are at risk of losing their careers if they should make a mistake. During the filming of *The Search,* in the scene in which Steve tells Jim his mother is dead, Clift reputedly ad-libbed the line, "No, dear, she won't." "He asked Zinnemann to scrap that take and would not explain why, but he wrote [to a friend] that if that scene were printed, the audience was sure to think him homosexual for having said 'dear' to a boy."[13]

It is not homosexuality that is implied in this scene but pedophilia, a far more disturbing issue often presented as synonymous with homosexuality by homophobic sources. Even if we reject the connection, other scenes make the idea of child abuse unavoidable. While Father Logan speaks softly in French to a boy who comes for confession, there are no scenes in which anything improper could happen. In *The Search,* on the other hand, Steve grabs a half-dressed boy off the street, physically restrains him as he struggles and kicks, and uses a threatening tone to get him to sit still in the Jeep. Slinging the boy over his back to carry him into the house, Steve calls out to his friend, "Hey, Fischer. I got a present for ya," and locks the kid in a room with barred windows. When the boy hides behind a bar, Steve finds him and they engage in a prolonged, unseen tussle. Steve emerges once to exhort the boy to "relax, will ya?" Later, he bullies the child into holding still by threatening him with a hypodermic needle. Steve momentarily establishes control and begins to tend to the boy's damaged feet when Fischer shifts the terms of the relationship by asking, "Who picked who up?" Noticing the concentration-camp tattoo on the boy's arm, the older men believe the boy is afraid because he thinks they are SS men. That isn't the only thing he might fear.

The Production Code prohibited the very thought of child molestation; consequently Hollywood films could not raise the issue. But Italian films could. In light of the obvious influence of neorealism on *The Search,* I don't believe the issue of pedophilia implied in this scene can be dismissed as a modern imposition on a film that was made in a more "innocent" time. The possibility that children might be vulnerable to sexual exploitation in the chaotic aftermath of the war was one that was recognized at the time and was featured in the very films to which *The Search* was paying homage. Both *Germany Year Zero* in 1947 and *Bicycle Thieves* in 1948 have scenes in which young boys are tempted or seduced by older men who feign friendship but are clearly predatory.[14]

While fans may resist (or enjoy) these unauthorized interpretive flights as pernicious, inappropriate, tasteless, or irrelevant, it is impossible to block out such readings regardless of what we might know of the intentions of the actors or filmmakers, the logic of the narrative, or even our own desires. Although fans have the luxury of indulging in endless play with texts, what we think of specific scenes and characters could have a devastating effect if attributed to the actor as part of his "real" life.

Clift wasn't the only one worried about appearances. As late as July 1957, *Compact: The Young People's Digest* had a story on Clift subtitled "He Has Hollywood Baffled." With the usual innuendo and dramatic ellipses, we are invited to "meet Hollywood's most unusual personality . . . a strange young man whom no one really knows . . . not even his closest friends."[15] If his closest friends didn't know, what they would learn was that being close to someone of "questionable sexuality" could damage them, too. The pressure even led some of them to betray him.

Kevin McCarthy was one of Clift's closest friends during Clift's first years in Hollywood. In this anecdote he illustrates, somewhat guilelessly, how he became familiar with Hollywood homophobia. "I'll never forget the conversation. . . . It was in Henry Hathaway's office at Twentieth Century–Fox on Fifth Avenue. I went up to see him about doing a part in a film, and suddenly he said: 'People are talking about you. They're saying that you're shacking up with your buddy, Monty Clift.' I said: 'Jesus! Where did that come from?' . . . He meant that . . . Monty and I were a little too close, that there was a hint of a homosexual relationship. . . . Hathaway said, 'Lose that guy . . . he's killing your career.'"[16]

This is the version of the story quoted by LaGuardia. Bosworth has a slightly different version, which shows which details remain fixed in Mc-Carthy's telling and which vary over time. (This second version is also funnier.) When Hathaway barks, "You better stop shackin' with him," Mc-Carthy relates his shock. "I'm sitting there at the 20th Century–Fox offices on Fifty-sixth Street and Tenth Avenue, and I looked at him stunned and said, 'What the hell are you talking about?' and he said, 'Everybody in Hollywood thinks that!' and I said, 'You're not serious?' and he said, 'I am. Do yourself a favor. Lose that guy.' Here I was with a life to think about and a career to think about, and I couldn't believe what I was hearing. It was totally untrue. Monty and I had never had a homosexual relationship—we had a man-to-man relationship." He concludes, "I never had a clue he was gay all those years. *If* he was gay. Later I was reproached for not having my eyes open, for not being aware."[17] (When McCarthy says he had "a life to think about and a career to think about," *life* might be a misprint or misstatement for *wife*. In a moment of panic like this, some men are quick to establish their heterosexual bona fides.)

Regardless of whether the rumor of homosexuality was sufficient to spur

Clift's friends to avoid him, his alcoholism and drug use gave those around him numerous excuses to break with him. Alcoholism came to be nearly synonymous with homosexuality in references to Clift, another "failing" Clift was susceptible to and could never quite give up. One can also see how the topics of alcohol and drug abuse provided a screen (what one might call "plausible deniability") for what would otherwise look like simple homophobia.

McCarthy and his wife banned Clift from their home around this time (the mid-fifties) because they felt that, with his bad balance and bad judgment when drunk, he might accidentally harm their children. Alfred Lunt and Lynn Fontanne, who had given Clift his break on Broadway and considered him to be like a son, broke with him at the end of the decade. Biographer Margot Peters recounts that "Monty had become a problem the Lunts couldn't handle. . . . They had last met in Paris, where he was filming *The Young Lions*. Nervous and excited in the company of his idol, [Clift] drank too many martinis at dinner and in the elevator afterward collapsed against Alfred. His slurred apologies only further disgusted Lunt, who couldn't tolerate drunkenness in an actor." Like the McCarthys, the Lunts had "stopped asking [Clift] to their New York house, though," Peters adds, Clift "didn't stop thinking about them."[18]

Clift began drinking early in his career, but it did not become part of his public persona until after the accident. *I Confess* was one of the first films in which Clift's drinking contributed to tension between director and star. At the wrap party, Hitchcock goaded Clift into drinking until he passed out, but throughout the shoot Hitchcock had found subtle ways to express his hostility. Anne Baxter relates one way Hitchcock shut him out. "Hitchcock never talked to him. He had the assistant director, Don Page, handle everything."[19] In addition to the silent treatment, Hitchcock excluded Clift by speaking in German to costar O. E. Hasse. An account of the production in the *Boston Sunday Globe* (September 14, 1952) notes breathlessly that "Miss Baxter, Mr. Clift, and Mr. Hitchcock all speak French and Mr. Hitchcock also speaks German when he talks with actor Hasse."[20] This simple maneuver achieved several things: Hitchcock could play favorites, bond with the German actor by bringing up the old days (Hitchcock came into his own as a director in Germany in the twenties), and isolate Clift at the same time. (We might note also that Hasse and his character both bear a resemblance to the director.)

After *I Confess,* alcohol's effect on Clift's work began to elicit comment, though the gossip remained mostly behind the scenes. Fred Zinnemann, who had given Clift an early starring role in *The Search,* was troubled by a noticeable physical and professional decline when they began making *From Here to Eternity.* For this film, Clift seems to have increased his alcohol consumption, partly to help him "play" drunk and partly to prove his manliness to author James Jones and costar Frank Sinatra. The effects are noticeable in two notes Clift sent to Zinnemann during the production. Less lively and less detailed than the script ideas he sent Zinnemann regarding *The Search,* these tend to focus on alcohol. Referring to a scene in which Clift and Burt Lancaster play drunk, Clift writes, "Dear Fred, The Sarge and I finished yr bottle—Two measly drinks. Jesus man—how can I be a fuck-up on just one measly drink? Goodnight sir, M." Zinnemann later recalled this scene as one in which Clift was so genuinely bombed he couldn't say the final line correctly (when laying Maggio's body in the truck); Zinnemann eventually had to cut that part of the scene altogether. For Zinnemann's birthday, Clift sent an invitation. "*Old man*— Would you like to have drink *[sic]* with me on *This* night? Ask your social secretary to confirm or deconfirm. Happy B. Love M." On the back he writes in large print: "*ANCIENT.*" Zinnemann, who had fought Harry Cohn at Columbia to have Clift cast in the part, was not only not amused; he began to worry.

The effects of chronic alcohol abuse worsened throughout Clift's life with the addition of prescription (and nonprescription) medications, especially the powerful painkillers he took following his car accident. But alcoholism alone would have been problem enough. It had deep-sixed the careers of many actors, gay and straight (John Barrymore, to name one).

In biographies, references to Clift's drinking are pervasive. LaGuardia lists forty-five separate references to drinking in his index, covering ninety-one pages of text. (Drug use receives a relatively modest twenty-six references spanning fifty-five pages.) This is in 1978. By 1991, Barney Hoskyns's *Montgomery Clift: Beautiful Loser* attributes Clift's major problems not to alcohol but to drugs. Hoskyns calls him "a star . . . addicted to every known prescription drug."[21] Hoskyns's book does not have an index, but the trajectory Hoskyns sets out for Clift's life is obvious from the chapter titles alone: "Acting Out," "The Misfit as Superstar," "Glazed and Confused," "The Inner Circle of Hell." From 1959 on, Hoskyns asserts, Clift "would spend the remaining six and a half years of his life, leading what he called a 'phenobarbital existence' in his own personal twilight zone."[22]

While Hoskyns's reading is entirely consistent with the stereotype of the "self-loathing homosexual," it is important to remember that it was not necessarily closeted homosexuality that made Clift drink or made him a target. The modern understanding of alcoholism as a physical-chemical dependency—a medical issue rather than a moral weakness or failing—has never prevented biographers from proposing detailed psychological theories to "explain" Clift's abuse of alcohol. Clift's own explanations of why he drank tended to focus on fame. Bosworth recounts a story in which Clift sees himself on-screen and has a premonition. "I watched myself in *Red River* and I knew I was going to be famous, so I decided I would get drunk anonymously one last time." He ended up in jail.[23] This story implies that Clift was already used to the experience of getting drunk in public and felt he was going to miss it. An alternative reading suggests that Clift was afraid of fame not because it would interfere with his drinking (it obviously didn't) but because it would interfere with his personal life, specifically expressions of sexuality (i.e., drinking as cover). Regardless of whether the actor recoiled from the possibility of fame, such speculation is bolstered by the fact that Clift's drinking did intensify with his move from stage to screen. The myth of stardom as both a goal and a curse holds with either motive: as soon as Clift became a star, he couldn't throw it away fast enough.

While friends like Kevin McCarthy distanced themselves (whether to avoid becoming collateral damage of the homophobia directed at Clift or because of his drinking), others exploited Clift's alcohol abuse. In his unfinished novel *Answered Prayers,* Truman Capote uses Clift's drinking as the pretext for a story. Capote invites a few friends to a party in honor of Clift and his new film, *Red River.* The other guests are Dorothy Parker and Tallulah Bankhead (who already knew Clift, having worked with him in the theater, though Capote doesn't mention it). Clift arrives hours late, scratching and meowing at the front door. ("I've invited three alcoholics to dinner!" cries the host. "*One* is bad enough. But *three.*")[24] Capote's novel reconstructs the drunken behavior familiar from the biographies: Clift "fell into the room" and declared he had been sleeping off a hangover. When he takes a martini, we are told, the narrator "noticed that his hands trembled as he struggled to hold it."[25] Clift and Dorothy Parker discuss suicide by pills and the tragedy if one should fail.

The story's big set piece turns on Clift's beauty as modified by the twin "failings" of homosexuality and alcoholism.

> Clift dropped a cigarette into his untouched bowl of Senegalese soup, and stared inertly into space, as if he were enacting a shell-shocked soldier. His

PLATE 1. Clift circa 1950. Silver Screen
Collection, Hulton Archive, Getty Images.

PLATE 2. Glamour photo of Clift in *Screen Stories* (May 1950): 34.

PLATE 3. *Movie Life* cover (March 1950): "Liz and Monty on Location" (with Keefe Brasselle and Shelley Winters).

PLATE 4. Lobby card, *I Confess,* 1953:
Clift and Anne Baxter in the rain,
In the flashback scene.

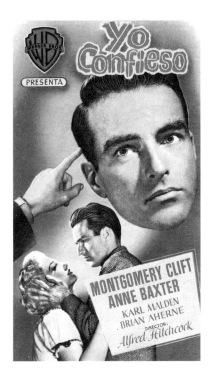

PLATE 5. *Yo confieso:* poster for
the Spanish release of *I Confess.*

PLATE 6. Lobby card, *I Confess:* Baxter and Clift on the ferry.

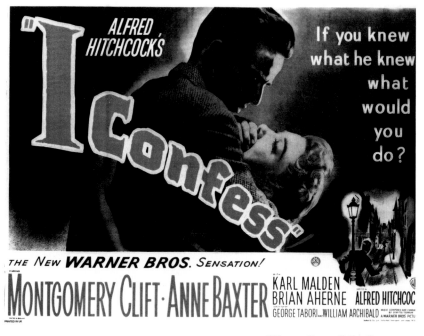

PLATE 7. Warner Bros. *I Confess* poster.

PLATE 8. Clift in a publicity still for *From Here to Eternity*, 1953.
Courtesy Random House.

PLATE 9. Clift on location for *Raintree County*, 1957. Corbis.

PLATE 10. Spanish poster for *Los dioses vencidos (The Young Lions)*, 1958.

PLATE 11. Lobby card for *Indiscretion of an American Wife*, 1954: Clift (Giovanni) in custody.

PLATE 12. Lobby card for *Freud: The Secret Passion*, 1962: Clift (Freud) and Susannah York (Cecily).

PLATE 13. Publicity still for *Suddenly, Last Summer,* 1959: Katharine Hepburn (Violet) and Clift (Cuckrowicz). Burt Glinn, Magnum Photos.

companions pretended not to notice, and Miss Bankhead continued a meandering anecdote. . . . While she talked, Miss Parker did something so curious it attracted everyone's attention; it even silenced Miss Bankhead. . With tears in her eyes, Miss Parker was touching Clift's hypnotized face, her stubby fingers tenderly brushing his brow, his cheekbones, his lips, chin. . . .

"He's so beautiful," murmured Miss Parker. "Sensitive. So finely made. The most beautiful young man I've ever seen. What a pity he's a cocksucker." Then, sweetly, wide-eyed with little girl naiveté, she said: "Oh. Oh dear. Have I said something *wrong?* I mean, he is a cocksucker, isn't he, Tallulah?"

Miss Bankhead said: "Well, d-d-darling, I r-r-really wouldn't know. He's never sucked *my* cock."[26]

At first, it seems that Clift's drinking and drug use, his ultimate drunken stupor, set up the gag, and his being gay serves as the punch line. The real punch line, though, upsets such easy assumptions. When Parker asks her disingenuous question ("he is a cocksucker, isn't he?"), Bankhead answers it not on the basis of knowledge but using a comically perverse reasoning ("He's never sucked *my* cock"). By rewriting herself as a phallic female, Bankhead makes bodies irrelevant—along with any assumption that sexuality is biologically determined. The true issue is Clift's inaccessibility; sexuality provides one more enigma, another way for Clift to remain blank and unreadable.

The closer you look, though, the more it seems that Capote's story isn't really about Clift at all. Even Clift's sexuality can hardly be said to belong to him. A topic of conversation, subject of speculation, "his" homosexuality is presented as an obstacle for others (Parker despairs of ever possessing such beauty because its owner is gay). Every other character in the story, including the author and host, is more vivid than the sphinxlike Clift. Composed of pure surface and unexplained oddities of behavior, Clift mirrors whomever he is talking to or remains impenetrably opaque. He is the cipher at the heart of the tale.

As Clift's persona has evolved, alcoholism and homosexuality have often served as masks for each other. In Clift's films, whenever the topic of sexuality is raised, the character's proposed sexual identity is rendered unstable by the palimpsest of the actor's biography. The same is true of his characters' drinking habits. In *From Here to Eternity,* the actor's drinking and the character's are at times inseparable. (Playing drunk in the scene immediately preceding the death of Sinatra's Maggio, Clift was in fact so inebriated he could hardly stand.) Excessive drinking may have been more costly to the actor in social terms—and was his only real failing in terms of professional discipline—but homosexuality was the bigger threat to his career. Despite the risk, in *From Here to Eternity* Clift makes both alcohol abuse and the possibility of alternative sexualities simultaneously invisible and out in plain sight.

FROM HERE TO ETERNITY

Many aspects of James Jones's novel had the potential to raise objections that could have made the film unproduceable. Excessive drinking wasn't one of them. The red flags for the Production Code office included the novel's use of "bad language," depictions of unregulated male promiscuity, and scenes of prostitution—the same problems that had arisen with *Red River*. The questions raised about leadership in *Red River* become and all-out assault on authority in *From Here to Eternity*. Published eight years after the end of World War II, *Eternity* depicts the army as festering in waste and corruption. This posed a particular problem because director Fred Zinnemann wanted to shoot the film on location at Schofield Barracks in Hawaii and use military personnel instead of extras, making the cooperation of the U.S. Armed Forces essential.[27]

Screenwriter Daniel Taradash's Oscar-winning adaptation of the book did everything necessary to turn the sprawling novel into a two-hour film. Characters were condensed, relationships revised, events eliminated. In deference to the Production Code, brothels became social clubs and prostitutes were transformed into hostesses. For the army, the book's wholehearted disgust with the U.S. military is deflected by the film's wholehearted endorsement of the war. Because most of the story takes place before Pearl Harbor, the film can imply that the careerism and hypocrisy we see are the result of peacetime conditions in which soldiers have nothing worthwhile to do. Once Pearl Harbor is attacked at the film's climax, everything changes. A peacetime army may be an unwieldy, unstable edifice, but an army at war is something to behold.

The most substantial alteration in the transition from novel to screen is the film's complete erasure of homosexuality, a topic that takes up a surprising amount of space in Jones's novel. If this aspect of the book raised hardly a word of protest when it came to making the film, it was because everyone understood that it had to be eliminated in every way, shape, and form.

Considering how much the book concerns itself with the homosexual activity of men in uniform and the book's status as a best seller, it is surprising that the subject could disappear so utterly from the film with so little comment. The postwar period was one of the first times mainstream novels openly explored gay topics without fear of censorship. When these works were adapted for film, though, the "gay issue" was either dropped or replaced by comparable "weaknesses" or prejudices (alcoholism sans gay subtext in 1945's *The Lost Weekend,* pathological anti-Semitism in 1947's *Crossfire*). While it would be difficult to call Jones's novel positive in its representation of homosexuality and gay characters, the matter-of-factness of Jones's attitude is remarkable nearly sixty years later. *From Here to Eternity,* published in 1951, everywhere sustains the 1948 Kinsey report's assertion that homosexual experiences are commonplace for a significant percentage of American men. Ostensibly immune to gay desire, Jones's characters nevertheless demonstrate a persistent, unabashed, functional bisexuality. If there is hardly a trace of this in the film's script, the staging, or the actors' performances, there really didn't have to be. Jones's book, which enjoyed a positive critical reputation in addition to its widespread popularity, was an ever-present comparison point for the film's original audience.

In this context, Clift's decision to take the role of Robert E. Lee Prewitt is especially intriguing. As one observer noted, "No actor has ever plotted his career more carefully or selected his roles with such caution."[28] Of course, the actor and the producers of the film could depend on any homosexual undercurrents being disguised by the homosocial settings required by the genre (as happens with westerns like *Red River* and military films like *The Search* and *The Big Lift*). And Prewitt, like other characters Clift played, can be (and has been) easily read at face value. In his resistance to social and institutional pressures to compromise or conform, Prewitt has an unyielding integrity and refusal to violate a private moral code that recall Father Logan in *I Confess.* As a soldier, Prewitt brings to mind Steve and Danny, but the hardheaded, bugle-playing former boxing champ gives Clift the chance to transform the earlier characters' fundamental innocence into a hard-won individualism. Moreover, as a model of stoic endurance in the face of persecution, Prewitt can be seen as a hero to anyone who has felt isolated or subjected to unjust treatment. Because of these traits, Prewitt is for many Clift's finest self-portrait.

A shot of Clift opens the film. He marches up to the camera through the last few opening titles, wearing a well-pressed uniform and a hat, with a duffle bag slung over his shoulder. Significantly, as soon as he sees Maggio

(Frank Sinatra), a friend doing chores out in the yard, Prewitt begins to fidget with his uniform. He takes his hat off (a dress hat with a rigid top and a visor) and runs a hand through his hair. Bouncing the hat a few times in his hands, he taps it like a tambourine, then smushes it back on his head, only this time it is set at a jaunty tilt, well away from his forehead. Pacing back and forth in front of the building to which he has to report, he clenches and flexes his fingers, hesitating while his nervous energy urges him forward.

Inside, Prewitt shoots some pool, lining up a trick shot as Clift did in *A Place in the Sun.* As in that film, pool seems to be a solitary pastime, a game for people who are more comfortable being alone. Both George and Prewitt seek out an abandoned pool table when they find themselves in stressful social situations. (As Angela suggests in *A Place in the Sun,* this can also be seen as the sign of a misspent youth.) Prewitt's game is interrupted by Sergeant Warden (Burt Lancaster), who immediately tries to put him on the defensive. Warden barks out challenges and veiled threats, suggesting that he has heard all about Prewitt, who has just transferred in. Instead of being intimidated, Prewitt is impressed and amused. He half-smiles and says, "I heard about you too, Sergeant," as if Warden is just the kind of man he has been looking for—a model military man.

In this opening scene, Clift suggests Prewitt's resistance to pressure through subtle means. As Prewitt waits to see the captain, Maggio chats with him through a window and tells him he is the best bugler on the island. Prewitt acknowledges the compliment in a subtly self-mocking way, undercutting any hint of arrogance by saying, "That's—true," as if he had just realized it. When the captain walks in and Warden calls "Attention!" Prewitt does not snap to. He simply rises and stands more or less straight. Not superstraight—his chest is not shoved forward, as in Burt Lancaster's hyperbolic Popeye carriage—but there is also nothing about his posture that could be objectionable, technically. Simply by slowing down the tempo of his movements, Clift establishes that Prewitt is an excellent soldier but not subservient to anyone. He is not externally motivated.

Called into Captain Holmes's office, Prewitt does not march in a clipped, precise gait, but steps quietly and carefully, as if he is carrying out his duties as he sees fit, to his own standards, rather than trying to make an impression. Questioned about why he requested a transfer, Prewitt's response, "It's a personal matter," stakes out his right to have personal values without denying the values of the group (not to mention the right to keep things secret). When he says he won't be joining the boxing team (again standing his ground and keeping his motives private), Holmes tells him, "Looks to me as if you're trying to acquire a reputation as a lone wolf, Prewitt." Prewitt says nothing but maintains steady, constant eye contact. He will not argue but he will not back down, either.

When a supply sergeant offers his first impression of Prewitt, "Looks like a good man," Warden disagrees. "I know his type. He's a hardhead." The rest of the film will attempt to reconcile these terms. Prewitt in turn bestows the title "good man" on Warden and Maggio, the two men whose lead he might follow.

Warden is a company man, dedicated to the army but bitter about what careerists (in other words, commissioned officers) like Holmes have done to it. Around Warden, Prewitt wears a range of uniforms, trying out different military identities. Pulling weeds by hand on his knees in the yard, he wears a Smokey the Bear–style campaign hat that evokes the cavalry. On cleanup detail, swabbing the floor of the gym or scrubbing pots in the kitchen (assignments designed to humiliate him for not boxing), he wears dark denim jacket-style shirts and dark pants. Sometimes he rolls up his sleeves and wears his shirt unbuttoned over a T-shirt, making the uniform fit him instead of him trying to fit it. The stiff denim makes him look more like a prison inmate than a soldier.

Maggio is the antithesis of Warden. Anti-army first and last, he refuses to be the model soldier-turned-inmate. Maggio even declares, "We're not prisoners," shortly before he is arrested and dragged off to the stockade. In terms of dress, it is Maggio who introduces Prewitt to lighter fare and the critique of the army that goes with it. On payday, a sullen and mistreated Prewitt lies stiffly on his cot, his arms under his head and jaw shut tight, dressed in full uniform. Maggio provides a lively contrast, speaking nonstop, spilling talcum powder all over his upper body as he prepares to dress. In a sleeveless undershirt, he is a neutral palette. Instead of army regulation, he chooses Hawaiian (what he calls his "loose, flowing sport shirt" in place of Jones's term, "gook shirts")[29] and casually tosses one to Prew, complete with philosophy, "We just dress up in civvies and we're as good as the rest of the world, ain't we?" Maggio's rebellion against the army culminates when he goes AWOL from sentry duty and Prewitt finds him half-naked on a park bench, shoes, shirt, and undershirt gone, wearing only dog tags and pants.

Although Lancaster as Warden demands most of our attention in the first half of the film (his character being more intense and conflicted, his acting style more exuberant), the film is built around Prewitt, with Maggio and Warden presenting the opposite poles of Prewitt's character. While Maggio is locked in a struggle to the death with the army, Warden suggests that it might be possible to make a life in the military, complete with heterosexual romance and marriage.

The most famous scene in the film involves Warden and Holmes's wife, Karen (Deborah Kerr), having sex on the beach. Sexual relations between men and women throughout the film are riddled with power imbalances, economic exploitation, and the kind of emotional violence and cold-blooded neglect that breed a bone-deep bitterness in both of the film's female characters, Karen and Lorene. Sex itself (heterosexual relations indicated in the film) is presented as a positive if temporary respite, blocking out the characters' awareness of everything else that makes these relationships impossible. Desire springs eternal, but it cannot be sustained.

What is not often noted is that the beach scene is part of a series of scenes juxtaposing Warden and Karen's affair with Prewitt's difficult relationship with the bar hostess Lorene (Donna Reed). The crashing waves on the beach dissolve to the postcoital cigarette smoke of Prewitt and Lorene in the madam's private room upstairs at the New Congress Club. Later, when Warden and Karen have an argument in the car, we cut to Prewitt about to propose to Lorene (who turns him down). Both women refuse to marry common soldiers. Karen wants Warden to become an officer; Prewitt, who was a corporal before he transferred, offers to get his stripes back to satisfy Lorene's hunger for middle-class status and financial security.

Prewitt's manner toward Lorene is dramatically different from Warden's combative, confrontational stance toward Karen. Because Prewitt is not an articulate man, Clift depends on his body to communicate Prewitt's shifting moods as the relationship develops. For instance, when Lorene meets Prewitt in a crowded bar, Clift, in what is almost a characteristic stance (turned three-quarters away from the camera), redirects our attention from his barely visible face to his expressive posture—his bare forearm, the loose silken shirt sleeve skimming his biceps, his tensing shoulder and curved back. In a two-shot, with Clift and Reed on opposite sides of the screen, Clift drops his forearm on the bar, visually connecting the space between them. Gazing at Reed, Clift transfers our attention from his eyes to his back and shoulders when he props his arm on the bar and uses it to support his head, blocking his face even more decisively.

Clift's body is that of a dancer, thin, wiry, all muscle, trained to be useful rather than sculpted for display. As Prewitt, the tenor of Clift's physique, the perfect complement to his soft-spoken, self-sufficient, independent characters, is in stark contrast to the aggressive physicality of Burt Lancaster's Warden. Not only are we invited to see our fill of Lancaster's broad shoulders, massive chest, small hips and waist, and long legs in the scene on the beach, scenes of him in uniform draw even more attention to the shape, size, and condition of his body. When Maggio starts a fight with Sergeant Judson (Ernest Borgnine) in a bar, Warden jumps up, smashes a bottle, and strikes an "Incredible Hulk" pose. Shoulders rounded in, he is poised to explode, his chest muscles straining against his shirt, his thighs taut in his pants legs. Evoking his acrobatic background, Lancaster balances this impression of massiveness with a lightness in his movements that suggests the possibility of imminent, sudden action. Shouting at the men to stop, Warden fills up the space vocally as well as visually. Warden is too big a presence to be contained, just as his body is too big for his uniform.

Now compare Lancaster's physical hyperbole to Sinatra. Maggio, putting on his Hawaiian shirt, jokes that his sister sends them to him and they are always too big. In the first half of Sinatra's career, one of his most commonly noted features was skinniness. If we compare him with Clift on that basis, there is not much difference. In matching uniforms or in matching shirts, the men resemble each other. As characters, though, Prewitt is defined as a fighter; when pressed, he can hold his own, even against much larger men. Sinatra's Maggio is more vulnerable. A little shorter than Prewitt, a little thinner perhaps, Maggio is also much less guarded. Constantly talking, all his feelings out in the open, Maggio is emotionally exposed, not having learned to hold himself back like Prewitt. Maggio impulsively starts fights that other, wiser men have to step in to finish for him. When Maggio fights with Judson (who has insulted Maggio's sister), Warden smashes a bottle and breaks it up. After Maggio dies as a result of Judson's sadistic abuse, it is Prewitt who steps up to avenge him.

The relationship between the actor's body and his character/affect brings up one specific moment that seems negligible in the film but has a disproportionate importance for Clift fans. In all of his seventeen films, there is only one scene in which Clift's body is on display, unmediated by wardrobe: Prewitt with his shirt off in *From Here to Eternity*. Forced to dig a hole as part of "the treatment" (his punishment for refusing to box), Prewitt rests for a moment, standing beside his shovel in the tropical heat, his skin glistening with sweat. The gleaming hairlessness of Prewitt's pecs suggests the shaved ideal described by Steve Cohan in his book on 1950s stars, *Masked Men*. In what he dubs the "Age of the Chest," the ideal 1950s man was exemplified by beefy hypermales like Burt Lancaster, Kirk Douglas, Rock Hudson, and Charlton Heston. Simultaneously smooth and boyish, a hairless chest was de rigueur.

Clift's profession and his celebrity required that his body be on semipermanent public display, where it could be subjected to inspection and evaluation. It was Clift's responsibility not only to monitor his and his characters' sexuality, but also to show his willingness to accede to social pressure by policing his body's appearance. As an actor, Clift simultaneously had to display his body and hide its "faults." Like a woman, he was exalted for his beauty while at the same time being made to feel self-conscious and ashamed, inadequate. Held up to impossible and contradictory criteria, even someone as beautiful as Montgomery Clift could never be beautiful enough. As it happens, Clift and his friend and costar Elizabeth Taylor shared the same unforgivable "flaw"—noticeable body hair. Taylor and Clift had similar coloring: in Taylor's case, jet-black hair that set off her light eyes and pale skin. The vivid contrast of hair and skin exacerbated the appearance of body hair and provoked ridicule. By the time she made *A Place in the Sun*, Taylor's "failing" had made her the butt of jokes. Bosworth reports that one makeup artist crudely suggested that Taylor be given "a razor and shaving cream for her arms."[30] Clift also has noticeable hair on his forearms, but it was another site that prompted him to take extreme measures.

Though a classic secondary characteristic of maleness, the hair on Clift's chest provoked reactions more appropriate for a "secret shame." According to Bosworth, Clift underwent months of electrolysis before shooting began on *From Here to Eternity* in order to have "a thick pelt of hair removed from his shoulders and chest."[31] Before and after this film, Clift had found ways to avoid baring his chest. Cast as the romantic lead in *A Place in the Sun*, he was asked on the first day of shooting to take off his T-shirt for the scene by the lake with Elizabeth Taylor. He refused. In *The Big Lift*, a T-shirt comes in handy again. Clift's character returns to his room, fresh from a shower, wearing a robe; beneath it is the customary T-shirt—just to be safe. Once again Clift as an actor was required to balance impossible contradictions, embodying masculinity in terms of musculature while erasing other evidence of testosterone-related sexual traits. And again, there was a lot at stake. If he failed to measure up to these socially determined aesthetic demands, he would not only suffer professional penalties, he could be excoriated and ridiculed.

Clift was. Instead of gaining points for manliness ("that'll put hair on your chest"), Clift was dehumanized. In addition to her reference to Clift's "pelt," Bosworth quotes "fans" who glimpsed Clift vacationing at a friend's place in the woods. "I don't recall he ever swam—I had the feeling he was embarrassed at being so hirsute."[32] Others are less diplomatic. "In a bathing suit he looked like a monkey."[33] Another calls him "hairy as a bear."[34] LaGuardia's *Monty,* on the other hand, presents a series of candid shots of a shirtless, swimsuit-wearing Clift with his chest unshaven. There is hardly cause for alarm.[35]

The homosocial setting of *From Here to Eternity* allows for increased physical interactions as well as intimacy among the men. Male bodies are on display everywhere, whether the men are hanging out around their bunks in sleeveless undershirts and boxer shorts or sparring in the gym. Casual touching is routine. During the treatment, when Prewitt is being marched up a mountain with a full pack, the man supervising him lets him rest and have a cigarette. As he bends for a light, Prewitt cups the man's hands in both of his own. Alcohol acts as a social lubricant to ease any "fears" of homosexuality in this testosterone-rich environment. Even Warden, the film's torch-bearer for heterosexuality, the tiger on the beach, drinks too much one night and finds himself sitting in the middle of the street with Prewitt, their knees touching. At one point Warden reaches out in an openly affectionate way and strokes Prewitt's hair, asking, "How's your girl?" At this exact moment, Maggio comes crashing out of the bushes and winds up in Prewitt's arms.

More than any other character, Maggio relates the film to the book and in the process reintroduces the possibility of homosexuality within the homosocial. Once they have donned their "too-big" Hawaiian shirts, Prewitt and Maggio stroll down the crowded streets of a red-light district, looking strikingly alike in their light-bodied shirts covered with busy prints (Prewitt's suggestive of flowers, Maggio's of leaves). They also look like a couple. When Prewitt bumps into a woman and turns to look after her, Maggio takes his arm and steers him back, pointing ahead to the sign of the New Congress Club, where Maggio is a member (and Prewitt learns that his first name is Angelo).

This is where the film and the book diverge. As the film shifts its focus to Prewitt's relationship with Lorene, it leaves behind the part of Prewitt's relationship with Maggio that takes place off base. In the film, Maggio repeatedly pops up whenever Prewitt is alone with Lorene. When Prewitt and Lorene are upstairs at the New Congress Club (in a Production Code–placating "sitting room" as opposed to a bedroom), Maggio interrupts their

FIGURE 23. Lobby card for *From Here to Eternity:* Clift (Prewitt), with Frank Sinatra (Maggio) in his arms, and Burt Lancaster (Warden).

private session. As Maggio entertains them with patter, Lorene kisses Prewitt's neck, both of them competing for his attention. As if unconsciously, Clift/Prewitt lets his left hand fondle Reed's hair, but he watches Sinatra, smiling and laughing. Lorene may have Prewitt's body, but Angelo has his affection and his attention. The film also implies later that Prewitt's relationship with Lorene has led him to neglect Angelo, even betray him unknowingly. When Maggio is thrown in the stockade (Sinatra marching through gorgeous clear, sharply focused shots of blank walls and right angles), we dissolve to Prewitt and Lorene strolling through an idyllic (almost parodic) leafy arbor to her new rental—to which he has a key. In this shot, he wears the Hawaiian shirt Maggio lent him, symbolically including Maggio in the scene, and suggesting that it is his relationship with Maggio (and Maggio's absence) that has made this idyll with Lorene possible. Prewitt's happiness is the indirect result of Maggio's suffering.

In the book, Angelo Maggio is Prewitt's connection to the Honolulu gay scene. Having lost his pay in a poker game, Maggio declares, "To hell with it. I'll take me fifty cents and go to town and pick me up a queer. I aint never picked me up a goddam queer, but I guess I can do it if other people can. It hadn't ought to be too goddam hard."[36] Running into Prewitt a few weeks later at the New Congress, Maggio tells him "the triumphant story"—how Maggio arranged for what he calls "my queer, Hal" to pick him up, take him to dinner, buy him drinks, and lend him money (237). He invites Prewitt out on a double date.

Maggio is not introducing Prewitt to anything new. Earlier in the book, we learn that more than one member of Prewitt's company has a sideline as a would-be gay hustler, an activity that involves an elaborate and well-known protocol. When asked how he plans to return to base without cab fare, one soldier casually mentions, "Bloom's got a queer lined up out in Waikiki he thinks we can roll, a guy with quite a bit of dough" (146). Out of nowhere, Prewitt breaks in, speaking with the voice of authority. "How long you been in Wahoo? You oughta know by now that Honolulu queers don't get rolled. They never carry money with them." Everyone, it seems, knows that. Prewitt also speaks with the voice of experience. "Maybe he's pimpin for this queer," he warns. "You're liable to end up gettin' made." He then tells the soldier what to do "if the guy turns out to be a jocker and you get pogued" (147), inviting the reader to imagine the shared knowledge that would make the impenetrable slang comprehensible. These outbursts occur right after an aside on Prewitt being raped in a boxcar "at the tender age of twelve" and killing another "queer" "at the not-so-tender age of fifteen." "If you want to go queer huntin'," he advises, "go by yourself" (148). When Prewitt hits the town, however, he accompanies Maggio on their double date.

A twenty-page scene follows in which Prewitt and Angelo meet Hal and another man in a restaurant, then go back to Hal's place (371–94). After a tense evening, Maggio stumbles out drunk and gets arrested after being found half-undressed on a park bench. Prewitt feels guilty because "Angelo had been playing the queers for quite a while now, he had been coming down to Hal's place often, and nothing like this had happened before" (410). Another elaborate set piece follows when the local police round up all the soldiers to try to stop the cruising. Prewitt, we are told, "might not have gotten to see Angelo again at all, if it had not been for the queer investigation the city police started downtown" (411). When Maggio arrives at the police station, he sees that "almost half the company had been called in on that queer investigation" (569). "My god," Maggio cheers. "This here looks like a regular G Compny [sic] roll call, or else convention" (417)—

though even here, as the book contends about the U.S. Army as a whole, there is favoritism and injustice. "There were at least six queer-chasers from G Company as persevering and proficient as any queer-chaser present," Maggio observes, "who had not been called at all" (411).

The suspicion that some of those engaged in this rampant sex trade might actually desire the men from whom they accept money drives one character to suicide. The one character in the book who may be homosexual by desire rather than economic circumstance is Sergeant Bloom, a character who has been completely eliminated from the film. (He is the man Maggio fights in the bar when Warden steps in, not Sergeant Judson. He is also the fighter Prewitt boxes in the yard.) Jones gives Bloom a long internal monologue after half the company is questioned by the police. "Why was it none of them had been suspected of being queer? Of course that bitch Tommy had spread it all around how Bloom had let him talk him into it that one time. . . . But what about all the others that had tried it, too? What about them? They all tried it sooner or later," Bloom thinks before pulling the trigger (569).

The fact that the book depicts homosexual activity as widespread in the military does not mean that Jones avoids stereotypes. Far from it. What is unexpected, however, is the unpredictable emotional effect stereotypically "gay" behavior elicits from the nominally straight author. For instance, there is the matter of interior decorating. After Maggio first visits Hal's place, he cannot stop telling Prewitt how nice Hal's apartment is. When they visit together, Maggio is still amazed. "'Aint this place something?' Maggio said to Prew. 'How would you like to have a place like this here? . . . Just imagine it, livin in a place like this. Jesus!' The two of them stood just inside the little entryway, looking around at the neatness and the order and the niceness of the apartment" (382). Later, Jones offers three pages on how one soldier discovered Django Reinhardt's music. "A rich queer had picked Andy up. . . . Learning that Andy was a guitarman, [he] had taken him up to [his] very expensive and exclusive apartment. . . . It was a lovely bachelor apartment, so lovely Andy had felt transported to some unreal other earth . . . a place so rich and beautiful and harmonious and clean. . . . Oh, he remembered all of it, every last detail."[37] The beauty of class outweighs any stigma regarding sexuality. As long as they can decorate an apartment, "queers" are jake with Jones.

Negative stereotypes abound, as well. When the self-loathing, self-destructive Bloom kills himself, Prew muses, "I wonder what the hell made him *do* it?" Maggio answers "sagaciously," "he was afraid he had gone queer." Jones confirms this when he has Bloom say to himself right before his suicide, "You're a queer. . . . You did it, and you liked it, and that makes you a queer" (573). Prewitt, on the other hand, lives in denial, maintaining what the reader knows to be a false belief. "Hell, Bloom was no queer," Prew snaps. "If I ever saw a not-queer, it was Bloom." Angelo concludes with the inscrutable observation, "Theres a difference between being queer and thinking you're queer" (584). But when it comes to "thinking queer," it should be noted that when Jones presents the stream-of-consciousness rumination leading up to Bloom's suicide, it is a six-page aria, requiring Jones to enter as deeply into Bloom's psyche as he will do later with the internal monologue that culminates with Prewitt's death.

In the film it is Prewitt's feeling for Maggio that prompts him to break his commitment to himself not to fight. Prewitt is motivated to fight as much by Maggio's mistreatment as by his own. Fixing the lawn on his hands and knees, Prewitt asks a compatriot who has just been released from the stockade how Maggio is doing and hears that he is being beaten regularly by Sergeant Judson. (The informant adds that Judson hits Maggio in ways that won't show, a nicety that clears the army of complicity and makes "Fatso" Judson a lone bad apple.)

As Prewitt crawls on the ground in a denim shirt unbuttoned to the waist, big white legs enter the shot and we hear a hostile voice say, "Still on your knees, huh, Prewitt?" Prewitt keeps his eyes on the ground until Sergeant Galovitch (who earlier spilled a bucket of spit in Prewitt's direction in the gym) steps on his hand. Pushing Galovitch back as he rises on one knee, Prewitt immediately begins undoing his cuff to roll up his sleeve. When someone tries to step between them, Prewitt shouts, "Get outta the way," and pushes the peacemaker away. (In the book, Prewitt fights Bloom, and it has no connection to Maggio.[38] When Bloom commits suicide, one of the things eating at him is having lost the fight with Prewitt, who considers this another tragedy his boxing might have caused [569].)

Boxing, it seems, would provide many shots of bare-chested men wearing trunks, as when Galovitch was seen working out in the ring earlier. But Clift's body is covered for the climactic fight. This could be, in part, a way to minimize the glaring physical differences between Clift and the actor who plays Galovitch (John Dennis). Simply put, they are not in the same weight division. Galovitch looks like a heavyweight (over 175 pounds), while Prewitt is at best a middleweight (147 to 160), and at the lighter end of the scale. (Bosworth puts Clift's average weight at around 150. A 1950 interview lists him at an optimistic 155.)[39] Anything lighter and Clift/Prewitt would fall into the welterweight range (136 to 147 pounds), two divisions under heavyweight. Such classifications matter, especially in the 1950s, when television established itself in millions of American homes via the hugely popular Friday night bouts. Weight could well have been a factor in producer Harry Cohn's preference for Aldo Ray to play Prewitt. Although Ray might have played the part without the nuance, depth, or sensitivity Clift brings to it, just as undoubtedly his body would have been better suited to this aspect of the role, complete with the bullet-headed buzz cut of a soldier and fighter's build.[40] Nevertheless, casting Clift opposite a larger opponent emphasizes Prewitt's vulnerability and plays into the character's psychology.

Prewitt is, by choice, an outsider. During the first half of the fight, he is surrounded. At first he wastes time exchanging body blows with his larger opponent. Hitting Galovitch in the face would be more likely to balance out the difference in weight, but Prewitt avoids the face because of having blinded a friend in a sparring match years before. When he does become incensed and starts to focus jabs to the head, he begins to win, though at the cost of his scruples.

PREWITT AS PERFORMER

Bosworth describes Clift playing the bugle in *From Here to Eternity* in physical terms: "His entire body seems forged with the notes blaring out from his horn."[41] Like Clift, Prewitt expresses his deepest feelings by throwing himself into his art. There are three scenes in which he performs publicly. In the first two, he's drunk. In all of them he performs as a musician or, as Prewitt puts it, "bugler." We already know that he gave up "bugling" rather than reconcile himself to injustice. He admits several times that he is good at it, that it is as fundamental to his sense of self as is his stubbornness. Half-joshing when he agrees with Maggio that he is the best bugler on the island, he is shyly self-confident when he tells Lorene later that it is something he is genuinely good at (head lowered, chin tucked in, looking up from under his eyes). We do not hear him play until halfway through the film. In a bar, restless from "the treatment," he takes a bugle away from an inferior player and ad-libs to a jukebox playing "Chattanooga Choo Choo." Unlike Clift's earlier encounter with this song in *The Big Lift*, the character here is not self-conscious or out of place. He is completely invested in the music. Prewitt swings it, and Clift makes it all about the body. Rising out of his chair, in a three-quarter turn away from the camera, he curves himself into a *C,* folding himself around the bugle. With his back turned, Clift gives the impression that Prewitt is expressing himself unconsciously. Because Clift cannot actually play the instrument, he finds a visual equivalent to show us that this is Prewitt's form of expression.

The second performance is the second version of "Re-enlistment Blues." The first time we hear it, it is played on a guitar in the barracks by someone else as Prewitt lies on his bunk, separated from the others, in his undershirt, smoking. This time he is part of a threesome, lying on a porch with his head propped against a post. This scene is staged in a way directly opposite to the "Chattanooga Choo Choo" scene, in which he can't stay in his seat, rising up as if drawn by the music. Here he is relaxed, with one knee propped up and swaying. He plays a solo on just his mouthpiece, which sounds like a kazoo. In the context of the song, it sounds like a Bronx cheer, but that is not altogether a negative thing; it shows that Prewitt can express his ambivalence about the army in a humorous way using the artistic skills the army gave him.

Prewitt's third performance is one of the most famous moments from the film—playing "Taps" after Maggio's death. Maggio's death precipitates Prewitt's break with the army. In the book Maggio lives, escaping the stockade with a Section 8 and a dishonorable discharge.[42] It is another soldier's death that motivates Prewitt to kill Judson (657). Two soldiers, in fact, are murdered by guards in front of Prewitt when Prewitt (not Maggio) is being tortured in the stockade. All of this is erased in the film, and the dying Maggio is given a line that implies it wasn't Judson's beatings that killed him but an accident, when he fell off a truck while trying to escape. Here, Taradash is repurposing a line in the novel: another character uses the "fell off a truck" line as a deeply cynical attempt to cover up a beating death at the stockade.[43]

Unlike the earlier bugle-playing scenes, when he plays "Taps" Clift does not present us with a physical acting-out of the emotion of the music. Clift lets the music express the character's feelings. The actual bugle player (Manny Klein) softens the transitions between notes, slurring them rather than articulating separate notes. This adds an interpretive dimension to a standard song. Because the audience is familiar with each note and its timing, we can read any alteration as artistic choice, personal feeling, character response—or all at the same time. When a note is played ahead of the beat, it gives the bugler time to elongate the phrase; lagging behind the beat makes us wait as a sense of anticipation builds, leading to the inevitable note.

Zinnemann constructs the scene to spotlight Clift, setting it apart as a key moment. Before we even see him, we see the men inside the barracks being drawn to the music. One says, "I bet that's Prewitt." Close-ups of Clift with tears on his face alternate with shots of listeners commenting on or illustrating the effect the music has—emphasizing that this is an unusually moving rendition of "Taps." These reactions cue the audience to read the music as Prewitt's transformation of ritual, his expansion of private grief onto a large public scale. In the midst of this heavily telegraphed "important" scene, the close-ups of Clift are not particularly expressive. Tears run down his face (though the lighting makes it appear that a single tear slides down Prewitt's cheek, which is more of a cliché), but his expression is blank—necessitated to some degree by the facial positions required when playing the bugle. The selling of the emotion—the editing, lighting, close-ups, reaction shots—may be too much; Clift's performance isn't. Prewitt's tears tell us the intensity of his emotion, but he suppresses emotion so that he can express what he feels more perfectly through his art.

In this scene, everything Prewitt is comes together. But it is not solely in the music. After he has finished playing "Taps" once, he adjusts the megaphone and plays it again. When he is done, instead of ending the scene Zinnemann includes two more shots. In a medium shot, Prewitt takes his mouthpiece, hands the bugle back to the other bugler, and walks out of the shot. In the next he passes Warden, who had come outside to listen. What do these shots add? First, that Prewitt's playing was voluntary, a matter of choice. Prewitt is not the company bugler—he refused the job because Holmes made it contingent on fighting. For this scene, Prewitt has stepped in and taken the regular bugler's place of his own volition. This makes it "a personal matter" (as he told Holmes at the beginning). To that extent, it shows Prewitt's hardheadedness, his tendency to be willful rather than submit to orders. At the same time it demonstrates that Prewitt can express himself, his deepest feelings, within the army. Playing "Taps" is a military ritual Prewitt freely submits to. He performs the army's rituals but transforms them to serve a deep personal need. Also, through the army's ritual he can pay tribute to someone who died in opposition to the army, who wouldn't conform and couldn't fit in. As Prewitt walks past Warden, it is in Prewitt/Clift's version of military bearing. The two men in uniform share the shot, though Warden is fixed in place, having just learned from listening to "Taps" how much of yourself can be expressed within military form. Prewitt, on the other hand,

FIGURE 24. Lobby card for *From Here to Eternity:* Ernest Borgnine (Sergeant "Fatso" Judson) and Clift.

is passing through, hand in pocket, withheld, not totally at attention, not marching. A human being within a uniform, he is himself first, which finally puts him at ease in the army and at ease as he leaves it.

This is the last time we see Prewitt in uniform. The next scene finds him outside the New Congress Club, wearing Maggio's Hawaiian shirt, waiting for Fatso.

Bosworth details the "heroic" lengths Clift was willing to go in preparing for a role, and everyone agrees the actor suffered physically when performing physically rigorous scenes such as the knife fight with Judson. From the beginning, Clift considered acting a physically and psychologically risky business. "When you become angry, tearful or violent for a part. . . . it takes a tremendous toll of the performer emotionally and physically. . . . I can't pace myself the way some other actors can. I either go all out or I don't accept the picture. I have to dredge it out of me. I'm exhausted at the end of a picture."[44] The same intensity applied to the act of watching others: "One must know a bad performance to know a good one. . . . I can't be middle-of-the-road about a performance, especially my own. I feel that if I can vomit at seeing a bad performance, I'm ahead of the game."[45]

For Clift, acting (his own or that of others) is understood at a deep physical, internal level, its value measured by physical cost. On *A Place in the Sun* he was described as "work[ing] with such highly charged concentration and intensity as George that he would often finish a take drenched with sweat."[46] On *The Young Lions,* director Edward Dmytryk describes finding Clift rehearsing a scene in which his character almost drowns: "Sweat was running off his forehead. He looked exactly like a man who had rescued himself from death."[47] To act was to risk everything, even death; the fact that it was "faked" did not lessen its effect. As Clift told Elizabeth Taylor, "Your body doesn't know you're acting. It sweats and makes adrenalin just as though your emotions were real."[48] For other actors, Clift became the personification of an extreme brand of professionalism that held nothing back.

In the accounts of coworkers, Clift's physical sensitivity testified to an emotional sensitivity. "If someone kicks a dog ten miles away, Monty feels it," director Edward Dmytryk once said. "Every cruelty, every indecency pains him."[49] This emotional sensitivity in turn was seen as feeding his professional work. Robert Kass in *Films in Review* referred to Clift's performance in *From Here to Eternity* this way: "He is perfectly cast as . . . a shock absorber for the insensitivity around him."[50] Brother Brooks Clift says, "Monty was affected by everything—a man without skin. It's amazing to me how he was able to survive, despite all his mental, moral, physical and legal problems, to the ripe old age of forty-five."[51] It was not only his family who worried. *Photoplay* reported, "The intensity he brings to each role is, at times, terrifying to his colleagues, some of whom feel that each part he plays takes a severe toll of his nervous system."[52] Clift even asked himself the rhetorical question "How to remain thin-skinned, vulnerable and stay alive?"[53] Given his hypersensitive body, no one doubted that, for Clift, acting could be a matter of life and death.

Such stories equate the suffering of the character with the suffering of the actor, a view that is especially resonant when Clift plays characters who are persecuted. In the fight with Galovitch, Clift's character is surrounded by a jeering crowd and facing off against an imposing opponent who has the support of the corrupt army brass. Not coincidentally, fight scenes elicit the most consistent criticism of Clift, often taking the form of gender-based ridicule, especially the old canard that he "punches like a girl." Jokes about Clift's lack of manly prowess (fighting, riding) started with *Red River* and continued in descriptions of the fight with Galovitch. In the latter,

Clift's inclination to turn his back to the camera makes it easy for Zinnemann to substitute a stuntman as needed. (Clift also displays bad form during the fight scenes in *The Young Lions*, but there it is completely appropriate because his character is untutored in the "sweet science.") No one, however, jokes about the knife fight with Judson. Costar Borgnine reports that both actors were covered with bruises after hours of shooting punches and falls that required them to land repeatedly on bare concrete.[54] The scene is grueling to watch, grim and suspenseful, and lacks the cheering crowd that turned the earlier fight into a spectator sport. In that fight there was a clear winner. Here, Judson ends up dead and Prewitt seriously hurt.

If action scenes are not Clift's forte, scenes that require him to convey a complicated mix of psychological and physical pain with the minimum of dialogue or obvious gesture show Clift at his best. Appearing at Lorene's house with his hand on the wound at his side, he stands at the top of a short staircase, and then falls down the stairs. It's a terrific fall. He begins to fall forward onto his knees, but because there is no ground below him he falls sideways down the stairs. Because he is holding his left side with his right hand, when he falls to his right he doesn't put an arm out to catch himself. His body is completely undefended.

Life as a civilian (surrounded by women after Angelo's death) does not suit Prewitt, and the next time we see him he is unshaven, wearing an undershirt, his hair mussed, trying to write a letter with a bottle of booze and an ashtray full of cigarette butts in front of him. The way he sits slumped at the table (so that it meets him well above mid-chest) makes it look as if he's sinking. His grumpiness contrasts with the first time we saw him at this table, in an idyll of domestic bliss, with Lorene (the soon-to-be star of *The Donna Reed Show*) pouring him coffee and Prewitt (sitting up straight and leaning forward, not back) kissing the inside of her arm before asking her to marry him.

The disintegration of their relationship is cross-cut with the end of Warden and Karen's relationship. Neither Lorene nor Karen will marry the men as they are. Lorene recoils at the thought of being tied to someone poor, and Karen wants Warden to become an officer. When he tells her he cannot be an officer to please her, she walks away, past a street sign that says, "Pearl Harbor, 8 mi." Actually, it's closer to two minutes. The big blow-up comes in rousing action scenes that allow Lancaster to play superhero, single-handedly shooting a Japanese Zero out of the sky and watching with great satisfaction as it crashes into a big ball of flame under an American flag flying high over the Pacific.

Prewitt, meanwhile, twists on his bed in pain as Lorene and her roommate hover over him, listening to a radio broadcast on the attack. His eyes closed, he seems feverish, as if suffering for his army and his country. But he is also flat on his back and feminized by a kimono-style top.

The last ten minutes of this scene are staged as a series of long takes in which Prewitt has almost no dialogue. Nearly every part of the character's decision-making and emotion must be communicated through physical means. The film cuts from the violent action at Pearl Harbor to Prewitt emasculated, wounded, feminized. He is alone, listening to the radio, sitting with a towel in his hand and fresh shaving cream around his ears. As he wipes away the shaving cream, his jerky, angry movements express frustration and tension at the same time. He looks left, then right, without an object, and then raises himself to his feet, leaning on the radio console. As the radio announcer urges everyone to "stay in your homes," Prewitt walks away from the camera. Turning his back, he tears off the kimono-style top, revealing a large bandage around his waist. Exiting the shot, he puts a hand on the wall to steady himself, and then pulls it away suddenly as if impatient with his own weakness. As the women return from shopping, breathlessly relating the destruction they've seen, he emerges shirtless, unnoticed, the bandage on his left side even larger when seen from the front. Instead of pajama bottoms he is now wearing his khaki uniform pants. He carries his shoes and shirt tenderly, the way he carried Maggio's earlier, when he tried to save him from the MPs.

As the radio announcer says, "Your attention, please. Listen to this carefully and keep calm," Prewitt stops to listen. The women catch sight of him and freeze. He crosses gingerly screen left, leading the camera away from the women, and slams the radio console door shut. "Who do they think they're fightin'?" he asks, in a quiet, unsteady voice. "They're pickin' trouble with the best army in the world." (Clift's notations in his copy of the script suggest that this line was added on the set, perhaps by Clift himself.) Sitting to put his shoes on, he ignores Lorene, who demands, "Where you going?"

As he lifts a knee to put on his socks, he begins to say, "I gotta go back—" but catches his breath in pain. He repeats, "I gotta go back to company" in a rush, with a rise at the end as if he had been holding his breath the whole time and just got it out. Standing, he deftly slings on his Hawaiian shirt with one arm (unable to lift the arm on his wounded side). When Lorene hugs him, he winces in a combination of emotional and physical pain. He stops and closes his eyes as she tries to convince him to stay, but he does not melt or yield. He opens his eyes again and blinks, not obdurate but not torn either. When she offers to marry him, he opens his eyes wide, his mouth open in surprise. Then he sighs, lowering his eyes and tightening his lips. He looks away from her and says a guttural "Sorry" as he's pulling away, his hands at her waist guiding her away from him. (When he proposed earlier, in this same room, he put his hands on her waist to pull her onto his lap. Now he pushes her away, gently but firmly.) Concentrating on some object in the foreground, he walks past her into the middle of the frame, trying to button his shirt one-handed. He picks up a pack of cigarettes from a coffee table and puts them in his shirt pocket, his left arm hanging useless.

As Lorene grows angrier, attacking the army for what it has done to him, Clift gives Prewitt a series of reactions, underplaying in contrast to Reed's near-hysteria. Throughout the film, Lorene's obsessive bitterness is more persuasive than her alleged seductiveness. This scene gives us Lorene at her most intensely shrewish. Something unattractive happens to her mouth when she's angry; her lips get weak and formless as she becomes almost unstable with bitterness. As Lorene harps at him, attacking his devotion to an army that murdered his friend, Prewitt keeps his eyes on the ground, only flashing her a look from under his brow for a fraction of a second, as if he could get mad if he were to listen. The third time he looks at her, he makes eye contact and maintains it as he walks past her toward the door. He doesn't begin to respond to her tirade until he passes *behind* her and is blocked from our view. (This dedramatizes what might otherwise be a big moment for the star, giving an effect of naturalism.) "What do I want to go back to the army for?" he asks quietly in amazement. "I'm a soldier," he says with almost a smile, his eyes wide open and clear as he mounts the stairs. He is not dressed like a soldier, though, and because of his wound he cannot stand up straight.

Prewitt stops at the top of the stairs and reminds the women before he leaves that he has to turn out the lights because of the blackout. The women are framed on the left, below him in their domestic space, while Clift takes the right half of the screen. His back is to the camera as he hugs a featureless modern wall and door. As he turns off the lights, the women are left in the dark and by a trick of the light, his Hawaiian shirt (plate 8) suddenly seems brighter than before.[55] In the dark, the light palms against a dark background jump out at us like a negative image—the jungle on Prewitt's back dramatically incongruent in this modern grid house.[56] When he leaves, the camera pans right to eliminate the women as he walks out the door, the wild print disappearing through the blank wall.

Trying to rejoin his unit as sentries patrol the beach, Prewitt emerges from a stand of reeds. Crossing from behind one tree to the next, he suddenly leans forward with his eyes closed, catching himself, taking short breaths, his left hand holding his side the whole time. There is a close-up of blood seeping through the busy shirt. Ordered to halt, he tries to run in a zigzag but is finally hit and jackknifes into a bunker. Hitting the sand, he rolls over twice. When identifying the intruder, Warden is asked if Prewitt was a friend. Picking up the bugle mouthpiece from Prewitt's hand, he pronounces Prewitt's epitaph: "He was always a hardhead, sir."

The ending of the film significantly softens Jones's indictment of the army in the novel. In the film while Prewitt holes up at Lorene's, AWOL and suspected of Sergeant Judson's murder, two officers descend from army-investigator heaven and magically put everything right. Holmes is forced to resign, Galovitch is busted from sergeant to private, boxers are demoted, and professional soldiers are rewarded. A new commanding officer restores Warden's faith in leadership. Redeemed in time for Pearl Harbor, the army just barely escapes the jeremiad mounted against it throughout the rest of the film. Prewitt's recommitment to the army at the end is riddled with unresolvable problems. While the film tries to soften the army's responsibility for Maggio's death, it is more difficult to soft-pedal Prewitt's killing of a superior (which cannot even be defined as self-defense because Prewitt starts it—though it is a fair fight). Prewitt's recommitment is met by irony in the music; as Prewitt lies dead we hear an instrumental rendition of "Re-enlistment Blues." In the novel, Prewitt composed this song and saw it as his one major accomplishment in life. The composition takes place across several chapters and Warden finds a copy in Prewitt's pocket after Prewitt's death.[57] If that plot point had been included in the film, the music's presence on the sound track when he dies would suggest that Prewitt lives on in his music. Without the backstory, the use of the music is more mocking. "See what it gets ya?" it implies. In the film Prewitt tells Lorene he loves the army, despite how he has been treated. He tells her, "Just 'cause you love a thing doesn't mean it has to love you back." In the book Jones paraphrases Oscar Wilde to sum up Prewitt's position. (And what red-blooded all-American GI wouldn't cite Wilde?): not every man kills the thing he loves; sometimes it kills him.[58]

Like Father Logan, Prewitt is a man of faith. Willing to die for what he believes in, each man refuses to compromise his principles even when he is humiliated, ostracized, scorned. Neither will be swayed, whether by physical violence or kindly advice. Accused of failing to uphold the values of the institutions to which they belong, Logan and Prewitt are shown to be more constant in their devotion than those around them. The struggle to reconcile personal loyalties with official codes of conduct humanizes each character as it elevates him, establishing his ability to understand abstract virtues on a deeply personal level. Although his loyalty to individuals leads each character into major trouble (Prewitt killing Judson, Logan refusing to provide an alibi because it might sully Ruth's reputation), in both films it is devotion to an institution and its ideals that will get you killed.

But where Logan is defined by his refusal to articulate his motives (withholding himself emotionally, a quality augmented by Clift's determined inexpressiveness), Prewitt openly states his commitment, love, and gratitude to the army in several memorable lines of dialogue, delivered without irony or cynicism. The soldier's inarticulateness is more expressive than the priest's silence. Prewitt's love of the service is all the more touching when, despite the risks (from the sentries, his wound, and ultimately the military police), he offers up his life to the army without hesitation or plan. Unlike Logan, it is Prewitt who dies a martyr: unwavering, pure of heart, and, finally, too good for this world.

The film's last scene shows the women leaving the island on a ship. By chance, Lorene and Karen, who have never met, are standing next to each other on deck. Lorene tells Karen that her late fiancé was a heroic flyer who died fighting on December 7. He was from an old southern family, she says, and named for a general. "Robert E. Lee Prewitt. Isn't that a silly old name?" Karen recognizes it from Warden's accounts and realizes that Lorene's prettified account is a lie. The last shot is of two leis floating in the wake of the ship, flowers turning into garbage.

James Jones's novel, published in 1951, was a postwar critique of prewar conditions. The film *From Here to Eternity* (released in August 1953) is wracked by its own ambivalence. Prewitt is both a sensitive man and a killer, a rebellious misfit and unquestioningly loyal to the army. His rededication to the army leads immediately to his death. His self-sacrifice ends as waste in the wake of the ship. The film not only wants to have it both ways; ultimately it doesn't know what it wants.

For many fans, this is where it ends.

In Steve Erickson's novel *Zeroville* (2007), Clift's ghost haunts a Los Angeles hotel, eternally suspended between completing *A Place in the Sun* and beginning *From Here to Eternity*. The book's main character, Vikar—a metaphoric vicar of the new religion of movies—presents himself under the sign of Clift, the famous kissing scene from *A Place in the Sun* tattooed on his shaved head. (It is an impossible image. At no time in this scene are Clift's and Taylor's faces visible in the same shot, but then the essence of this scene—the kiss itself—has always been imaginary.)[59]

A tabula rasa, Vikar is a "cinautistic" cineaste, with films etched on his brain. The religion Clift symbolizes in the book rejects the Judeo-Christian heritage of Abraham and Isaac in which fathers kill their children in favor of a pagan vision of God as a child, a Platonic ideal of soulmates, and a vision of eternal return.[60] All times are now; all films are now. Working as a film editor, Vikar comes to realize that "there's a secret movie that's been hidden, one frame at a time, in all the movies ever made."[61] When they meet in a hallucination near the end of the story, Monty explains to Vikar cinema's mystical precedence over the world as we know it:

"That Secret Movie? The one that's hidden frame by frame in all the other movies?"
"Yes."
"Maybe we're not dreaming it. Maybe it's dreaming us." (321)

For Erickson, Clift's spirit lives in Los Angeles ("All the Los Angeles movies are the same movie"), in Room 928 of the Roosevelt Hotel (115). Immersed in repetition and preserved in a moment in time—the eternal life cinema provides—Clift is, as usual, a keen critic of his own image. Referring to the accident, he observes, "I would have been Jimmy Dean if I'd died then. Hollywood is *full* of people who would trade their lives in a heartbeat just to be legends. Would have traded mine in a heartbeat not to go through the next nine years" (317).

In Erickson's fictional eschatology, Clift's status as patron saint rests exclusively on his first eight films. For Erickson, it would have been better if everything that followed never happened. But if Erickson means to have Clift disavow his own work, it is an opinion directly contradicted by the actor. In 1963, after all but his very last film, the actor said, "Looking back on my career, I can honestly state that I've never done anything that I'm ashamed of."[62]

Whatever difficulties he was beginning to struggle with while making *From Here to Eternity,* Clift proved what he could do when he had a sympathetic director and a good script. In the films that followed, both would be harder to come by and the actor's circumstances much worse. *From Here to Eternity* would mark the peak of Clift's popularity, critically and at the box office. After it, his work as an actor would be overshadowed as his life and the condition of his body became front-page news.

FIGURE 25. Clift on location in 1960 for *The Misfits*. Ernst Haas, Hulton Archive, Getty Images.

FIVE

Mortification of the Flesh

KARL MALDEN ONCE SAID of Montgomery Clift, "He had the face of a saint but when you looked into his eyes you saw a tortured soul trying to make its way out of utter bewilderment."[1] Barney Hoskyns, in his 1991 biography, asks rhetorically, "How was it, then, that this perfect boy, this actor with *a face of almost impenetrable beauty,* was so *diseased,* so racked by emotional and sexual doubts?"[2] Tortured, diseased. How did we get here, from the face of a saint to what David Thomson calls "a sainted mess"?[3]

THE ACCIDENT

After completing *From Here to Eternity* (released in August 1953) and *Indiscretion of an American Wife* (which was shot before *Eternity* but not released until June 1954), Clift took a three-year hiatus. During this period he did a play off-Broadway and took no new film roles.[4] In 1956 he accepted a part in *Raintree County* because it would give him the chance to work with Elizabeth Taylor again. One night in May, halfway through filming, he left a party at Taylor's house and drove into a telephone pole. The crash split his career in two—eight films before, eight after, with *Raintree County* on either side. It altered his face and made the question of his health (physical and mental) subject to public speculation. No one doubts that Clift suffered a great deal for a long time following the accident. Descriptions of that suffering form a major part of most accounts of Clift's life.

Details about the accident itself are constantly debated, contradictions swirling through competing accounts: Clift was drunk, he was sober, he was sleepy and had to be on the set early, he could not sleep and had taken pills, he was playing a trick swerving back and forth, he was struggling with the darkness of unlit canyon roads. While what really happened that night is ultimately indeterminable, biographers and critics carefully grade degrees of responsibility in order to establish Clift's "innocence" or "guilt." Is the damage we see written on his body due to factors beyond his control (age, illness, accident) or is it the result of self-destructive acts such as excessive drinking, drug use, and risk-taking? (One encyclopedia avoids the issue of responsibility altogether with the inelegant phrasing "he got in a car accident.")[5] Two things are undisputed: he was seriously hurt, and he was surrounded by an all-star cast—Kevin McCarthy saw the whole thing, Rock Hudson pulled him out of the wreck, and Michael Wilding called the police while Elizabeth Taylor cradled Clift's head in her lap.[6] It is alleged that photographers arrived before the police.

Although Clift had suffered from a variety of ailments all his life (the childhood surgery that left a scar on his throat, the chronic colitis that made him ineligible for the draft), the visible consequences of the accident made the condition of Clift's body suddenly central to discussions of his life and work. (The accident itself was traumatically visible through news photos of the car, the wreckage standing in for Clift's ravaged body.) As soon as the accident occurred, people took the marred surface of Clift's body as license to speculate on what was inside, under the skin. The following litany is but one example. "His face was severely swollen; he had numerous cuts, especially under the eyes; his lips had been lacerated badly, and a hole gouged right through the middle of his upper lip; two front teeth had been knocked down his throat; his jaw was broken in four separate places; his nose was broken in two, and one whole upper cheekbone was broken, with cracks running into the sinus area."[7]

Not satisfied with visible scars, fans, critics, and biographers pressed for more intimate knowledge, concerning themselves not simply with Clift's appearance (though that always elicited comment) but with his body's *internal* condition. Mary Desjardins describes the mutation of star biography into the genre of pathography—"a life narrative of illness or disability that foregrounds the somatic experience of the body, especially its experience of pain, as a fundamental constituent of identity."[8] Once a pathographer gets started, there is no stopping the lust for details. LaGuardia discusses Clift's "peculiar blood pressure," "sebaceous cysts," "amoebic dysentery and colitis" ("his intestines had already been partly wrecked").[9]

We are told that Clift developed a thyroid condition that made his eyes bulge, and that the pains in his head from his injuries in the car accident were "excruciating."[10] In *Montgomery Clift: Beautiful Loser,* Hoskyns describes Clift three years after the accident: "By the spring [of 1959], he was in bad shape, losing his memory and his balance and suffering from alcoholic hepatitis. His physician . . . having discovered premature cataracts in his eyes, further diagnosed 'spontaneous hypoparathyroidism,' a condition that prevented Monty's parathyroid glands from producing enough calcium, causing cramps and spasms."[11] Some of the other medical conditions compulsively recorded by Clift's biographers include vitamin B_1 and thiamine deficiencies caused by heavy alcohol consumption, leading to bad balance, memory loss, tremors, and mood changes.[12] "Then he developed phlebitis in both legs."[13]

Paige Baty argues that the use of supposedly neutral medical language reduces the star to a collection of body parts, organs to be weighed and measured, robbing the star's "image of its transcendent qualities."[14] As a consequence, the star's body assumes a contradictory purpose, doubling as "a deified, holy, and iconic body and a defiled, horrific, and seamy body."[15] Although Baty's main focus is representations of the star's corpse (e.g., Marilyn Monroe's autopsy), prurient interest in the inner workings of Clift's body began long before his death.

Some stars are loved because of their suffering.[16] Sympathy and admiration arise as fans learn of the star's triumph over hardship, in the cases of Judy Garland, Maria Callas, or Marilyn Monroe. Viewers read the star's performance style as verification of the biographical material they have uncovered through close readings of publicity, gossip, and fan magazines. For instance, Jane Feuer argues that Garland's "singing style [in the second half of her career], with its histrionic excess and awkward gestures," transformed performance into "a means of expressing tragedy, heartbreak, alienation."[17] Comparisons with Garland began soon after Clift resumed his career. Steve Cohan quotes a 1958 *Photoplay* article in which the author asserts, "Clift is tougher than he looks. Like Judy Garland, he will—I am persuaded—go on for many years staging apparent collapses, disappearing, but always rising again to perform better than ever."[18] Garland outlived him by one year.

Stars like Garland and Clift possess what Desjardins calls a "somatically apparent relationship to suffering."[19] The never-ending physical ailments become legible, but attain their fullest meaning only when read as signs of psychological torment. Adrienne McLean explains how, over time, "ambivalence and pain became a major component of Garland's star image";

these were then "commuted into 'an emotional register,' in Dyer's words, 'of great intensity which seems to bespeak equally suffering and survival, vulnerability and strength, theatricality and authenticity, passion and irony.'"[20] One encounters many of the same qualities in exploring the relationship between Clift's work and his biography. After the accident, Clift's life does not simply erupt into our awareness of his work as an actor but threatens to block it out.

In photographic representations of fictional characters, indexicality encourages viewers to sidestep the character in favor of the actor. Consequently the body Clift prepared to represent a character is read as a direct reflection of his soul. Clift's face, previously read as the indicator of positive internal spiritual qualities, becomes a warning sign of the chaos that lies within. Scholars, fans, biographers, and publicists take the changes to Clift's face as their cue to disregard the actor's performance and begin scrutinizing the inside of Clift's body instead, searching there for the key to *his* character—the "real" Montgomery Clift.

There is a difference between the serious physical effects this event produced for the actor and the way the accident has been used by fans. For fans, the accident has come to serve many purposes: to explain changes in the actor's appearance, to serve as a key to interpreting his performances, or to provide an excuse for speculating about his physical and mental condition. For many, the accident achieves its greatest resonance in connection to Clift's beauty. Although changes in the actor's appearance could be attributed to the wear and tear of hard living, the idea of Clift being scarred by a sudden traumatic event elevates simple aging to the level of tragic loss. Watching his early films today, such fans study his face, searching for what will be lost. Watching the later films, we measure what is left.

The accident obscures another reason for changes in Clift's appearance. In fact, Clift had aged rapidly in the three years that passed between completing *From Here to Eternity* and beginning *Raintree County.* Early publicity photos for *Raintree County* are often hard to distinguish from those taken after the accident (see plate 9). As one biographer wrote, the "physical damage [to Clift's face] is barely discernible on screen but any child could see he looks a good ten years older."[21] Comparing stills from before and after May 12, 1956, we see that, in Clift's case, age is inseparable from injury.

Clift's performances in this period (and representations of him in publicity material) were all too easy to read for signs of physical and mental suffering. His alleged drug addictions, alcoholism, and simple exhaustion were now purportedly visible in his crumpled posture, striking weight loss, and prematurely aged face. While it may not be possible to pinpoint the source of the changes to Clift's appearance, the very argument—accident or age?—deflects attention away from performance and toward the materiality of the body. Clift's acting is no longer subsidiary to his beauty; now it is overshadowed by his endlessly intriguing physical pathology. Absorbed into a larger story of crises and physical and mental torment, viewers can lose sight of the fact that Clift was still an active participant in shaping his performances.

FOUR FILMS

Immediately after the accident, Clift completed *Raintree County* (released in December 1957), followed by *The Young Lions* (April 1958), *Lonelyhearts* (March 1959), and *Wild River* (May 1960). These films share many of the same problems, so I will discuss them as a group. Above all, Clift is miscast in every one of them, called on to play roles that are directly contradicted by the actor's appearance.

In all four films, Clift's characters are supposed to be young. *Raintree County* begins with John Shawnessy having just graduated from high school. (Clift was thirty-six.) In *The Young Lions* Noah Akerman is explicitly referred to as "a boy." Even before the accident, Clift was too old to play boys. In *From Here to Eternity,* at thirty-three, Clift can play a character in his twenties. At thirty-seven, in *The Young Lions,* he can't. While a later film such as *Judgment at Nuremberg* (released in December 1961) uses the changes in Clift's appearance to express aspects of the character he plays, *Raintree* and *Young Lions* cast Clift as the romantic lead as if nothing had changed. At the same time, these are two of the films in which Clift goes to the greatest lengths to alter his appearance—with fake beards and putty to change his nose and ears. In *The Young Lions* especially, the extensive makeup he wears in the early scenes makes his face odd and artificial—not handsome and not young.

The disconnect between the actor's appearance and the stated age of the character is amplified by each character's youthful idealism. In *Raintree County* John Shawnessy is a naive, poetry-loving romantic who is wooed away from his nice-but-bland high school sweetheart by a tempestuous southern belle in the years before the Civil War. Tricked into marriage, he becomes a teacher and respected member of the community as his southern wife, Susanna, becomes progressively unstable, driven mad by a trail of murder, arson, and miscegenation in her past. When she disappears with their son, John spends the rest of the film as a Yankee soldier, fighting his way across the South in search of his family. Finding Susanna hospitalized and the boy safe, he returns north with his family, only to have Susanna run into a nearby swamp and conveniently drown. Presumably, father and son live happily ever after.

Early in the film, John Shawnessy is a clean-living student-athlete, chosen to represent his county in a cross-country race. The character's youthful inexperience almost immediately begins to chafe against publicized elements of the actor's biography. Before the race, John is challenged to list his vices. Given the possibilities—chewing tobacco, smoking it, or "poking it up your nose," he brags, "I do all three at the same time." Taunted into a drinking contest, he asks ingenuously, "Bourbon? Me?" (Clift makes a nice entrance into the saloon, snapping the swinging doors open like the star of a western, the character fully aware of the pretense involved.) More subtly, and perhaps insidiously, John's teacher, whom he idolizes, warns him about trying to fly too high; this man, too, looked for the mythical raintree and, failing to find it, "became slowly the pitiful harmless creature you behold today." Cut to a shot of Clift caught in quicksand (metaphorically) and sinking fast.

Slow-moving and turgid, *Raintree County* was Clift's first film in color; other than that, the film has little to recommend it except for Clift. Clift did not have a high regard for the material; in November 1955, he wrote two words on the back of the first page of the script: "Conventional, Humourless."[22] Nevertheless, the actor worked diligently to make the film better, as we can see from his extensive comments on the script.

Clift's first appearance in *Raintree County* is as an absence. Eva Marie Saint as good girl Nell calls out for Johnny, and Clift's voice answers back, "He's not here." Indications are that Clift wrote this line himself (before the accident). In a copy of the script dated March 25, 1956, Clift writes "John (hiding): He's not here."[23] Then he crosses out two paragraphs of description and two lines of his own dialogue, leaving only one word, "Nell."

Although all the comments are in Clift's handwriting, some of the revisions might have been suggested on the set (by the director, writer, etc.), with the actors noting the changes on their scripts. Some comments, however, would be of concern only to Clift. For instance, he routinely eliminates descriptions that tell him how his character feels. When John realizes he loves Susanna (Elizabeth Taylor), the script goes into lyrical overdrive: "A marvelous full-blooded keenness of the senses, a delightful, high pitched frenzy seizes him. . . . So he dances this ritual of love." Susanna says, "I think you're wonderful." John says "You are the goal of my life." Clift draws a big box around all of this and crosses it out, leaving himself one line: "Let's go home."[24] On page 142 of the same script, Clift has written "cut cut cut" and drawn a big question mark in the margin beside half a page of dialogue.[25] Clift also frequently cuts his—and others'—dialogue.[26]

When he saw *Raintree County,* Clift was as critical as ever of his own work: "excepting a couple of moments I'm horrific—wooden, frozen, walking through. In my beard I look like Jesus Christ in a Union cap."[27] While he does not indicate what moments he found satisfactory, there are two scenes in the nearly three-hour film that provide glimpses of the techniques that will serve Clift in the more successful performances of the second half of his career. Both scenes show the character's growing disillusionment as John realizes that he has had a less-than-ideal teacher and a less-than-ideal marriage, and lives in a less-than-ideal country.

In the first of these scenes, John stands up for his philandering professor, who is being pursued by an outraged husband. Wearing a loose shirt, a thoughtful and somber John stands on the railroad tracks, holding a whip in his hands. Keeping his eyes down, working his lips, Clift/John contemplates the whip as if reluctant to use it but determined to stand his ground. Just how difficult that might be is made clear when the vigilantes appear, led by the physically imposing, big-bearded, big-bellied husband. It is not unusual for a Clift character to be in a position of physical vulnerability, and here the actor's slight stature is emphasized by his curved posture and the folds of his shirt, which make it clear how thin he is. John's heroism is defined by resoluteness to the point of self-sacrifice. He puts his body on the line for a friend in a situation where he is unlikely to prevail—he can only suffer.

The other worthwhile moment concerns John's growing maturity in regard to his marriage. Entering his wife's bedroom, he begins to let in the light, opening the curtains on the windows and those surrounding the bed. This reveals the slightly unnerving sight of Susanna and her doll collection, the dolls hanging suspended behind her. As she clings to the past and her own childishness, he comes to expose the truth. He reads to her (beautifully) from a newspaper editorial directed at John and Susanna's domestic life. "Teachers who use the schools as a platform" to teach "the inflammatory and seditious doctrine of abolition . . . had best look to the hypocrisy of their own leadership." He tells her that she can no longer keep the two female slaves she brought with her when they married. Susanna counters with southern tradition, but he retorts, "You're not South now. You can't have slaves here." When she personalizes the matter by complaining that he is always criticizing her, he replies, "Honey, I'm not picking on you. I just don't want slaves in my own house." Facing down her mounting hysteria, Clift presents John as the voice of reason, his voice literally slow and low in volume and tone versus Taylor's increasingly shrill, high-pitched delivery of non sequiturs and paranoia. Offering her options, he insists, "Get rid of the girls or pay them wages. Do whatever you want." In a classic melodramatic substitution of the personal for the political, she answers, "You don't love me. You never did love me." Clift's impact in this scene is partly due to the scene itself. This is the first time John stands up to his wife, the first time he insists that his point of view should prevail, the first time he makes it clear that he intends to live by his principles regardless of tantrums or emotional fallout. John is also a father (rare in Clift's work), and his determination to challenge Susanna's indefensible beliefs and actions will prove essential for his son's life and safety.

Clift was well aware of how others saw him. It was his profession. When *Raintree County* was finished, he knew right away that "audiences would see the picture to guess 'which is me before or after the accident.'"[28] At the premiere of *The Young Lions,* his next film, "after he made his first appearance on screen, a girl in the balcony screamed and fainted, and there were shocked murmurs of 'Is *that* him?' One of Monty's guests saw him tense visibly but he didn't move," Bosworth recounts. "He just continued to stare straight and unblinking at the unrolling film."[29]

Because *The Young Lions* was going to be Clift's first project filmed entirely after the accident, the actor was under enormous pressure. In May 1957, instead of showing up for filming in Paris, Clift disappeared.[30] As the reception of the film demonstrates, he had the right to be nervous. His disappearance prompted scandal-sheet speculation. On the cover of its June issue, *Motion Picture* blares, "Film Star Vanishes: Where is Monty Clift?" Inside is a story titled "The Disappearance of Monty Clift," but it is the photographs that tell the tale: on the left, a publicity still from *Red River* with the caption "This is the face of a Hollywood Dream Prince"; on the right a recent photograph with the legend "Ten Years Later. This is the Face of a Man No One Can Locate." As the introduction of John Shawnessy told us, "He's not here." Wherever Clift might have been, Hollywood's dream prince was gone.

Another would-be epic (at two hours and forty-seven minutes, it is one

FIGURE 26. *Raintree County*, 1957: Clift (John) confronting Elizabeth Taylor (Susanna).

minute shorter than *Raintree*), *The Young Lions* was Clift's second project with director Edward Dmytryk. The film follows the stories of three men, their war and their women. Noah Akerman's awkward courtship of a blonde, small-town Hope Lange (read: not Jewish), takes a backseat when he is called up to fight in World War II. At the draft board he meets Dean Martin, who is hoping to avoid active service—a character flaw that embarrasses his girl-friend, society lady Barbara Rush, who has also been friendly with an Aryan ski instructor–turned–SS officer, Marlon Brando. The film cuts back and forth between the Americans' experience and the German's. Although much was made of Clift and Brando costarring in the same film, their only scene together comes at the very end.

Again Clift revised the script by "cut[ting] his own lines to a bare min-imum," according to costar Lange.[31] As in *From Here to Eternity,* Clift plays a lightning rod for the hostility of others. See if this sounds familiar: Clift plays a soldier bullied by other soldiers on a military base until he proves himself in a series of fistfights. Urged to give up, Clift's character refuses to make things easy for himself. Although the plot seems like a direct rip-off of *From Here to Eternity,* there is a twist. Unlike Prewitt, Noah (Clift) *wants* to fight. A bookish Jewish intellectual (he reads *Ulysses* in boot camp), Noah feels compelled to refute his fellow soldiers' anti-Semitism and dispel their doubts about his patriotism and masculinity. Physically beaten by his fel-low soldiers whom he fights in a series of bare-hand contests, Noah expresses his mettle not by winning, but by standing and taking it. He endures and eventually succeeds. On the whole, *The Young Lions* is more optimistic than its predecessor. Instead of waiting until the end for the corrupt Captain Holmes to be disciplined in *Eternity,* here the evil commanding officer who originally singled Akerman out for abuse is instantly reprimanded and dis-charged by a sagacious superior. When Noah returns to the unit after briefly going AWOL, the men welcome him back wholeheartedly.

The fight scenes lead to a shot of Clift's face that is terrifying. At one point he is being patched up by a medic, looking like a prizefighter hav-ing his eye stitched by a corner man. His lip is split in two places, he has contusions on his chin and forehead, and his left eye is swollen shut and bloodied—all in all, a representation fans might have imagined after the accident but until this shot never actually had to see.

All of the actor's biographers recount Clift's pride in the meticulous work he put into creating this look. According to Hoskyns, Clift modeled Noah's appearance on Franz Kafka. Bragging about his "ultra-ascetic dieting—the cocktail of skimmed milk and raw eggs that [Clift] said 'keeps me starving but concentrated, at the peak of tension,'" he sounds like Kafka's Hunger Artist.[32] But the most striking change Clift made was to his face, having his "ears glued forward" to make them stick out and widening his nose with stuffing.[33] Clift not only wanted to look like Kafka, he was trying to "look Jewish." Unfortunately the actor's explanation of his efforts comes perilously close to parroting the anti-Semitic Nazi stereotypes the film was denouncing. Asked why he had "lost twelve pounds to play the part," Clift responded, "I wanted to look like a rodent, that's why. Lean and slim like a rodent. Or let's say a rat passing for a mouse."[34] If the heavy makeup also hid his features after the accident, all the better.

Regardless of his reasons, Clift's attempts to transform himself physically into the frail, intellectual Noah failed. (The figure of a rugged Jewish action hero would have to wait for 1960's *Exodus* and its tan and muscular Paul Newman.) It is not that Clift doesn't look good in *The Young Lions* or that he doesn't look young or that he doesn't look all that much like Kafka—in fact, he falls short on all counts. The real problem with his prosthetically altered face is that it doesn't look real. At times it is as if he is wearing a rubber mask. Even worse, as the actor himself acknowledged, the audience ignored his laborious attempts to build a character based on appearance. "They didn't see that. Oh no. All they saw was that my face looked different and they shrieked."[35]

In the film's climactic scenes, Clift's contribution is marginal, his performance a series of poor choices. Liberating a concentration camp, Noah and Mike (Dean Martin) represent the American response to the evil of the Holocaust. Led by Captain Green (a sympathetic officer who intervened on Akerman's behalf during the tensions at the barracks), Noah and Mike are surrogates for the audience, witnesses at a meeting between Green and the mayor of a town near the camp. When the mayor advises the American commander not to allow the surviving Jews to hold a religious service for those who died, the film sets up a rousing depiction of American backbone and decency. As Noah and Mike look on, preparing themselves for compromise and cowardice, Captain Green announces that not only will the Jews hold their service, but anyone who attempts to interfere will be shot. The film cuts to a two-shot of Mike and Noah's reaction. Clift has his back turned. Unfortunately, Clift's usual means for engaging the audience by making them imagine what he is feeling (rather than by trying to show it through facial expression) does not work in this situation, partly because of Dean Martin. In his first dramatic role, Martin demonstrates a flawless touch with a morally ambiguous character. The visceral revulsion

FIGURE 27. Costume test for *The Young Lions*, 1958.

on Martin's face as he listens to the mayor's excuses distracts us from Clift's unexpressive back as Martin vividly conveys the film's attitude.

Ordered by Green to get some fresh air, Noah and Mike go on a walk through the sun-dappled forest. As they stroll along, the GIs are overheard by Brando's German officer, Christian. Hiding in the woods, Brando/Christian begins to set up his rifle, preparing to shoot at them. He waits, aims, and then stops himself. Recognizing the pointlessness of fighting on, he stands up and begins smashing his rifle against a tree stump. Unarmed, he begins to walk downhill, prepared to surrender to the two Americans below. Mike sees him, yells "Kraut!" and shoots from the hip. Brando does an elaborate fall down a hillside and lands facedown in a puddle. We see a few bubbles. Clift's eyes tear up as if this last act was unnecessary: the enemy was unarmed, and Mike was too quick on the trigger. This last death is presented as ironic, accidental, a tragic casualty of war. But we can't really blame good old Mike, can we? The army buddies march on, the body facedown in the foreground—the only shot there will ever be of Brando and Clift together in the film. The film ends on a coda of homecoming as Noah, back in New York, hurries across the street to see his wife and baby. With Hope (the wife's name as well as the actress's), Noah can repopulate the Earth. Their new postwar life will have to proceed without us, however, as the film fades to black. We were here for the fighting.

Potential viewers are often drawn to the film by something promised but never delivered: Clift and Brando together at last! Promoted on the basis of something that never happens, the film cannot help but disappoint. Posters and publicity stills (see plate 10) inevitably substitute shots of the actors on the set for scenes from the film, supplying what the film lacks.

There are critics who like the film. Hoskyns calls Clift "mesmerizing."[36] Irwin Shaw, the author of the novel on which the film was based, thought Clift "was superb—the best and truest to the character I'd written."[37] One other person who liked Clift's performance was Clift himself. Bosworth reports that "Noah became an artistic expression of faith for Monty. It was his favorite role—the performance he wrought most painfully and carefully from his own experience, his own observations."[38] "Noah was the best performance of my life," she quotes Clift as saying. "I couldn't have given more of myself. I'll never be able to do it again. Never."[39]

The belief that Clift's face was radically altered by the accident rests on *Raintree County* and *The Young Lions*. Yet these films are not representative of Clift's looks throughout the second half of his career. Made immediately after the crash, the scenes shot on location for *Raintree* show him when parts of his face were still swollen and his jaw recently wired shut. In *The Young Lions*, his face was prosthetically altered, so one cannot tell based on this film what Clift himself actually looked like.

Lonelyhearts and *Wild River* are marginally better films than *Raintree County* and *Young Lions*, and in both Clift is not bad-looking at all. Although he is still cast as the romantic lead, there are now caveats. Both films emphasize his character's passivity with regard to women and establish a direct link among each character's troubles with women, lack of self-respect, and flirtation with alcoholism. Adam White *(Lonelyhearts)* and Chuck Glover *(Wild River)* are innocent young idealists. Adam befriends the wife of a newspaper editor, hoping for a job on the *Chronicle*. He is appointed to write advice for the lovelorn, part of a trap set by his bitter employer, Shrike (Robert Ryan), to disillusion the idealistic young man. Shrike also subjects Adam and Mrs. Shrike, played by Myrna Loy, to a constant barrage of cynical abuse. Chuck Glover in *Wild River* has been assigned the unenviable job of displacing backwoods people in the name of progress, in the form of electricity and the Tennessee Valley Authority. He must persuade them to sell or leave before their homes are flooded for a hydroelectric dam. Although he too befriends a local woman (Lee Remick), the locals are as abusive to him as Shrike is to Adam, routinely threatening him and eventually beating him unconscious.

Sexual inadequacy, mental and physical suffering, alcoholism, drug abuse, and scenes of humiliation twine in and out of both films. When Clift is cast opposite much younger women (both Remick and Dolores Hart in *Lonelyhearts* were in their early twenties), his age raises questions about his characters' status as unmarried men. Adam is keeping a secret from his girlfriend, Justy (Hart), from the beginning. By the time the film is over he will have added two or three more. When director Elia Kazan tries to establish Chuck's desire for Carol (Remick), the camera focuses obsessively on her tight-fitting jeans. In Chuck's reaction shots, his discomfort, signaled by an inability to sit still, reads more like embarrassment than lust.

Both Chuck and Adam begin as teetotalers and proceed to full-blown alcoholic binges. A cascade of double entendres linked to Clift's biography follows. In *Lonelyhearts,* Clift's boss takes one look at him and observes, "You're practically stoned." Watching him drink, a bartender tells him, "That's no way to handle the spirits." Clift gives him a long "no comment" look. Earlier, Shrike tells him that he will be dealing with people with mental disturbances—"and you are an authority on the subject." When drunk, Adam punches a friend in the face and, consumed with guilt, quits his job. Like Adam, Chuck in *Wild River* is ashamed of the morally ambiguous position he is in because of his work. After he is slapped around the first time, Chuck imbibes a large quantity of white lightning (sent by the man who hit him as a sign of no hard feelings). Going to visit the old woman he is trying to displace, he admits, "I had a drink, yes." Addressing her from the

FIGURE 28. Lobby card for *Wild River*, 1960: Clift (Chuck) and Lee Remick (Carol).

front yard as she stands on her porch, he tells her he has figured out the true reason for her reluctance to leave her home. "It's your dignity. It's your everlasting—ever-loving—*dignity.*" Waving his arms in sweeping gestures, he concludes, "It's your dignity. That's that," and begins to sink under the porch, curling up on the ground. "It's your dignity." (Clift preserves his own dignity—just barely—by playing the scene for comedy.)

Adam, posing as Miss Lonelyhearts, is overwhelmed by his inability to help the multitudes who write to him. When he requests another assignment, his boss demands a reason. Adam becomes impassioned, raising his voice: "I can't help them . . . and if I can't help, I am twisting the arm of all the broken—bewildered—desperate—despairing—sick of it all. . . ." Unable to explain himself, he collapses against his seat back, drops his shoulders, and takes a deep breath. "I would rather ignore them than lie to them. I would . . . rather be dead than laugh at them." Threatened with the loss of his job, Adam backs down. Chuck in *Wild River* conveys the government's promise to "bring" electricity to the poverty-stricken region. But by convincing the local population to adopt electricity, he is creating a need that will put people who are poor but self-sufficient into a condition of perpetual debt. There is a strong suggestion of masochism and self-hatred as Chuck gets himself repeatedly beaten by hostile locals. He is thrown headfirst into the river, slapped (offscreen) by a Klansman, knocked unconscious in the film's climax. Kazan arranges for Clift to end up facedown in the mud more than once, but the actor again plays the moments as comic. Waking up in the mud next to Carol, who was knocked out after rushing to his defense, Chuck makes himself comfortable, turning on his side and mentioning, "You know, I wish someday I could win maybe one fight."

Adam also pursues suffering and degradation. "The element which attracted Monty initially" to *Lonelyhearts* (according to Bosworth, "the element he wanted to drown in") was "the obsession of the Christ-figure hero for the miseries of humanity."[40] Characteristically, Clift wanted to pursue the darker path. Comparing Dore Schary's script to the Nathanael West novel, he asked indignantly, "Where's the corruption? the misery? the evil? the disease? Hysteria has been replaced by blandness,' he said. 'Miss Lonelyhearts, meet Andy Hardy.'"[41]

Of course, to find corruption, misery, and hysteria in these films we need look no further than the circumstances of their production. In this period, Clift worked with some of the most compromised figures of the McCarthy era. As a member of the Hollywood Ten, Dmytryk had gone to prison rather than cooperate with the House Un-American Activities Committee (HUAC). He recanted eventually and became a "friendly" witness, willing to name publicly friends who had been communists. Kazan testified twice, in January 1952 and again in April. Dore Schary, who wrote and produced *Lonelyhearts,* participated in the 1947 meetings that resulted in the Waldorf Agreement, whereby the studios banded together to fire the Hollywood Ten and blacklist suspected communists. He was the studios' spokesman, sent to explain the new facts of life to some of the people who would be hit hardest by the blacklist, members of the Screen Writers Guild.[42] Even Joseph Mankiewicz (who directed Clift in *Suddenly, Last Summer*) had failed to live up to his ideals. Elected president of the Screen Director's Guild in 1950, Mankiewicz "ended up endorsing the first mandatory loyalty oath in a Hollywood talent guild." Although he had run in opposition to the ultra–right-wing Cecil B. DeMille, signing the oath was Mankiewicz's first act as president.[43]

There are reasons Clift might have admired Dmytryk. He had been nominated for the Best Director award for *Crossfire* (1947), his exposé of anti-Semitism in the United States (and in the army). In *The Young Lions,*

Dmytryk acknowledges the Holocaust in several scenes (an SS officer's discussion of Auschwitz, a re-creation of the Allied liberation of a concentration camp)—something *The Search* had minimized ten years earlier—an intentional oversight to which Clift had objected strongly.[44] But Kazan?

Clift had worked with Kazan in the original theatrical production of *The Skin of Our Teeth* when Clift was twenty-two. Kazan was a big noise; between 1945 and 1955, he was arguably the most respected director in America. On the stage he had directed the premieres of *A Streetcar Named Desire* and *Death of a Salesman;* in Hollywood he made *Gentleman's Agreement* (1947), *Pinky* (1949), the film version of *Streetcar* (1951), *Viva Zapata!* (1952), *On the Waterfront* (1954), and *East of Eden* (1955). Kazan's work "dealt with problems of conscience, responsibility, and personal honor in a materialistic society."[45] One expert on the period argues that it was not just his unparalleled success but the evident commitment to social issues in Kazan's work that made his decision to name names so upsetting. It was an act that has tainted Kazan's reputation ever since.[46]

If Clift admired these men for their early socially conscious work, they were not particularly sympathetic toward him. Discussing the casting of *The Young Lions,* Dmytryk reports, "I had just finished an extremely long and difficult stint with Monty Clift in *Raintree* and I was looking forward to a few months rest. . . . Monty had a great drinking problem, and after *Raintree* I had sworn that, great actor, good friend, and exceptional person that he was, I would never work with him again—but who else could play Noah?"[47] In his memoir, Kazan calls Clift a "sexual borderline case."[48] (He also blames Clift for the car accident, saying Clift was "loaded with warm rosé wine and 'steadied' by two 'downers.'")[49] Although Kazan makes a show of trying to be kind, he always ends up insulting Clift, using terms like "sick," "quivering," "shaky," "wobbly," and "a tenderhearted shell of a man."[50] "He was still in some way or other a cripple," Kazan declares. "Some way, some subtle way, he wasn't entirely healthy."[51] Besides, Kazan admits, "I always wanted Brando"—for this film and every other project he was working on in this period.[52]

Like John Huston and other directors obsessed with manliness, Kazan was at great pains to separate himself from Clift. Kazan had conceived the character in *Wild River* as a reflection of himself.[53] What he wanted to see was Brando; what he got was Clift. "My hero was to be a resolute New Dealer engaged in the difficult task" of bringing change to resistant "country people," Kazan recalled. Talked into casting Clift, Kazan made an about-face. "I began to see how the part could be played as a rather uncertain and inept social-working intellectual . . . dealing with people who were stronger and more confirmed in their beliefs than he was."[54] The ruthless, brutal, amoral, animal sensuality of Stanley Kowalski was replaced by the hypersensitive, morally precise, stoic suffering of an Adam White or a Noah Akerman. Even without Brando, *Wild River* is rife with the kind of self-serving comments that stand out in Kazan's post-HUAC work. Chuck, for example, opines that "sometimes it happens that we can't remain true to our beliefs without hurting a great many people."

Clift's own political beliefs are a topic that has yet to be fully addressed in any biography. His film career spans one of the most politically contentious (and widely documented) eras in Hollywood and a crucial period in American history, from the HUAC hearings starting in 1947 to the arrest, trial, and execution of the Rosenbergs (1950–53). Attempting to ascertain the actor's position vis-à-vis McCarthyism and the blacklist, we find his politics in some ways more closeted than his sexuality. Perhaps it was the same closet.

The year 1950 saw a nationwide eruption of homophobia that originated in Washington, D.C., and came to be known as the Lavender Scare. Between February and November, roughly "six hundred federal civil servants" were dismissed from their jobs. The State Department, which had already fired ninety-one employees for "moral weaknesses," was soon firing "on average . . . one homosexual per day, more than double the rate for those suspected of political disloyalty."[55] Gay men and lesbians who worked for the government found themselves labeled "security risks" (the *nom du jour* for "sexual perverts" and "moral degenerates") and grouped with communists as being among those who posed the greatest threat to "honorable, loyal, clean-living American men and women."[56] Chillingly, in light of the political climate, a memo to President Truman concluded that "the country is more concerned about the charges of homosexuals in the Government than about Communists."[57]

If Clift ever came close to being caught up in the homophobic currents of the day, it would have been through his two-year relationship with Jerome Robbins. In accounts of the McCarthy era, Robbins is described as one of the friendly witnesses, naming names to HUAC, sometimes with little heed to whether his identifications were true or false.[58] Decades later Robbins would be outed as a gay man by these authors, though the directness with which this information is expressed varies. In *A Journal of the Plague Years* in 1973, Stefan Kanfer (who calls him "Robbins the meek") states that "the balding, fastidious dancer, choreographer and director had committed a number of personal indiscretions. The Committee caught up with them and with him in 1953. Robbins had been threatened with loss of network and film assignments, and with worse."[59] What "worse" might have been is suggested by Victor Navasky in *Naming Names* (1980), as is the nature of Robbins's indiscretions: "The choreographer Jerome Robbins was rumored to have turned informer to keep the Committee's investigators from publicizing evidence that he was a homosexual. . . . Robbins denies that this was his motive, although his demeanor before HUAC was so compliant that his appearance had about it the aura of social blackmail."[60] (Navasky also quotes Ring Lardner Jr., who said, "I don't know whether it's true or not, but if you were Jerry Robbins, wouldn't you like to have people believe that's the reason you did it?")[61]

Robbins not only denied the motive, he did not publicly acknowledge that he was gay. Because of his reticence, Clift's biographers in the late 1970s were forced to disguise Robbins's identity. Bosworth states that, "off the record," Clift was "emotionally committed to a Broadway choreographer [in the late 1940s]—a 'theatrical genius,' Monty called him early in their affair."[62] The sexual relationship between Robbins and Clift would not be publicly revealed until after Robbins's death.[63] *Dance with Demons: The Life of Jerome Robbins* by Greg Lawrence and *Jerome Robbins: His Life, His Times, His Dance* by Deborah Jowitt (both published in 2004) state that Clift and Robbins had a serious two-year relationship. As happens with any biographical endeavor, varying accounts are offered, none of which can be definitively established or proved. Robbins's biographers differ on how the relationship ended. Jowitt slights Clift, speculating that Clift left Robbins because the actor was on the verge of becoming a star and needed to stay closeted.[64] Lawrence, who is less sympathetic to Robbins, gives the breakup political resonance by repeating a story Brooks Clift told Bosworth: that Clift lost respect for Robbins after Robbins cooperated with HUAC.[65]

On the whole, Clift seems to have been an all-purpose liberal, opposed to prejudice in general and in favor of social change. His only overt political act was to speak at a rally at Madison Square Garden in support of Adlai Stevenson's candidacy for president in 1952.[66] This mild gesture precipitated a vitriolic outburst from his father, who saw it as an "utter betrayal," calling Stevenson "a Commie liberal."[67]

The film that comes closest to representing the atmosphere of absurdity and fear that characterized the various fifties witch hunts is, unlikely though it may sound, *Indiscretion of an American Wife*. In the performance Bosworth describes as "perhaps his most sexual one" (I think she means "heterosexual"), Clift plays Giovanni, an Italian in love with a married American tourist, Mary/Maria (Jennifer Jones).[68] When the couple is apprehended kissing each other passionately in a train compartment, Giovanni steps into the hallway to speak heatedly to the security guards. A moment later, he reenters the compartment and whispers to himself, "They're crazy." Struggling to explain matters to Mary, he shields his eyes with one hand as he rubs his temples, trying physically to get his mind around a thought. "It seems we're criminals."

At first, the idea that a couple would be arrested in Rome for kissing seems not only implausible but wildly disproportionate. The audience has to do mental gymnastics to account for this illogical plot development. We could assume *kissing* is a euphemism mandated by the Production Code: they weren't just kissing, but any sexual activity in excess of kissing could not be shown or alluded to. We can propose a moral-psychological reading: that the law crashing down on them for so slight a transgression serves as a metaphoric or unconscious acknowledgment of a deeper guilt regarding adultery; in other words, they are punished not for what they have done but for what they have desired. A third reading suggests itself via biography.

It makes more sense to consider the scene as queer. It is queer to be arrested for kissing. In a time and place where (homo)sexuality is literally policed, kissing—in fact any same-sex physical expression of affection—would be tantamount to committing a lewd act. (Clift was reportedly arrested more than once for cruising—in New York, New Orleans, and Rome.) The rest of the scene plays out as if their sexuality itself were a crime—as if they were gay—as Giovanni and his illicit love object are subjected to ritual humiliation. Paraded through the train station, they are pointed at, whispered about, and ultimately held to account by the commissar (see plate 11).

Waiting for the judge to arrive, Giovanni is most concerned about being looked at. He objects to passers-by peeking in the windows to see them. When they are finally taken to the commissar, they are questioned not about what they have done but about who they are. The commissar finds out that Mary is American, married, a mother, and leaving town that evening. Giovanni is silent. In the reconstructed version of the film called *Terminal Station*, Giovanni is asked one question—his profession. He hesitates, and then says quietly, "Teacher." That is all the judge needs to know. Both sides of this couple would have a lot to lose if they were to be exposed. When the scene is read as gay, the actions of the authorities and reactions of Giovanni and Mary make sense. As Clift knew personally, at any time he could find himself subject to whispers, exaggerations, salacious rumor, and public ridicule, his career ruined by scandal.[69]

In the corrosive era of the blacklist, those who could still work eventually ended up working together, regardless of their political pasts. Clift worked with Kazan *and* with Kazan's former friend and political opponent, Arthur Miller (who would also work with Kazan again). But on the whole, when Clift was at his most vulnerable, he was surrounded by some of the least sympathetic coworkers of his entire career. It is no surprise that he sought out allies wherever he could find them, and that they were usually women—Remick during the making of *Wild River;* Myrna Loy, Maureen Stapleton, and Dolores Hart on the set of *Lonelyhearts.*

Lonelyhearts allows Clift the opportunity for his most sustained performance among the four films under discussion, though the film as a whole is less successful. Based on the novel by Nathanael West and a play by Howard Teichmann, the film was directed by first-time director Vincent J. Donehue. Aided by veteran cinematographer John Alton, Donehue avoids the high-key lighting and close-up heavy shooting style typical of many television directors' first foray into film. Two weeks of rehearsal also eased the way for several long takes and complicated tracking shots.

Again, Clift's character is supposed to be young (twenty-eight) and naive. In his first scene it is established that he neither drinks nor smokes. He also shows how much he is willing to stomach to get a job. Having asked the editor's wife to introduce him, Adam has to sit by while Mr. Shrike insinuates that his wife sleeps around. Challenged to prove that he can write, he describes the encounter in the third person: "At first sardonic and unimpressed," the editor, Adam expounds, "went to the length . . . of insulting his wife [softly]. However [loud and clear], the young man . . . anxious to get his assignment . . . resisted an impulse to hit Mr. Shrike . . . and instead sat it out. [Pause] Mr. Shrike, obviously touched by the young man's ambition . . . [inhales] and amused at his lack of courage . . . decided to hire him."

Clift looks relatively good when Adam tells his girlfriend, Justy (Dolores Hart), that he got the job. Noticeably younger than Clift, Hart was a Fox contract player typecast as the healthy, wholesome girl next door, someone in the same vein as such unthreatening blondes as Nancy Olson in *Sunset Boulevard,* Barbara Bel Geddes in *Vertigo,* Hope Lange, and Eva Marie Saint. Their first scene together takes place at a drive-in theater in two relatively long takes (fifty-three seconds for the first shot, forty-five for the second). Considering Hoskyns's description of the making of *Lonelyhearts* ("By the time the movie began shooting in late 1958, Monty was so bombed on Nembutal and Seconals that he was unable to work beyond 2 p.m. each day" and "for the first time" had to "use the idiot cards that now became a staple feature on any set that had Montgomery Clift on it"), it is surprising to find that Clift can walk and act at the same time.[70] The long takes and elaborate tracking movements of this scene also demonstrate his ability to do several pages of dialogue without cutaways or cue cards (though multiple takes were required).[71] Walking past cars in night-for-night lighting, Adam breaks the good news to Justy, then buys her an orange soda from a vending machine. Although the shot seems effortless, it would be impossible to ignore the mannerisms that critics of the day began to complain about in Clift's work. He smiles, sparkles, straightens, and sags. When he and Hart face each other, he occasionally takes deep breaths that propel him upward a good four to six inches, until he collapses down again. (Hart remains admirably level.) Flopping his arms onto her shoulders for a hug, he seems like a marionette. Too old to be securing his first job (or to have a teenage girlfriend), Clift's Adam comes across as wired, his energy and excitement spilling over in all directions like someone trying too hard to seem happy. In the office scenes, simply by putting on glasses Clift becomes unrecognizable. Worse than that, he's ordinary. In a few scenes with Justy and her younger brothers, Clift is just right. Less jazzed, steadier, he sneaks up behind her one night on the front porch after she has stormed out over the boys' incessant game playing, and asks her, soberly, apologetically, with a glint in his eye, "You wanna play dominoes?" In moments like these, the age difference does not seem so severe, and we can see that whatever his eccentricities, Adam/Clift might be well balanced by Justy's sensible stability.[72]

If Clift alternates between jarring mannerisms and unexpected grace in his scenes as a young lover, his depiction of the character's descent into moral confusion is consistently well judged and executed. When Shrike dares him to contact one of his readers, Adam calls Fay Doyle (Maureen Stapleton). Like Jo van Fleet in *Wild River*, Stapleton is so powerful a force she could easily steamroll over Clift (which suits the scene and characters perfectly). Predatory Fay seduces Adam with her neediness and pain. Having invited her to his apartment, he sets out two chairs and thoughtfully leaves the door open. She closes it (for privacy, she says) and tells him with much hesitancy and shame about her sexual frustration. He turns to the window but she draws him back with her sobbing. Clutching his arm, she pulls herself up as he bends toward her. Asking for "one gentle kiss," she is soon in his arms;

FIGURE 29. *Lonelyhearts,* 1959: Clift (Adam) and coworkers.

fade to black.[73] Parting with him later in the backseat of a cab, she becomes vulgar and demanding. "When am I gonna see ya again?" When he fails to respond, she tells him, "You're not a very appreciative fella." Trying to explain that he did not have licentious motives when he contacted her, she cuts him off brusquely. "Who are you kiddin'? Listen. You wanted a sad story, you *got* a sad story. You also wanted some action. And so did I."

Adam heads straight for a bar, gets drunk, and then moves to the next bar, where he meets Shrike and his coworkers. As they laugh and joke about the kind of people who write to Miss Lonelyhearts, Adam becomes angry and punches a friend in the face. Unnerved by his own violence, he whispers into a towel, "I'm sorry, I'm sorry, I'm sorry." Looking up, he stutters, "For—Forgive me—" and exits as he starts to cry.

The next day Justy finds him in bed, hungover and unshaven. In a staccato rhythm, with a high, nasal voice, he tells her why he did not call. "Because I got drunk—I got stupid drunk. I hit—a man—and I wanted to hurt him." He looks away. "*And* . . . not only that . . . " She completes the sentence: "a woman." He exhales but does not answer and cannot look at her. In this close-up, with Clift's disheveled hair and five-o'clock shadow, his bushy eyebrows—the usual sign of "late" Clift—finally seem in proportion to his face. (This is also the scene with the nearly compulsory reference to Adam's youth; Justy tells him, unpersuasively, that when she saw him lying there he looked "so much like a little boy.")

In this scene, and throughout the second half of his career, Clift stops being careful, forgetting (or refusing) to hide things he took pains to cover up earlier, and it is vaguely disturbing. In scenes sprinkled throughout his last several films, the hair on his chest is plainly visible. Allowing the audience a slight glimpse might be read as accidental or unwitting; prolonged exposure—taking a bath in *Raintree County,* leaving his shirt unbuttoned after swimming a river in *The Young Lions,* wearing an open-neck shirt with no undershirt in a hotel hallway in *Wild River*—seems more like reckless abandon. In *Lonelyhearts,* especially, we again have the option of reading Clift's appearance as the conscious choice of a meticulous professional: it is the character, sick and hungover, who lacks the capacity to care what he looks like. Throwing on a robe, Adam hurries after Justy when she turns to leave. "Dear? . . . Dear? Will I see you tonight?" Pulling the robe close around his neck, he looks like a junkie begging for a handout. An odd dissolve takes us from Adam following Justy out onto the stairs to Adam and Shrike standing in his room. "Go away," Adam says. As he folds his pants and hangs them in a wardrobe, Shrike impugns what he assumes to be Adam's romantic notions about unemployment. In his strongest, deepest voice, Clift recites Adam's renunciation of Shrike. "Former boss. I don't want the South Seas. And I don't want the soil. And I don't want art in a garret." Above all, he says, he wants not to hit anyone, hurt anyone, or become violent ever again. In his rejection of Shrike, Adam refuses the coupling of cheap cynicism and clichéd romanticism as decisively as he rejects the link between masculinity and violence.

Despite Adam's repudiation of masculine aggression and his passivity when confronted by rapacious or scolding women, the film's marketing campaign struggled to depict Clift's character as a man driven by (heterosexual) desire. On a poster for the film, Clift's standing figure is divided horizontally by an image of a woman in a slip lying facedown on a bed. Beneath her is the slogan "His name was Adam . . . but he wasn't the first Man to Yield to Temptation."

Although Adam seems to cut ties to both his job and his girl, in the film's last scene, he and Justy are reunited and visit the office one last time so that Adam can say good-bye. Refusing Shrike's attempt to win him back, Adam is about to leave with Justy when Fay Doyle's husband arrives with a gun. As Shrike confronts the man, Adam quickly and quietly puts himself be-

FIGURE 30. *Lonelyhearts:* Dolores Hart (Justy), Clift, and Robert Ryan (Shrike).

tween Justy and the gun. Directing Doyle's attention away from Shrike, Adam interrupts. "Mr. Doyle . . . I'm Miss Lonelyhearts." When Doyle pathetically asks him, "Why did you follow her?"—having believed Fay's story that Adam was the aggressor—Clift/Adam pauses, then walks toward Doyle as the camera isolates the two of them in a close shot. Indirectly denying Fay's story, Adam nevertheless takes on all the responsibility for what happened. "I met her because . . . she *asked* to see me." Pause. Clift increases the volume, his use of a monotone emphasizing the staccato line reading: "I asked her to stay. She stayed. I wanted her to stay."

None of this speech is in the script dated June 20, 1958. A revised version dated July 16 adds the line "I met her because she asked to see me," but Clift writes in the next two lines—"She stayed. I wanted her to." Evidently the lines were not finalized until the scene was shot. The addition of the first line ("I asked her to stay") and the last word of the last sentence ("I wanted her to stay") establish the rhythmic repetition that gives the short speech such power.[74]

As Doyle crumples, the gun hanging limply from his hand, the film puts the last stamp of fifties middlebrow on West's parable of doom. Instead of being killed by Doyle, Adam steers Justy toward their happily ever after, leaving Shrike to think for the first time that it might be possible for him to reconcile with his long-suffering wife. Asked why Miss Lonelyhearts doesn't die in the film as he did in the book, director Donehue opined that writer Schary "didn't believe the Christ figure needed to be crucified."[75]

A SUPPORTING PLAYER

While playing young romantic leads was becoming more and more prob-lematic, Clift excelled when cast in supporting roles.[76] *The Misfits* and *Judg-ment at Nuremberg* shift attention away from Clift's romantic potential by emphasizing other qualities. *Misfits* screenwriter Arthur Miller originally thought of the character of Perce Howland as one of three men compet-ing for Marilyn Monroe's Roslyn (he describes Perce as "in his late twen-ties"), but because Clift's character does not show up until an hour into the film, passes out, and then remains emotionally withdrawn in the last scenes rounding up wild horses in the desert, Perce as played by Clift seems more like Roslyn's friend or confidant and less competition of any kind for Gable's rugged man's man, Gay.[77] Clift's Perce has dropped out of that rodeo.

The Misfits is another film in which the actor's performance is overshad-owed by stories of how he conducted himself during the shoot. Making *Lonelyhearts,* he was "bizarre"; for this film, *The Young Lions,* and *Wild River,* he was "good."[78] He "behaved." Dmytryk vouches for Clift when he de-clares that while shooting *The Young Lions* on location in Paris and Stras-bourg, "We had good luck and bad luck. The good luck was that Monty didn't cost us one hour."[79] In his memoir, Kazan pays tribute to the actor's resolve, characteristically undercutting the compliment at the same time. "He always showed up in the morning, quivering but ready and willing. . . . I'd extracted a solemn promise that he would not take a drink from the first day of work until the last. He kept his promise, surviving days of stress and physical discomfort without the help of a bottle until the very last day, when he arrived on the set swaying on his feet, then keeled over. When I got to him he was on the ground, he was asleep."[80] In this telling, Kazan leaves Clift in the dirt, rhetorically. In Bosworth he literally picks him up again. "He came on the set . . . and he fell on his face in front of me right in the mud. Drunk. I picked him up and he apologized. I told him it was all right because it *was* all right—up until then he'd done a wonderful job. I knew how rough it had been for him to boom—stop drinking. He didn't taper off—he just stopped."[81] While Kazan shows greater respect for Clift in the second version, in neither account does he suggest what might have precipitated the lapse. Bosworth links it directly to a near-tragedy. Lee Remick, Clift's chief ally and emotional support on the film, had to leave abruptly when her husband was seriously injured in a car accident. Between Clift's concern for Lee and memories of his own near-fatal accident, a temporary lapse would be completely understandable. (According to Bosworth, Clift did not actually stop drinking; he just kept his vodka well hidden.)[82]

Because *The Misfits* brought together a profusion of A-list celebrities, there was a great deal of interest in what was happening on the set. As a consequence, more behind-the-scenes gossip from reporters, participants, and photographers was publicly available than for any Clift film since *Raintree County*. A collection of photographs by the Magnum group, a book, and a documentary on the making of the film are some of the texts inspired by the production. In the middle of this mismatched array of talents, Clift could be a mirror for them all. A major star since the early 1930s, Clark Gable was the most dominating male actor Clift had appeared opposite since John Wayne in *Red River*. But now, like Clift, Gable was nearing the end of his career, his leading-man status becoming more and more compromised by his age. Eli Wallach was the intensely serious New York theater actor Clift had once been, now trying to negotiate his way from Method workshops to a Hollywood film career. Of all of his costars, Clift was most like (and compared most frequently to) Marilyn Monroe. Iconic, idolized figures, both were becoming progressively damaged by neuroses, drugs, and alcohol; the effects, now visible, were undeniable. A chameleon like most great actors, Clift could even play the part of Arthur Miller, the company's resident intellectual. Magnum photographer Inge Morath (who would become Miller's wife after Monroe) remembers Clift calling late at night to read German poetry to her over the phone.[83]

It is difficult to separate Perce in *The Misfits* from Clift on the set. Too much of Perce's drunk and drugged high jinks invite us to read the character as Clift on the verge, Clift doped up and flying, Clift barely in control. He whoops and hollers in the backseat as Gable drives them in to town; talks about the shots he was given in the ambulance after he was kicked in the head by a bull; and staggers around with the absurd bandage on his head unraveling all around him. Dancing with Monroe, Clift/Perce remains stiff and upright, an old man at a church social, opening his eyes wide when he becomes off-balance and dizzy and has to go lie down. As with *Nuremberg* (the film he made immediately after *The Misfits*), it is a struggle not to

FIGURE 31. Clift on location for *The Misfits:* hotel room with cowboys, 1960. Dennis Stock, Magnum Photos.

see the role as Clift-on-Clift, tragedy in one and self-parody in the other. Like John Barrymore, Clift would not be the first to have made the journey from great actor to joke, acting out the spectacle of who he used to be.

But reading Perce as a crypto-Clift risks undervaluing the actor's genuine achievement. As he had with all of his films, Clift spent weeks in preparation, once again putting his body on the line. He spent "up to six hours a day" riding, learning to rope a calf. The bridge of his nose was cut by a bull's horn, an injury that proved useful for the film.[84] In the film Clift sits on a skittish horse who smashes him into the side of a chute and tears his shirt across the back. Huston films this in a long take so that we can see it is really Clift being tossed around the dangerously enclosed space. We watch for a long, suspense-filled time before Gable's character opens the gate, allowing Huston to cut to a long shot of a stuntman. In the horse-wrangling scenes near the end of the film, Clift tries to hold a rearing wild horse, the rope chafing his hands because he did the scene without gloves. (According to Huston this was an accidental oversight. If Clift had worn gloves, it would have created a continuity error. Honest.) The physical damage the actor suffered suited the character, but read biographically it becomes questionable for Clift. Attributed to Clift the actor, it proves dedication to craft; attributed to Clift the neurotic it becomes a failing, another example of masochistic self-destruction.

Nevertheless there is one scene critics, coworkers, and fans alike agree is one of the best of his life—his first scene in the film, one hour in, when he calls his mother from a phone booth. This scene's popularity is testified to by the fact that in Clift's copy of the script at the New York Public Library's Performing Arts archive, this one page has been stolen. Somewhere a fetishist is smiling. Nevertheless, it would be hard to imagine that Clift could have indicated in the margins of one page all the things he does in this two-minute scene. Above all, in every shot Clift faces the camera, never turning his back.

The scene begins with Perce standing outside the car, being introduced to Roslyn by Gay, with Guido (Wallach) and Isabelle (Thelma Ritter) in the backseat. The phone rings in the booth behind him and he hurries to answer, explaining the trouble he has had getting through. The camera follows him. Picking up the receiver, he balances his white cowboy hat in his other hand as he shouts to the operator, "Hello? Hello? . . . Hello, Ma? This is Perce." Putting on his hat to talk to his mother, he embarks on a conversation that winds through pride, defensiveness, reassurance, irritation, resentment, love, and loss. The only voice we hear is Perce's. The first thing

FIGURE 32. *The Misfits,* 1961: Clift (Perce) riding in a rodeo.

he tells his mother is, "Yeah, I'm okay," and that he won a hundred dollars.
As the others watch from the car, he begins to apologize, closing the phone
booth door to dampen the sound. "Ma, I—I was gonna buy you a birthday present with it but . . . I was comin' outta my boots!" An explosive laugh
punctuates the last word but the pause that follows shows that his amusement is not shared. "No. No, Ma, I haven't been in the hospital since I talked
to you" (he reaches up and digs his finger into the door frame), "I just bought
some boots, that's all." He pauses and then, with an intake of breath, is instantly on the defensive. "Ma? What—What would I wanna get married
for? I just bought me—." His reaction to the injustice of the accusation
(similar to one made by George's mama in *A Place in the Sun*) is registered
by witnesses in another cutaway to the car. Returning to Perce, we see him
wiping his mouth with the back of his hand as he changes the subject. "Hey,
you know what?" He pauses and reopens the phone booth door. "On top
of the purse money, I won me a nice silver buckle." Describing it, he looks
down at his belt, his face momentarily hidden by his hat brim. Leaning
comfortably against the wall, he glances up, lifting his face so we can see

his eyes as he asks with shy eagerness, "Ya proud?" Listening to presumably kind words, he hurriedly cuts in to reassure her—"Oh no. No, no. My face is fine." He stands straighter as he wipes his hand down his face. "It's all healed up. It's as good as new." Arthur Miller was accused of insensitivity bordering on effrontery for giving Clift these lines, but Clift plays it with an amused obliviousness.[85] The next line, though, has greater weight. Huston cuts to a two-shot of Gable and Monroe listening as Perce lowers his voice to tell his mother, "You would too recognize me." Returning to Clift, we see him suddenly stand up straight when he hears that his time is running out. He hurries to give his mother a list of people to say hello to for him. His demeanor changes as he pauses, looks down at the floor, and then in a quiet, low voice, says resignedly, "Okay. Say hello to him too." Trying to avoid an argument, he waves it off with his free hand. "No, no, ma. Ma, it—it—it just slipped my mind, that's all." He leans against the wall, sunk lower in the frame than before. Getting angry, he says sharply, "Well, okay. I'm saying it now." He shuts the door, the hinge making a loud squeak. Although his voice is muffled again, his irritation comes through loud and clear. "Ma, you married him, I didn't. So say hello to him." Relenting, he tries to change the mood by changing the subject, suggesting that he will try to call for Christmas, but the call ends abruptly. "Hello? Hello . . . " Talking to a dead line, he lingers and then, defeated and a little bitter, adds, "God bless you, too."

One of a series of modern-day westerns marking the death of the mythical West, *The Misfits* is a difficult film to warm to. In films like *Lonely Are the Brave* (1962) and *Hud* (1963), the cowboys are anachronisms, disillusioned, disparaged, crushed (literally in *Lonely Are the Brave,* in which Kirk Douglas on a horse is no match for a semi on the highway). Perce and Gay live an imitation of a life that doesn't exist anymore. They think and dress and act appropriately, but their fidelity to the myth serves no purpose. Their skills have become part of a show (the rodeo), their horses replaced by truck and plane, while the only authentic remnants of the real West—the wild mustangs—have become good for nothing but meat. The film's palpable misogyny (vicious in the case of Guido, thoughtless coming from Gay) adds no joy, nor does Miller's heavy touch as he strains for poetry and depth. Overall, except for Clift's first scene, *The Misfits* leaves the viewer disappointed and dissatisfied.

Of all of Clift's later films, the most polarizing is the one that trades most heavily on public knowledge of Clift's physical and psychological struggles.

Where *Raintree County, Wild River,* and *Lonelyhearts* proceeded as if nothing about Clift had changed since his late twenties and *The Young Lions* used makeup to obscure Clift's features in favor of a putty-and-pancake fiction, only *The Misfits* and *Judgment at Nuremberg* integrated the forty-year-old actor's swollen nose, smeared upper lip, and unmanageable eyebrows into the characters he portrayed. More than any film since *Raintree County, Judgment at Nuremberg* invited the audience to explore the actor's face for proof of actual trauma, real scars. Imagine, the film insinuates, how powerful it would be to see Clift, this weighted image of manifest suffering, inserted into a narrative of travail.

PERFORMING/THE BODY ON TRIAL

The original definition of a trial was a physical ordeal that tested the capacity of the body to suffer, endure, triumph, or be defeated, at the risk of being destroyed. Rather than cede all expressivity to the mute communication of the body, however, I want to examine the way Clift *uses* his body as an actor fully aware of his effect. Three trial scenes filmed ten years apart (between 1951 and 1961) epitomize the two halves of Clift's career. As Logan on the witness stand in *I Confess,* George Eastman in *A Place in the Sun,* and Rudolf Peterson in *Judgment at Nuremberg,* Clift demonstrates that regardless of his personal problems, before and after the accident he was in control of his performances.

Unlike the disciplined and confident Logan, Eastman and Peterson both struggle with bodies that are overly expressive. Both have difficulty explaining themselves. While on the witness stand, they are forced to confront their weaknesses as they struggle and fail against the hostile regard of opposing counsel.

In the trial scene in *I Confess,* Clift/Logan is all rectitude, rock solid in his faith, including his faith in himself—everything Clift/George isn't on the witness stand in *A Place in the Sun* two years before. In the Canadian setting of *I Confess,* Clift's character stands when he testifies. Shot from a low angle, he is on a pedestal as he stands in the dock. In the U.S. trial, Clift's George Eastman sits. Each variation in posture expresses the differences between the characters. Logan stands tall, occasionally placing his hands on the railing before him, his arms out straight—but only when he is being emphatic, eager to proclaim the truth. George sits with his shoulders hunched, elbows on the chair's armrests (a posture Clift repeats in *From*

Here to Eternity after a spat with Lorene). Unlike the patient, stalwart Logan, George is unable to sit still, stuttering, hesitant, confused.

Above all, George is ambivalent about his own guilt. Born guilty according to the restrictive teachings of his fundamentalist upbringing and a pretender in terms of class position, he is guilty whether he acts on his desire (sleeping with a coworker) or dares to imagine the possibility of sex with a socialite. Steve Cohan argues that George's "unsuccessful defense rests entirely on the immateriality of his desire, its distinction from action."[86] If he did not actively kill Alice, as we see in the scene, did he really do everything he could to save her, or did he want her dead and passively let her drown? Logan, on the other hand, has no sexual guilt, no hidden desires. He has no desire for Ruth, therefore he can plainly state that even though they spent the night together in the summerhouse, there was "nothing wrong with being caught in a storm." The "storm" of potential lust, lies, and adultery does not touch him at a deep level. While George Eastman literally cannot say whether he is guilty (he had planned to kill Alice, he wanted her dead, she ended up dead though he took no direct action), when Logan is accused of murder, he *can* say, unequivocally and with a clear conscience, "It's not true."

Each film contains a similar shot when the character has the opportunity to answer directly the key question of his trial. Asked what happened when he met Otto in the church after Villette's death, Logan stares resolutely ahead and responds, "I can't say." This is one of the film's heavily symbolic shots—Clift suddenly seen in strict profile, screen right, with a crucifix balancing the image at screen left. Because the cross is in the background and on a different visual plane, Logan does not look at it, but it is "before" him. It represents the higher things he looks toward at the same time that it constrains his response.

In *A Place in the Sun,* when George testifies that Alice thought he wanted her dead, we cut to a close-up of Clift in left profile as he says, "I told her it wasn't true, I didn't want her to die." Here, the left profile suggests that we are getting only half the story, our ability to read his face suddenly restricted. As with Logan, George's face fills the right side of the screen, but what balances the left half is not a symbol of faith but members of the jury, specifically a man and a woman who stare at George. The space "before" him is filled with those who will judge him. Logan's "I can't say" is not an assertion of lack of knowledge or an equivocation ("I don't know," "It might seem incriminating if I said"), but a resolute refusal—"I choose not to answer because I submit to a higher law." George, on the other hand, may have told Alice he did not want her dead, but was it true? Was it true in general, was it true at the time, or was he just saying it to calm her down? Does he even know himself?

Cohan criticizes the acting in the trial scene, but it is not Clift, it is George who "testifies in a very dramatic (and overplayed) performance."[87] In addition to perspiring (glycerin drops quite visible on his forehead), Clift/ George leans forward, wriggling in the chair, his head bobbing down and rarely rising above his shoulders. He tightens his fists and brings the back of his hand to his mouth. "I didn't want to think such things." He holds his hands, trying to keep them from shaking. "I couldn't help myself, I couldn't." By the end of the scene, he is drained, pale, drenched in sweat, gulping and blinking as he timorously risks a look at the jury.

As Logan, Clift underplays. Most of the time he stands straight, prepared to answer any question. Whenever Logan is asked a question he can answer without giving away anything confidential, Clift leans back and lifts his chin, opening up his chest. He opens his eyes a little wider (they really do twinkle) and answers succinctly. George Eastman writhes, caught in complexities of guilt and ambivalence he can neither understand nor explain. Logan knows where he stands (literally), his confidence as fixed as his stance. In *I Confess,* the trial scene frustratingly refuses to be climactic. Logan's testimony ends with a loud "No" as he denies the crown's theory of the crime, but nothing has been resolved.

Compare these two scenes with Clift's last major trial, in *Judgment at Nuremberg.* Clift's role consists of a single fourteen-minute scene (sometimes misidentified as seven minutes) in which his character, Rudolf Peterson, testifies. Because his entire role in *Nuremberg* is contained in this one scene, Clift's performance on the witness stand has to express everything about Peterson, his temperament, his body, his life. Like Logan, Peterson knows the truth of his own experience—he is not the one on trial—but because of his inherent weakness, his inability to work his way through an argument or prevail against the manipulations of a hostile questioner, he is in an emotional position comparable to George Eastman's.

Like Eastman, Peterson sits but can't sit still. He pivots, using the chair's armrests to raise himself on his elbows, shifting in his seat as if he can't find a way to be comfortable. Peterson's testimony begins relatively easily. He is nervous, moving stiffly, cocking an ear forward as he pauses to be sure he has understood the question (and its translation through headphones in the multilingual tribunal). When he knows the answer, he straightens his head, abruptly nods, and gives a simple answer with extra emphasis, relieved to be back on solid ground. Asked more disturbing questions, he lowers his head, slumps in his chair, and then quickly perks up, his head rising as he extends his neck. He sticks his chin out so his face catches the light. When attacked, this sequence is reversed: his chin drops in; his shoulders hunch up, swallowing his neck; and he pushes his torso into the back of the chair, sliding lower like a child in a corner.

When Peterson tries to fight, he is even more vulnerable. Trying to be emphatic, he lifts his face and upper body while his right arm flails, but his lower body stays wedged in the chair, caught between resistance and defeat. When he is put on the spot and has to answer a question that will convict him of "feeble-mindedness," he is so physically uncomfortable that it is hard for the viewer to sit still. He stretches and turns within the chair, uncomfortable no matter which way he moves. His body rises up suddenly as if he has glimpsed a possible answer, then slumps just as quickly, the idea gone as fast as it came. Clift splays his fingers across his mouth, dragging and pushing his lips, his stiff, straight fingers a sign of rigidity and increasing tension. The lack of flexibility combined with his jerky movements physically signals the lack of fluidity in Peterson's thoughts.

The most striking difference between this scene and the trial scenes in the other films is the visible change in Clift's face as a result of the accident. James Elkins, writing about portraiture, argues, "The body becomes a fact, an object, or even a specimen, that can express itself *merely by being seen*."[88] Actors' bodies are presented to be read, but what their bodies express is an inescapable doubleness—the actor's body making legible the *character's* physical and mental state. Despite the fiction of a performance or a pose, as Friedrich Kittler argues, "the real of bodies . . . necessarily slips through all the symbolic grids."[89] But the "real of bodies" can still be harnessed, corralled, put to use for symbolic purposes. Naremore states that "all acting has a biological dimension, and biology often contributes powerfully to theatrical effect—witness," he writes, "the many cases where film exploits the decay of celebrity players (Montgomery Clift's ravaged face in *Judgment at Nuremberg*)."[90]

It is not surprising that Naremore uses Clift as his model for visible cinematic suffering. As we have seen, nearly all of Clift's postaccident work calls attention to the conjunction of fiction and biography, if only in the form of double entendres: in *The Misfits* ("You would *too* recognize me") and the endless drunk scenes—in that film, *Wild River, Lonelyhearts,* the 1964 recording of *The Glass Menagerie,* and so on.

FIGURE 33. Lobby card for *Judgment at Nuremberg*, 1961: Clift (Peterson) on trial.

According to Naremore, "involuntary biological process is seldom performed outright"; a film "must place [the actor's] suffering in the context of a story, if only the story of the film itself."[91] In *Nuremberg*, Clift's injuries are appropriated for Peterson. The character becomes a grab bag of references to Clift's real-life tribulations—memory problems, brain damage, victim of a traumatic event that left the sufferer permanently altered—physically and emotionally scarred and helpless to do anything about it. Most poignant is the character's (and possibly the actor's) pathetic awareness of his inability to measure up.

Those who conflate actor and character like this, who read the scene as Clift's suffering on display rather than Peterson's, reduce Clift's choices as an actor to involuntary symptoms. Mercedes McCambridge, who worked with Clift on *Suddenly, Last Summer*, attributes Peterson's tremors and sweating to Clift's alcoholism. A recovering alcoholic, McCambridge diagnosed Clift in *Nuremberg* as suffering the d.t.'s. However, Clift performed many of the same gestures on the witness stand in *A Place in the Sun*, tightening his fists, flexing his fingers, pushing against the armrests with his elbows. In *Nuremberg*, these gestures are intensified. When Peterson rejects the prosecutor's insinuations about his mother's "hereditary feeble-mindedness," Clift flattens his hand and pushes it toward the camera as if fending off attack, his arm stiff and fully extended. "That is—it's *not* true! Not true. Not true." Defending his mother, he weaves in and out of repetition. "My mother. What you say about her. She was a woman—a servant woman who worked hard. She was a hard-working woman, and it is *not* fair! Not fair! What you say." As he repeats "Not fair!" he points his left index finger and slashes his arm away from himself for emphasis. (The same gesture appears to totally different effect in *Freud.* Experiencing a dizzy spell whenever he attempts to visit his father's grave, Clift's Freud slashes his index finger away from his body as he diagnoses himself: "These are neurotic symptoms.")

Peterson's gestures are emphatic, not neurotic, but combined with his broken syntax and repetition of sentence fragments, Clift clearly suggests in his performance that the character is not in control of himself. But the actor is. When we see the recurrence of these gestures across time and roles, before and after the accident, it seems reasonable to call them choices characteristic of the performer. Clift is not a mess; he plays one. His decision to act out of control coincides with characters who are under enormous stress, who have a great deal at stake (his life and reputation in *A Place in the Sun,* his father's death in *Freud,* his mother's reputation here) and who see themselves losing. (Another example is his loss of coherent speech when he pounds on the door at the end of *The Heiress.*) Contradicting the assumption that all actors want to be loved (rewriting scripts to make their characters admirable, likable, strong), it is part of Clift's integrity as an actor that he never minded revealing his characters' weaknesses (in fact, he often wanted to emphasize them, for instance in *The Search, The Heiress,* and *Lonelyhearts*). He also did not mind looking bad. Bosworth reports that he told a friend he was off "to get a 'very bad haircut'" before shooting began on *Judgment at Nuremberg.* "Monty believed the poor slob he was playing would get a special haircut before testifying against war criminals."[92] He also bought a badly fitting suit. Whenever Peterson places his arm on the chair's backrest, his suit bunches up around his shoulders and neck, making him look even more helpless, even less in control.

The comments Clift wrote on his copy of the script provide persuasive evidence of the degree of thought Clift put into this performance. Multiple copies of the script show that Clift was constantly revising the dialogue. He inserts short German phrases, excises explanations, simplifies the dialogue in keeping with the character's mental capacity, and alters the grammar to introduce mistakes. When Peterson explains how he first came into contact with the authorities, Abby Mann's script says, "I went to work on a farm. It was necessary for the work to drive a truck." Clift rewrites it in a way that makes it more jagged, less fluid, the grammar more German than English. "I got a job on a farm—but for the work—to drive a truck it was necessary."[93] (Like Emily Dickinson, Clift rarely uses a period when a dash will do, something that makes his dialogue seem livelier on the page and more conversational than the formal sentences in the script.) Asked by the authorities to name Hitler's birthday, the original script offers, "My reply was" (already far too formal for Peterson) "that I didn't know when and was not interested in it either." The penciled-in line is punchier: "I told them that I didn't know and I didn't care either."[94] Clift then crosses out an entire exchange regarding Goebbels's birthday. In Mann's version, Peterson says that his mother "died of heart disease"; Clift's Peterson says, "She died of her heart."[95] At his most emotional, when the defense attorney suggests that his mother was "feeble-minded," the speeches become shorter and shorter in Clift's emended script. The original line read, "My mother was a woman who worked hard all her life. It's not fair to say things about a woman like that. It's not fair."[96] In this revised version from November 1, 1960, Clift only crosses out the "It's" of "It's not fair." But by January 20, 1961, the whole section has been drastically reduced to "Not true. Not true." On the facing page, Clift pencils in the new version, adding repetition and incoherence. "My mother—My mother was a woman—a servant."[97] As Mann's character turns to the court with a clearly stated appeal, Clift inserts ungrammatical fragments instead. "I have her picture here with me" becomes "I have here her picture." "I would like to show it to the Tribunal" becomes "I want—I would like you looked at it."[98]

Asked to prove his mental competence by making a sentence out of the words *hare, hunter,* and *field,* Peterson becomes flustered, frustrated, and highly emotional. When the defense counsel points out that Peterson is not in control, Mann's character originally explains, "I am not! I know I am not! I never have been since that day! I have been half-paralyzed, half dead! But I wasn't like that before!" On his copy of the script, Clift starts refining, taking out "paralyzed" and crossing out words. Finally he crosses out every line except for "I am not! I know I am not!"[99] Evidently Clift was still not satisfied. There is a memo dated "Friday afternoon" addressed to "Monty." "Here is the verbatim transcript of the Second Take of 'Hare, Hunter, Field' you asked for." Evidently this part of the scene has already been shot twice, but Clift wants to go over it again. The dialogue in this take ended, "Since—since—since that day I haven't been half—I was."[100]

FIGURE 34. Spencer Tracy congratulating Clift at the end of a take in *Judgment at Nuremberg.* Allan Grant, Time & Life Pictures, Getty Images.

In the fourth version of the script (January 20, 1961), Clift wrote opposite the speech, "Since that day—I've been half I've ever been." In the film, it has been condensed even further.

Those who try to calibrate how much of Peterson is performance and how much is Clift inevitably zigzag back and forth, attributing this aspect to work, that one to symptom. Hoskyns weights the performance more toward Clift-as-actor, though "personal" attributes pop up in his description. Watching his performance as Peterson, Hoskyns argues, we see "a typically Cliftian insertion of genuine disturbance into the ponderous flow of what is effectively just another courtroom drama." To achieve the performance, however, Clift must win the struggle against himself. "Despite the huge, glassy eyes, with their only too obviously contracted pupils, he is very definitely *there,* with all his shrugs and flinches, his squirming distress, his touchingly uneasy smiles."[101] Director Stanley Kramer had no doubt that Clift's performance was a performance, though he too could not completely separate biography and work. "Monty was playing a man who was a little retarded and stumbling. Monty's condition gave the performance an aura as though it were being shot through muslin: the way the words tumbled out and the disjointed, sudden bursts of lucidity out of a mumble. It was classic!"[102]

One reason the linkage of biology and character in *Nuremberg* is especially unsettling is that the role isn't really about the character's face. Just as an early scene in *Red River* calls on us to imagine Clift being branded on the rump like a steer, this scene is built around the audience in and out of the film imagining the state of Clift's character's genitals—as inadequate, damaged, marred. The crime of which Peterson has been a victim is a court-ordered castration. The opposite of that old confidence-builder "imagine your audience naked," Peterson presents himself to be looked at by people who are speculating about the "inferior" condition of his masculinity. Humiliation is unavoidable. As Thomas Leitch says about Logan in *I Confess,* "The scrutiny to which he is subjected is obscene."[103]

Peterson's loss or lack becomes the basis of the struggle between prosecution and defense, with the hostile defense attorney (Maximilian Schell) implying that Peterson's castration is no great loss because he is "feeble-minded" anyway. When Peterson attempts to describe the trauma ("I had to lie there, like an animal"), Schell asserts, "We don't know how you were before." But the audience knows what *Clift* was like. When close-ups of Clift are intercut with close-ups of the highly polished Schell, it only reminds us that Clift was that handsome once, even more handsome perhaps. Peterson/Clift acknowledges how much he has lost: "Since that day—I'm *half*—I've ever been." One could say the same of Clift, or imagine him saying it to himself.

Earlier, a 180-degree shot invites prolonged scrutiny of Clift's features as the camera circles around him in a medium close-up, traveling from his right profile around the back of his head, calling attention to the four- or five-inch scar visible beneath his jawline. (As we have seen, this scar dates from Clift's childhood and had nothing to do with the accident. It is invoked in *The Big Lift* when Clift's character pretends to be a wounded German war veteran who can no longer speak. It is also easily visible in a scene in *A Place in the Sun* when he is sitting in a convertible with Elizabeth Taylor shortly before he is arrested.) In the long tracking shots around Clift/Peterson, we can also detect a scar across the middle of his nose, and make note of his left eyebrow, bushy and wild, out of control (especially in the last shot). Clift's face is the stand-in—damaged, scarred, there for all to see—that signals a physical trauma that can be neither shown nor undone.

The logic that offers Clift's broken face as proof of Peterson's castration poses a threat to Clift as an artist. When his appearance is read as a collection of inherent physical traits rather than as the result of conscious artistic decisions, Clift's performance, his work as an actor, disappears. Clift, like Peterson, presents himself to the public, knowing he will be judged hopelessly marred by comparison to his past self.

There is also a distinct threat in terms of sexual identity. In *Nuremberg,* the violence directed toward Peterson puts the matter in the starkest terms. With the revelation of Peterson's literal castration, the film presents an ominous portrait of the social forces that can be brought to bear on an individual. This is what "the law" can do to you. Peterson recounts how fascist thugs in the street became city officials, the courts ratified their authority by appeal to supposedly neutral laws, and the medical community carried out the assault through scientific, surgical means. Peterson's dysfunctional sexuality is not a sign of self-destructive behavior or neuroses, it has been imposed on him by a hostile world. He has been martyred in sexual terms.

Clift's performance in *Judgment at Nuremberg* was well received for the most part (it marks his last Oscar nomination), but its extremes make it a take-it-or-leave-it performance. More than any other character, Peterson requires the viewer to choose between Clift-as-performer and Clift-as-victim, the remnants of a shattered life on display.

Let the martyrdom begin.

SIX

A Gay Martyr

MANY OF CLIFT'S ROLES point to the danger of sexuality of any kind.[1] His characters' sexual relationships with women rarely turn out well. In *The Heiress*, he is outsmarted by a woman he had conned earlier. In *The Big Lift*, he is taken in by a duplicitous schemer. In *A Place in the Sun*, sexual longing leads him to the electric chair. In *I Confess*, the character's potential for sexual activity in the past is used against him. He is arrested and then has his heart broken in *Indiscretion of an American Wife*, and he meets mostly frustration and misunderstandings with a dance-club hostess before his death in *From Here to Eternity*. Heterosexuality does not become easier in his later films: in *Raintree County*, he marries the intense but insane Elizabeth Taylor and ends up in an unpersuasive, uncomfortable détente with Eva Marie Saint, a state of affairs that applies equally to his relationships with other wholesome blondes, including Hope Lange in *The Young Lions*, Lee Remick in *Wild River*, and Dolores Hart in *Lonelyhearts*. Repeatedly his character is presented as jokily inadequate: in *Wild River* and *Lonelyhearts*, he is often too beaten up, drunk, or hungover even to think about consummating a relationship. When healthy and sober, he is elusive; the women pursue him. In *The Misfits*, his character has half a dozen reasons why he cannot respond "properly" to Marilyn Monroe—alcohol, painkillers, bruised ribs, possible concussion . . . pick a reason. As soon as Monroe conclusively shifts her attentions to Clark Gable, Clift's Perce stops drinking. He can relax and be a friend because there will be no more embarrassing, unspoken demands.

FIGURE 35. Lobby card for *Suddenly, Last Summer,* 1959: Clift (Cuckrowicz) and Taylor (Cathy).

Little wonder, then, that it is such a relief when the typical Clift character stops trying so hard and becomes someone for whom sexuality is not a central motive. In *I Confess, Freud,* and *Suddenly, Last Summer,* his characters are asexual by profession; in *The Search* (fortunately), sexual desire isn't an issue at all. In his asexual roles, Clift no longer has to either pass or hide.

In these films, Clift's characters are fully present for those around them, deeply engaged with their lives, sensitive to their problems. There is an emotional contact, love even, that is not simply the product of desire. Even in a historical romance like *Raintree County,* Clift's character moves away from romance and sexual desire and into what will become his familiar "listening" mode as his wife's mental illness worsens. As a priest or doctor in these films, heterosexual desire is as restricted as homosexuality. Sexual activity of any kind would not only be unethical, it would constitute a betrayal and an assault. In terms of refraining from sexually exploiting women and children, Clift's characters are exemplary, completely trustworthy, integrity personified.

In this collection of films, celibacy is preferable to an uneasy heterosexuality. The third possibility—a positive, untroubled homosexuality—is barred, not least by the Production Code. There are moments, however, when Clift is so open (his body literally relaxed into an unfolded posture) we can almost glimpse what a performance of an unself-conscious, un-closeted gay relationship might be like. The most notable of these rare moments would be his relaxed, teasing exchanges with John Ireland (Cherry) and his deeper connection with John Wayne in *Red River*, and the way he enjoys Stieber's tales of how to live a guilt-free double life in postwar Berlin in *The Big Lift*. This happiness does not last, for many reasons, and the repudiation of active sexuality becomes the favored option in Clift's later films.

In his last two leading roles Clift is no longer cast as the "boyish" young man. In *Suddenly, Last Summer* and *Freud*, he plays adults, doctors brought in to resolve the mayhem and madness produced when social structures are upended by sexuality. Despite their regulatory function, neither of these men promotes patriarchal or conservative solutions. Instead of presenting themselves as voices of authority, Clift's doctors listen. Caught between "hysterical" women, gay men, dictatorial bosses, and overwhelming mothers, Clift's doctors are supportive but not gullible, demanding but not exploitative, calm without being indifferent, critical and sympathetic in equal measure. In the process, Clift redefines masculinity, once again, in a way that appeals to both men and women, and attracts feminist and queer readings.

Coming toward the end of his career, both films feature endless echoes of earlier work. In *Freud*, Clift interviews one of his former selves, asking a male patient under hypnosis, "You row to the middle of the lake. What happens then?" The compulsive rower, racked with guilt, tells the iconic story: "I stand up. The boat rocks. I'm falling. The boat turns over. I'm in the water." While he searches for his brother rather than *A Place in the Sun's* Alice, the result is the same. "I swim 'round the boat but I can't find him. My brother's gone. Drowned."

There is a scene in *I Confess* that foreshadows the climax of *Suddenly, Last Summer*. Logan is acquitted by the jury but the judge publicly questions the verdict, once more casting Logan's innocence into doubt. Bearing the weight of the public's suspicion and resentment, Logan walks out of the courtroom and into a hallway. Hissed by bystanders, he hurries down a winding staircase, going down and down, past hostile eyes, until he emerges into the street. The street is blocked by a sea of faces, among them "a group of rough-looking young men leaning like vultures over the roof of an automobile."[2]

This silent confrontation is foreshadowed earlier in the film when Logan finds himself face-to-face with an unsettling group of young men. Leaving the police at Villette's house, where the body has just been found, Logan sees four or five young men lolling about across the street. He hesitates as they (visually and metaphorically) block his path. Photographed from behind, Logan suddenly turns right and exits, avoiding a showdown. When we see them again later in the film, their number and hostility have been magnified. This time, Logan cannot turn away. He has to move forward. Why? As Truffaut says, Logan's walking "concretizes his integrity." He must go on. But Logan's will, his refusal to retreat or avoid confrontation, is not enough to allay the tension. As he ploughs through the crowd trying to get to a waiting car, the mob (almost exclusively male) erupts, crushing in on him as if to destroy him.

In *Suddenly, Last Summer,* made six years later, this scene is reenacted, but with every aspect reversed. In contrast to Logan's long trek down the interior courthouse stairs, the character of Sebastian runs "up and up" a winding Spanish hillside lined with empty white walls, indifferent old women, and the occasional skeleton. Logan wears black, Sebastian white. Where Logan steps out of the courthouse to face a sea of young men, Sebastian (played by a man whose face we never see) arrives at an empty open space at the apex of his journey. The mob that Logan faces is silent and unmoving; Sebastian is being chased by a group of boys who play raucous "music." At the film's climax Sebastian is torn apart, devoured like a perverse sacrificial meal. As Logan tries to get through the crowd to a cab, the mob becomes agitated and begins to swallow him up. In each case, the man's peril is witnessed by a woman, his life and reputation dependent on her ability to speak the truth and make herself heard.

Joseph Mankiewicz's adaptation of Tennessee Williams's Southern Gothic play was the surprise hit of the 1959 Christmas season, despite the fact that the most passionate responses to the film were negative.[3] One critic called it a sewer. Williams himself reportedly disliked the film so much he threw up when he saw it.[4] Recently, though, the film has found champions in the field of queer studies. Richard Kaye calls *Suddenly, Last Summer* "the apotheosis of Eisenhower-era camp sensibility."[5] D. A. Miller and Kevin Ohi clearly appreciate the sublime absurdity of the film's most intense moments, but their work also addresses the "queer logic" behind the film's overheated mix of religion, homosexuality, medical science, poetry, Darwinian musings, and hysteria.[6] As producer Sam Spiegel quipped, a dash of incest, rape, sodomy, and cannibalism never hurt at the box office.[7]

FIGURE 36. (a) Frame grab from *I Confess:* Logan descending. (b) Frame grab from *Suddenly, Last Summer:* Sebastian ascending.

Religion, homosexuality, Darwin, and Melville are all topics of interest for Sebastian Venable, a poet who saw the face of God while retracing Melville's trip to the Encantadas. The enigmatic figure around whom the narrative revolves, Sebastian is dead when the film begins. Never represented directly in the image, never present as himself, Sebastian exists as the product of other characters' words and their fragmented visual memories. All of the characters define and reveal themselves by the way they relate (or relate to) Sebastian's story.

A tug-of-war over who gets to define Sebastian—to say what happened "suddenly, last summer"—takes place between two women: his mother, Violet (Katharine Hepburn), and his cousin, Catherine (Elizabeth Taylor). Catherine has returned from the trip abroad during which Sebastian died. "Babbling" horrifying and unbelievable accounts of what happened, she has been confined to an asylum. Sebastian's mother, Violet Venable, offers a large donation to a local hospital if they will give Cathy a lobotomy to prevent her from tarnishing Sebastian's reputation. Clift, as Dr. Cuckrowicz, plays the part of medical science, adjudicating the women's competing claims, determining who will be heard and whose story will be held to be true. An allegedly neutral observer, Dr. Cuckrowicz is dispassionate, receptive, critical. Introduced as a brain surgeon performing lobotomies in "primitive" conditions (the film is set in the 1930s), he has forsaken surgery by the end of the film in favor of the talking cure (with an assist from psycho-pharmaceuticals such as sodium pentathol).

The figure of the "listener" is a type that would come to be a speciality for Clift in the second half of his career. In these roles, the male character's professional disinterest is tempered with warmth, concern, and compassion in place of a more predictable sexual or romantic goal. Such qualities are precisely what Cathy says she appreciated about her cousin Sebastian. Like Cuckrowicz, Sebastian seems to have been a man who enjoyed the company of women. This is what made him an appealing alternative to the rapacious heterosexual men who have victimized Cathy, the southern debutante. (She was raped by a married man after a dance and has been sexually harassed by a gardener and a mob of lust-crazed inmates at the convent/mental hospital to which she has been confined.) Because they do not make sexual demands, Sebastian and Cuckrowicz express their pleasure in women by their willingness to listen. The first half of *Suddenly, Last Summer* consists for the most part of Clift listening to Katharine Hepburn, and the second half of him listening to Elizabeth Taylor.

All of Clift's "listener" roles disrupt the usual Hollywood depiction of male-female relations through the characters' rejection of mandatory heterosexual behavior. Of course, each listener has a cover story to soften the radical nature of his refusal. Father Logan's celibacy is mandated by the church; Doctors Freud and Cuckrowicz's refusal to respond sexually to female patients is required by professional ethics. The characters' fundamental heterosexuality can be taken for granted, with the absence of action presented as a positive sign of self-control. On the other hand, Sebastian's attentiveness to his mother and cousin is exposed eventually as a cloak for a different kind of rapaciousness, and his relationships with women exploitative in a different way. Sebastian not only problematizes the issue of Clift's characters' motives for not sexually pursuing women, his character raises the possibility that the real reason for heterosexual reticence may be homosexual desire.

Both *I Confess* and *Suddenly, Last Summer* revolve around the mystery of one character's identity—who is he really, beneath the socially acceptable surface? In both films the key to identity is posited as sexual, and flashbacks are used to reveal the purported "truth" of the male character's sexuality.[8] In *I Confess* the flashback reveals Logan's supposedly free expression of his heterosexual desire as he kisses Ruth in rapturously soft-focus medium-shots. Our confidence in this representation is undermined as we become aware that Logan's passion is part of the interpretive template Ruth has imposed on the past through her selective memory. If Sebastian is presented at all in *Suddenly, Last Summer,* it is as a figure half-seen, glimpsed fleetingly in Cathy's drug-induced flashback. While Logan's presence is proclaimed by numerous close-ups of his face, Sebastian's face is never seen. All we see are isolated body parts or a man's back. (Queer theorist D. A. Miller has a field day with this, as discussed below.)

Like Logan, Sebastian has been displaced from his own story by the very women who tell it. Logan's refusal of heterosexual activity is silenced by Ruth; Sebastian's active homosexuality is presented as unspeakable *especially,* it seems, for heterosexual women. Sebastian's mother wants Dr. Cuckrowicz to "cut the memory" of Sebastian's sexuality "out of [Cathy's] brain." Violet is willing to kill to keep Sebastian's secret. Cathy, suicidal early in the film, is willing to die rather than remember. Both go mad. Sexually rejected, they are women scorned, and it drives them insane. But why? In Clift's life, it was men who were most violent in their reactions to his homosexuality (except for Jennifer Jones, who, according to Truman Capote, had a nervous breakdown and threw a fur coat down a toilet when she learned that Clift was gay).[9] In this film, however, male homosexuality is supposedly a threat to a woman's very sanity. In his article on *Suddenly, Last Summer,* "Visual Pleasure in 1959," D. A. Miller offers an explanation. As women tell the story of male homosexuality, they erase their own existence.

In Miller's reading of the film, Cathy is merely "a device for giving utterance to the story of Sebastian."[10] Her image is subsumed by Sebastian,

Cathy being presented at times "literally as her cousin's figurehead."[11] (In another essay on the film, Kevin Ohi literalizes this metaphor when he says, "the film seems at times to co-star Elizabeth Taylor's breasts, which, crammed into the most improbable dresses, often quite literally precede her.")[12] Despite being extravagantly female and helplessly heterosexual, Cathy nevertheless cannot hold her ground, cannot defend the value of, or express, her own subjectivity. Her body, Miller argues, "is implicated in male homosexuality not merely as its sign . . . but as its very evidence."[13] Because of the editing of the last sequence (what Miller calls "the logic of succession that has introduced her"), "her figure can't help appearing an equivalence for the gay male object-choice."[14] The exaggerated presentation of Elizabeth Taylor's body is not enough to establish Cathy as a subject, present as herself. Even when Cathy/Taylor's figure is most on display (on her knees wearing the bathing suit that was supposed to have become transparent in water according to her narration, but doesn't in the image), Miller still finds "the male homosexual . . . mysteriously present under the perfectly unaltered luscious appearances of a woman's body."[15] Twenty years later, Miller tells us, fashion designer Calvin Klein "design[ed] for himself a 'flesh-colored charmeuse swimsuit that turned translucent when it got wet.'" "It is still impossible to say," he concludes, whether Klein was "copying Cathy's famous bathing suit, or finally explicating it: trying to be this woman or revealing her to have always already been a gay man."[16]

The film's narrative logic demands that we see Cathy as Sebastian's stand-in. The story she tells about her trip to Cabeza de Lobo with her cousin "last summer" begins with Sebastian using her body to lure young men for his sexual satisfaction. "Consider," Miller asks, "the striking paradox, contradicting common sense and practical experience alike, that we are here being asked to accept: through their sexual attraction to a woman who looks exactly like Elizabeth Taylor, a town's whole population of toughs turns queer."[17] Cabeza de Lobo—where *la dolce vita* meets *la vida loca*.

Not only is Catherine's body not hers, functioning as a sign of something radically other, her physical existence as a woman is an obstacle. When she finally begins to tell the climactic story, she is both a sign and a screen. Miller comments, "If her voice could once successfully channel what the play's enigmatic narrative structure made us want to know, her body is now in the way of what [the film] . . . has made us want to see. No longer satisfied with her epistemology of the closet, we demand the plein-air gay pornography of which she is blocking our view!"[18] "Isn't that what everybody wants," Cathy asks earlier, "me out of the way?"

As Cathy narrates what happened last summer, her image progressively becomes a close-up, a head pushed to the edges of the frame while her "body is required to fade from the narrative." At times her image becomes transparent, dissolving away "much as saintly apparitions are said to do." Reduced to a mere voice, like Echo, the woman is "without substance."[19] Sebastian, on the other hand, is exclusively visual, but instead of being a face, as Miller points out, there is "the famous fact that [he] is shown only from the back."[20]

While Miller sees the dissolves as merging "Cathy's Front" with "Sebastian's Behind" to form the "Gay Male Woman" ("a crossbreeder weirder than anything dreamt of in Mendel: half woman, half gay man"),[21] to me, the images reproduced by Miller actually support Kevin Ohi's take on the film: a swooning Taylor, mouth half-open, gives us an image of "ecstatic orality."[22] In "Devouring Creation: Cannibalism, Sodomy, and the Scene of Analysis in *Suddenly, Last Summer*," Ohi describes the film as "relentlessly oral." Cathy recounts "Sebastian's obsessively oral metaphors for sex: boys are 'delicious' or 'not delicious,' Sebastian becomes 'famished for blondes' [sic]."[23]

The film's obsession with orality takes many forms, especially in reference to the compulsive speaking of the women in the film. Both Catherine and Sebastian's mother, Violet, give long, vivid descriptions of scenes in which victims are "devoured." In her morbid garden filled with carnivorous plants, Mrs. Venable describes a moment with Sebastian in the Encantadas when they saw "the hatching of the sea turtles [spawn] a feeding frenzy."[24] "The sky was in motion," Violet intones, "full of flesh-eating birds [with] their horrible savage cries. . . . They were diving down on the sea turtles, turning them over to expose their soft undersides, tearing their undersides open, and rending and eating their flesh." (This monologue is the highlight of what Miller describes as the film's "insane Darwinism." In Clift's script, the actor has written one word next to this speech: "SHIT.")[25]

Motherhood is also depicted as devouring, as demonstrated by the very structure of Violet's long speeches. As Ohi points out, "Mrs. Venable's language grows out of a . . . nonregenerative recursive structure. . . . Her lines turn back on themselves. . . . 'We were a famous couple. People didn't speak of Sebastian and his mother or Mrs. Venable and her son. No, they said, Sebastian and Violet, Violet and Sebastian.' . . . The recursive structure of Mrs. Venable's speech, emphasized by Hepburn's inimitable delivery, connects the madness of Mrs. Venable's obsessive motherhood to the 'devouring creation' linked to sodomy and cannibalism."[26] The equivalence of cannibalism and sodomy demonstrates the film's "confusion of orifices," a confusion of "the oral and anal pleasure of gay sex."[27] (Ohi does not address the assumption that gay sex alone involves oral and anal pleasure.)

The film's "ecstatic orality" achieves the status of "sodomitical rapture" not in what we see of Sebastian's death, but in Cathy's telling of it. Finally able to speak the unspeakable, Cathy's language begins to resemble Mrs. Venable's in its repetition and compulsive forward momentum. "He—he was lying naked, on the broken stones. And this you won't believe. Nobody, nobody, nobody could believe it. It looked as if—as if they had devoured him. As if they had torn or cut parts of him away with their hands or with knives or those jagged tin cans they made music with. As if they had torn bits of him away and stuffed them into those gobbling mouths."[28]

The speech is bracketed by opposites. At the beginning Catherine says, "I heard Sebastian scream. He screamed just once." After his death, she recounts, "There wasn't sound any more. There was nothing." In the beginning "Cousin Sebastian" is "lying naked on the broken stones"; at the end Cathy finds "Sebastian, Sebastian, lying on those stones, torn and crushed." Catherine's speech culminates in this description of the cannibalized and/or sodomized body, marking what Ohi calls "the concrete appearance of this figure in its mute and lurid materiality."[29]

For Ohi, both Violet's disquisition on nature's brutality as the true face of God and Catherine's description of Sebastian being chased, overtaken, and devoured indulge "the fascinating allure of taboo" as appetite leads to cannibalism and cannibalism serves as "a figure for gay male sex."[30]

If Catherine is merely a conduit for the story of Sebastian, a surrogate or screen for the real thing (gay sex), it is hard to imagine what women could find to enjoy in the film except its camp delirium, epitomized by the performances of its female stars. While Ohi ridicules Taylor's body and Miller erases Catherine altogether, Taylor's Catherine is essential when it comes to Tennessee Williams's zeal for proclaiming the truth about sexuality. In *Cat on a Hot Tin Roof,* released a year before *Suddenly, Last Summer,* Taylor fulfills a similar function. As Maggie, she is accused of being a failure as a woman, specifically of failing her husband sexually. As her mother-in-law tells her, when a marriage is on the rocks, "the rocks are here" (slapping the marital bed). But Maggie refuses to accept the blame and instead insists on speaking the truth—that her husband Brick either loved/ desired his best friend, Skipper (who has committed suicide), or that (in the movie version) her husband refuses to accept that Skipper loved/desired him. Maggie's argument, like Joanne Dru's in *Red River* (only without the shotgun), is, "just admit that you love each other." Neither censorious nor judgmental, Maggie, like Catherine, is exhausted from wasting so much time fighting the "mendacity" of people who won't face a simple fact. In both these films it is Taylor's character who—*as a woman*—insists on two things. The first is that homosexuality be recognized. Violet tries to eliminate any sexuality, insisting that Sebastian was "chaste." "Do you mean celibate?" Cuckrowicz asks. "Do you believe that he never—?" Violet: "Yes, never. As strictly as if he'd taken a vow." Second, Catherine insists that homosexuality—like any sexuality—is not inherently positive and can be perverted through violence or exploitation. As a woman, she has suffered the consequences of a socially mandated closeting of sexuality, the obfuscation and the lies, the impossibility of saying what she knows or of telling the truth about her own experience. It is important to remember that Catherine is not only telling Sebastian's story—she is telling her own. Unlike Maggie the cat, though, Catherine has an ally.

Cuckrowicz navigates the pressures brought to bear by the wealthy Mrs. Venable and his supervisor, the hospital administrator, patiently running interference as he leads "Miss Catherine" to the point where she can (and does) say everything. Why Cuckrowicz does this, who he is as a character, is harder to get at because of the subtlety—and simplicity—of Clift's performance.

There are three key aspects to Dr. Cuckrowicz's character, all having to do with speech. When we first meet him, his face is covered by a surgical mask, which directs attention toward his words rather than his appearance. After performing brain surgery in what looks like an old library with empty bookshelves, rickety railings, and unreliable lighting, Cuckrowicz snaps off his surgical gloves and denounces the conditions in no uncertain terms. (The film is supposed to be set in 1937, but the women's clothes, hats, shoes, and handbags contradict it.) Storming into the office of the head of the hospital (Albert Dekker), Cuckrowicz cuts off Hockstader's apologies and excuses, drowning him out and standing his ground. Laying down the law, Cuckrowicz establishes that he has high standards and will fight for what he believes in. For Cuckrowicz, fighting takes the form of speaking his mind.

When he speaks to women, though, his demeanor is dramatically different. At first, both Violet and Catherine interrupt him at will, each desperate to establish her perspective on the situation. When Cuckrowicz does speak, it is in a supportive way often associated with the way women speak. He makes brief interjections rather than declarative statements ("Yes?" "And after that?" "Go on," "Tell me about it") or repeats the last few words spo-

FIGURE 37. Taylor and Clift in separate dressing rooms while making *Suddenly,*
Last Summer. Burt Glinn, Magnum Photos.

ken to him. These are all methods used to prolong communication and to
signal that one is listening. An active listener, Cuckrowicz watches the
speaker, which makes him seem interested, concentrating, respectful. (In
the script, Clift notes that at one moment Cuckrowicz's and Catherine's
"EYES LOCK" [written in caps] and draws a padlock below.)

The only time Cuckrowicz interrupts women or takes a harsh tone is when
he is speaking out against an abuse of power. When an officious nun tries
to silence Catherine and remove her after an emotional breakdown (a communication breakthrough), Cuckrowicz snaps loudly, "Sister, get out of here.
Get out and don't come back till I call you." He is also more forceful with
Violet Venable when it becomes clear that her interests are at odds with
Catherine's well-being.

There is a pallid attempt to provide Dr. Cuckrowicz with a (hetero)sexual
motive for helping Catherine. In the script there is a comically melodramatic moment when Hockstader threatens to remove him from the case.
Cuckrowicz was supposed to say "(desperately): No! Don't . . . don't do that!
Not yet." In his copy of the script, Clift rewrites the line in a way that is
more consistent with Cuckrowicz's alpha-dog demeanor toward his boss.
"Do that," he retorts, daring Hockstader to cross him. This exchange has

been cut from the film. Now when Hockstader walks in on Catherine and Cuckrowicz in an embrace, he barely reacts and says nothing.

Catherine kisses Cuckrowicz twice. The first time, in the convent/asylum, she impulsively gives him a quick kiss on the lips, but then begins berating herself for having done something that will make her look libidinously insane. As Cathy asserts that she should not have done it, Clift/Cuckrowicz casually leans back on his heels, says in a reassuring tone, "Why not? It was a friendly kiss, wasn't it?" and smiles kindly. Before the climactic scene in which Catherine will reveal all, she asks Cuckrowicz to hold her. "Hold me. I've been so lonely." Because of the contrast with his dark suit, we focus on Catherine's arms, in long white sleeves, embracing the doctor. Moving her hands to his face, she asks (mirroring Maureen Stapleton's character in *Lonelyhearts*), "Let me. Let me," as she begins to kiss him feverishly. Throughout this exchange, Clift/Cuckrowicz stays still, not embracing her in return or responding noticeably to the kiss. In both cases, he does not pull away or reject her either; he is receptive but not intrusive. He does not introduce his own desire into the situation or reprimand Catherine for expressing hers.

The final sign of Cuckrowicz's attitude about speech occurs when he insists that *others* listen. As Cuckrowicz is establishing the conditions that will allow Catherine to face and speak the truth, Violet tries to discredit her on the matter of a detail. Cuckrowicz, inoculating Catherine from criticism or doubt, says flatly, "Whatever she wants to say, I want her to say it." He moves a chair and sits directly in front of her, focused on her every word. A man of integrity, indifferent to pressure and devoted to the truth, he shows Catherine how to be the same.

As Violet and Cathy struggle for control of the memory and image of Sebastian, where does that leave Cuckrowicz or, as Violet calls him, "Dr. Sugar"? (The name *Cuckrowicz* is said to mean "sugar." Is he going to be dessert?) Both Violet and Cathy confuse him with Sebastian—Cathy "confuses the doctor with the 'items' on Sebastian's 'menu': 'This one's eyes are so blue,'"[31] while Mrs. Venable, when she goes mad, addresses the doctor as if he were her son, ascending through the top of the frame in her private elevator in the film's last shot.

If Logan descending the stairs in *I Confess* can be seen as the mirror image of Sebastian's last journey, Cuckrowicz is another Sebastian twin. Ohi points out that "the film pairs him with Sebastian: in the oblique shots of [Sebastian], he looks remarkably like the doctor, who shares his penchant for the color white and whose looks and dedication to his 'art' remind Mrs. Venable of her son." This association brings with it the "taint of homosexuality," even though "Sebastian's 'homosexuality' is assumed even as it is never explicitly articulated." Ohi argues that despite "the doctor's professional and desexualized altruism," Cuckrowicz "cannot simply distance himself from Sebastian by desiring Catherine, for to thus assure himself of his heterosexuality would be to take Sebastian's bait" (i.e., Catherine, Miller's "Gay Male Woman").[32]

The other shadowy gay figure Cuckrowicz cannot avoid being paired with is Montgomery Clift. Ohi suggests that if Cuckrowicz is "perhaps the character whose desire most needs to be straightened out," it is in no small part because of the star's persona.[33] "That the good doctor was played by Montgomery Clift, whose oddly blank and unreadable allure in the film is . . . generated in part by his aura of sexual ambiguity and by his status as a gay icon, is no doubt significant."[34] Assumptions about Clift's sexuality are not restricted to the post-LaGuardia or Bosworth period. Ohi quotes an especially nasty review of the film that appeared in *Time* magazine in January 1960: "Dr. Clift, whose gestures have in recent years been more and more reduced to twitches, sometimes looks even queerer than his patient." ("Queer" had its antigay meaning in 1960—indeed, that usage dates in the United States to the 1920s. But in 1960, it held enough of its other meaning of "strange" or "weird" to allow *Time* simultaneously to insinuate homosexuality and disavow doing so.) "The logic of this (twitchy) formulation," Ohi points out, "is a bit evasive, confounding, among other distinctions, the doctor's and the actor's 'art.' . . . Also interesting is the slippage between Clift, Dr. Cuckrowicz, Catherine, and Sebastian—who is queerer than whom?"[35]

With his own desires left unspecified, Cuckrowicz becomes one of a series of figures who endlessly reflect one another. Cuckrowicz is mistaken for Sebastian by those who knew Sebastian best, and Cuckrowicz is played by Clift. A professional listener, Cuckrowicz is like Logan and moves closer and closer to being like Freud. Critics from 1960 (*Time*) to 1999 (Ohi) suggest that the secrets of Sebastian's life might actually be explained by stories about Clift. Like Sebastian, Clift's youth was characterized by endless travel abroad with a suffocatingly close mother. Like Clift, a key sign of Sebastian's ailment is ocular. "He wasn't well. His eyes looked dazed," Cathy says of Sebastian, though she could just as easily be describing Clift. Sebastian was endlessly "popping little white pills"—another phrase that applies equally to Clift.[36] Ultimately, Catherine recounts the true nature of the calamity that struck Sebastian as devastatingly as it did Clift. "Suddenly, last summer, he wasn't young anymore."

One more figure slip-slides through this nexus of Logan-Sebastian-Cuckrowicz-Freud-Clift. Sebastian is identified early in the film with a large reproduction of Botticelli's 1474 painting of Saint Sebastian pierced with arrows. In "Losing His Religion: Saint Sebastian as Contemporary Gay Martyr," Richard A. Kaye explores the legacy of representations of Sebastian. "For a myth to prove as resilient as a cultural narrative as that of Sebastian, it must generate broad, multiple, and even contradictory meanings."[37] Like Clift, Saint Sebastian can be seen as simultaneously a religious figure and a gay icon.

Images of martyrs present the body as the spirit made legible. In the midst of the most vivid suffering, the saint's face remains beatific, transcendent, the promise of the spirit conveyed through the body. Paintings of Saint Sebastian are the ultimate examples of this triumph of beauty over pain, death, and decay. Above all, Sebastian is young, preserved forever by an early death. Because he survived his horrific accident and years of abusing his health, youth was something Clift could not maintain.

The archetypal Saint Sebastian was established in the fourteenth and fifteenth centuries.[38] Botticelli presents Sebastian as a bare-chested, pretty young man with curly hair and a calm manner. Instead of suffering, this saint could best be described as preoccupied, lost in thought, hardly troubled by the six arrows sticking out of his body, one in his inner thigh. In one scene, Cuckrowicz stands directly beneath a larger-than-life copy of this painting in Sebastian's studio.

Throughout the Renaissance the location and number of arrows varied, as did the saint's reaction to them. Mantegna's Sebastian (1459) has an arrow piercing his chin and coming out his forehead. He keeps his eyes cast heavenward, but frowns as if he has a really bad headache. In this painting there are fourteen arrows altogether. Often, an arrow has lodged under the saint's loincloth, pointing upward. This placement is not unusual, nor are compositions that depict the martyr as seductive or erotic. In the late fifteenth century Perugino presents his Sebastian in a sexy little loincloth, nearly transparent and worn provocatively low, his genitals perceptible through the fabric. A soft, white youth with upturned eyes, this Sebastian's arms are tied behind his back, the better to broaden his chest and display his hairless feminine torso with its tiny nipples and decorative assortment of arrows. Such images have provided the foundation for endless erotic fantasy. According to Richard Kaye, each of these images "provides the opportunity for an unobstructed, unmediated erotization." The presentation of "an ecstatically self-preoccupied nude male . . . grant[s] erotic permission . . . paradoxically, to every viewer."[39]

Perhaps the most frequently reproduced depiction of Saint Sebastian is Guido Reni's dark martyr of 1615. Muscular but young, with full, bow-shaped lips and quizzical eyes raised to God, his arms are tied above his head, his muscles bulging under his pale skin as an arrow pierces one armpit, another jutting out from under his ribs. Reni's painting is perhaps the archetypal image of Saint Sebastian.[40] More than any other, it is this rendition that came to epitomize the late nineteenth century's "shift from a stress on homosexual *acts* to an emphasis on homosexual *identity*."[41] This is the painting Oscar Wilde was referring to when he first conferred a gay identity on the saint (later taking the name Sebastian to travel incognito after his release from prison). In the film *Mishima* (1985), this is also the image that instantly awakens the sexuality of Japanese novelist Yukio Mishima as a boy, an event described in his autobiographical *Confessions of a Mask* (1949).[42] In these instances, paintings of Sebastian do more than display a legible homosexuality; they speak to and arouse homosexuality in others.

As "eroticized religious hero," Saint Sebastian has become "simultaneously sacred and heretical."[43] The tension in the paintings stretches between the saint's casual stance and the pain indicated by the biting arrows. At all times, though, his face is untroubled—an expression that can be read as transcendent at best or (at worst) bored. Either way, "the martyr's self-absorbed detachment . . . is a fundamental aspect of his intricate mythology."[44] By the last part of the twentieth century, "the martyr's classic poses of exquisite satisfaction and pained detachment" had become comic, part of "the camp dimension so integral to Sebastian's appeal."[45]

The scandal of representations of Saint Sebastian lies not only in his gay or "polymorphously perverse" erotic appeal, but also in the unsettling fact that his suffering so frequently crosses the line into ecstasy.[46] For Kaye, "the archetypal Renaissance image of the saint as *ecstatically receptive* to arrows suggests, of course, a desire for penetration and thus embraces associations of male homosexuality. The penetrated (and therefore feminized) male in the Renaissance paintings of Saint Sebastian is, significantly, a figure of *visibly triumphant bliss*."[47]

By the late nineteenth century, bliss no longer needed to be read; it was openly proclaimed. In the Debussy-D'Annunzio opera *The Martyrdom of Saint Sebastian*, the saint (played by a woman) cries out as he is being shot full of arrows, "Encore! Encore!"[48] (A similar effect [the blurring of ecstasy and suffering] is produced by Bernini in his sculpture of Saint Teresa, another ecstatic figure pierced by a confusion of arrows and eros.)

The saint occupies a field of representation familiar from Clift's films. Like Sebastian, Clift has been read as "camp token, political comrade, or patron saint." And lest we forget, Sebastian was a soldier—captain of the Roman archers, in fact. Clift plays soldiers or returning veterans in a third of his films. Like Sebastian the saint, Clift in his early films could be described as "alluringly ambiguous," an "exquisite, beardless youth of Apollonian beauty."[49] When one combines the ritualized physical punishments he is subjected to in *Red River, From Here to Eternity, The Young Lions,* and other films, with the widespread knowledge of his offscreen physical pain after the accident, Clift can be said to share "the soldier Sebastian's aura of morbid sensuality."[50] If we add the nonmilitarized instances of public mortification *(Lonelyhearts, Wild River, The Defector),* it would be safe to read a Clift character as possessing what Faulkner, in another context, calls "the voluptuous ego of the martyr."[51] Kaye argues that "while generations of men of homosexual inclinations have understood Sebastian as a homoeroticized icon, for others he has denoted a homosexual eros that is *menacingly narcissistic and suicidal in kind.*"[52]

As poet Richard Howard warns in a poem about Kafka being asked to pose for a painting of Saint Sebastian: "Don't pose as a saint or you might become one."[53] The frenzied murder of Sebastian Venable, *Suddenly, Last Summer*'s perverse sacrificial victim, demonstrates "the perils of a too-close identification with the saint's aura of deathly ecstasy."[54] The dark, morbid qualities associated with the saint spread outward to envelop the character of Sebastian, and then Clift. What Kaye says of the saint applies equally to all three: he is "at once a stunning advertisement for homosexual desire (indeed, a homoerotic ideal), and a prototypical portrait of a tortured closet case."[55]

Clift's place in this chain—from Cuckrowicz to Sebastian to Saint Sebastian—is cemented by a story reported by Bosworth in which Clift *becomes* Sebastian Venable, subject to the same "devouring creation" in life that the fictional Sebastian found in the Encantadas and Cabeza de Lobo. An assertively heterosexual friend tells Bosworth about once accompanying Clift to a seedy bar. Losing track of Clift's whereabouts, but curious,

he ordered a drink—straight Scotch—which he gulped down, and then he moved to the end of the room and pulled back the leather curtain.

He was practically knocked down by a blast of music, the smell of urine and beer. . . . Directly ahead of him was a circle of about thirty people. They appeared to be observing some sort of performance. "My first thought was they're watching an illegal cock fight," but as he moved closer and stood at the edge of the circle he saw they were watching Monty, who was stretched out on a table, passed out fully clothed in his grey flannel suit while butch dykes, drag queens, transvestites, guys in leather jackets crawled all over him humming like insects.[56]

It's a marvelous story, well crafted and probably told many times. It begins by establishing suspense (a real man would need a good stiff drink to face what this man's about to face). The hero embarks on his arduous journey while being bombarded with sensory overload (the blast of music, the smell of urine). There is some literary misdirection that serves as foreshadowing (maybe an illegal cockfight?). Reconfigured in dream logic, this image is used by the teller as a screen to help him disavow what he already knows. And, as in a dream, the centrality of the illegal cock is eventually confirmed, though sexual pleasure is displaced from the penis and dispersed across Clift's body as a whole. Thus, the climactic revelation: the theatrical curtain (made of telltale leather) is pulled back, the witness-hero moves through the crowd to behold the revelation of numerous irreconcilable, incomprehensible boundary transgressions—women dressed like men, men dressed like women, people sounding like insects. While the rest of paragraph calls to mind the orgiastic "nightmare" in *Rosemary's Baby, Suddenly, Last Summer* is well in evidence as Clift is again placed in the role of Sebastian Venable, the sacrificial victim laid out to be devoured by a dehumanized mob.

As the accident had, this anecdote raises questions about Clift's participation in his own martyrdom. Despite the brutality of his treatment by others, Clift's lifelong abuse of alcohol and drugs has been read repeatedly as a deliberate pursuit of self-destruction (not to mention Clift's decades of chain-smoking, a habit that led to at least one life-threatening fire). As mentioned in the discussion of *I Confess,* any trace of willingness negates martyrdom; Claude Chabrol and Eric Rohmer question Father Logan's motives when they suggest that he *wants* to be a martyr. The version of the script that received the strongest negative reaction was the one that included Logan's proclamation that he was eager—in fact, he had been chosen—to die for others. Sprawled unconscious in the back room of a sleazy bar, his body available to all comers, Clift can be seen as abandoning himself in an ecstasy of self-abnegation and debasement.[57]

If Clift is seen as consenting to his abjection (*posing* as a saint, staging his own suffering, playacting), he becomes less a victim of persecution and more a collaborator, assisting those who would persecute him and alienating potential allies in the process. The otherwise sympathetic Robert La-Guardia draws a picture of Clift carefully manipulating the image of himself as victim. At parties, he writes, Clift "talked with another person as if he expected to be hit, drawing sympathy without actually asking for it. . . . If approached, Monty would hunch up even further, a saintly posture of which he was obviously intensely proud."[58]

The suggestion that Clift's was a willed and willful martyrdom might account for the marked cattiness evident among some of Clift's gay contemporaries.[59] In addition to Truman Capote and Tennessee Williams, another writer who had reservations about Clift's character was screenwriter and playwright Arthur Laurents. At least he had a reason. Laurents was less than enchanted when Clift made a play for Farley Granger—the man Laurents was living with at the time.[60] (This did not stop Laurents from thinking Clift would have been ideal opposite Granger in Hitchcock's *Rope* [1948], for which Laurents wrote the screenplay. The part was ultimately played by John Dall.)[61]

Among the most dismissive was writer Christopher Isherwood, who charts his own disenchantment with Clift in his diaries. Even though he states that he had "fallen for" Clift the moment he saw him in *The Search* in July 1948, by the end of the year the spark was gone. Writing of himself in the third person, Isherwood recounts that "whenever Clift and Christopher met, they playacted enthusiasm for each other, but they were never to become real friends. Maybe Clift found Christopher cold and standoffish. Christopher found Clift touching but ugly minded and sick."[62] The "sickness" (perhaps the "touching" quality, too) is always linked to alcohol. "On December 31, [1948,] Christopher saw the New Year in at Salka Viertel's. I think Montgomery Clift was there among others and that this was the night when Clift insisted on drinking blood brotherhood with Christopher."[63]

By August 1955, Clift's drinking is a commonplace—and juicy—dish. "I had supper at Salka's, with Virginia and a nice couple—the Fred Greens—who are friends of Montgomery Clift—now reportedly drinking himself out of his career in the elderly arms of Libby Holman."[64] Clift's drinking provides stories for another evening's entertainment when Isherwood and friends get together to hear "horrific tales" of "adventures with the *Raintree County* company (Clift's drinking and the love life of Elizabeth Taylor)." "Marguerite tells us that when Clift is very drunk on the set the crew have passwords—bad is 'Georgia,' very bad is 'Florida,' worst of all is 'Zanzibar.'"[65]

Like Capote, Isherwood enjoys dining out on stories about Clift but has doubts about inviting him over. The woman who is currently "mothering" Clift "wants to bring him to supper on Saturday night—promising that he will probably smash everything and have to stay the night. The prospect doesn't charm me." However, on the night in question (September 24, 1956), "Clift behaved neither worse nor better than I'd expected. He arrived drunk, crumpled somewhat during supper but didn't spill anything and left soon after." The coldness in tone is not offset by Isherwood's professing to have been "really shocked by the change in his appearance since I saw him last. Nearly all of his good looks have gone. He has a ghastly, shattered expression."[66] The party does not go well. "Both Don and I felt we could have handled Monty better without Marguerite. It is obvious that she arouses his sadism. She fusses at him the whole time, subconsciously provoking violence." But the criticism is again followed by qualifications. "Monty is touching, and very anxious to be friendly," Isherwood notes, "—but, oh dear, how sorry he is for himself!" Five months after most of the bones in his face were fractured, Clift's pain is dismissed as self-pity. Evidently whatever sympathy Isherwood possesses has its limits. By September 1957, Isherwood's lover, Don Bachardy, is off "to take Marguerite's red Dior dress to the cleaner's because Monty Clift vomited over it or made her vomit."[67]

Obviously, being configured as a gay icon/martyr does not protect Clift from attack by gay critics, who could be scathing. LaGuardia, the most gay-friendly of Clift's early biographers, summarizes gay opinion from Fire Island in the early 1960s: "Almost universally, they looked upon him as a *Boys in the Band*, sunken-ship type: a man, a *famous* man, who had destroyed himself over the guilt and disappointments of homosexual life. He became a popular ikon [sic] for all the self-indulgent semi-alcoholic gays who loved to gossip about the big movie stars who 'were' and what they had done to themselves as a result. It was moronic, vacuous talk, unfair to the man Monty was and had been. They reduced him, in their own minds, to just another sad faggot."[68] A quarter-century later, a similar acidity can be detected in Brett Farmer's assertion that any "exploration of queer engagements with Montgomery Clift would be incomplete without a discussion of Clift's 'tragic' death at age forty-five."[69] The quotation marks around *tragic* say it all.

For one gay critic, Clift's suffering can be seen as a model "of gay self-loathing fueled by internalized homophobia and 'dangerous masochis[m],'" therefore it—and Clift—must be rejected.[70] Others are more sympathetic and would hold on to Clift-as-icon—and his suffering—as a means of understanding the social and political past. Brett Farmer singles out gay critic Richard Lippe as someone who "castigates mainstream critical evaluations for their failure to recognize that the primary source of Clift's tragedy was not his sexuality per se but 'the degradation and mental anguish he experienced as a gay person living and working in a homophobic society.'"[71]

Which brings us to John Huston.

HUSTON AND *FREUD*

Despite the increased drinking and drug use and the effects of the accident, as Clift continued to work it was his sexuality that put him at greatest risk. If the wrong person were to find out, they could make his daily working life hell. This was especially true if that person were a director. Not all the directors Clift worked with were homophobic, and not all directors were cruel. Feelings on the set of *Suddenly, Last Summer* were famously contentious, but what seems to have bothered director Joseph Mankiewicz most was what he saw as Clift's unprofessional behavior, resulting from his alcohol and drug use.[72] (The same things had worried Dmytryk and Kazan, who both distanced themselves.) Hitchcock despised the extent of Clift's drinking, but unlike Mankiewicz, Hitchcock was simultaneously homophobic and homo-fascinated. John Huston, by contrast, seems to have been overwhelmed to the point of homophobic panic.

Legend has it that John Huston brought Montgomery Clift in to work on *The Misfits* because he thought Clift would have a soothing effect on Marilyn Monroe. And, compared to Monroe, Clift was as good as gold. Huston did not have a problem working with Clift during the shooting of *The Misfits,* and he certainly did not object to working with heavy drinkers (for instance, Bogart in *The Maltese Falcon* [1941], *The Treasure of the Sierra Madre* [1948], *The African Queen* [1951], etc.). On earlier projects, Huston appears not to have had a problem working with gay men. He had brought in Truman Capote to work on the script of *Beat the Devil* in 1953. This "some of my best friends" argument, however, may serve as an alibi for tenacious, deep-seated fears.

In light of his violent reaction to learning about Clift being gay, Huston's relationship with Capote is curious. In Lawrence Grobel's book *The Hustons,* Capote describes his relationship with Huston on the set of *Beat the Devil:* "Everybody thought Huston and I were having an affair since we were living in the same rooms." Humphrey Bogart "spread it everywhere—

the sounds that he could hear in the room at night between me and Huston, Huston had finally gone that way. . . ." According to Capote, "Huston played straight into it because he thought it was funny," even though there were professional and social consequences for playing that game. "Half the crew were barely speaking to him, they were so appalled. I enjoyed it. I didn't mind a bit."[73]

Far from taking offense, Huston fueled the rumors by appearing at an impromptu costume party in drag. Grobel prints an astonishing picture of Huston in a flowing "harem-style" outfit and full makeup, being carried on a litter by some beefy coconspirators. The picture alone suggests too much was going on to be altogether innocent.[74]

Huston could flirt, cross-dress, be accused and teased, embrace the stereotype, and push it to an outrageous limit because, through exaggeration, he could show that any question about his sexuality was absurd, incredible, ridiculous (like Huston in drag). Spending entire nights in a hotel room with Truman Capote was no threat to Huston's self-image because Capote was "obvious." But ambiguity was Clift's stock-in-trade. People could "know" and "not know" at will. Some, like Kevin McCarthy, could insist without the slightest self-consciousness that their relationships with Clift were strictly "man-to-man," and their protestations of ignorance might be entirely true. Clift did not court self-destruction by outing himself to those who might shun him.

At the beginning of his career, Clift had been warned. Alfred Lunt told him "being gay could ruin his career," adding the somewhat surprising explanation, "You can't ordinarily be a pansy in the theater and survive." Lunt's biographer adds, "Clift listened to the warning from an actor who was obviously tortured himself."[75] As an actor and as a gay man, Clift diligently monitored his behavior and his appearance, most famously when he asked director Zinnemann to reshoot the scene in *The Search* in which he called the little boy "dear."

While Clift was "careful" on film, in his personal life he took more risks. His refusal to date starlets for publicity, occasional arrests (presumably covered up by the studio), rejection of "Hollywood," and insistence on living in New York could be seen simultaneously as a rebellion against what he saw as false values (fame versus art, stardom as opposed to "real" acting) and as an unwillingness to participate in heterosexual masquerades. The rebellion of the high-minded artist was the preferred reading in the fifties and sixties and is well documented by Steve Cohan. The second reading (a resistance to masquerade) became more common beginning with the biographies of the late seventies. Clift was never as deeply closeted as other actors in the fifties such as Rock Hudson, who went as far as marriage to quell rumors, but neither was he "out" in the way Truman Capote and Tennessee Williams were. (Huston also worked with Williams, directing *The Night of the Iguana* in 1964.) Years later Williams said, "Monty disliked me because I was so open about being gay and he wasn't."[76] Being open, however, did not spare either Capote or Williams from alcoholism and drug abuse.

Did Huston know that Clift was gay? Capote knew. Capote was available to work on *Beat the Devil* because he was already in Italy, having been brought in to work on another chaotic project, the Vittorio De Sica, Montgomery Clift, Jennifer Jones, David O. Selznick tug-of-war, *Indiscretion of an American Wife.* Other Huston coworkers had Clift pegged as gay from the start. While making *The Misfits,* Clift lit a cigarette in the middle of a speech by Clark Gable's character. Gable raged, "That god-damn fag stole the scene from me!" When he saw the dailies, however, Gable admitted that Clift's contribution improved the scene. "That faggot is a hell of an actor," he said. Gable knew.[77]

How could Huston not know? According to LaGuardia, "Huston had already heard that Monty was homosexual, but refused to believe it. He considered it merely malicious gossip."[78] What changed his mind? Well, it was like this. There was a revelation, a primal scene in which nothing was seen but suddenly everything was all too clear. Details vary. Huston invited Clift to his castle in Ireland to talk about *Freud.* Either Clift brought a "companion" or he flirted with an English reporter (perhaps he was French)— either way, the next morning Huston realized that the man had slept over.[79] Suddenly he *knew* Clift and the man had had sex. They had done it in Huston's home, under his roof—in effect, while Huston had been *right there,* having (in Huston's words) his "nose rubbed in it."[80] This violation, this eruption of homosexuality into Huston's own private space, tipped Huston over the edge into full-blown homophobic panic.

Huston biographer Lawrence Grobel tries to maintain some sympathy for Huston, but eventually has to admit that "John's revulsion was so great that everything about Monty offended him." When Huston complains about Clift during the making of *Freud,* tellingly, what obsesses him is any manifestation of Clift's body as a body. In short, Huston can't stop imagining himself in physical contact with Clift's body. He tells Grobel, "His behavior was simply revolting. He had a plastic bottle filled with grapefruit juice and vodka. I never took a drink out of it. I didn't want to touch *any-*

thing that his lips were near."[81] Ostensibly Huston's main complaint during the production of *Freud* centered on Clift's memory problems, the consequence of years of drinking and drug use, but he returns compulsively to descriptions of Clift's body. "There was an *odor* that just came out. . . . He *belched* and he *farted*. It was terrible, terrible, just *repelled* one."[82]

Like other heterosexual, homophobic men, Huston resented the attraction Clift held for heterosexual women. "All females felt protective toward Monty. It was a strange thing. They became *moist* over him. Particularly if they were a few years older." Clift was close to Huston's stepmother, as he had been with Myrna Loy while making *Lonelyhearts* and with Libby Holman through much of the fifties. Huston imagines these quasi-Oedipal relationships in physical detail (the women becoming "moist"), and with equal distaste. (Kazan also had contempt for women who wanted to mother Clift.) Again, Huston's visceral reaction tells us more about Huston than it does about Clift. The possibility of bisexuality (Clift's relationships with older women) does not mitigate accusations of homosexuality as much as it allows Huston to distance himself from women as well—anyone who might be taken in by Clift, be sexually aroused by him, and thus be insensible to the loathsomeness of his physicality. "But he was in his last stages," Huston continues. "There was brain damage there and he couldn't remember a line. He was *revolting*. It was a combination of drugs, drink, his being homosexual, the whole thing became a soup that was *gag-making*."[83]

In imagining Clift's body, Huston resorts to images of uncontrollable physical eruption. If Clift belches and farts, those around him gag or become "moist." Bodies, male and female, are sent spinning out of control, exposing their distasteful secrets. Clift's insides become present, expressed and unavoidable, through vision, smell, taste, and hearing. The properly masculine response is an equally uncontrollable, reflexive rejection, especially at the thought of oral contact (anything his lips touched).

On the set of *Freud*, hostilities were engaged, sides taken.[84] Barney Hoskyns suggests that Huston encouraged a barely submerged anti-Semitism among the crew when shooting in Munich and Vienna. "There have been suggestions that [Clift] was the victim of anti-Semitic feeling in Germany. After *The Young Lions*, people had begun to wonder if he wasn't actually Jewish, and now here he was in Germany—just months after appearing in *Judgment at Nuremberg*—playing 'the Jew Freud.'"[85] (Bosworth identifies *Nuremberg*'s Peterson as "a feeble-minded Jew who is sterilized by the Nazis," but nowhere in the film is he identified as a Jew. He *is* a self-identified communist who is also mentally challenged—either being sufficient to have made him a target of National Socialism.)[86] On the set of *Freud,* neither side made life easy for the other. Clift had trouble remembering his lines as Huston continually rewrote the script, reinventing the chaos that had existed on the set of *Beat the Devil* years earlier.[87] Describing that experience in a 1957 interview, Truman Capote recalled, "The cast [of *Beat the Devil*] was completely bewildered . . . sometimes even Huston didn't seem to know what was going on. It was totally mad, but it was meant to be. I was always just one day ahead, sometimes I was down there in the morning distributing the script to the cameraman and the poor actors."[88]

In his copies of the *Freud* script, Clift diagrams the chaos. In five weeks there are five different versions of the scene in the garden where Freud and his patient Cecily experiment with free association. The white pages of the original script are swamped by yellow and blue rewrites, new pages being added on December, 9, 11, and 12, 1961.[89] One page of the scene, preserved in the New York Public Library, illustrates Clift's futile attempt to impose order as the script unravels before him. He draws circles around phrases and arrows leading from one section to the next. Numbers establish the correct order of the lines and three different writing instruments are needed to keep it all straight—a pencil and two pens with different color inks (pink and blue). The numerous changes scribbled on the December 9 script are formally incorporated by December 12. Although that version is close to what we see in the final film, Huston made the actors shoot the scene again a month later, and again a few days after that. On January 12, Huston reinserted a speech that had been in the script the first time they shot the scene on December 9. The last version was filmed on January 16, 1962—the ninety-sixth day of shooting.

Huston had cue cards placed around the set, but Clift could not read them because of his worsening cataracts. Things came to a head one day in Clift's dressing room. Again, accounts differ. Grobel relates Huston's version of the climactic confrontation: "Huston admitted to getting rough with Clift, even once entering his dressing room and slamming the door so hard that a mirror fell off and shattered. John wanted to shake Clift up to get a performance out of him, but instead Monty just looked at him blankly and asked Huston if he was going to kill him. John glared at him and said he was seriously considering it."[90] Clift's version is more dramatic and comes via LaGuardia: "He came into my dressing room and told me to take my choice. Either I'd remember my lines or he'd break every bone in my body. I just stood there quietly—didn't raise an arm—and told him, 'Why don't you hit me? Why don't you strike?'" LaGuardia observes that "Huston in frustration began demolishing the room, destroying one piece of furniture after another as if he were destroying pieces of Monty."[91] (Of course, in order to strike Clift, Huston would have had to touch him. As Freud says to Breuer when they first meet, "You're not afraid to touch the leper?")

Bosworth combines the two versions: Huston "decided to stage a fight to frighten [Clift] into shaping up. 'I even considered using physical violence. I wasn't trying to destroy him. I wanted to save my movie!' They met in an empty room. . . . 'All we did was glare at each other,' Huston recalled. Finally Monty asked him, 'Are you going to kill me?' Huston ended up saying nothing to him."[92]

Here, the fight is only "staged to frighten," and Clift needs to "shape up." In Huston's account to Grobel, there was violence but it was inadvertent—the door was slammed so hard the mirror happened to fall. Clift's account is more active. He stands up to a bully, courageously daring him to take his best shot, and reduces him to mute destruction. Bosworth also leaves Huston anticlimactically "saying nothing." Just as Clift gave himself the benefit of his account, Huston (screenwriter of the hard-boiled *The Maltese Falcon* and *The Asphalt Jungle*) weights the story his way and gives himself a snappy comeback. Monty, "blank" and presumably frightened, asks if Huston is going to kill him. "I'm seriously considering it," he says he said.

The intensity and brutality of Huston's reaction suggest that his response to Clift was primarily defensive. Regardless of whether he threatened to kill him, Huston *did* try to ruin Clift's career. When principal photography was finished, Huston told everyone that Clift had destroyed his film. He sued, alleging that Clift's "self-inflicted" alcohol- and drug-related memory problems, plus his worsening medical condition (at one point, shooting was interrupted so that Clift could have cataract surgery), caused the production to go over schedule and over budget, thus preventing the film's successful completion. The fact that the film was complete and playing in theaters at the time undermined Huston's claims, and Clift was exonerated to an extent.

Whoever was most to blame for the turmoil and confusion on the set, the film that emerged rests securely on the foundation of Clift's performance. His Freud anchors every scene.

As he did in *Suddenly, Last Summer*, Clift plays a man who listens to women. Because D. A. Miller and Kevin Ohi present queer readings of the earlier film that emphasize female pathology, even going so far as to suggest that male homosexuality drives women insane, their readings fail to account for the appeal these films might have for women. Both Cuckrowicz and

Freud are intensely focused on women, though not as objects of desire. When Cuckrowicz and Freud listen to women, they evince interest, openness, and respect. This is not to say that the relationships are easy. Both Catherine and Freud's patient Cecily (Susannah York) challenge their doctors: Catherine to see whether she can trust him and Cecily to see whether she can manipulate him. Neither doctor acts out of chivalry, riding to the rescue or fighting the women's battles for them. Instead, by listening closely, by taking the women seriously—at their word, so to speak—each man opens up the space that makes it possible for the women to speak. Each man defies cultural and institutional authority in order to help women tell their own stories.

In *Suddenly, Last Summer* and *Freud,* each doctor has an absorbing interest in one female patient, a woman defined as "sick." Both films (to a greater or lesser degree) recognize that this "sickness" is an expression of the impossible position the women have been placed in by society—a society that defines them as ill in order to discredit and silence them. In *Suddenly, Last Summer,* for instance, Cathy is a victim of sexual violence. When she tells the truth about being raped at the Dueling Oaks, exploited by Sebastian, and harassed at the asylum, she is shunned by her social circle, reviled by her aunt Violet, and maligned by the nuns who are supposed to be taking care of her. Cuckrowicz not only listens to her, he makes everyone else listen. Instead of helping a sick, weak woman, he stakes his career on her strength.

Freud and Cuckrowicz ally themselves with women in a common goal to find the truth. The medical, scientific "truth" they find, however, is deeply unsettling socially because its implications go far beyond the etiology of one person's "illness." The very process each man pursues disturbs the social order by requiring him to break away from a position of institutional, heterosexual, and patriarchal privilege and ally himself instead with women, homosexuals, and "neurotics."

In *Freud,* women do not have to be sick for their words to be valued. From the beginning it is clear why female audiences would like Freud—he listens to his mother. Publicly embarrassed by the head of the hospital when he tries to prove that a female hysteric is "telling the truth" (i.e., not faking), Freud's response is a voice-over that leads us into the next scene: "Mother, what should I do?" Rosalie Crutchley, the actress who plays Freud's mother, is not an obviously maternal presence. Thin, beautiful but severe, with a low voice, careful diction, and an English accent, she is also close to Clift's age (born the same year).[93] But her performance as Freud's mother depends less on appearance and more on similarity of temperament—she is a good listener. Although she seems to be concentrating on her sewing as Freud complains about Professor Meynert (Eric Portman) and muses about the possibility of studying hysteria with Charcot, her perceptive questions reveal that she has been listening carefully. When she offers advice, her ideas are insightful and incisive. "Of course you're going to Charcot." He backs away, surprised. "I am? . . . How do you know?" "By your voice when you talk about him," she says simply, foreshadowing the talking cure. Freud: "Oh?" She even provides the first verbal description of the unconscious at work when she says she wouldn't be surprised if his plan to study hysteria hadn't all been decided before he had his fight with Dr. Meynert.

Traditionally hysteria was defined as a female complaint. In the first scene, the hysteric we see is a woman; because she is a woman, Meynert casually declares that she is faking her symptoms in order to get attention. But when Charcot demonstrates the use of hypnosis to alleviate hysterical symptoms, his exemplars are a woman and a man. It will be the male patients who unhinge Freud the most. Although Meynert, Freud's fiercest opponent, denounces him publicly when he presents a paper on his observations of Charcot's methods, Dr. Breuer (Larry Parks) invites Freud to join him in investigating theories of hysteria and begins referring patients to him. Visiting a young male patient for the first time, Freud is confronted by evidence of the Oedipus complex long before he is capable of understanding it or ready to face what he sees. Karl von Schlosser (David McCallum) has attacked his father and is afraid of being sent to an asylum. When Freud hypnotizes him, Karl removes his father's military tunic from a mannequin standing in the corner, revealing a female form underneath. As Karl begins to caress the mannequin, calling it "mother," Freud freaks out. Entering the shot, Clift/Freud forcibly pulls Karl's hand off the dummy and drags him to the right of the frame. Positioning himself firmly between Karl and the female figure, Freud hesitates, breathing heavily and not knowing what to do. As a film, *Freud* is all about opening doors, shedding light, and opening one's eyes. Here Clift closes his eyes, covering them with his hand (doubling his refusal to see in a classically overdetermined manner) as he says quickly, without pause or pattern—"You will remember nothing of this when you awake. Nothing. I'm going to wake you. 1–2–3–4–5" (said in quick succession). "Wake up!" He snaps his fingers. "Eyes open," he barks, "wide awake." During this outburst disguised as method, Clift keeps his eyes down, unable to look at Karl. At the last second he risks a glance as he hurries out of the frame. Karl is left alone, disoriented and vaguely surprised. Freud rushes out, locking the door behind him.

If the implication in the scene with von Schlosser is that Karl's hatred of his father and desire for his mother are something that Freud recognizes within himself, the scene with Meynert provides another example of "unacceptable" sexuality that Freud must accept at a personal level. Breuer finds out that Freud has abandoned their studies in hysteria and asks who his last patient was before he made this decision. Freud, in classic Freudian fashion, doesn't remember. Then word comes that Professor Meynert is dying. Earlier, Meynert had warned Freud not to let in the light on certain things that belong in the dark (scorpions are his case in point). The dying Meynert enlightens Freud with a long speech about Meynert's life in the closet, code-name "neurosis." We begin with "gay-dar": "Neurotics form a brotherhood. They learn to recognize each other as I did you. They have only one rule—silence in the presence of the enemy. Our common enemy. The normal people would knock our deformities, torment and degrade us. You, Freud, belong to the brotherhood. I feared you because you seemed determined to betray us. So I did what I could to discredit you." Meynert now feels that he has wasted his life by refusing to accept his own identity. "My life has been a sham. I misused my talents, hiding the truth even from myself. I suppressed my real being. . . . I don't know who I am. It is not I who lived my life, but another—the creation of my vanity."

Meynert encourages Freud to speak out, regardless of the hostility he may encounter. "Break the silence. Do what you set out to do—betray us. We need a traitor." He characterizes such an act in terms of a heroic journey or mythical act: "Go to the heart of our darkness. Hunt out the dragon." Freud responds in religious terms: "Angels and saints slay dragons. I am neither." But Freud's biggest failing, what keeps him from seeing himself as an angel or a saint, is his guilt regarding Karl von Schlosser. Although the sexual desire he enacts is toward his mother, David McCallum's performance is heavily coded as gay: delicate, soft-spoken, worried about what he should wear, eager to please his handsome guest. It is strongly suggested that the "neurosis" shared by Meynert, von Schlosser, and Clift's Freud is homosexuality. Rather than reject Meynert's claim that Freud is part of "the brotherhood," Freud heads directly to the von Schlosser house and asks to see the young man. Told that he died six months earlier in the asylum he feared, Freud (half-hidden behind bars and shadows, only half-seeing) begs his forgiveness: "Karl. Forgive me, Karl."

The scene with Meynert also frees Freud to resume his work with Cecily. Just as Cuckrowicz never protests when Catherine or Violet points out his resemblance to Sebastian, Freud openly acknowledges his resemblance to Meynert *and* Cecily after he experiences his own "neurotic symptoms" at his father's funeral. He faints upon approaching the cemetery. Asking Breuer to return with him, he finds the dizziness beginning again and turns back. "I'm a neurotic," he proclaims, wagging his finger, "these are hysterical symptoms." Describing the symptoms to Breuer, he explains, "my legs won't support me." In the next scene, Cecily uses the exact same phrase about a childhood fainting spell—"my legs wouldn't support me—the doctors didn't know why"—cementing the similarity of doctor and patient.

It is Freud's identification with Cecily—along with another discussion with his mother—that makes it possible for him to develop "his" ideas. (Though, to be fair, when he stops using hypnosis with Cecily and tries to interpret her dreams instead, he defines it as a mutual achievement: "Do you realize what's happened in this room today? You and I have found our way into the unconscious without hypnosis.") Breuer is willing to settle for surface improvements with Cecily, the temporary elimination of her symptoms; Freud pushes further. When Cecily, under hypnosis, tells both men about her father dying in a Protestant hospital in Italy, Breuer accepts the story but is disappointed when Cecily's symptom remains. Freud pushes on and, by questioning inconsistencies in Cecily's account, establishes that her father died in a brothel. Freud's intervention does cure her symptom—an inability to see clearly—though she screams at him to leave because she does not like what she "sees."

Freud learns from women because he *recognizes himself in them.* But there are dangers from too great an identification (or rather, an uncritical one). While Cuckrowicz does not question Catherine's accounts of her victimization, Freud invents/imposes two readings of Cecily's life, in each case led (or misled) by his own experience. First he persuades her that she was molested by her father when he believes his father molested his sister. He questions the correctness of this theory for Cecily only when he finds out that it does not apply to him. The fact that she is still fond of the doll her father gave her nags at him until he talks to his mother and finds that his father could not have molested his sister because she had not yet been born. This is when he realizes it was a fantasy he invented to cover his own desire for his mother. (We dissolve from his realization that Cecily loves the doll her father gave her to Freud studying a toy train he had as a child. Mother: "Memory plays queer tricks." Freud: "And always to a purpose.") Because his father could not have molested his sister, Freud deduces that Cecily must also be fantasizing—a deduction that modern audiences might find rushed and not altogether persuasive. Freud's turning away from the seduction theory in favor of the wholesale substitution of fantasy remains controversial. In this particular scene, this hypothesis is especially dubious coming so quickly on the heels of a scene with just the opposite explanation. Because Cecily is a fictionalized composite and not based on an actual case, it is impossible to say whether Freud is correct in choosing fantasy over trauma as the root of her condition. It is clear that Cecily is herself a kind of fantasy character for the film, because with this one patient Freud is able to prove the existence of the unconscious; develop the techniques of hypnosis, the interpretation of dreams, free association, and Freudian slips; support his own insight into the Oedipal complex; and recognize the phenomenon of transference.

Although Freud berates himself for "betraying" his father by inventing this slander against him, he repeatedly betrays father figures throughout the film. He drops the watch his father gave him as a gift (an example to be used later to illustrate the concept of one kind of Freudian slip—"there are no accidents"); he "betrays" Meynert by studying with Charcot; he is called to Meynert's when the older man is dying just as he is called to his own dying father's bedside; he breaks with Breuer when Breuer questions the theory of infantile sexuality and forbids Freud to present his findings. More to the point, Breuer says, "As your spiritual father, I forbid you to read this paper." Freud's response, the last thing he ever says to Breuer, is "The time comes when one must give up all one's fathers and stand alone."

Freud's severing of his sentimental connections to patriarchy is a crucial step in allying himself with women. All fathers have to be replaced. Freud himself refuses to assume that role when it is offered to him. Cecily tries to insert him into the role of the father, revealing, in doing so, how corrupt that role is. Whether she was molested by her father or fantasized a scene based on her own desire, the only way Cecily can imagine appealing to her father or to father figures is to make herself up as a prostitute. Meeting Freud in the street in the red-light district, she tells him, "Doctor, you can have me for nothing. You made me able to walk again. You deserve something— a reward." When he refuses, she denounces herself for having lied (though her excessive reaction seems more like denial). "I don't deserve the father I had. The most loving father that ever lived. And I—his daughter—accused him of such an unnatural, unspeakable act. Only a born harlot could tell such a lie." As she becomes more hysterical, insisting, "You must believe me. You must!" she runs to a bridge and threatens to kill herself. Although Freud is too quick to believe her denial, he does recognize the part his own desire played in his (mis)interpretation of her past. "I am the guilty one," he tells her. "It was my lie, not yours."

It is at this very moment that the only detectable traces of the chaos on the film set become evident, in the form of postproduction dialogue replacement. On the bridge when Freud asks Cecily not to jump, we hear him say as a voice-off, "for my sake"—but the voice is not Clift's. The line has been dubbed by someone else. Tellingly, John Huston makes a slip in his incarnation as a voice-over when Freud is beginning to doubt his theory on the origin of Cecily's illness. Until now, Huston as the all-knowing voice-of-God narrator speaks of Freud in the third person, but here he says, "Perhaps the answer lies still farther back, as in my own case"—making himself synonymous with Freud-as-patient. The next scene Freud has with Cecily—the last time we see her—also starts with a voice not Clift's own. Offscreen we hear someone we have never heard before saying, "Do you remember as a child dreaming of your mother's death? Why do you," then we blend into Clift saying "think you dreamt such dreams?" He then explains everything—"Shall I tell you your story?"

In their final scene together, Freud makes Cecily confront her final symptom.

> CECILY: And now I'm cured you will never see me again.
>
> FREUD: I will see you again. Because you're not cured.
>
> CECILY: My symptoms are gone.
>
> FREUD: Yes. All but one.
>
> CECILY (cringing): Which?
>
> FREUD (flatly): Your love for me.

Cecily, on her hands and knees at the reduction of exalted emotion to pathological marker, says, "That's not a symptom." (Earlier, Freud's wife, Martha, had said much the same when Freud explained that Cecily sent him flowers only because he reminded her of someone else, and that this might be what all relationships are based on.) Freud does not reject Cecily, though. He explains that since he too is a father figure, and before him Breuer, and before him her father, that like Freud himself, for her there will come a time when she too will be able to give up all her fathers and stand alone. Cecily asks, "Then you accept this love?" Freud: "As a sacred trust." When he asks her to "believe me," she answers like a wife—"I do" (see plate 12).

It must be noted that in the film Freud is not perfect in his respect for women. The one woman he does not listen to is his wife, Martha (Susan Kohner). When he catches her trying to read his latest paper, he tells her, "I'd rather you didn't. . . . That's not for your eyes." Martha is the only figure in the film who is encouraged not to see, to keep her eyes closed. Freud re-institutes the professional-amateur, male-female hierarchy when he tells her, "It's for physicians to read, not one's wife." Badly underwritten, Martha's character lacks character. When Freud has his first nightmare and wakes calling out "mother, mother, mother," Martha in bed next to him has to introduce herself. "No, dear, it's Martha. Your wife, Martha." Although she is literally put in the position of his mother, unlike his mother Martha does not know Freud very well, limiting her ability to contribute to his work. Jealous when Cecily begins to send him flowers, she does not know what we have seen in his interaction with Cecily and what Breuer so strongly proclaims in the last scene, that Freud has scrupulous ethical standards. For all that, she is still the good little woman, and when her "Siggy" is troubled, Martha throws open the curtains and encourages him to press on.

By learning to identify with his patients in their shared imperfections rather than defensively separate himself from them (as he did with Karl von Schlosser), Freud transforms weakness into strength. Because they can openly acknowledge their human frailty, Cecily and Freud, Catherine and Cuckrowicz are ultimately stronger than the tyrannical Meynert or Violet Venable, both of whom collapse in the face of the truth. They also triumph over weaker men and weak women. The puffed-up head of Cuckrowicz's hospital and Freud's mentor Breuer lack the courage to acknowledge publicly what they know privately; Cecily's mother and Cathy's mother resign themselves to the way things are, crying a lot but taking no action to help their daughters.

When Breuer introduces himself to Freud, it is presented as an act of courage: "You're not afraid to touch the leper?" Freud asks. Breuer shares his secret interest in the "dark art" of hypnosis, but only *as* a secret. When he proposes they work together, publishing the results as "Freud and Breuer," he is hiding behind Freud as much as he is being modest. When Freud pauses a bit too long before suggesting that it should be "Breuer and Freud" (reluctantly taking his place as the less-established member of the team), his hostility to father figures peeks through. Unlike Freud, Breuer hides from himself. Flattered by Cecily's devotion and dependence, he becomes too involved, and then runs away. Freud confronts him rushing down the stairs: "Breuer! You can't leave her like this. . . . You're her doctor, she needs you." Breuer responds, "I must go to preserve my marriage," this time hiding behind his wife, whom he accuses of "imagining" an improper attachment between doctor and patient. Breuer eventually, inevitably, betrays Freud. (Blacklisted despite having testified before HUAC, Larry Parks still finds himself—in his last good role, his last film—cast as a moral weakling.)[94]

When Freud presents his theory on infantile sexuality despite Breuer's having forbidden him to do so, he finds himself publicly reviled—like Catherine being jeered at by the other patients in *Suddenly, Last Summer*. As the men in the audience rap on their desks and erupt in shouts when Freud tries to speak, a moderator adds to the cacophony by repeatedly ringing a bell and calling for order. Freud (wearing glasses) continues his speech. Raising the issue of the child's "desire for the mother herself—" he is again drowned out by catcalls, and pauses as three men approach, stop in front of him, and spit on the floor in disgust before walking out. Unwavering, Freud ploughs ahead, concluding on the need to stand up and face the truth about ourselves regardless of society's possible disdain. "*Each*—each human being is confronted with the task—of overcoming [the Oedipus complex] within himself. If he succeeds—he will be a whole individual; if he fail—he will become a neurotic—and himself wander forever—blind, homeless." Amid the shouting, he addresses the crowd with heavy irony. "'Gentlemen. I am deeply grateful for your kind attention.' [More shouting almost drowns him out.] 'You have not ceased to display the detachment' [silence] 'the love of truth for truth's sake—' [Someone calls out, 'What truth?' and the shouting begins again] '—that ennobles our profession.'"

As Freud takes his seat on the stage next to the podium (the living future of science framed next to a skeleton from its dead past), one gentleman rises and directs his question not to Freud but to Breuer, sitting in the audience. At first Breuer rises to Freud's defense. As he declares, "There are many here who would do well to have his scruples and professional conscience," the others laugh. Turning on them, he raises his voice—"How *dare* you? And how dare you ask me for references regarding Dr. Freud?" However, when he is asked directly if he supports Freud's theory of infantile sexuality, Breuer bows his head and folds. "I do not believe in it. I have never believed in it. And I can never accept it—never accept it." Waving the thought away with his hands, he leaves the room, literally turning his back, incapable of looking Freud in the face.

It might seem that in the shift to psychoanalysis (from Logan to Cuckrowicz and Freud), we have moved firmly past religious mystification into the clean, clear world of reason. Having made the transition to scientific discourse, however, we find that religious sentiment has not disappeared, it has merely gone underground. For Kaye, it was Saint Sebastian who could be seen at the end of the nineteenth century as the "embodiment of the transition whereby homosexual desire, once a theologically construed sin, was increasingly understood in the late-Victorian epoch as medical illness."[95] As the scientific study of sexuality took root, religious concepts could still be found buried deep within the scientific paradigm. According to Foucault, Western culture "subordinated its soul to sexuality by conceiving of it as what constituted the soul's most secret and determinant part."[96] In this new dispensation, sexuality, instead of eliminating the soul, became the soul's disguise. "A mysterious and undefined power,"[97] sexuality was endowed with a near-mystical force as it became, as the soul had been, the key to one's being. The *real* you. The thing that could reveal at last who Montgomery Clift really *is*.

But while psychoanalysts, fans, and other soul-searchers debate the ever-elusive truth of the real Montgomery Clift's inner being, there remains the documented, historical trace of the actor's work. If, by shifting the focus to his continuing ability as an actor, I have attempted to counter both the cult of Clift's beauty and the "tragic myth" that has dominated accounts of his career since 1956, then his performance in *Freud* is some of the best evidence I have. Furthermore, as mythical figures, Clift and Freud are perfectly matched. Both demonstrate the same kind of courage and single-minded commitment to their work. Willing to put themselves at risk, they expose their own weaknesses for the higher goals of medicine and art. Neither wilts in the face of public ridicule or professional persecution. As with Freud, integrity, intellectual excitement, perseverance, and stoic endurance are all qualities the actor was known for. Regardless of his physical or psychological condition during filming, or the extent to which his problems were exacerbated by working with Huston, as Freud Clift was able to summon all of his strengths as an actor, providing the film with a hero who is everything Huston or anyone else could have wished. Nevertheless, *Freud* was not a commercial success. In a last-ditch effort to attract some kind of attention, it was retitled *The Secret Passion*.

Despite Huston's having lost his lawsuit against the actor, Clift, who had been considered uninsurable since 1959 (when Elizabeth Taylor insisted on his being cast in *Suddenly, Last Summer*), did not appear in a film for the next four years.[98] Fans of the actor and the director are still taking sides. Clift biographer Hoskyns writes, "If it was true . . . that Monty had 'deteriorated to a shocking degree' since *The Misfits,* that did not excuse the appalling treatment the actor received on the set of *Freud* in Munich. Brooks

Clift was not alone in believing that Huston's vicious bullying of Monty all but killed his brother."[99] For those who would wish to demonize John Huston (and I would not necessarily try to stop them), it is an inconvenient fact that Clift did not die as a result of his struggles on the set of *Freud* any more than he prevented the film from being completed. His "tragic" "early" death again refused to arrive in a timely fashion. This meant his persecution could continue full-bore, reaching new lows.

SEVEN

Nothing Sacred

ALTHOUGH HE WAS FREQUENTLY (if disparagingly) spoken of in terms of Christlike suffering, the closest Clift came to Christ-on-film was when George Stevens considered casting Clift in his biblical epic, *The Greatest Story Ever Told.* The idea of reteaming Clift with the director of *A Place in the Sun,* combined with the overtly religious subject matter, makes this project an irresistible what-if.

Much of an actor's career takes place in the imagination. Before we can see a performance, many people have to imagine it first. Those casting a film have to be able to picture the actor in the role, as does the actor himself. (It may be difficult to imagine Clift in a biblical cloak or a toga but, as *Freud* proved, he did look very good in a beard.) Audiences have famously had opinions about casting prior to a film's production. After an actor's death, fans are left imagining what might have been: the projects unrealized, the films eventually made with actors in roles originally slated for someone else.

Some projects are easy to picture because they call to mind earlier performances. Louella Parsons announced in March 1954 (one year after *I Confess*) that Clift "has been asked to play a priest in 'The Leather Saint,'" a project written by someone said to be "a close friend of Monty's" who "wrote it with Clift in mind."[1] The story of "a young priest who takes to the prize fight ring to raise money for the poor children of his Mexican parish," the project is described as "another 'Going My Way,'" suggesting that perhaps it is better that the film was never made. Selznick nixed him for the role of

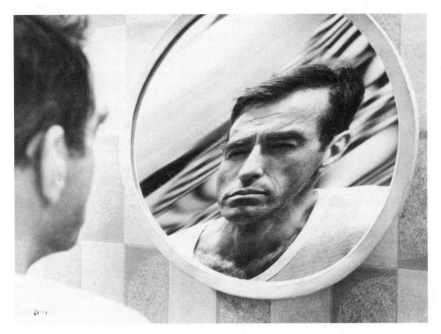

FIGURE 38. Lobby card for *The Defector,* 1966: Clift (Bower) in a mirror.

the psychiatrist husband of an unstable Jennifer Jones in *Tender Is the Night,* even though it would have been Clift's third psychiatric specialist and his second film with Jones. Jason Robards Jr. played the part.[2]

Other roles are so far off type as to be close to unimaginable. For example, Clift was suggested for the role of Dmitri in Richard Brooks's 1958 adaptation of *The Brothers Karamazov.*[3] As played by Yul Brynner, the character is all animal magnetism, sex and rage, and what used to be called rude good health—not qualities Clift was known for. The thoughtful seminarian Alexi (soulful, sense of humor, good with children) would have been ideal for the younger Clift, but by 1958 that time had passed. (The part was played by William Shatner.)

Then there are the roles that cut too close, making them easy to imagine and painful at the same time. At the end of the 1950s, Clift turned down the Dean Martin role in *Rio Bravo,* even though it would have meant another chance to work with Howard Hawks and John Wayne.[4] No longer the young rebel, Clift would have played the drunken sheriff, a pathetic shadow of his former glory.

In the summer of 1962 people were imagining Clift in Galilee. A flurry of telegrams and phone calls shows how close the idea of Clift as religious icon came to being realized. They also illustrate how unemployable Clift had become since completing *Freud.*

Early in his career, Clift took an active part in soliciting and shaping his roles, as demonstrated by the detailed letters he wrote to Fred Zinnemann before *The Search.* Now the job was left to a dedicated acolyte. Without consulting Clift's agent, Clift's new, relatively unknown publicist, Irwin Franklyn, contacted director Stevens about considering Clift for his immense, years-in-the-making biblical extravaganza. On July 17, 1962, Franklyn sent a telegram suggesting that Stevens call Monty: "Registered as Mr. Montgomery at El Convanto/Old San Juan, Puerto Rico. He'd like George to call him collect."[5] The first question Stevens asked Franklyn was loaded but bland. "How's he feeling?" Reassured that "He's feeling wonderful," "Mr. Stevens spoke with Montgomery Clift at 6:10 P.M." The conversation must have gone well because it was followed by a telegram from Stevens that same evening: "Dear Monty: I enjoyed talking to you very much this evening, and am rushing the enclosed script to you so that you can give it your consideration. I see magnificent moments in the story of [for?] you that the suggestions in the script only lightly point to." On July 31, Clift sent a telegram from Antigua. Stevens replied on August 2. "Dear Monty: Having just hung up the phone after talking with you I must tell you how pleased and excited I am at the idea of you in the Greatest Story. I must tell you in all honesty that I have felt from the beginning that no one could play this part but you. I was hoping that you would see and feel the possibilities here and our just completed conversation has given me a feeling of great excitement. Looking forward to seeing you in New York. Yours as ever." ("Yours" has been crossed out and replaced by a hand-written "Best.")

Stevens and Clift agreed to meet on August 13 at the St. Regis, but there is no written account of what happened there. The last word on the subject comes a month later (September 5), when Franklyn puts in a somewhat desperate plea to Stevens. "There is nothing which can delay or deter this production, because it is right and no matter how rigorous your schedule, Monty can deliver and would. I hope you will not think me presumptuous in the steps I have taken. I am not an agent, but a press agent, I will continue to work for Monty, whether or not he is in Greatest Story . . . but he just must be in that picture. . . . [No one] can deliver a performance in that role as honestly and with as much *integrity* and *beauty* as Monty could." Reassuring Stevens about Clift's physical (and photographable) condition, Franklyn encloses visual proof. "The attached photos of Monty

Clift are blow-ups from snapshots taken this summer in Puerto Rico by Libby Holman on a small box camera." As to exactly which role Clift could play with such honesty and beauty, Franklyn guilelessly asserts: "Libby feels, as I do, that Monty was born to play Judas." Only in Hollywood could this pass as a compliment.

Clift was evidently no longer in the running for Jesus. Bibliographer Mary Kalfatovic says he was considered for the part but not offered it.[6] A couple of weeks later (September 21), his actual agent, Sy Samuels, sent Stevens a list of clients to be considered for major roles:

Stuart Whitman—for Judas or Herod

Trevor Howard—for Pilate

Monty Clift—for Judas

Karl Boehm—for Judas or one of the apostles.

Clift is not at the top of the list, nor is he the only one "born to play Judas." A month later, even Judas was out of the question. On October 23, Samuels suggested Clift for Herod, though he was still second to Whitman, who had made a big impression as a tortured pedophile in 1961's *The Mark*. Whether it was drinking, painkillers, the accident, or stories about difficulties on the set of *Lonelyhearts, Suddenly, Last Summer,* or *Freud,* Clift was no longer bankable, insurable, or castable for a major Hollywood film.

Franklyn's efforts were not a complete waste. Judas was eventually played by David McCallum, whose film debut had been the one scene he played opposite Clift in *Freud.* Saint Peter was played by Gary Raymond (Cathy's brother in *Suddenly, Last Summer*). Franklyn also represented Clift's good friend Roddy McDowall (eventual costar of Clift's last film, *The Defector*), whose performance as Octavian in the Mankiewicz-Taylor *Cleopatra* had yet to be seen. Franklyn sent pictures of McDowall in Roman costume to Stevens, helping McDowell land the part of Saint Matthew.

Although it might have seemed that the mainstream press was becoming more sympathetic to Clift as he aged (stories emphasizing his suffering include "The Agony and the Ecstasy of Montgomery Clift" [*Modern Screen,* March 1963] and "Montgomery Clift: Film's Fall Guy" [*Cosmopolitan,* May 1963]), the fact that his career was coming to an end did not prevent those who would attack him from doing so.[7]

About this time Clift himself neatly expressed the way the sacred and the absurd coexisted in his life when he discovered that his sexuality, his reputation, in fact every part of his body was available for the prurient speculations

FIGURE 39. Clift with a beard, circa 1955. John Kobal Foundation, Hulton Archive, Getty Images.

of others. In the unexpurgated European version of Kenneth Anger's *Hollywood Babylon,* there is a discussion about the size of Clift's genitals, what Thomas Waugh refers to as "Clift's ranking on the peter-meter."[8] According to Bosworth, when Clift read an advance copy of the book, he cried out, "Jesus H. Christ! Is nothing sacred?!" His lawyer handled it with the threat of a libel suit and the scurrilous material did not appear in the American version.[9] Clift was not completely helpless, after all. But no, nothing is sacred when it comes to actors. And nothing is private, even in death.

After Clift died, stories about his body were still making the rounds. At a party in 1978, twelve years after Clift's death, New York medical examiner Michael Baden and "his wife joked about Montgomery Clift's 1966 autopsy (which Baden conducted). In particular, the Badens laughed at the size of the late actor's genitalia."[10] Baden was fired and the story made the pages of the *New York Post.*[11] (Baden has since found a more congenial venue for purveying the details of celebrity deaths on cable television.)

After Clift's death, biographies and documentaries about him began to circulate, providing new material out of which readers and viewers could build their own images of Clift. Instead of an actor producing a performance, Clift was transformed into a character produced by others. As previously discussed, the biographies tended to veer between scandalous revelation and unexamined hagiography, depicting Clift as a "beautiful loser" and a "sainted mess." The works that followed continue to bounce back and forth between reverence and scorn, picturing Clift as either a victim of fate or a self-destructive gay martyr.

To be a martyr, it is not enough to suffer. Your suffering must have meaning for others. Roughly thirty years after Clift's death, the alternative rock band R.E.M. finally cast him in the role that had eluded him on screen.[12] In "Monty Got a Raw Deal" on the album *Automatic for the People,* Clift is addressed as an intimate. "Monty, this seems strange to me." The song is about suffering, the iconography religious as fans occupy the position of Mary and John kneeling at the foot of the cross. "I saw you strung up in a tree. A woman knelt there said to me, 'Hold your tongue.'" Attention must be paid to the suffering endured by figures in popular culture, especially those who are required to keep their sexuality closeted and are persecuted just the same. But what can the fan do for the star, dead years before the fan knew he existed? "Just hold your tongue." The demand for respect is a demand for privacy. Clift's exclamation "Is nothing sacred?" is another way of asking, "Is nothing private?" The fact that R.E.M.'s lead singer, Michael

Stipe, publicly came out about this time makes the song's insistence on respecting a star's privacy seem all the more heartfelt.

In R.E.M.'s ethics of fandom, the true fan doesn't presume, doesn't ask, doesn't speculate. The desire to form an emotional connection with a dead idol exerts a powerful attraction ("heroes don't come easy"), but according to R.E.M., cheap sympathy must be resisted. The chorus renounces any urge to get the inside scoop on Clift's deepest secrets (telling the star, "You don't owe me anything"). At the same time the song refuses to disguise prurience as compassion or as an expression of political solidarity. The singer knows how the star feels—"You don't want this sympathy"—and in turn advises himself and other fans, "Don't you waste your breath."

As with Father Logan, when we confront the impassive surface of someone whose character and spirituality are so deeply internalized, we had best keep our grubby curiosity to ourselves. Logan's integrity as a priest and Clift's integrity as an actor rely on not making a display of their innermost feelings. To quote poet Richard Howard, "The self, divine in each of us, is not to be fully entered into."[13]

A few years earlier, the British rock group The Clash wrote another song about Clift, "The Right Profile." ("Shoot his right profile" is the cynical advice supposedly given by Hollywood executives looking for a way to continue making money from Clift after his face was damaged in the accident.) Compared to the elegiac mood of R.E.M.'s Cliftian ode, The Clash has a raucous good time skewering sacred cows. The song borrows from *The Boys in the Band*'s stock of characters, opening with a disoriented Clift staggering down 42nd Street, surrounded by hustlers and pimps and assailed by "fans." At first they do not recognize him, a list of his accomplishments only calling attention to how far away they all seem. "Where'd I see this guy? In *Red River* or *A Place in the Sun*." Maybe it was *The Misfits* or *From Here to Eternity*. The chorus restages the shocked commentary of a disbelieving public, the distance between Clift the star and the pathetic has-been before them: "Everybody say 'He sure looks funny.' / That's Montgomery Clift, honey." Clift himself, heavily medicated ("Nembutal numbs it all"), can find solace only in the past, watching films a modern audience barely remembers.[14] "Go out and get me my old movie stills. / Go out and get me another roll of pills," he begs. His last line is indecipherable gibberish. There is no better example of the refusal to weep softly at the foot of Clift-as-martyr.

The song's satirical attack is so merciless it is hard to say whether the ridicule and disgust are directed at Clift or he is being presented as an example of popular culture's penchant for toppling its idols. The title indicates the latter, but the lack of sympathy for the actor is so pronounced, the song could be seen as verging on homophobic. (Although its members were politically progressive, The Clash was not a gay band.) Nevertheless, "The Right Profile," written fifteen years after the period it portrays, presents a gay-based contempt that matches precisely the attitudes of some gay men quoted by LaGuardia. (The song was released in 1980, LaGuardia's biography in 1977.)

THE LOW RESONANCE OF A MAN'S VOICE

Clift's career did not end with *Freud* or his failure to secure a role in *The Greatest Story Ever Told*. Between *Freud* and *The Defector* (1966), Clift may have seemed a voice in the wilderness, lost, unseen, his memory worsening and his health continuing to deteriorate, but he was still acting. Fully aware of the kinds of personal attacks being made against him in a climate of doubt and contempt, Clift was eager nevertheless to take whatever work he could find, even if it meant working in a less-exalted venue than the Hollywood feature film.

Although television was often the medium of choice for former Hollywood stars seeking to prolong their careers in the late fifties and early sixties, Clift's television appearances were few and far apart. His first role on television, however, was historic. As a member of the cast of the 1939 Broadway production of Noël Coward's *Hay Fever*, Clift participated in one of the very first television broadcasts in the United States. A performance of *Hay Fever* was aired during the New York World's Fair as part of the introduction of television. It is not likely that any recording of the broadcast exists.

After this auspicious beginning, Clift's appearances on the small screen were sporadic. He appeared as himself on Ed Sullivan's *Toast of the Town* in March 1954, then on a show called *Here's Hollywood* in January 1962. About this time Clift was a guest on the game show *What's My Line?* (a cruel title for an actor with a bad memory). The blindfolded panelists had to identify the profession of the unemployed actor on the basis of his answers to their questions. They might have guessed his identity from his voice alone. It was through his voice that he continued his career and would eventually give one of his best, but least-known, performances.

Clift's voice-over work for the television documentary *William Faulkner's Mississippi,* which aired in April 1965, provides a suggestion of what Clift could do in one of the avenues still open to him as a performer. There are two narrators—Zachary Scott handles the informational side, speaking of Faulkner in the third person, while Clift reads directly from Faulkner writing in the first person. Unlike Zachary Scott, who has a soft drawl, Clift is not a southerner and does not approximate a southern accent. Where Scott's voice is purely nasal, giving his simplest statement a sneering quality regardless of the actor's goodwill or intent, Clift's voice is roomier—not lower than Scott's but more resonant, interior, the tone rounded in his mouth. He does not mumble, but he does find a way to give the impression of intimate communications, as if we were overhearing Faulkner's private musings. First heard in *Raintree County* (when he reads aloud a Faulknerian editorial about slavery and hypocrisy), this is Clift's postaccident voice. It is also his adult voice—lower thanks to time, more nasal since the accident. While earlier in his career Clift used vocal mannerisms such as a tendency to swallow lines and hesitation as a sign that his characters were struggling with complex ideas, in *Faulkner's Mississippi* he speaks with the loud, solid, well-enunciated style heard in *Suddenly, Last Summer* and *Freud*—the style he uses when his characters are taking a stand, speaking with the voice of reason, or possessed of moral certainty. In *Suddenly, Last Summer, Freud,* and Clift's vocal work, there is a sense of arrival, of coherence, as everything falls into place. The characters are no longer at odds with the actor's biography. Clift and his characters do not pretend to be young anymore; they are not pressured to ape heterosexual desire.

Clift's vocal performances have been overlooked for several reasons.[15] There is no major economic or corporate interest in preserving, promoting, or distributing audio drama. As a consequence, audio recordings have been rare and (before the advent of eBay) hard to come by. Even with this amateur form of distribution, audio recordings have a limited audience. A taste for live radio drama is esoteric, to say the least; those who listen to plays on LPs are even rarer. Because they fall outside traditional commercial structures, audio works have been accorded a limited status in studies of actors' careers. Until recently, no actor has been widely applauded, rewarded, or even reviewed for his or her reading of a book on tape.

Of course, the rarity of audio texts only enhances their potential to become highly prized fetish objects. Once an actor has died, his body of work becomes finite. Fans, having seen all his films, are left trolling for fragments. Whether they are completists (collectors always wanting more) or fetishists (investing something with private importance in excess of its public value), fans treasure what is rare or lost. Materials that are not widely available become highly sought after by those who define themselves as the most passionate, the most devoted, the actor's "biggest" fans.

For such fans, listening to a recording of a live radio broadcast from the forties or fifties creates a sense of intimacy beyond that experienced watching films from the same period. The contingencies of "liveness" confer on these recordings an aura of transience and fragility that underscores how easily these texts could have been lost forever. The sense of presence is also exaggerated when listening is done as a private act and hearing is the only channel of information. All these factors combined might account for the uncanny sensation one feels listening to what Jeffrey Sconce calls "voices from the void."[16] Add to this a text that is ownable and infinitely repeatable, and fetishism is virtually guaranteed.

One important thing Clift's audio recordings reveal is how his voice and the use of it—his judgment as an actor—change over time. To emphasize the actor's agency in the use of his (changing) voice, I will compare two audio-texts, one made early in Clift's career and one late. Clift plays the same role in both. The first is a recording of a live radio broadcast of *The Glass Menagerie* from 1951. The second is a recording of *The Glass Menagerie* on two long-playing albums made in 1964 by Caedmon Records.

Clift had done live radio early in his career (and, according to one source, hated it).[17] In April 1949 he did an hourlong production of "Wuthering Heights" for *Ford Theater*, with Joan Loring as Cathy. Clift's performance as the "handsomely sinister" Heathcliff (discussed in chapter 2) was not a success.[18] In January 1951 he was in "The Metal of the Moon" as a nineteenth-century boy inventor who discovers a practical way to extract aluminum. "The Dupont Company of Wilmington Delaware, makers of 'Better Things for Better Living through Chemistry,'" presented this episode as part of its *Cavalcade of America* series. Through this character, the image of Clift as the open-faced Broadway juvenile lives on. Polite and hardworking, the nice young man is properly shamefaced when he accidentally blows up the family's shed. In September 1951, however, Clift was cast in a project that held genuine promise—a version of *The Glass Menagerie* for a *Theater Guild on the Air* production, sponsored by U.S. Steel. Shortened to a forty-five-minute running time, the play was performed before a live audience at the Belasco Theater in New York. A "world premiere on radio," this production starred Clift as Tom; Helen Hayes as his mother, Amanda Wingfield; and Karl Malden as the Gentleman Caller.

The play opens with a first-person introduction as Tom Wingfield (Clift) sets the scene. The first thing one notices is that Clift's voice sounds very high-pitched, higher than in any of his films.[19] He rushes through the introduction, sounding like a young adolescent. "The story is memory . . . memory of a tenement. Down a back alley near a streetcar line. Streetcars stopping, starting, all night long. Down a back alley next to a dance hall." He describes the building in detail, as if to make up for the absence of set design. As he fills us in on the dramatis personae ("I'm a character in this story. The other characters are my mother, Amanda, a little woman of— of g-great but confused vitality [. . .] and my sister, Laura") audio sound bites are inserted of Amanda and Laura saying lines representative of their characters.

The most surprising choice of the production is to present the play as a comedy. When Tom, in his opening monologue, introduces his (absent) father as "a telephone man who fell in love with long distance," we hear a murmur of amusement from the live audience. Later, Amanda Wingfield confronts her son about his late hours. When he tells her he goes to the movies, she retorts, "Nobody in their right mind goes to the movies night after night"—and gets a solid laugh. Telling her how much he hates his job, he says he thinks "how lucky dead people are"—another big yuk. Act II is no better. The next day Tom tries to apologize for storming out. His mother has but one request. "Promise me you will never be a drunkard." That line, plus an observation Amanda makes on the background of the gentleman caller Tom has invited to dinner, produce the biggest laughs of the evening. "Irish on both sides and he doesn't drink," she states in disbelief.

After a brief intermission, Clift returns to deliver Tom's description of the dance hall across the street. Slurring his words, as called for by the script, he flubs a line in the live broadcast. "You could see [the young couples] kissing behind ashpoles. . . ." There is an embarrassingly long pause until Clift recovers—"ash pits and telephone poles." Decades later, at least one person who heard the original broadcast was so disturbed by Clift's mistakes he was convinced (and still believes) that Clift was actually drunk.[20] Maybe he was.

The second *Glass Menagerie*, in 1964, was made for a medium with a smaller audience than TV or radio. A two-LP set available in libraries for educational purposes, this *Menagerie* was the "premiere production" of a Caedmon Records series designed to preserve "the entire heritage of world theatre." A booklet included in the boxed set lays out the goals of Caedmon Records and the newly constituted Theatre Recording Society, and explains how this particular play came to be chosen: "Tennessee Williams is a playwright who uses language as an art form, in the great tradition of

FIGURE 40. *The Glass Menagerie,* 1964. Left to right: director Howard Sackler, Julie Harris (Laura), Jessica Tandy (Amanda), Clift (Tom), and David Wayne (the Gentleman Caller) recording at Caedmon Studios, New York.

drama. He proves that the American idiom can be rendered sensitively and literately, without resorting to the fashionable grunts, monosyllabic phrases and plodding pedestrianism which constitute an alarming percentage of current productions. By the very nature of our recording project, we decline to inflict upon the ear two or three hours of banality or worse."[21] The determining factor, though, was something else. The "unusual presence simultaneously in New York" of Clift, Jessica Tandy, Julie Harris, and David Wayne "enabled us to fulfill our cherished dream of perfect casting for this modern classic."[22]

In the 1951 version, the play starts with the line "The story is memory" and provides a detailed description of the setting. The 1964 version is less concerned with providing visual information or audio snapshots of the main characters. The introduction dwells more on "the social background of the play," as Tom tells us about "that quaint period, the thirties, when the huge middle class of America was matriculating in a school for the blind. Their eyes had failed them—or they had failed their eyes—" [he inhales raggedly] "and so they were having their fingers pressed, forcibly down, on the fiery Braille alphabet of a dissolving economy." The dark, political references (to the Depression, fascism in Europe, Guernica, labor protests—"sometimes . . .

pretty violent") provide a ruminative perspective, similar to the tone Clift would adopt for Faulkner. By the time Tom says, "The play is memory," the tone has already been substantially altered from what it had been in the earlier production. (Having been recorded in a studio rather than in a theater with an audience, there are no laughs.)

On the radio, Clift's Tom is young from all angles. His voice is high, his delivery hurried, energetic, and restless. Thirteen years later, Clift plays youth from a distance. He occupies a dual point of view, the character both living in the past and remembering it many years hence. As an adult he understands how much his younger self needs to separate from the family. And as an adult, he recognizes the lasting sorrow that has come from having done it (and having had to). Clift's voice repeatedly settles into words, bottoming out as he ends a sentence with a downward inflection, the air moving through each word as it moves in his throat. For instance, when he describes his father's last postcard from Mazatlán, "Two words: Hello. Good-bye. And no address," Clift's voice falls to its lowest point on the second syllables of "Good-bye" and "address," followed each time by a pause.

At the end of the first act, Tom and his mother, Amanda (Jessica Tandy), fight and he storms out, breaking pieces of Laura's glass collection. A brisk two minutes and twenty seconds in the radio version, their argument is nearly twice as long in the later production, allowing for more detail in the dialogue and greater variety in the actors' delivery as the confrontation builds to an emotional climax. The scene in 1964 starts with Laura (Julie Harris) trying to keep the peace as she gently steers her mother away, saying, "Mother, Tom's trying to write." Amanda, in a voice acid with contempt, mutters, "So he is. So. He. *Is.*" At first he tries casually to rebuff her interest, saying, "Mother, please go busy yourself with something else. I'm trying to write." But when she persists, he explodes, loud and profane. "What in *Christ's name* am I supposed to do? *Huh?*" When she asks if he has gone out of his senses, he insists in two staccato phrases—"I have. That's true. [adding volume] *Driven* out."

Clift/Tom is out of control and filled with complaint, but he is matched at every point by Jessica Tandy's imperiously critical Amanda. Full equals, sizing each other up in a fight to survive, they go at each other with all they've got, neither giving an inch. Bitter because she has taken his copy of D. H. Lawrence back to the library, Tom begins, "Yesterday you confiscated my books. You had the *nerve*—" but she cuts him off, insisting that she will not have "such filth brought into my house." He cuts her off in turn, shouting, "*My* house. *My* house. Who pays the rent? Who makes a slave of himself—"

She interrupts, drowning him out, "Don't you dare—*dare* to talk to me—" He shuts her out in turn, talking to himself with prissy sarcasm, "Oh, no no no. I mustn't say anything. I've just got to keep quiet."

As Clift works the dynamic range of his voice by increasing the volume or lowering the pitch, Tandy's voice shoots upward into shrill, harsh tones, cracking and scraping the listener's nerves. Their duet of overlapping dialogue becomes an aria of rage as Tom rebels against her self-serving self pity. When she says she is at the end of her patience, he counters, "What do you think I'm at the end of? [pause] Aren't I supposed to have any patience to reach the end of, Mother?" Resentful at being taken for granted, burdened by having to support the family, he tells her with grim monotony how he feels about his job. "Look. I'd rather somebody picked up a crowbar and battered out my brains than go back mornings. [pause] But I go. [Pause] Every time you come in yelling that goddamn 'Rise and shine, rise and shine,' I say to myself—how lucky dead people are. [pause] But I get up. [pause] I go." The speech culminates with his refusal to be held: "Don't—*grab* at me, Mother." Clift delivers this line, the climax of the speech, as the outburst that punctuates what he has been trying to say all along.

In the radio version, the exchange is handled quite differently. Tom, fundamentally, is an obedient, well-brought-up youth. (The profanity, of course, has been excised for the radio version.) He says, "Don't grab at me, mother" quietly, swallowing the line as if cowed and embarrassed and tired of always having to say it. When Helen Hayes's Amanda asks young Clift where he is going, he pauses, and then says in an exhausted but bound-to-be-comic way, "I'm going to the movies." This gets a big laugh, and Hayes waits for it. When she accuses Tom of lying, he responds simply, "All right. I'm going to opium dens." (Another big laugh as the actors wait.)

As with much else in the 1951 version, Tom's speech at the end of this scene has been severely condensed and treated lightheartedly. This is partly due to Helen Hayes's Amanda, who seems forceful (telling him she will not stand his insolence) but never unreasonable. (Helen Hayes happens to look like Clift's mother, Sunny, with whom Clift had some notorious shouting matches; in a photo of Clift's mother emerging from her son's funeral, the resemblance is particularly striking.)[23] The young Clift's stance toward his mother is more bemused and frustrated than furious. After the audience laughs, Clift informs her with an air of surprise, "I—I'm a hired assassin, Mother." (Laugh.) "They call me Killer Wingfield." (Laugh.) "Y'know what?" he asks in a friendly voice. "My friends plan to dynamite this place.

They're gonna [pause, then loudly] blow it all sky-high some night, and *you* [pause]—are gonna go up on a broomstick over—" The laugh here is so prolonged that Clift has to pause in the middle of the line, backtrack, and then ad-lib, elaborating on the line so that he can regain his momentum: "—*way high* over Blue Mountain—" He finishes all in a rush, saying almost under his breath, "with all your seventeen gentleman callers, you ugly, babbling old witch."

The entire speech is six lines.

When Clift responds to Tandy in the later version, the moment is transformed. Hearing him declare that he is "going to the movies," she retorts, "I don't *believe* that lie!" Accusing him outright, she throws down a gauntlet with full force. Instead of responding with a pallid "All right," Clift reacts this time with a challenge of his own. "No?" he asks, drawing out the word into rising syllables. Turning the tables on her, his voice self-satisfied and insinuating, he says, "Well, you're *right*. For once in your life, you're *right*." The singsong rhythm Clift uses underscores the sarcasm of Tom's praise and sets up a torrent of excess, accented at the end of each line by the way he spits out the bitter word "Mother."

> I'm going to opium dens. Yes, opium dens, dens of vice and criminal hangouts, *Mother*. I've joined the Hogan gang, I'm a hired assassin. I carry a tommy gun in a violin case. I run a string of cathouses in the valley—they call me Killer. [Suddenly louder] *Killer* Wingfield! I'm leading a Double Life. [Quietly] A simple honest warehouse worker by day, [switching to an insinuating tone] and by night—a Dynamic Czar of the underworld, *Mother*. . . . [Darker, more threatening] Oh, I could tell you things to make you sleepless [his voice diving deep].

Hoskyns suggests that Clift was not adept at conveying anger or even raising his voice; he never heard this recording.[24] Whether arguing with Hockstader in *Suddenly, Last Summer* or being combative with Meynert in *Freud*, Clift had offered glimpses of anger before. Here, at last, he sheds the stoicism that typifies earlier characters like Logan, Prewitt, and Noah Ackerman and finishes the speech at full volume. Instead of swallowing the injustices done to him, Tom is filled with justifiable anger at not being allowed to be who he is. An aspiring writer no longer content to be the good son and work in a warehouse for sixty-five dollars a month, Tom cannot keep it all inside anymore, whether as a young man prone to adolescent outbursts in 1951 or as a character choking on rage and frustration in 1964.

(To give *The Young Lions* its due, there is one scene in the film in which Clift's Noah is tired and fed up and lets everybody know it. Crouched down in a field beside an unconscious comrade, he finds himself a target for jumpy American sentries. Insulted at being shot at and exhausted from having just saved a fellow soldier from drowning, he summons all his energy and yells at his fellow GIs, "Cut it out!")

If anger is rare, it is even rarer for a Clift character to be part of a family. In half of his films he plays a loner. In eight of them, there is not so much as a reference to a family *(The Search, The Big Lift, I Confess, From Here to Eternity, The Young Lions, Suddenly, Last Summer, Wild River,* and *The Defector).* He is an orphan in *Red River* and *Judgment at Nuremberg,* having lost his parents in traumatic circumstances. The families that do exist are rarely complete. In *The Heiress* his only living relative is an older sister, and in *Lonelyhearts* Dad is in prison for having murdered Mom. When he does have a mother, he keeps her at a distance, staying in touch by phone *(A Place in the Sun* and *The Misfits).* Both his parents are alive at the beginning of *Freud* (though none of Freud's children are shown to exist and his sisters are nonentities). Although he refers to his parents' happy marriage in *Indiscretion of an American Wife,* the only time we see Clift as part of a whole, healthy family is early in *Raintree County.* In *The Glass Menagerie,* by contrast, he cannot escape his role as son and brother, both of which put him in an impossible position. Tom cannot tolerate his mother's overbearing presence, suspicion, and criticism, but if he leaves, he becomes the absent, abandoning father. Leaving also means cutting himself off from the only person he loves and who loves him—his sister, Laura.

The epilogue returns to Tom in the present and addresses what he has lost (Clift's voice, landing with special emphasis on the italicized words). "I didn't go to the moon, I went much further. For time is the longest distance between two *places* [. . .] The cities swept about me like dead *leaves.* Leaves that were brightly colored—but torn away from the branches—" Clift leaves this sentence with an upward intonation, turning it into a sentence fragment rather than a continuation of the previous sentence. He pauses, inhales for a second, then inhales again and says, carefully and deliberately, "I would have stopped—" [again leaving the sentence hanging in the air, as if looking for a way to express something unexplainable] "—but I was pursued by something."

As *The Glass Menagerie* ends, Tom is caught in a permanent state of mourning at having failed his sister. Although we might imagine the 1951 Tom as a young idealist beginning his career as a soon-to-be-famous writer by lighting out for the territories, the older Tom is more than a rebel defying the expectations of the petite bourgeoisie. As that Tom looks back, we can read Clift's ragged, expressive voice—loosed by rage, sapped by remorse— as the voice of wisdom, perspective, and regret.

Much of Clift's vocal work is elegiac in purpose and tone, which calls to mind E. L. McCallum's formulation of fetishism as a means of mastering loss. Because of its precarious status, the ephemeral nature of its existence, the voice (especially the disembodied voice) is the ideal fetish object. The reassurance of the voice, its constancy as a balm in the face of loss, is attested to by the daughter of famous radio personality Alistair Cooke. Comparing listening to her father when she was young and he was away from home, and listening to his voice again after his death, she said, "You crawl into people's voices the way you crawl into people's laps. It's very consoling."[25] As long as the voice can be heard, loss can be denied, presence seemingly restored and sustainable through repetition.

There can be pleasure, even bravado, in the face of loss. Listening to a recorded voice, the auditor constructs an intimate connection with an absent body. In his essay "The Grain of the Voice," Roland Barthes proposes listening in a way that privileges the voice over language, sound over sense, so that we may attend to "the voluptuousness" of sound, "the materiality of the body" that "exceeds culture" and "sways us to *jouissance*."[26] "I am determined," Barthes asserts, "to listen to my relation with the body of the man or woman singing . . . and that relation is erotic." Through vocalization of any kind, the losses of melancholia can be met, refuted, and transcended by another kind of loss—the loss (or willful misplacing) of the self in ecstatic union.[27]

My own effort to describe Clift's voice on the 1964 recording of *The Glass Menagerie* is an attempt to capture both the physical thrill and emotive power of (in Alumit's terms) the "low resonance of a man's voice" in this, my most prized Clift text since childhood. In doing so, saying, "*This* is important, *this* is where it happens, listen to this part," I recognize the proselytizing urge Willemen identifies as characteristic of the cinephile (and, we can now add, audiophile). But although I use the occasional, never-adequate adjective and resort to italics, punctuation, and capital letters in a vain attempt to describe the actor's line readings, no matter how I struggle to describe Clift's voice, I find myself reproducing Tennessee Williams's dialogue.

Mladen Dolar, in his book *A Voice and Nothing More,* warns against reducing the voice to language, "reducing the heard to the meaningful, reducing the audible to the intelligible." Listening, as opposed to mere hearing, he argues, "implies an opening toward a sense which is undecidable, precarious, elusive." But for Dolar, aware of the metaphysical heritage of thinking about the voice, there is more to be gained from listening than mere *jouissance*. Listeners are "on the lookout" for "something that announces itself in the voice," something "beyond meaning" *and* the body.[28] "The voice, by being so ephemeral, transient, incorporeal, ethereal, presents for that very reason the body at its quintessential, the hidden bodily treasure beyond the visible envelope, the interior 'real' body, unique and intimate, and at the same time it seems to present more than the mere body."[29] This sense of "a world beyond representation which only shimmers through in certain moments" (as Willemen puts it) takes us to the metaphysical heart of the matter: "The voice carried by breath points to the soul." Irreducible to the body, "the voice is the flesh of the soul, its ineradicable materiality."[30]

Once more we come to Clift via religious discourse, no longer a mere actor but someone who, by having become a voice, reveals his soul. In metaphysics the voice has long been held to have a privileged relation to the spirit. In that discourse as well as for Dolar, the voice would be the manifestation of the soul for any actor (for any person), regardless of talent or skill or will. So why would Clift's voice be any more moving than Jessica Tandy's, or Zachary Scott's, or even his own, thirteen years earlier?

Because I cannot speak to the condition of Montgomery Clift's soul, regardless of how much I like his voice, I must conclude that metaphysics is not what I'm after. Clift's sainthood, like his martyrdom, is the product of his fans' relation to texts, some made with Clift's participation, some produced by others. Out of all the materials available, fans take what they want and use the details they select in order to make a story that has deep and lasting personal meaning for them.

The fan's reading of texts is conditioned not only by content and medium, but by history. The importance of the voice, for instance, is tied not just to performance, but to the historical, material circumstances of reception. Clift's original fans could see his work, for a limited time only, in theaters during each film's original release. In the sixties, as Noël Alumit illustrates in *Letters to Montgomery Clift*, people could see the films multiple times, in any order, whenever they were played on television. In the eighties, they could rent, buy, or own video copies of the films, which also made it possible to select out favorite scenes and watch them over and over. But in the early seventies, the only Clift performance that was available to be played at will in the home was *The Glass Menagerie*.

In her work on "how texts become meaningful within personal and social horizons," Barbara Klinger argues that the intense affective response fans have to a film or recording "is substantially enhanced when films and other media enter private space and become part of an intimate repertoire of domestic objects infused with personal meaning."[31] My relation to this particular Clift text was intensified by all of these factors: it was ownable, repeatable, and rare. My preference for his later films is a by-product of my relation to *this* voice, his postaccident voice, and not the voice of the first part of his career. A longtime indifference to his youthful beauty was also conditioned by the preference for vocal texts that grew out of these circumstances—as did a certain impatience with those who would privilege the "young" Clift over the older actor on the basis of his looks.

But even a fan can hear too much. Among the new works made after Clift's death are biographical documentaries that intersperse clips from his films with "new" (i.e., previously unseen) material such as outtakes, candid photographs, and home movies. Such works promise the audience a glimpse of Clift "himself," unscripted moments that reveal the person in his everyday life as opposed to an actor performing a role. While candid photographs and such have long been part of the repertoire of studios' promotion of stars (and are often as carefully posed and thought out as any other type of publicity material), candid audio recordings are less common and carry with them a disproportionate capacity to disturb.

The voice overheard, recorded without the speaker's knowledge, carries few of the markers of self-consciousness so easily detectable in "candid" photos. Because sound unfolds in the present—can only exist *as* sound at the moment in which it is heard—and because the sound of the voice is created inside the speaker's body and heard or registered inside the body of the listener (something accentuated by the use of headphones), the listener experiences the voice of the other in a uniquely intimate way. When listening to a recording of a voice (always distanced from the listener in terms of time and space—a distance compounded by the death of the speaker), the listener revivifies the voice by incorporating it, acting as host body to a disembodied consciousness, spirit, or relic from the past.

Because the voice of the speaker brings with it traces from the interior of the speaker's body (an interior "without defenses," a body that may no longer exist), the listener is granted a uniquely intimate access to the other. Dolar points out the drawbacks of such intense intimacy. "There is a too-much of the voice stemming from the inside—it brings out more, and other things, than one would intend. *One is too exposed to the voice and the voice exposes too much.*"[32]

In a televised documentary, Brooks Clift provided audio recordings of his telephone conversations with his brother, circa 1960.[33] Issues of fraternal betrayal aside, the tapes are presented as having biographical value, especially when Clift in his own words deflates the myths of his rebelliousness and indifference to fame. In a conversation recorded November 2, 1962, for example, he indicates how much he loved being popular and how desperate he is to win an Oscar for *Judgment at Nuremberg.* He had set so much store on that performance resecuring him the respect of the industry that he had waived his salary. Talking about this to his brother late one night, his words slurred, he begins crying: "Boy, it would sure be wonderful." Dolar notes, "The voice comes from some unfathomable invisible interior and brings it out, lays it bare, discloses, uncovers, reveals that interior. By so doing it produces an effect which has both an obscene side (disclosing something hidden, intimate, revealing too much, structurally too much) and an uncanny side—this is how Freud, following Schelling, described the uncanny: something that 'ought to have remained . . . secret and hidden but has come to light.'"[34] It should have stayed private; even a fan might feel ashamed to have heard.

LOST TEXTS

Even if fans create their own Montgomery Clift, he is not an entirely imaginary figure. The most important contributor to Clift's image among all the publicists, biographers, documentary filmmakers, novelists, playwrights, songwriters, gossips, and raconteurs was Clift himself.

Of all the roles he might have played, the role Clift was imagining himself in the year he died seems the most unlikely of all. In September 1966, Clift was set to begin filming *Reflections in a Golden Eye,* Elizabeth Taylor again having secured him the job.[35] He would be back in uniform, playing an officer this time, a closeted gay man who lusts after a young soldier. Clift was ready to take that risk. He was even willing to work with John Huston again, who was set to direct. (After Clift died, Brando played the part.)

Prior to embarking on one more sojourn into midcentury Southern Gothic, Clift decided to make a low-budget film in Europe. *The Defector,* the film that turned out to be his last, was shot in Munich in early spring. Although the film does not show Clift at his best, it should not be excluded out of misplaced respect for the actor. Much of his performance is consistent with what is most admirable about Clift's career as a whole.

The Defector is not terrible; it is not good either, just ordinary. On paper it had promise. Clift was back in Europe, where he had made close to half his films, including *The Search, The Big Lift, Indiscretion of an American Wife, Suddenly, Last Summer* (set in the United States but shot in London), *Judgment at Nuremberg,* and *Freud.* Twenty years after beginning his film career, he was still eager to work with promising European directors (as he had done with Zinnemann and De Sica).

The Defector has impeccable French New Wave credentials. Raoul Levy, the film's writer and director, had worked as either writer or producer on Roger Vadim's . . . *And God Created Woman* (1956), Marguerite Duras's *Moderato Cantabile* (1960), and Jean-Luc Godard's *Two or Three Things I Know about Her* (released in 1967). The film's cinematographer was the legendary Raoul Coutard, and the music was composed by Serge Gainsbourg. Clift's female costar was Macha Meril, the star of Godard's *A Married Woman* (1964). Director Levy even had a part in *Two or Three Things* (as "John Bogus the American"), a favor Godard returned in *The Defector,* where he turns up in a wordless cameo as a famous Russian spy.

Although the final result may seem little more than a routine genre picture, the genre itself was a defining one for the first half of the sixties. Films about Cold War espionage provided some of the decade's biggest commercial successes (five James Bond films between 1962 and 1967), serious dramatic films such as *The Spy Who Came in from the Cold* (1965), and a number of high-profile misfires (from Hitchcock's *Torn Curtain* [1966] and *Topaz* [1969] to *Casino Royale* [1967, John Huston et al.]).

Considering its provenance, *The Defector* may in fact be a film that is better imagined than seen. Seeing —seeing Clift—is one of the film's problems. As Professor James Bower, Clift appears in nearly every scene of the film. While the "damaged" quality of his face had been an asset for the actor in *Judgment at Nuremberg* and a nonfactor in *Suddenly, Last Summer, Freud,* and *The Glass Menagerie,* here Clift's face signifies in excess of his character—which is a fancy way of saying he looks god-awful. When he first appears in the harsh light of a Munich winter in the film's first scene, his face is lined and scarred. The use of color emphasizes variations in his skin tone caused by age, sun, and smoking. The bones under his skin are accentuated by his wasted appearance, making his forehead out of proportion to his indrawn cheeks.[36] A shriveled body lost inside an oversize coat, he calls to mind Judy Garland, who would die the next year, similarly withered and frail, age forty-seven but looking sixty-seven. Meeting a friend from the CIA (Roddy McDowall) in an underpopulated zoo, Clift/Bower is not favored by the natural lighting or the choice of camera angles. That kind of glamour photography would be out of keeping with both the New Wave and the Cold War spy genre. Instead we see him in the cold, clear light of day, a kind of "dead man walking" breaking into a ghastly smile as he rushes up to embrace McDowall and the plot is set in motion. (Mc-Dowall's character introduces some double entendres de la closet: "It is very, *very* important that no one see us talking together" and "You've got to begin to be a devious man.")

An American physicist, Bower is asked to help the CIA by persuading an East German physicist to defect to the West. Bower refuses, but when he is threatened with the loss of government funding for his research, he agrees to collect some top-secret microfilm from the East German's contacts. This is of the utmost importance, he is told, because it "could determine who's going to get to the moon first." Watched by security forces from the moment of his arrival in Leipzig, Bower goes through the usual steps—innocuous meetings with pharmacists and impromptu doctor's appointments that turn out to be part of a plan to contact the secret network through which his counterpart can communicate with him. At the same time, everyone in this world knows the rules of the game. Bower is quickly summoned to meet with a "public relations" officer, Peter Heinzman (Hardy Kruger), who lets him know that they know what he is up to, and now that he knows that they know . . . and so on. Soon thereafter Bower finds himself trapped in a psychedelic hotel room designed to break him down psychologically so that he will cooperate. (The faucets spew ink; a spotlight pursues him at night; the walls become mirrors, then walls; people appear and disappear, their voices heavily filtered, their images distorted.)

In the midst of these familiar tropes of the genre, Clift begins to remind us what an actor can contribute, regardless of the quality of the material. Not treating the work as routine, Clift begins adding small touches to scenes that make his physical condition moot and his intelligence as an actor central. In his first interview with Kruger, Clift/Bower sits aslant in a chair, smoking languidly. Playing cat and mouse with surprising sophistication, he boldly exposes the entire charade. "You're um . . . you're not a public relations man, are you?" he says to Heinzman. "I would guess that you're a representative of state security—or whatever they're calling it nowadays." In his rigged hotel room, Clift's Bower looks more wiry than frail in a white T-shirt (reminiscent of *A Place in the Sun* and *From Here to Eternity*). Fed

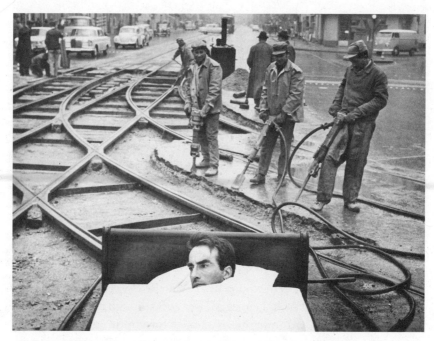

FIGURE 41. Lobby card for *The Defector:* Clift in bed in the street.

up with the attempts at mind control, he begins to smash up the room. Unexpectedly, breaking things helps him reestablish a sense of cause and effect. Repeatedly dropping a salt shaker onto a plate cover, he is reassured by the predictability of the sound and the weight. Leaning against a wall, he speaks to his unseen listeners: "You can't make a schizophrenic out of me—at least today . . . tonight, or whatever time it is." Making a joke at his own expense by admitting that he doesn't know what time it is, Clift's tone undercuts the typical hero's bluster but proclaims his defiance just the same.

A fake romance gives Clift/Bower a chance to poke fun at the playboy style of the era's flashier secret agents. Arranging a date with Frieda (Macha Meril), the assistant to the doctor who is his contact, Bower finds himself hauled away from her apartment by the secret police. On his way out, he leans over to kiss her on the lips for show—a gesture that is equal parts bravado for the police and a shared joke with her. As their relationship develops (holding hands in the snow, being watched by the secret police), he becomes even more relaxed. Lolling around on her bed one afternoon (looking like an exclamation point in his black turtleneck and black pants), he asks her about the books she reads. "It's *very revealing,*" he tells her, "to know what books one takes to bed with one." (Hers is a French comic book.) She asks him in turn, "And what do you take to bed?" He responds coyly, "How do you mean?—Oh! Books." Although his gay best friend act soft-pedals the heterosexual desire that supposedly fuels the scene, Clift's comic takes are never seriously at odds with the character. Unlike Brando, who often ridiculed his characters and would find ways to make otherwise acceptable films worse by his overweening contempt, Clift's jokes make his character more playful and interesting.

Being French, the film portrays the machinations of the United States and the Soviet Union as equally distasteful. Heinzman and Bower find they have more in common than not. The son of a physicist, Heinzman too has been promised the chance to do research on condition that he play along with the state. Both men struggle with the ethical quandary they find themselves in. When Bower finally receives the microfilm, he turns it over to Heinzman, explaining that it is worthless. When Bower tries to escape back to the West, stealing boats and swimming through heavily guarded riverways at night, Heinzman helps him at the last minute by directing him away from a minefield. In a last twist, it is Heinzman, not the physicist or Bower, who becomes the defector of the title, leaving East Germany for the West. In a twist on that twist, Heinzman's defection turns out to be a cover story to sneak him into America as a double agent. But the Americans are on to him as fast as the East Germans were on to Bower, and being just as ruthless, the CIA has Heinzman summarily run over by a truck. Bower, unaware of the last three plot twists, is devastated. The End.

Although *The Defector* is not the lost gem fans might hope for, when it was completed Clift would still be right to say he had never made a film that he was ashamed of.[37] Various biographies detail the difficulties Clift had during the making of the film, especially with his memory, but at least he was surrounded by friends. Mira Rostova came back to help and Roddy McDowall was in the opening and closing scenes.[38]

Although chronology may demand that we end here, with Clift's last film, there is one more text that has fallen out of time, the kind of lost film fans dream of when they have exhausted the known canon of the actor's work. It is difficult to place and hard to describe in methodological terms, but like the LP set of *The Glass Menagerie,* its idiosyncratic position outside the usual categories makes it likely to be valued all the more.

Terminal Station (a title both redundant and meaningless in English) is the 1983 reconstruction of Vittorio De Sica's *Indiscretion of an American Wife*. Shot before *From Here to Eternity*, *Indiscretion* was released after the success of that film, having been severely reedited by producer David O. Selznick until a mere sixty-three minutes remained. (The reconstructed version is eighty-seven minutes.) Bosworth states that Selznick saw the picture "as a vehicle" for his wife, Jennifer Jones, and that he eliminated "most of De Sica's colorful but unnecessary vignettes with other travelers."[39] When the two versions are compared, however, it is soon clear that the vignettes are still there—it is scenes involving the stars that Selznick dramatically reduced. Not only are the shots in a different order, but the reconstructed version uses different camera angles, different shot lengths, and different takes of the same shot. Some of the differences are subtle: a tighter close-up, a longer pause between phrases. A long take in one version is interrupted by reaction shots in the other. Often the only way to be certain that a different take is being used is when the dialogue changes. In one close-up, for example, Clift says, the name "Maria" three times. In the reconstructed version, he says it four times. (In the tighter close-up for this take, his face is partly obscured by the back of Jones's head in a way inescapably reminiscent of the extreme close-ups in *A Place in the Sun*.)

Long dismissed as a blatant imitation of *Brief Encounter*, this film about the end of an affair was never respected enough for the reedited version to make much of a splash, but when compared to the version Selznick distributed in 1954 (and the one that continues to circulate), the 1983 version is a revelation. Our response to the characters and our understanding of their motives are fundamentally changed as it becomes clear that Selznick removed any sign of adult sexuality in favor of sentimentality and romance. The consequences of Selznick's editing are especially clear in the first extended scene Clift and Jones have together. The fourteen-minute scene in the reconstruction is twice as long as the one in the Selznick version. Because opportunities for large-scale physical action are limited, these scenes place more emphasis on the actor's voice, eyes, and facial expressions. Unlike *A Place in the Sun* or *From Here to Eternity*, where Clift communicates through silence and with his back turned, here he faces the camera and speaks. The medium shots and close-ups of Clift's interaction with Jennifer Jones provide a classic example of film acting.

Giovanni (Clift) arrives at the train station just as Mary (Jones) is about to leave Rome. He persuades her to wait for the next train and they look for a place where they can speak privately. As they find a table in a nearly empty restaurant, he begins to sort out what has happened. In the American release, Clift is in profile on the right side of the screen in a medium two-shot. After an uncomfortable silence, he addresses the idea of her leaving. "You start to leave Rome after these weeks, this month, after yesterday." In the restored version, *she* begins the conversation, saying, "I can see you're not going to help me." There is a cut to Giovanni, seen in an over-the-shoulder medium shot. "I may be wrong but if—if I understand you—I'm the one who's entitled to help." Upset and confused, he begins to lay out his feelings, working at the table with his hand (much the way Perce digs at the wall of the phone booth in *The Misfits*).

GIOVANNI: You start to leave Rome after—these weeks—this month—after yesterday. [growing louder and angrier] Or don't you remember yesterday. What did you say to me then?

MARY: That I loved you.

In the American version, this part of the conversation ends here. In the longer version, he begins to interrogate her.

GIOVANNI: More than?

MARY: More than all the world.

He repeats this quickly: "'More than all the world.' *And?*"

MARY: Anyone in it.

In both films he asks her, in a close-up, "Wh—what am I—t-to you—suddenly? Some . . . an old guidebook that you don't really want anymore?" She replies with a melodramatic "Don't want! Then you don't know what wanting is." He responds, insulted, "Oh, don't I."

As the lovers reminisce about their first meeting, their motives change from one version of the film to the other. In both Giovanni says that until he saw her he "didn't know what wanting was." In the longer version he expands on this. He tells her outright that he was motivated by desire. "I liked your legs." He flashes a quick smile and comments wryly, "I wouldn't have looked at you, maybe, if it hadn't been for those legs." Mary, on the other hand, misunderstood who he was from the start. "I thought you were an Italian," she simpers. "Because my mother was American doesn't make me less Italian," he assures her. "In this country, it's the men who count." He leans back, his eyes cast down, in too much pain to look at her. "You American women are too emancipated."[40] Each film uses a different take of this brief sketch of Italian machismo. In the restored version, Clift is out of focus for the first two lines, but when he leans back his face (and his pain) become sharper instantly as his voice falters on the word *emancipated*—playing the subtext in classic Stanislavski/Bobby Lewis/Alfred Lunt fashion.

Mary's dialogue is cut so that any sign of physical desire on her part is removed, to be replaced by dreamy generalities. When Giovanni asks her why she came with him for coffee the day they met, in Selznick's American version Mary ascribes everything to kismet—"It was you. It was Rome. And I'm a housewife from Philadelphia." In the Italian version the character shows a greater awareness of her own behavior and her own desire. "I've never done anything extraordinary, except that. Letting you—pick me up." After blaming it on Rome, she begins to rationalize: "But I only thought it would be a small adventure," she tells him, adding that perhaps it was something she could tell her sister or write to her husband. "A small adventure," he muses. "I see."

The childish irresponsibility of her flirtation is reinforced when she tells him he is her "beau ideal," a figure dreamed of since she was a girl, like her high school crush, Percy Tuttle. Amused, he asks her, "Do you think I look like your Mr. Tuttle?" She cautions him: "Percy was so handsome." Clift, in mock exasperation, spoofs her childish romanticism, speaking almost in a falsetto as he repeats, "'Oh he was so—.'" He sighs and shakes his head, disbelieving, "I'm not?" At this moment it is impossible to imagine he could ever *not* be handsome.

Surprisingly, when Mary describes her love for her daughter, Cathy, and defends her marriage, Selznick cuts her dialogue substantially. In the Italian version, there are signs of premeditation. When she insists she could never leave Cathy, Giovanni points out, "In all the conversations we've had, in all the plans we've made, have I ever suggested you should give up Cathy?" The American version keeps the last part of the sentence but leaves out the plans and conversations. More seriously, in the Italian version Mary says that Cathy was very ill at birth and that Mary and her husband, Howard, swore, "really swore," on their daughter's life never to break up her home. In the Selznick version, this is gone.

Selznick would have known as well as anyone that while divorce may have been grudgingly accepted, at this particular historical moment the public had a strong antipathy to the thought of a mother abandoning her child because of an affair. In 1949–50, Ingrid Bergman, who began her Hollywood career under contract to David O. Selznick, had left her husband and daughter in Los Angeles while she went to Italy to work with Roberto Rossellini. Bergman's affair with Rossellini (also married at the time) caused an uproar that was only compounded when they had a child out of wedlock. As Adrienne McLean points out, it was not the affair, divorce, or the new baby that sparked the deepest indignation, but the idea of the child Bergman left behind, her preteen daughter.[41] This is also the probable reason that, in the earlier exchange, Mary could allow that she loved Giovanni but, in the American version, not "more than all the world" and definitely not "more than anyone in it," lest viewers assume she means her daughter.

But it is Mary's defense of her husband that pushes Giovanni over the edge. In the American release, Mary's regal proclamation, "I am Howard's future. Cathy and I," ends the conversation as she and Giovanni are asked by a waiter to leave the empty restaurant. The Italian version makes Mary's view of her marriage more prosaic and at the same time more compelling. "Giovanni, you—you can't live with a man for eight years and bear his child. . . . You can't do that without caring what happens to him." She goes on about Howard's vulnerability and helplessness. "He can't even find his socks." "Oh, stop," Clift groans, turning his head away in disgust as if it is all so much sentimental hogwash. "I'm sorry," he continues, "I just don't want to hear about the lovable husband who doesn't know where his socks are." Facing her bluntly, he provokes her: "What are you supposed to do—spend the rest of your life finding them?" Defensive, she primly replies, "If you want to put it that way." Expelled from the restaurant, they take a small table in a crowded public space in the midst of the terminal.

The second part of the scene risks the likability of both Mary and Giovanni. Mary's betrayal of her husband and daughter is compounded by her mistreatment of Giovanni. Unlike *Brief Encounter,* in which both parties are married and anguished about their affair, here only Mary is unfaithful. Giovanni is single and ready to commit himself to her, as shown by his discussion of how he imagined their future would be. On the other hand, Giovanni's anger, while understandable, is intense and a little unsettling. As they sit opposite each other in the noisy café area, he demands that she take off her hat. When she hesitates (in a reverse shot), he commands her again (in voice-off) to take it off. Suddenly, he reaches into the shot and pulls the hat off her head, explaining, "It's a smug little hat." The close-up of Jones/Mary makes clear her imperiousness as she bristles at being ordered about. When he snatches her hat, she is not only shocked and angry—she looks icy and vindictive. In the American version the whole scene is done in a long shot, as we hear Clift say (once, with his back to the camera), "Take off that hat," then quickly reach over and take it. In the long shot, Jones's reaction seems more confused than harsh, and the shot ends at a moment when she flashes a brief smile—minimizing the scene's force.

In a closer shot, Giovanni explains his outburst. "I was starting to hate you, starting to hate everything you said but . . . [melting into a smile] I can't." In the Italian cut, again he emphasizes physical desire. "You are so— quite beautiful. Your hair—you're really—. Oh, let's get out of here," he implores. "It's too crowded, huh?" In this 1983 version he asks her twice to go back to his place. Perhaps the most striking addition in the reconstruction is Mary's openness about her own sexual desires. When Giovanni tempts her with an invitation to his apartment, she warns him (in a tight close-up), "We're not saints, darling. At least I'm not." Again Selznick moves to save his wife's reputation by robbing her character of any trace of anger or sexuality, though it is not hard to see why he cut this particular exchange. Jones herself had divorced her first husband, Robert Walker, with whom she had two children, to marry Selznick. Walker committed suicide shortly before filming began on *Indiscretion*. All of this biographical information had to be negotiated in reference to Jones's film persona. Though often cast as lustful and wild (*Duel in the Sun* [1946], *Madame Bovary* [1949], *Gone to Earth/The Wild Heart* [1950], *Ruby Gentry* [1952]), the part for which she was best known was a saint. Jones won an Oscar (something Clift never did) for her first major film, *The Song of Bernadette,* in 1943. (This makes her even holier than Ingrid Bergman, whose 1948 *Joan of Arc* was not nearly as celebrated.) In the reconstructed film, Jones/Mary continues, "I'm sorry I'm not a saint, Giovanni. [Pause.] But if I went to your apartment there never would be a train for me."

The one part of the scene that does not change from film to film (except for a line about Cathy at the very beginning) is a two-shot of Mary and Giovanni that lasts over two minutes. Describing their future as he had imagined it, Giovanni tries to rekindle their relationship and persuade Mary to go back to his place. As he says (in both versions), "At least for a little while, we'll have known what it could have been like." Technically, Clift conveys desire in a relatively simple way—repeatedly returning his gaze to Jennifer Jones's half-opened mouth, he gives the impression that he can't take his eyes off her lips. Nevertheless, the emotional consequences far exceed the technique. Even though Bosworth had seen only the Selznick cut, in which the character's strongest feelings had been omitted, she has no problem ze-roing in on what makes Clift's performance so powerful. "He plays the cliché situation . . . with drama and urgency and a sense of style. Passion clings to his every move, every gesture, every look."[42] No longer the passive lover (as in his scene in the fog with Joanne Dru in *Red River*) or hidden in the dark (as with Shelley Winters in *A Place in the Sun*), Clift plays each mo-ment with Jennifer Jones as if his life depended on it. When Peter Bog-danovich said that "Clift never once [gave] a performance without the same riveting intensity, the same soulful integrity," and, for a time, a "magical perfection of pitch," regardless of whether he had seen it, he was describ-ing *Terminal Station*.[43]

CLIFT SEES SELF II

Bogdanovich met Clift once. One day in the early 1960s, Clift escorted Mrs. Walter Huston to a screening of *I Confess* at a New York City revival house. At one point, Clift left the auditorium. Bogdanovich, who programmed the film series, approached him in the lobby and asked him what it was like to see the film after all that had passed. "It's hard, you know," Clift re-sponded. "It's very . . . hard."[44]

What Clift meant cannot be pinpointed, but it can resonate. His words cover a range of possibilities. It might have been hard for him to see him-self and know he would never look like that again. It would certainly be hard not knowing if he would ever work again. (He was in the midst of a four-year stretch of unemployment.) He might have missed the fame. When Bogdanovich showed him the theater's guest book, in which fans had specifi-cally requested more Montgomery Clift films, Clift began to cry. Then again, given his standards, he could have simply felt that his performance was just not good enough.

If a star is an imaginary figure created by fans, then anything anyone has ever said about Montgomery Clift would be true, with the construction of Clift-as-saint being merely one more attempt to make sense of or impose meaning on the vast array of materials produced around the actor's name, life, image, and voice. Nonetheless, it is important to remember for a mo-ment that there actually was someone named Montgomery Clift. He went on the stage when he was fourteen and made his living as an actor for thirty-one years. His work was widely admired. For six years he was an unrivaled star. He had a face of almost indescribable beauty. That changed. In the last part of his career he was considered "damaged," unreliable, and finally unemployable. He died in his sleep in July 1966 of a heart attack. Since his death, his work continues to circulate, its meaning changing over time as new works are produced and old ones rediscovered.

While the feelings or thoughts of Clift the person are never fully knowable, there are certain conclusions we can draw based on the readings of his work and life that have been explored here. We know, for instance, that like all actors he made his body and his voice (and parts of his life) available for the emotional, imaginary engagement of others. Like his fans, he too invested himself in an imaginary being (each character he played) and felt most himself when absorbed in that imaginary union.[45]

If we accept the proposed construction of Clift as a figure for whom acting is a matter of life and death, such a figure upends assumptions about acting being the antithesis of sincerity and sainthood the model of absolute commitment. For this Clift, acting *is* his faith, what he holds on to whether he is being persecuted or acclaimed, celebrated or dismissed.

The qualities people associate with saints crowd the landscape of Clift's films and accounts of his life. In his early films, he provides a vision of glowing promise, an innate goodness demonstrated by his sympathy for the suffering of others (starving war survivors in *The Big Lift*) and his sensitivity to their needs (friend and teacher to a war orphan in *The Search*, patient, considerate leader to frightened and tired men in *Red River*). In these films, the groundedness and maturity of Clift's characters never overwhelm their sense of humor and fundamental kindness. When this image of goodness is complicated by Clift's portrayal of morally ambiguous characters (*The Heiress, A Place in the Sun*), he is able to maintain and even increase audience sympathy, guiding us to understand the characters in ways they do not understand themselves. More immature than actively evil, Morris Townsend becomes a vulnerable figure when confronted with the consequences of his childish machinations. Developing an acting style that requires a greater degree of viewer engagement than usual, Clift leads the audience to supply George Eastman's thoughts of murder, guiding us to understand the character without setting ourselves apart from him—and without minimizing the fact that even indecision can have terrible consequences.

In *I Confess* and *From Here to Eternity*, the integrity attributed to the actor is compounded by that of characters whose commitment to institutions never wavers even when those institutions (the church, the justice system, the military) fail him personally. The zeal, fortitude, endurance, and lack of complaint in the face of persecution shown by these characters are qualities that can be claimed for Clift the actor as well, given the circumstances in which he worked.

Even though an actor can never control the films in which he appears (whether it be preproduction influence that limits the story that can be told *[I Confess]* or postproduction interference such as Selznick cutting half an hour from *Indiscretion of an American Wife*), Clift is depicted as an actor who put everything on the line. He risked his body and his health for projects that were ultimately not worth the effort (returning to *Raintree County* before he had fully healed from the accident; incurring multiple injuries in preparing for and shooting the rodeo scenes in *The Misfits;* swimming in frigid water in *The Defector*). Remarkably indifferent to vanity, he presented his face to the camera after the accident, knowing how he would be judged. He continued working despite having to play scenes that might hold him up to ridicule or contempt (the drunk scenes in *Lonelyhearts* and *Wild River*) or worse (the horrified reactions to his makeup in *The Young Lions* and the supposed lack of it in *Judgment at Nuremberg*). In his later films, when he was impossible to work with and the hostility on the set was at its most intense *(Suddenly, Last Summer; Freud)*, Clift's performances nevertheless conveyed an unwavering sense of courage, stability, and steadfastness. When he could no longer find a job in film, he put his soul into his voice *(The Glass Menagerie)*.

Clift's roles were limited by conventions that predetermined what was expected of a leading man. Heterosexual love stories appear in every Clift film except *The Search* and *Judgment at Nuremberg* (with *Suddenly, Last Summer* and *The Misfits* settling for hints of romance), including those made when Clift was close to forty and cast opposite women in their early twenties *(Lonelyhearts, Wild River, Freud)*. This compulsory heterosexuality was enforced by political, professional, and social pressures that Clift, as a gay man, had to navigate in order to continue his career—whether that meant dodging the national zeitgeist (HUAC and Washington's Lavender Scare) or withstanding hostility from directors (Hitchcock, Huston, Mankiewicz), cast, and crew. He also endured private betrayal when friends distanced themselves, and public derision when scandalmongers spread salacious gossip. Nevertheless, he continued to work, tireless in his commitment to his art.

Clift's pathography may prove that he was not a saint in the standard sense of the term—too much sex, drugs, alcohol, and more drugs. But, as with saints, death changes things. Writing about Clift's performance in *The Defector*, Bosley Crowther (who had called Clift "hollow," "glassy-eyed," and "lackluster" in *The Young Lions*) was generous to the recently deceased actor. "Mr. Clift is apt in his last film—lonely, bewildered, courageous."[46] Despite the tendency to portray Clift's death as a defining element in his star persona, it too is available to be read in multiple ways, even as relatively unimportant. Only those whose lives paralleled Clift's found it necessary to alter or soften their opinions of him after he died. For modern-day fans, Clift is perpetually a contemporary figure, part of their lives now. Always youthful *and* declining, bright with promise and approaching the end of his career, Clift exists outside of time—always already dead, always present, and always just about to be (re)discovered.

Since the Vatican reserves to itself the authority to proclaim sainthood, it is fitting to let them have the last word on Clift. According to Hoskyns, "Among the many obituaries that appeared in the world's newspapers after Clift's death, none was more extraordinary than that published by the Vatican City weekly, *L'osservatore della Domenica.*" This is what the Vatican had to say: "We shall not recall or pass judgment on aspects of his life that were or seemed questionable. But it is a fact that there was in his solitary life an example to remember, the example of his integrity as an artist, of his disinterestedness, of his contempt for easy success."[47]

Or, as Clark Gable said, he was "a hell of an actor."

NOTES

INTRODUCTION

1. Barney Hoskyns, *Montgomery Clift: Beautiful Loser* (New York: Grove Weidenfeld, 1991), 6.

2. Caryl Rivers, *Aphrodite at Mid-Century: Growing Up Catholic and Female in Post-War America* (Garden City, NY: Doubleday and Company, 1973), remembering seeing *Red River* as an eighth grader, 99. This line is quoted in Patricia Bosworth, *Montgomery Clift: A Biography* (New York: Harcourt Brace Jovanovich, 1978), 144, and in Robert LaGuardia, *Monty: A Biography of Montgomery Clift* (New York: Avon Books, 1978), 73.

3. Patricia Bosworth quoted in *Mysteries and Scandals*, "Montgomery Clift" (1998), produced by Joel K. Rodgers, E! Entertainment Television.

4. Elizabeth Taylor narrating a Turner Classic Movies short tribute to Montgomery Clift.

5. Karl Malden, with Carla Malden, *When Do I Start?* (New York: Simon & Schuster, 1997), 229.

6. Bosworth begins her biography with the accident, a prologue against which everything else is measured (*Montgomery Clift*, 1–3).

7. S. Paige Baty's *American Monroe: The Making of a Body Politic* (Berkeley: University of California Press, 1995) addresses the hagiographic tendencies of postmortem writing about the actress; Claudia Springer, *James Dean Transfigured: The Many Faces of Rebel Iconography* (Austin: University of Texas Press, 2007); Erika Doss, *Elvis Culture: Fans, Faith and Image* (Lawrence: University Press of Kansas, 1999). Doss points out that some Elvis fans strongly resent their devotion being compared to religion (see chap. 6, "Saint Elvis," especially 72–75).

8. Bosworth, *Montgomery Clift*, 237.

9. Springer, *James Dean Transfigured*, 9–10.

10. Jackie Stacey, *Star Gazing: Hollywood Cinema and Female Spectatorship* (London: Routledge, 1994), 138–45.

11. Stacey, *Star Gazing*, 142, 143.

12. Richard Dyer is specifically referencing critics of the fifties and sixties who dismissed Judy Garland's gay male fans as hysterical exhibitionists (*Heavenly Bodies: Film Stars and Society* [New York: St. Martin's Press, 1986], 147).

13. Stacey, *Star Gazing*, 143.

14. Stacey describes how the impact of seeing "the star of your dreams" on-screen can mark "the beginning of a lifetime's devotion" (*Star Gazing*, 141).

15. Steve Cohan, *Masked Men: Masculinity and the Movies in the Fifties* (Bloomington: Indiana University Press, 1997).

16. Emile Vuillermoz, quoted in *French Film Theory and Criticism,* ed. Richard Abel, vol. 1: *1907–1929* (Princeton, NJ: Princeton University Press, 1988), 108.

17. Edward Dmytryk, Fred Zinnemann, and Stanley Kramer, quoted in Lyn Tornabene, "Montgomery Clift: Film's Fall Guy," *Cosmopolitan* (May 1963): 74–81 at 74.

18. Tornabene, "Montgomery Clift," 76.

19. Quoted in Tornabene, "Montgomery Clift," 76–77.

ONE. THE FACE OF A SAINT

1. "Speaking of Pictures," *Life* (December 6, 1948): 22–23.

2. "Life's Cover," *Life* (December 6, 1948): 35.

3. Peter Bogdanovich, *Who the Hell's in It?* (New York: A. A. Knopf, 2004), 92.

4. Quoted in David Shipman, *The Great Movie Stars: The International Years* (New York: St. Martin's Press, 1972), 90.

5. Quoted in Bosworth, *Montgomery Clift* (see intro., n. 2), 138.

6. See Bosworth, *Montgomery Clift*, 133–34.

7. Sharon Marie Carnicke, "Lee Strasberg's Paradox of the Actor," in *Screen Acting,* ed. Alan Lovell and Peter Kramer (London: Routledge, 1999), 79. See also James Naremore, *Acting in the Cinema* (Berkeley: University of California Press, 1988), esp. 197–200.

8. For an excellent discussion of the evolution of acting styles and training from the nineteenth century to the first half of the twentieth, see chap. 3 of Naremore's *Acting in the Cinema*, "Rhetoric and Expressive Technique" (34–67).

9. According to a recent biography, Lunt and Fontanne would sit knee to knee, going over their lines again and again, trying to perfect their timing—to fix precisely when the lines should overlap (Margot Peters, *Design for Living: Alfred Lunt and Lynn Fontanne* [New York: A. A. Knopf, 2003], 71).

10. Bosworth, *Montgomery Clift,* 83–84.

11. Sandy Campbell, quoted in Bosworth, *Montgomery Clift,* 114.

12. Bosworth, *Montgomery Clift,* 138. Actual veterans had been used in films throughout the war years and the postwar period to bring increased credibility to the staged sequences of newsreels and "serious" fictional representations of the war and its aftermath, most famously in *The Best Years of Our Lives* (1946).

13. Bosworth, *Montgomery Clift,* 128. LaGuardia expresses a similar sentiment: "It would be wrong to say that Monty simply loved children; the fact is, he treated them as real people. . . . By the time they got in front of the camera, Monty and Ivan seemed so close it almost seemed that the camera was intruding" (*Monty* [see intro., n. 2], 69).

14. Bosworth, *Montgomery Clift,* 128–30; LaGuardia, *Monty,* 68–70.

15. LaGuardia and Bosworth relate that mutual friends were struck by Stevenson's resemblance to Clift's good friend, actor Kevin McCarthy (LaGuardia, *Monty,* 68). Bosworth says it was Clift's mother who told him, "You act like Kevin on the screen" (*Montgomery Clift,* 139).

16. Letter from Montgomery Clift to Fred Zinnemann, June 25, 1947. From the collections of the Margaret Herrick Library, Academy of Motion Picture Arts and Sciences, Beverly Hills, CA.

17. Bosworth, *Montgomery Clift,* 127.

18. Bosworth, *Montgomery Clift,* 131.

19. Clift to Zinnemann, June 13, 1947, from the collections of the Margaret Herrick Library.

20. Wire from Zinnemann to Clift, June 18, 1947, from the collections of the Margaret Herrick Library.

21. Christopher Isherwood, *The Lost Years: A Memoir,* ed. Katherine Bucknell (New York: HarperCollins, 2000), 149.

22. Mary Ann Doane calls it "the *domain of the inarticulable* in the film viewing experience"; *The Emergence of Cinematic Time* (Cambridge, MA: Harvard University Press, 2002), 226; see also 225–32.

23. Jean Epstein, "The Senses I (b)," in Abel, ed., *French Film Theory and Criticism* (see intro., n. 16), 1.243.

24. Quoted in Paul Willemen, "Through a Glass Darkly: Cinephilia Reconsidered," in *Looks and Frictions: Essays in Cultural Studies and Film Theory* (Bloomington: Indiana University Press, 1994), 223–57 at 233.

25. Willemen explores these issues in two essays collected in *Looks and Frictions:* "*Photogénie* and Epstein" (124–33; first published in 1982) and "Through a Glass Darkly" (written in the early 1990s). Christian Keathley's *Cinephilia and History, or The Wind in the Trees* (Bloomington: Indiana University Press, 2006) positions Willemen's later essay as central to the definition of cinephilia. In a review, Jennifer Pranolo describes Willemen's essay as providing "a theoretical blueprint" for Keathley's book (*Film Quarterly* 61, no. 3 [Spring 2008]: 84–85).

26. Willemen, "Through a Glass Darkly," 231.

27. Willemen, "*Photogénie* and Epstein," 129.

28. Willemen, "*Photogénie* and Epstein," 129.

29. Willemen, "Through a Glass Darkly," 234. The other possibility Willemen raises only to deny is on page 239 (I paraphrase): "I know one thing. It's not a religious experience."

30. Epstein, "Magnification," in Abel, ed., *French Film Theory and Criticism,* 1.235–36. It is probably not chance that film performers were transformed into (or first experienced as) stars at the same time that classical editing patterns were introduced. Not only did viewers such as Epstein revel in the intensity of a close-up of a face, they knew they could lose it in the microsecond of a cut—an inevitable loss they were powerless to predict or prevent. (See also Mary Ann Doane, "The Close-up: Scale and Detail in the Cinema," *Differences: A Journal of Feminist Cultural Studies* 14, no. 3 [2003]: 89–111, esp. 92–93.)

31. Epstein, "The Senses I (b)," 243. Jinhee Choi quotes Epstein's "On Certain Characteristics of Photogénie" (1924): "It is only the mobile aspects of the world, of things and souls, [that] may see their moral value increased by filmic reproduction," in "The Bergsonian Vogue and Epstein's Theory of Photogénie," presented at the Society for Cinema and Media Studies conference, March 2007.

32. Willemen, "Through a Glass Darkly," 233.

33. Epstein, "The Senses I (b)," 243.

34. Epstein, "The Senses I (b)," 243.

35. Epstein, "Magnification," 235.

36. Epstein, "Magnification," 239.

37. Abel, ed., *French Film Theory and Criticism,* quoting Vuillermoz, 1.108.

38. Epstein, "Magnification," 239. Abel's translation is "It's not even true that there is air between us."

39. According to Abel, Epstein "described what occurred between screen image and spectator *as a mysterious relay of energy,* as in breathing or *taking the sacrament*" (*French Film Theory and Criticism,* 1.205; my italics).

40. Doane, *Emergence of Cinematic Time,* 226.

41. Epstein, "Magnification," 236.

42. Epstein, "The Senses I (b)," 243.

43. Epstein, "On Certain Characteristics of *Photogénie*," in Abel, ed., *French Film Theory and Criticism,* 1.317, 316.

44. Epstein, "For a New Avant Garde," in Abel, ed., *French Film Theory and Criticism,* 1.352.

45. Willemen, "Through a Glass Darkly," 232. "The whole argument around realism," he asserts, "hinges on the revelation of the soul . . . whether it was the soul of the viewer being projected onto the screen, the soul of the actress being revealed in Rossellini's *Stromboli* or the soul of Hitchcock being revealed in *I Confess*" (232).

46. Willemen, "Through a Glass Darkly," 230. The difference between revelation and epiphany is primarily one of emphasis and position. With a revelation, information is conveyed. The subject is passive and has something unveiled, revealed to her. (In Catholic terms, the Annunciation would be the model.) While a revelation can be perceived as a gift from a messenger, epiphany is the realization itself. An epiphany marks the recognition that one already knows, has always known. It is in me. Inseparable. Indivisible.

47. King in Willemen, "Through a Glass Darkly," 235.

48. Willemen, "Through a Glass Darkly," 234.

49. Willemen, "Through a Glass Darkly," 239.

50. Quoted in Jonas Barish, *The Antitheatrical Prejudice* (Berkeley: University of California Press, 1981), 58.

51. Noël Alumit, *Letters to Montgomery Clift* (San Francisco: MacAdam/Cage Publishing, 2002).

52. A Web site called The Montgomery Clift Shrine describes this scene in religious terms: "One night Bong Bong finds a new saint on the late show."

53. Barbara Klinger, *Beyond the Multiplex: Cinema, New Technologies, and the Home* (Berkeley: University of California Press, 2006), 154.

54. Klinger, *Beyond the Multiplex,* 177.

55. In an interview on the Web site The Montgomery Clift Shrine, Alumit traces his interest in Clift to having seen *Suddenly, Last Summer* as a child. *Suddenly, Last Summer* may seem an odd choice to appeal to children, but it has a classic fairy-tale structure: a young princess locked in a tower needs a prince to free her from the evil queen, who lives in a castle surrounded by a frightening, blighted landscape. Alumit also explicitly mentions Clift's appeal to children, supporting his experience as an observer of performances with biography, e.g., "I hear he was good with kids."

56. Although Klinger mentions that the "dynamic" of textual refashioning and associative possibilities "is substantially enhanced when films and other media enter private space and become part of an intimate repertoire of domestic objects infused with personal meaning" (*Beyond the Multiplex,* 177), in the novel, as soon as Bong has *Freud* on tape, he learns some shocking family secrets and flees—presumably never to watch the film again, let alone fast-forward or incessantly replay his favorite scenes.

57. Among the most interesting Web sites are The Montgomery Clift Shrine; Montgomery Clift's Page, by Alexanderthegreat9.tripod; and Montgomery Clift Dot Com. The first two are fan sites, the last an "official" Web page that offers access to copyrighted photographs of Clift and the legal rules for acquiring them.

58. E. L. McCallum, *Object Lessons: How to Do Things with Fetishism* (New York: SUNY Press, 1999), 140.

59. See McCallum's concept of "incorporation, rather than impersonation"

(*Object Lessons,* 128) in her discussion of Judith Butler on parody and melancholia (127–41).

60. My italics.

61. McCallum continues: "Repetition is not entirely a private matter; repetition is how the fetishist relates to the outside, public world through the fetish" (*Object Lessons,* 140).

62. There are a few false notes in the novel. Even though he lives in Los Angeles, Bong does not visit the site of Clift's car accident. Having read Bosworth, he still maintains that he does not know where Clift lived in New York (Alumit, *Letters to Montgomery Clift,* 101), even though Bosworth lists the street address of Clift's first apartment on page 215 (207 East 61st Street) and locates his second "one block away" (*Montgomery Clift,* 348). She even gives directions to the plaque marking the building where he died (414).

63. Murray Pomerance, in *Johnny Depp Starts Here,* argues that "imitation is intimacy," not only when a fan copies a star but in any relationship characterized by "apprenticeship and personal affiliation"—including the process by which an actor attempts to embody a character, especially one based on a historical figure (New Brunswick, NJ: Rutgers University Press, 2005), 24.

64. Amy Hollywood, "Acute Melancholia," *Harvard Theological Review* 99, no. 4 (October 2006): 391–92.

65. Hollywood, "Acute Melancholia," 393.

66. Hollywood, "Acute Melancholia," 395.

67. Leora Batnitzky, summarizing Paul Tillich, in *Idolatry and Representation: The Philosophy of Franz Rosenzweig Reconsidered* (Princeton, NJ: Princeton University Press, 2000), 153, 152.

68. Batnitzky, *Idolatry and Representation,* 152.

69. See the Protestant Second Commandment: "Thou shalt not make unto thee any graven image, or any likeness of any thing that is in heaven above, or that is on earth beneath" (Exodus 20:4, King James Revised).

70. Adrian Fortescue, "Iconoclasm," in *The Catholic Encyclopedia,* 15 vols. (New York: Encyclopedia Press, 1908–13), 623.

71. Adrian Fortescue, "Images, the Veneration Of," *The Catholic Encyclopedia,* 669.

72. Christopher Smart, *Jubilate Agno (Rejoice in the Lamb)* (London: R. Hart Davis, 1954), 310. "Earning" might be a misprint or an anachronistic spelling of "yearning."

73. William James, *The Varieties of Religious Experience,* ed. Martin E. Marty (New York: Penguin Books, 1982). Quoting "Professor Starbuck of California," James points out how "growth into a larger spiritual life . . . is a normal phase of adolescence in every class of human beings. The age is the same, falling usually between 14 and 17." (This is also a prime age for cinephilia or fandom of

any kind.) "Theology," says Dr. Starbuck, "takes the adolescent tendencies and builds upon them" (199).

74. Klinger discusses "cinema's therapeutic potential," especially in relation to multiple viewings, in *Beyond the Multiplex,* 164–66.

75. McCallum, *Object Lessons,* 124.

76. McCallum, *Object Lessons,* 140–41.

77. Rivers, *Aphrodite at Mid-Century* (see intro., n. 2), 99.

78. Discussion with the author, ca. 2002. See also David Thomson, "All Along the River," *Sight and Sound* (Winter 1976–77): 9–13.

79. Rivers, *Aphrodite at Mid-Century,* 99–100.

80. Rivers, *Aphrodite at Mid-Century,* 99–100.

81. Stacey uses the phrase "love at first sight" to describe a worshipful fan's "romantic recreation" of how she came to adore a particular star (*Star Grazing* [see intro., n. 10], 142).

82. Bosworth, *Montgomery Clift,* 120; LaGuardia, *Monty,* 60.

83. A memo to Howard Hawks from Joseph I. Breen, August 22, 1946, declares the script to be "thoroughly unacceptable under the provisions of the Production Code." To wit, "the various killings by Dunson and Matthew seem to us to be outright murders for which they are not punished. The brutality of Dunson toward the various men seems excessive and could not be approved." A second memo to Hawks, summarizing a meeting with Breen's office, dated August 26, 1946, reiterates that an acceptable compromise would require that "none of the killings by Dunson or Matthew would be deliberate or unprovoked." From the collections of the Margaret Herrick Library.

84. LaGuardia, *Monty,* 59.

85. Bosworth, *Montgomery Clift,* 120. Stuntman-actor Richard Farnsworth is identified as the person who performed the riding and stuntwork for Clift in *Red River.*

86. Garry Wills, *John Wayne's America: The Politics of Celebrity* (New York: Simon and Schuster, 1997), 145.

87. "New kind of western": Suzanne Liandrat-Guiges, *Red River* (London: BFI Publishing, 2000), 38.

88. Wayne and others described the film as a landlocked *Mutiny on the Bounty* (Wills, *John Wayne's America,* 335, n. 11).

89. The Breen office warned Hawks that "the brutal treatment of animals in this story could not be approved under the provisions of the Code," then instructs Hawks to contact the American Humane Society. Memo to Howard Hawks from Joseph I. Breen, August 22, 1946, p. 2, from the collections of the Margaret Herrick Library.

90. Jon Lewis, *Hollywood v. Hard Core: How the Struggle over Censorship Saved the Modern Film Industry* (New York: New York University Press, 2000), 301–02, 307.

91. Steve Cohan talks about the sexuality of cowboys historically in relation to *Red River* in *Masked Men* (see intro., n. 15), 209–10.

92. The shots of Matt and his men galloping toward the endangered wagon train feature an odd Expressionist moment rarely encountered after the 1940s—a canted angle that makes it seem as if Clift and the men are riding downhill. An equally odd moment comes, surprisingly, in the famous scene at the beginning of the cattle drive when the sound of the men hooting and hollering is oddly discordant, having been recorded indoors on a soundstage and not outdoors, where the images were shot.

93. Breen to Hawks, August 22, 1946.

94. Breen to Hawks, August 22, 1946.

95. Shipman, *Great Movie Stars,* 90.

96. Hoskyns, *Montgomery Clift* (see intro., n. 1), 171. Hoskyns cites Abby Mann as the source on *Nuremberg*'s premiere. Under pressure from Paramount, Clift agreed to accompany Elizabeth Taylor, the costar of his next Paramount film, *A Place in the Sun,* to the premiere of *The Heiress.* This is how they met (82). He attended the opening of *A Place in the Sun* with Judy Balaban and the premiere of *The Young Lions* with Libby Holman (96, 144).

97. Clift made only two films under this deal. After *The Heiress,* he was to have been in *Sunset Boulevard,* which he turned down (Hoskyns, *Montgomery Clift,* 71, 81). He was released from the contract on July 24, 1951, after completing *A Place in the Sun.*

98. According to Bosworth, "Monty refused to do any publicity" before making *The Heiress* but caved in after shooting was done (*Montgomery Clift,* 139, 145).

99. Quoted in Shipman, *Great Movie Stars,* 90.

100. Montgomery Clift, as told to George Scullin, "My Own Story," *Modern Screen* (October 1949): 51, 73.

101. Clift, "My Own Story," 73. Original italics.

102. Clift, "My Own Story," 74.

103. Clift, "My Own Story," 75.

104. Clift, "My Own Story," 74.

105. Bosworth, *Montgomery Clift,* 147.

106. Bosworth, *Montgomery Clift,* 147.

107. "Clift Sees Self," *Life* (December 6, 1948): 24.

TWO. THE BOBBY-SOXERS' IDOL

1. Clift, "My Own Story" (see chap. 1, n. 100), 50. Photo credited to Paramount.

2. The color photo with the blue background accompanies a story titled "Calling Monty Clift!" by Anne Hale, in *Screen Stories* (May 1950): 34–35.

3. In addition to fantasies of romantic love and marriage, sexual fantasies would be likely too, though they are seldom discussed as such in the popular press. Even

the faithful found it difficult when looking at an idealized image of a face or a body to separate spiritual from carnal thoughts. There is a remarkable account of a monk in the early centuries of the church who felt tempted by the flesh whenever he looked at an image of the Virgin Mary hanging in his cell in the monastery. He wrote to his bishop and asked if it would be possible to remove the painting as a means of avoiding sinful thoughts. The bishop instructed the monk to keep the image. Its power to turn his thoughts to the heavenly aspects of Mary was more valuable than any risk it posed in providing an occasion for sin (Fortescue, "Images, the Veneration Of" [see chap. 1, n. 71], 668).

4. Hoskyns, *Montgomery Clift* (see intro., n. 1), 59.

5. Ackbar Abbas, "On Fascination: Walter Benjamin's Images," *New German Critique* 48 (1989): 50.

6. Samantha Barbas, *Movie Crazy: Fans, Stars, and the Cult of Celebrity* (New York: Palgrave, 2001), 181.

7. Barbas, *Movie Crazy,* 179.

8. Barbas, *Movie Crazy,* 161.

9. Barbas also notes the "movie-struck girl" of the teens, the naive shop girl of the twenties, and the "mindless 'gum-chewing gals'" who "craved the 'idiotic slop' [of] 'fan mag guff'" in the thirties (*Movie Crazy,* 60, 173).

10. Barbas, *Movie Crazy,* 181. See Barbas's chap. 7, "The Fandom Menace," 159–84.

11. Quoted in Barbas, *Movie Crazy,* 206, n. 3.

12. Quoted in Barbas, *Movie Crazy,* 179.

13. *The New York Times,* April 6, 1947, quoted in Barbas, *Movie Crazy,* 159–60.

14. Quoted in John Kobal, *People Will Talk* (London: Aurum Press, 1986), 405.

15. Stephen Heath, "Difference," *Screen* 19, no. 3 (Autumn 1978): 51–112 at 56.

16. Linda Williams, "Film Bodies: Gender, Genre, and Excess," *Film Quarterly* 44, no. 4 (Summer 1991): 2–13.

17. *The Random House College Dictionary,* rev. ed. (New York: Random House, 1975), 419.

18. D. N. Rodowick, *Reading the Figural; or, Philosophy after the New Media* (Durham, NC: Duke University Press, 2001), 22.

19. James, *Varieties of Religious Experience* (see chap. 1, n. 73), 46.

20. James, *Varieties of Religious Experience,* 48.

21. Sigmund Freud, *Moses and Monotheism,* trans. Katherine Jones (New York: Vintage Books, 1967), 172.

22. *Today's Woman* (October 1947), quoted in Barbas, *Movie Crazy,* 160.

23. Nancy J. Lawrence, interview with the author, 2003. "Him" refers not to the character George Eastman (called Clyde Griffiths in *An American Tragedy,* which she *has* read), but to Clift.

24. Nancy J. Lawrence, interview with the author, 2003.

25. Cohan, *Masked Men* (see intro., n. 15), 223.

26. Cohan, *Masked Men*, 225.

27. Cohan, *Masked Men*, 223.

28. *Ford Theater,* "Wuthering Heights," April 1, 1949.

29. Bosworth, *Montgomery Clift* (see intro., n. 2), 146.

30. Ralph Richardson had already played Dr. Sloper in a production of the play in London (Hoskyns, *Montgomery Clift,* 63).

31. According to LaGuardia, Wyler was particularly dissatisfied with Clift's carriage (*Monty* [see intro., n. 2], 76).

32. Brett Farmer uses a publicity still for the film of the impossibly pretty forties pinup to illustrate the title of his chapter on Clift, "Papa, Can't You See That I'm Flaming?" in *Spectacular Passions: Cinema, Fantasy, Gay Male Spectatorships* (Durham, NC: Duke University Press, 2000), 198. A cropped version of this still is on the back of the dust jacket of Hoskyns's biography of Clift.

33. Dennis Bingham argues that "it is precisely this ageing make-up which lends [Wayne] the special power which allows us to foresee better roles to come" (*Acting Male: Masculinities in the Films of James Stewart, Jack Nicholson, and Clint Eastwood* [New Brunswick, NJ: Rutgers University Press, 1994], 29). For me, the white applied to Wayne's sideburns is more a mark of artifice—another way for the audience to separate actor from role.

34. LaGuardia, *Monty,* 76.

35. Nancy J. Lawrence, interview with the author, 2003. *Vulnerable* is a word frequently used to describe Clift, appearing as early as 1948 (LaGuardia, *Monty,* 74).

36. Epstein, "Magnification" (see chap. 1, n. 30), 239. Clift's fans enjoy endless opportunities to identify with the actor's suffering. From first to last, his films reiterate his ability to portray physical and mental anguish. Although endurance and stoicism are paramount, Clift's performances offer an impressive variety of ways to suffer. He is a boxer who is beaten for refusing to fight in *From Here to Eternity* and its virtual remake, *The Young Lions.* He accepts repeated beatings from stronger men in *Red River* and *Wild River* and is smashed around by horses and bulls in *The Misfits.* He undergoes trials by water—slogging through swamps in *Raintree County,* swimming rivers to save others or himself *(Young Lions, The Defector).* He undergoes legal trials in *A Place in the Sun, I Confess,* and *Judgment at Nuremberg.* As a doctor, he takes on the suffering of others *(Suddenly, Last Summer; Freud);* as an amateur, he is almost destroyed by others' neediness *(Raintree County* and *Lonelyhearts).* As a young soldier he tries to comfort those caught in the aftermath of war (a boy in *The Search,* a woman in *The Big Lift*). Despite, or because of, their integrity, when Clift's characters are at their most heroically selfless, they find themselves accused, denounced, and humiliated *(I Confess, Freud).* Even when he plays potentially villainous characters (*The Heiress* and *A Place in the Sun),* their tragically star-crossed moments of genuine bliss encourage the audience's sympathy and pity.

37. A valuable recent essay on the film discusses its recent reevaluation as an

exploration of urban sites and the construction of identity in postwar/early Cold War Berlin (Ralph Stern, "*The Big Lift* [1950]: Image and Identity in Blockaded Berlin," *Cinema Journal* 46, no. 2 [Winter 2007]: 66–90). Although he identifies Clift as the film's "luminary," Stern does not focus on acting and discusses the star's persona only briefly (87, n. 6).

38. LaGuardia, *Monty,* 29–31; Bosworth, *Montgomery Clift,* 85, 87–89; Hoskyns, *Montgomery Clift,* 41.

39. Another favorite tool of theatrically trained, "technical" actors is the use of costume. Actors act with their bodies, which are for the most part fixed assets. Costumes, however, mark the intersection of the actor's body and the role. Laurence Olivier, for example—the epitome of a "technical" actor—created characters from the outside in. (When Clift was nominated for an Academy Award for *The Search,* it was Olivier who won—for *Hamlet.*) Olivier's use of makeup was so overt it became prosthetic (visibly altering his nose and hairline, for instance). And like many actors he felt that he could not "know" the character he was playing until he put on a costume.

40. In *The Big Lift,* as Danny lists the penalties for being found out of uniform, Herr Stieber begins to take off his pants. This is an odd moment. All of Cliff's lines of protest are delivered with his back to the camera and seem postrecorded. The effect invites speculation about what the gesture of Stieber undoing his belt would suggest if all the army-related objections weren't being voiced. When Kowalski comes looking for Danny, he meets Stieber wearing the robe Danny wore. As in *I Confess,* Hasse and Clift trade clothes more than once, suggesting an underlying equivalence, one not otherwise apparent.

41. Music Harry Warren, lyrics Mack Gordon.

42. Stern notes that the film was cut by twenty-five minutes for its German release and given a happy ending ("*The Big Lift,*" 86, n. 3). Retitled *It Began with a Kiss,* it was known as *Two Corridors East* in Great Britain.

43. A burst gland became infected (LaGuardia, *Monty,* 10–11; Bosworth, *Montgomery Clift,* 28–29; Hoskyns, *Montgomery Clift,* 22). According to LaGuardia, Clift was nine; Bosworth and Hoskyns say he was seven.

44. Cohan, *Masked Men,* 232.

45. The effect is so intense it is little wonder that a book about film's emotional impact, Charles Affron's *Cinema and Sentiment* (Chicago: University of Chicago Press, 1982), reproduces this sequence on its cover. Affron emphasizes the close-ups as emblematic of intimacy (113–15).

46. Edgar Morin, *The Stars,* trans. Richard Howard (New York: Grove Press, 1960), 179. Quoted in Richard Dyer, *Stars* (London: BFI, 1979), 51.

47. Vuillermoz, quoted in Abel, ed., *French Film Theory and Criticism* (see intro., n. 17), 108; Epstein, "Magnification," 239. Epstein particularly prizes suffering. When he declares, "It is in me, I consume it," the pronoun's referent is purposely obscured: "it" is simultaneously the image of the face and suffering itself.

48. For Cohan, this moment establishes bisexuality as fundamental to the viewer's relation to the image/star, to Clift's persona, and to George and Angela's relationship. George and Angela act as mirrors for each other, with George's "reflexive, narcissistic" desire "entirely bound up in his being desired by Angela" (*Masked Men*, 232). Like Matthew Garth in *Red River*, George "does not act upon desire but excites it in the person who looks at him," whether male or female, character or audience member (216–17).

49. Cohan, *Masked Men*, 232. As "their close-ups become perfectly symmetrical in size," Cohan argues, "one beautiful, similarly featured face becomes almost indistinguishable from the other."

50. Farmer pinpoints the methods by which Clift achieved the effect of interiority. "The aura of withdrawal and introversion that is a standard feature of Clift's acting style . . . [is] frequently achieved with pained expressions and long, vacant stares" (*Spectacular Passions*, 235). However, I find Clift just as likely to turn his back as to depend on facial expression when he wants to "amplify certain elements of psychological turmoil" (235).

51. Peters, *Design for Living* (see chap. 1, n. 9), 44.

52. Charles Affron notes that "cinema has an affinity for the telephone and its figurations of intimate discourse" (*Cinema and Sentiment*, 113).

THREE. ACTOR AS SAINT

1. Hoskyns, *Montgomery Clift* (see intro., n. 1), 101. The quotation continues "entrancing us with the quaint music of his speech and the inadvertent mime of his hands."

2. Miriam Hansen, paraphrasing Roland Barthes on Valentino ("Pleasure, Ambivalence, Identification: Valentino and Female Spectatorship," *Cinema Journal* 25, no. 4 [Summer 1986]: 24–25).

3. Roland Barthes, "The Face of Garbo," in *Mythologies,* ed. and trans. Annette Lavers (New York: Hill and Wang, 1957), 56–57. "Garbo still belongs to that moment in cinema when capturing the human face still plunged audiences into the deepest ecstasy" (56). He calls Garbo's face a "deified face" that "gives rise to mystical feelings" (57–56).

4. Dyer, *Stars* (see chap. 2, n. 46), 17. He continues, "this *belief* in the 'capturing' of the 'unique' 'person' of a performer is probably central to the star phenomenon" (italics in original).

5. Balazs, quoted in Dyer, *Stars,* 17.

6. Barry King, "Articulating Stardom," repr. in *Star Texts: Image and Performance in Film and Television,* ed. Jeremy G. Butler (Detroit: Wayne State University Press, 1991), 129.

7. King, "Articulating Stardom," 129.

8. Doane, *Emergence of Cinematic Time* (see chap. 1, n. 22), 227–28, discussing connections between Willemen on cinephilia and Miriam Hansen on indexicality.

9. Carol Mavor puts it nicely when she says, "Even the maids and cooks were exposed as Virgin Marys, Ophelias, Beatrices, and mountain nymphs" (*Pleasures Taken: Performances of Sexuality and Loss in Victorian Photographs* [Durham, NC: Duke University Press, 1995], 46).

10. Mavor, *Pleasures Taken*, 47.

11. Cameron, *Annals of my Glass House*, quoted in Mavor, *Pleasures Taken*, 43.

12. Mavor, *Pleasures Taken*, 44.

13. Mavor, *Pleasures Taken*, 46.

14. Fortescue, "Images, the Veneration Of" (see chap. 1, n. 71), 671.

15. Coded visual signifiers (iconography) were associated with saints and holy figures and served to verify that the figure represented was consistent with the named subject of the image.

16. Estelle Jussim, *Slave to Beauty: The Eccentric Life and Controversial Career of F. Holland Day, Photographer, Publisher, Aesthete* (Boston: David R. Godine, 1981), 122.

17. Jussim, *Slave to Beauty*, 121.

18. Jussim, *Slave to Beauty*, 126.

19. Jussim, *Slave to Beauty*, 126.

20. Jussim, *Slave to Beauty*, 133.

21. Jussim, *Slave to Beauty*, 134.

22. Jussim, *Slave to Beauty*, 135.

23. Jussim, *Slave to Beauty*, 132.

24. Jussim, *Slave to Beauty*, 133.

25. Sadakichi Hartmann quoted in Jussim, *Slave to Beauty*, 129.

26. Jussim, *Slave to Beauty*, 123. Jussim also notes that Day was a close friend of Aubrey Beardsley, who died a few months before Day made *The Last Seven Words*.

27. Doane, *Emergence of Cinematic Time*, 190.

28. Jussim, *Slave to Beauty*, 134.

29. Quoted in Barish, *Antitheatrical Prejudice* (see chap. 1, n. 50), 50.

30. Quoted in Barish, *Antitheatrical Prejudice*, 61.

31. Barish, *Antitheatrical Prejudice*, 2.

32. Barish, *Antitheatrical Prejudice*, 4.

33. Barish, *Antitheatrical Prejudice*, 400. "Fraught with passion and charged with contradiction," antitheatricalism, time and again, comes down to a deep ambivalence about actors. Barish notes that "even a protheatrical bias . . . seems to contain the seeds of its own opposite. . . . In the theatergoing public of the late Roman Empire or of eighteenth-century France, . . . the same ambivalence [could be found] on a mass scale," combining "the hysterical adulation of the actors with cruel legal proscription."

34. In Ingmar Bergman's *The Magician* (1958), an actor tells an acrobat that the reason actors have greater status than circus performers is because "you only risk your necks—we risk our vanity."

35. Matthew Wikander, *Fangs of Malice: Hypocrisy, Sincerity, and Acting* (Iowa City: University of Iowa Press, 2002), xv.

36. Wikander, *Fangs of Malice*, 196. "When spontaneity and sincerity are perceived as virtues, repetition and rehearsal appear as vices" (196–97).

37. Barish, *Antitheatrical Prejudice*, 277. See Barish's chapter "Puritanism, Popery, and Parade" (155–90, esp. 159), and Wikander, *Fangs of Malice*, 24–27.

38. Wikander, *Fangs of Malice*, 36.

39. Wikander, *Fangs of Malice*, xvii.

40. Barish, *Antitheatrical Prejudice*, 194.

41. Barish, *Antitheatrical Prejudice*, 25.

42. Barish, *Antitheatrical Prejudice*, 281.

43. Rousseau quoted in Wikander, *Fangs of Malice*, xiv, xv.

44. Quoted in Barish, *Antitheatrical Prejudice*, 281.

45. Wikander, *Fangs of Malice*, 191.

46. Barish, *Antitheatrical Prejudice*, 281.

47. Barish, *Antitheatrical Prejudice*, 277.

48. Barish, *Antitheatrical Prejudice*, 276.

49. Barish, *Antitheatrical Prejudice*, 208–09.

50. Robin Wood, *Hitchcock's Films* (New York: Paperback Library, 1970), 41.

51. Donald Spoto, *The Art of Alfred Hitchcock: Fifty Years of His Motion Pictures* (New York: Doubleday, 1979), 224, 226.

52. *Daily Film Renter* (March 23, 1953), in the Warner Bros. Archive, University of Southern California, Los Angeles.

53. Peter Bogdanovich, interviewed in "Hitchcock's Confession: A Look at *I Confess*," a short film written, directed, and produced by Laurent Bouzereau, on the DVD *I Confess*.

54. Neil P. Hurley, S.J., *Soul in Suspense: Hitchcock's Fright and Delight* (Metuchen, NJ: Scarecrow Press, 1993), 46, caption, and 253.

55. In terms of Hitchcock's oeuvre, we have seen these streets before. *Murder!* (1930) begins in the street outside the scene of a crime. The figure glimpsed in the shadows is again the killer disguised as a figure of authority—in this case a policeman. The killer's true identity is little more than a series of disguises shielding multiple secrets, sexual, racial, and professional. From the opening scene to its theatrical conclusion, *Murder!* shows how easily identities can be doffed and witnesses fooled.

56. Quebec's dual nature as both North American and European disoriented an early reader of the script, who found "the whole atmosphere" of the story to be more European than American. "The way the people think and act strikes me as being not American. [The whole town] seems to be, for example, popu-

lated entirely by Catholics. That just doesn't happen here" (letter to Kay [Katharine Brown, MCA], signed Lee [Lee Wright of Simon and Schuster], October 24, 1947; Warner Bros. Archive, USC).

57. Will Leonard, *Chicago Daily Tribune,* September 12, 1952. Shooting on location caused serious delays in production. The daily production and progress reports from the *I Confess* file at the USC Warner Bros. Archive suggest that the crew held Clift partly responsible for delays that plagued the shoot. During the scene in which Logan carries a candle into the church and finds Otto praying, the report notes, "Co. held up by Montgomery Clift making dialog changes 4:05–4:25" (September 2, 1952). Filming in an actual church also presented difficulties. The daily report noted that the crew had to "WAIT for 2 funerals to be held at church 9:30–11:10 AM." Sometimes local extras ruined a take (September 1, 1952). But the main problem was the weather. Day after day it rained. Shooting began on August 21 and finished on October 22, 1952, seven days behind schedule. The last shots completed were process shots with Clift and Baxter (the ferry scene), Logan's walk past the clothing store, his close-up outside the church, and the post-recording of dialogue by Hasse on November 3.

58. Quoted in Cohan, *Masked Men* (see intro., n. 15), 223.

59. Jay Carmody, "Hitchcock's Touch Is Evident in Making of His Movie," *The Evening Star,* Washington, D.C., September 22, 1952, A-14; in Warner Bros. Archive, USC.

60. Jonathan Sterne, *The Audible Past: Cultural Origins of Sound Reproduction* (Durham, NC: Duke University Press, 2003), especially chap. 2, "Techniques of Listening," 87–136.

61. Michel Foucault, *The History of Sexuality: An Introduction,* vol. 1, trans. Robert Hurley (New York: Vintage Books, 1990), 61–63.

62. Thomas M. Leitch, *Find the Director and Other Hitchcock Games* (Athens: University of Georgia Press, 1991), 160–61.

63. For a discussion of the Production Code Administration's five-year engagement with Hitchcock regarding *I Confess,* see Amy Lawrence, "Constructing a Priest, Silencing a Saint: The PCA and *I Confess* (1953)," *Film History* 19, no. 1 (2007): 58–72.

64. Jack Larson, interviewed in "Hitchcock's Confession: A Look at *I Confess.*"

65. George Tabori script, dated August 9, 1952, pp. 63, 55A.

66. Quoted in Donald Spoto, *The Dark Side of Genius: The Life of Alfred Hitchcock* (Boston: Little, Brown, 1983), 339.

67. Farmer, *Spectacular Passions* (see chap. 2, n. 32), 235.

68. See Naremore, *Acting in the Cinema* (see chap. 1, n. 7), 46–67.

69. Farmer, *Spectacular Passions,* 235.

70. Hurley, *Soul in Suspense,* 253.

71. Hurley, *Soul in Suspense,* 253.

72. Keith A. Reader, "The Sacrament of Writing: Robert Bresson's *Le journal d'un curé de campagne* (1951)," in *French Film: Texts and Contexts,* ed. Susan Hayward and Ginette Vincendeau, 2nd ed. (New York: Routledge, 2000), 89–99 at 92.

73. Reader, "Sacrament of Writing," 92.

74. Quoted in Reader, "Sacrament of Writing," 92.

75. Reader, "Sacrament of Writing," 97.

76. Reader, "Sacrament of Writing," 90, 92.

77. Reader, "Sacrament of Writing," 92.

78. Wood, *Hitchcock's Films,* 45.

79. Claude Chabrol and Eric Rohmer, *Hitchcock,* trans. Stanley Hochman (New York: F. Ungar, 1979), 116.

80. Barish, *Antitheatrical Prejudice,* 166.

81. Hurley, *Soul in Suspense,* 253.

82. This backstory about the dead brother was, however, instantly familiar to me, as if I had seen it on television a long time ago. I have been unable to track it down.

83. Paul Anthelme, "*Nos deux consciences,*" *L'Illustration,* suppl. to no. 3117 (November 22, 1902): 3. This version is available from the Library of Congress, but only in French. The dedication reads "À Monsieur Constant Coquelin, Hommage d'affectueuse reconnaissance."

84. Undated memo (ca. 1948–49) on stationery from "Hotel Ritz, Place Vendôme, Paris," signed V. S. W.; Warner Bros. Archive, USC.

85. Simply assigning appropriate credit required a memo of Byzantine complexity from Hitchcock associate Barbara Keon to Carl Stucke at Warner Bros. Among the versions and contributors Keon lists as of October 29, 1952, are a translation of the play, "original story," and screen treatment by Louis Verneuil (dated September 1947); a treatment by Alfred Hitchcock and Alma Reville (March 20, 1948); a screenplay by Wm. A. Rose (August 11, 1948); a screenplay by Leslie Storm; a treatment by Paul Vincent Carroll (May 5, 1950); a comparison chart to keep them all straight; a fifty-one-page incomplete screenplay by George Tabori (May 12, 1952); "Story line by Alfred Hitchcock and Barbara Keon" (May 17, 1952); screenplay by George Tabori (May 26–June 23, 1952); a shooting script with tentative dialogue by Hitchcock and Keon (May 28–July 3, 1952), and another with "dialogue changes from Tabori" (May 27–July 10, 1952). From July 31 to August 25, Tabori revised scenes on almost a daily basis for the Breen office's approval (Warner Bros. Archive, USC).

86. Compare Logan's bomber-pilot philosophy to the postwar musings of characters in *Rope*—the play, the film, and the life of the film's star, James Stewart (Amy Lawrence, "American Shame: *Rope,* James Stewart, and the Postwar Crisis in American Masculinity," in *Hitchcock's America,* ed. Rick Millington and Jonathan Freedman [New York: Oxford University Press, 1999], 55–76). An in-

triguing note in the USC Warner Bros. Archives says, "REWRITE (by Tabori) of your Larreau-Michael scene . . . includes reason why Michael became a priest." This could be more talk about the war.

87. Historically, the postwar period is considered a golden age of vocations, with a dramatic increase in the number of candidates for ordination—a trend that continued into the 1960s.

88. In *John Wayne's America* (see chap. 1, n. 86), Garry Wills says that Howard Hawks discovered Clift (and wanted him for *Red River*) when he saw him "in New York, doing a Tennessee Williams play" (133).

89. Tennessee Williams and Donald Windham, *You Touched Me!* (New York: Samuel French, 1947), 29–30.

90. Williams and Windham, *You Touched Me!* 6, 5.

91. Williams and Windham, *You Touched Me!* 5.

92. Williams and Windham, *You Touched Me!* 30.

93. Bosworth, *Montgomery Clift* (see intro., n. 2), 127.

94. Williams and Windham, *You Touched Me!* 31.

95. Anthelme, *Nos deux consciences,* 19.

96. Anthelme, *Nos deux consciences,* 18, 19.

97. Bosworth, *Montgomery Clift,* 235.

98. See Anthelme, *Nos deux consciences,* 19.

99. François Truffaut, *Hitchcock,* with the collaboration of Helen G. Scott (New York: Simon and Schuster, 1984).

100. Hoskyns, *Montgomery Clift,* 100. In *Dark Side of Genius,* Spoto lists Hasse as one of the gay actors who fascinated Hitchcock (along with Clift, Ivor Novello, and Charles Laughton), though he does not give a source for this information. "Hitchcock was not openly contemptuous, nor was he uneasy about their [Clift and Hasse's] sexual conduct. He simply found the two men endlessly interesting" (340).

101. Bosworth, *Montgomery Clift,* 236.

102. Quoted in Bosworth, *Montgomery Clift,* 236.

103. David Sterrit, *The Films of Alfred Hitchcock* (New York: Cambridge University Press, 1993), 85. He also describes the film as "suspension carried to the point of paralysis."

104. In *The Priest: His Character and Work* (New York: Benziger Brothers, 1903), James Keatinge notes, "It is forbidden to wear secular dress even on a journey. The clothes should be black or of a dark colour. In the house it is most fitting to wear the cassock and biretta. The Roman collar must be worn not only . . . when exercising the sacred ministry, but always" (305). In the postwar period, the strictures on priestly dress were loosened dramatically. When Logan is not wearing his cassock he is always indoors in the rectory and never in public or in the church proper.

105. Wood, *Hitchcock's Films,* 45.

106. Spoto points out that "all the characters . . . have depended on their public roles to define their lives" (*Art of Alfred Hitchcock*, 226).

107. Wood, *Hitchcock's Films*, 42.

108. *I Confess* script, box 11A, folder 2, Billy Rose Theatre Collection at the New York Public Library for the Performing Arts. Script dated August 9, 1952, p. 111B.

109. *I Confess* script of August 9, 1952, 122; NYPL.

110. *I Confess* script of August 9, 1952, 124; NYPL.

111. Letter from Joseph Breen to Alfred Hitchcock, August 6, 1952, p. 3; Warner Bros. Archive, USC.

112. Anthelme, *Nos deux consciences*, 18.

113. *I Confess* script of August 9, 1952, 9; NYPL.

114. Dolly Haas in this role bears a strong resemblance to Peggy Ashcroft, who plays a similar character in *The 39 Steps* (1935).

115. Spoto, *Art of Alfred Hitchcock*, 222.

116. Letter to Kay (Katherine Brown), signed Lee (Lee Wright), October 24, 1947; Warner Bros. Archive, USC.

117. Alfred Hitchcock and Alma Reville treatment, March 20, 1948, 50–51; Warner Bros. Archive, USC.

118. Louis Verneuil treatment, September 3, 1947, 115, 119; Warner Bros. Archive, USC.

119. Verneuil treatment, September 3, 1947, 122; Warner Bros. Archive, USC.

120. *I Confess* file, Warner Bros. Archive, USC.

121. Hoskyns, *Montgomery Clift*, 101.

122. The phrase "torn between the spiritual and the sensual" recurs in the film *Le confessional*.

123. Farmer, *Spectacular Passions*, 203–04, summarizing Francis Pasche, "Symposium on Homosexuality (ii)," *International Journal of Psycho-analysis* 45 (1964).

124. Pasche, 211–13, quoted in Farmer, *Spectacular Passions*, 204.

125. Victor Peers wrote to Morris Murphy on July 31, 1952, saying that a new ending "is at this moment being rewritten," beginning at "the point where [the killer] escapes from in front of the courthouse until his death in the Château Frontenac"; Warner Bros. Archive, USC.

126. An excellent discussion of Fane can be found in Jessica Brent, "Beyond the Gaze: Visual Fascination and the Feminine Image in Silent Hitchcock," *Camera Obscura* (2004): 76–111, especially 100–104, nn. 29, 30, and 31; and in Tania Modleski, *The Women Who Knew Too Much: Hitchcock and Feminist Theory* (New York: Methuen, 1988), 31–42.

127. Chabrol and Rohmer, *Hitchcock*, 114.

128. Quoted in Chabrol and Rohmer, *Hitchcock*, 115–16.

129. Lesley Brill, *The Hitchcock Romance* (Princeton, NJ: Princeton University Press, 1988), 105. Originally I thought the line was "They mock you."

130. George Tabori script, August 9, 1952, 145; NYPL.

131. Quoted in Rohmer and Chabrol, *Hitchcock,* 114.

132. Bogdanovich, interviewed in "Hitchcock's Confession."

133. Hurley, *Soul in Suspense,* 253.

134. Jack Larson, interviewed in "Hitchcock's Confession."

135. *Look* (April 21, 1953): 110.

136. Jack Larson, interviewed in "Hitchcock's Confession." Trying to explain what specifically "they" were "on to," all Larson can come up with is "his style, or something like that."

FOUR. FACING PERSECUTION

1. Blurbs reproduced in the paperback edition of LaGuardia, *Monty* (see intro., n. 2): "Women—and men—couldn't resist him"; "In the end, drugs, alcohol, and his own conflicting sexual desires consumed him"; "Here, for the first time, is the definitive, emotionally charged biography of a brilliant American actor. Here is Montgomery Clift, the haunted man behind the boyish fire that ignited the screen."

2. Bosworth, *Montgomery Clift* (see intro., n. 2), jacket of hardcover copy.

3. LaGuardia, *Monty,* inside cover of the Avon paperback.

4. Thomas Waugh pinpoints the main differences between Bosworth and La-Guardia in "Montgomery Clift Biographies," in *The Fruit Machine: Twenty Years of Writings on Queer Cinema* (Durham, NC: Duke University Press, 2000), 93–100.

5. "Montgomery Clift's Tragic Love Story," *Photoplay* (May 1954): 40, 97–98. The story may be based on Clift's relationship with Judy Balaban, discussed in Bosworth, *Montgomery Clift.*

6. "Montgomery Clift's Tragic Love Story," 40.

7. *Motion Picture* (January 1950); *Movieland* (June 1950).

8. "The Triangle Got Lopsided Because . . ." *Screen Album* (August–October 1955): 19.

9. See Bosworth, *Montgomery Clift,* 337; Hoskyns, *Montgomery Clift* (see intro., n. 1), 189.

10. Hoskyns, *Montgomery Clift,* 71, 81. Libby Holman had a taste for American tragedy. In addition to her scandalous first marriage (her socially prominent husband committed suicide), she had a serious affair with Phillips Holmes, the boyish star of the first screen adaptation of Theodore Dreiser's *An American Tragedy,* the 1931 Sternberg film of the same name.

11. Richard Kayne, *Single Man at the Party* (opened April 21, 1959, and closed May 7). *Cue* (May 2, 1959) described the character as "a young Jewish boy from Brooklyn whom the movie moguls are carefully nurturing as the bobby-soxers' delight." *The New Yorker* (May 2, 1959) describes the heroine as "a Broadway ac-

tress who has slept with many men. The hero is a young movie star from Brooklyn who has also slept with many men but has now fallen in love with the actress. He sometimes worries about his integrity." A columnist exposes him. One review stresses the similarities to *Sweet Bird of Youth* by focusing on the older actress-star and the young man on the make—"The comedy-drama which concerns the plight of a once-famous movie queen when she meets and falls in love with a young actor bent on using her to further his career." But others highlight the gay male starlet. The play "has a Greenwich Village locale." Ruth Warwick, who played the actress, had also been in the stage version of *Miss Lonelyhearts* (presumably playing the Myrna Loy role).

12. LaGuardia, *Monty,* 71.

13. LaGuardia reports the line as "Don't cry, dear" (*Monty,* 71).

14. An article in the July 1950 *Photoplay* cites *Shoeshine* and *Bicycle Thieves* as two of Clift's favorite films and identifies him as "a staunch admirer of Vittorio de Sica, Italian director of 'The Bicycle Thief' *[sic]*" (Joseph Steele, "Restless Rebel," 48–49, 78).

15. Eleanor Harris, "Montgomery Clift: He Has Hollywood Baffled," *Compact: The Young People's Digest* (July 1957): 35. The term *young man* is qualified on the contents page: "Montgomery Clift has been around for quite a while, but hardly anyone has been able to discover anything about his personal life. Now at last you can read all about Hollywood's man of mystery."

16. LaGuardia, *Monty,* 137.

17. Bosworth, *Montgomery Clift,* 195.

18. Peters, *Design for Living* (see chap. 1, n. 9), 299.

19. Quoted in Hoskyns, *Montgomery Clift,* 100.

20. "Tourists in Quebec Throng to See Hitchcock Make Movie," *Boston Sunday Globe,* September 14, 1952. A French-language newspaper disagrees as to the actors' competence in French. Anne Baxter "parle un excellent français, Clift parle lui aussi, le français, mais avec plus de difficulté" ("Baxter speaks excellent French. Clift speaks it too, but with more difficulty."): Madeleine Fohy Saint-Hilaire, "On tourne [Shooting] dans les rues de Québec," *Photo Journal* (September 11, 1952).

21. Hoskyns, *Montgomery Clift,* 146.

22. Hoskyns, *Montgomery Clift,* 160.

23. Bosworth, *Montgomery Clift,* 123–25.

24. Truman Capote, *Answered Prayers* (New York: Random House, 1987), 99–109 at 104. A *New York Times* story puts Clift at another party where the guests were identified by their relation to alcohol. The reporter asks an Andy Warhol associate about "the wildest party" he and Warhol ever had. "The Judy Garland was the most fabulous one, with Nureyev and Tennessee Williams and Montgomery Clift. . . . It was the first time we ever had alcohol at the Factory, because Judy was coming. Because everybody—we just took amphetamines or

LSD or smoked grass or something. Nobody did alcohol. So we did a special setup, with whiskey and cubes, and she was totally happy" (Campbell Robertson, "Boldface," August 5, 2005, A 17).

25. Capote, *Answered Prayers*, 107.

26. Capote, *Answered Prayers*, 108, 109.

27. Lawrence H. Suid discusses the negotiations necessary to secure military cooperation in the production (access to barracks, airfields, planes, and personnel) in *Guts and Glory: Great American War Movies* (Reading, MA: Addison Wesley, 1978), 126–27.

28. Tornabene, "Montgomery Clift: Film's Fall Guy" (see intro., n. 17), 78.

29. James Jones, *From Here to Eternity* (New York: Charles Scribner's Sons, 1951). Angelo continues, "Wonderful things, gook shirts, aint they *[sic]*, Baby Doll? So loose and cool. Plenty of room to move. I love gook shirts. Do you love gook shirts?" (236). This "going to town" outfit is described earlier as the "undress uniform for town, the gook shirt and cheap slacks and two buck shoes" (150).

30. Bosworth, *Montgomery Clift*, 186.

31. Bosworth, *Montgomery Clift*, 186.

32. Bosworth, *Montgomery Clift*, 274.

33. Bosworth, *Montgomery Clift*, 186.

34. Bosworth, *Montgomery Clift*, 273.

35. In a list of unconnected factoids presumably provided by the star himself, Clift admits, "His beard is heavy and he has to shave twice a day when working" (Steele, "Restless Rebel," 78).

36. Jones, *From Here to Eternity*, 149.

37. Jones, *From Here to Eternity*, 464–66.

38. In the novel, when Prewitt fights Bloom (488–93), another topic is raised that never made it into the film—anti-Semitism. Bloom suspects that others think this way about him, but Prewitt wants to make it clear that that had nothing to do with the fight. "He had fought Bloom because he had had to fight somebody, or else bite himself and go mad" (499).

39. Bosworth mentions that when Clift lost twenty pounds for *The Young Lions*, he went from his usual "150 to 130 pounds" (*Montgomery Clift*, 315). Steele, "Restless Rebel," 78.

40. "Zinnemann felt the character needed 'spirit, particularly strong, indomitable spirit, a kind of nobility. And Monty had that beyond a question of a doubt, more than anybody I knew'" (Suid, *Guts and Glory*, 125).

41. Bosworth, *Montgomery Clift*, 249.

42. "They sent him back to the States. The Board recommended a yellow Dishonorable Discharge . . . [signifying] mentally unfit for service" (Jones, *From Here to Eternity*, 639).

43. Jones, *From Here to Eternity*, 657.

44. Quoted in Graham McGann, *Rebel Males: Clift, Brando, Dean* (New Brunswick, NJ: Rutgers University Press, 1993), 58.

45. Bosworth, *Montgomery Clift*, 320–21.

46. Bosworth, *Montgomery Clift*, 182.

47. Bosworth, *Montgomery Clift*, 319.

48. Bosworth, *Montgomery Clift*, 182.

49. Hoskyns, *Montgomery Clift*, 124.

50. Quoted in Hoskyns, *Montgomery Clift*, 114.

51. Brooks Clift, "Foreword," in Judith M. Kass, *The Films of Montgomery Clift* (Secaucus, NJ: Citadel Press, 1979), 7.

52. Richard Gehman quoted in Cohan, *Masked Men* (see intro., n. 15), 228.

53. Bosworth, *Montgomery Clift*, 162.

54. Bosworth, *Montgomery Clift*, 255–56.

55. The print on his shirt is still in production. Titled the Montgomery Clift print, it is available from Elukai, Honolulu, Hawaii.

56. The still photographer for the film was Irving Lippman. He may be the photographer of this shot (see color plates).

57. Jones, *From Here to Eternity*, 467–71, 474, 795.

58. Jones, *From Here to Eternity*, 789: "It was not true that all men killed the things they loved. What was true was that all things killed the men who loved them."

59. Steve Erickson, *Zeroville* (New York: Europa Editions, 2007). The designer of the book's cover substitutes a two-shot from a later scene in which George meets Angela in her car right after the idea of murder first occurs to him.

60. In light of the book's focus on Abraham, it is surprising that Nicholas Ray's film *Bigger Than Life* (1955) is not mentioned. Considering Vikar's reaction when people misread his tattoo as representing James Dean and Natalie Wood in *Rebel without a Cause* (1955), perhaps Erickson prefers to avoid Ray altogether.

61. Erickson, *Zeroville*, 320. Erickson's novel provides the clearest example I know of the generational specificity of cinephilia, a historical dimension suggested by Paul Willemen ("Through a Glass Darkly" [see chap. 1, n. 24]), Mary Ann Doane in *Emergence of Cinematic Time* (see chap. 1, n. 22), 225–29, and Christian Keathley in *Cinephilia and History* (see chap. 1, n. 25).

62. Clift quoted in Tornabene, "Montgomery Clift: Film's Fall Guy," 80.

FIVE. MORTIFICATION OF THE FLESH

1. Malden, *When Do I Start?* (see intro., n. 5), 229.

2. Hoskyns continues, "How could he have been so loved and so lonely?" (*Montgomery Clift* [see intro., n. 1], 6; my italics).

3. David Thomson, "Montgomery Clift," *The New Biographical Dictionary of Film* (New York: Alfred A. Knopf, 2002), 164.

4. The play was Chekhov's *The Seagull* (Bosworth, *Montgomery Clift* [see intro., n. 2], 265). *I Confess* was shot in the fall of 1952, *Indiscretion* in the winter of 1952–53, and *Eternity* in the spring of 1953.

5. Encarta. The full quote: "Actor Clift got in a car accident on the way home from a party at actor *[sic]* Taylor's house during the film's production. Though the accident didn't kill him, he was badly injured and partially paralyzed [his face], and the actor became subsequently addicted to painkillers and other drugs." This is listed under the heading "Trivia."

6. LaGuardia, *Monty* (see intro., n. 2), 149–54; Bosworth, *Montgomery Clift*, 297–99.

7. This appears in McGann's *Rebel Males* (see chap. 4, n. 44), 67–68, but is mostly a paraphrase from LaGuardia, *Monty*, 153–54. A substantial percentage of this chapter is plagiarized, the opening paragraph lifted from David Shipman, and the rest a patchwork of uncredited quotations from Bosworth, LaGuardia, Joan Mellen (*Big Bad Wolves* [New York: Pantheon, 1977]), Alexander Walker (*Stardom: The Hollywood Phenomenon* [New York: Stein and Day, 1970]), etc.

8. Mary Desjardins, "Star-Sick: Feminist Autopathography, Hollywood Stardom, and the Public Sphere," from the Society for Cinema and Media Studies panel "From Pathology to Hagiography: Imaging and Narrating the Suffering Body" (2001). See also Desjardins, chap. 5, "Star Bodies/Star Bios," in *Recycled Stars: Female Stardom in the Age of Television and Video* (forthcoming, Duke University Press).

9. LaGuardia, *Monty*, 182–83.

10. LaGuardia, *Monty*, 183.

11. Hoskyns, *Montgomery Clift*, 160.

12. Bosworth, *Montgomery Clift*, 350.

13. LaGuardia, *Monty*, 269.

14. Baty, *American Monroe* (see intro., n. 7), 162.

15. Baty, *American Monroe*, 146.

16. For Cohan, "The comparison to Garland repeats *the collapse of authenticity into performativity* that had always been central to the Clift persona" (*Masked Men* [see intro., n. 15], 226); my italics. The actor's "true self" is found in performing, and that willful persistence is heroic.

17. Jane Feuer, *The Hollywood Musical*, 2nd ed. (Bloomington: Indiana University Press, 1993), 119.

18. Cameron Shipp, "Hollywood's Most Shocking Rumor," *Photoplay* (1958): 87, quoted in Cohan, *Masked Men*, 225.

19. Desjardins, "Star-Sick."

20. Adrienne McLean, "A Special Relationship to Suffering: Judy Garland and the Kinesics of Pain," paper presented at the Society for Cinema Studies, 2001; quoting Dyer, *Heavenly Bodies* (see intro., n. 12), 155.

21. James Christopher, *Elizabeth Taylor: The Illustrated Biography* (London: Andre Deutsch, 1999), 50.

22. Montgomery Clift papers, Billy Rose Theatre Collection at the New York Public Library for the Performing Arts, box 14, folder 4, "Complete" script, November 22, 1955.

23. Montgomery Clift papers, NYPL, box 14A, folder 1, script marked "2–6–56" and stamped "Mar. 26, 1956," p. 7.

24. Montgomery Clift papers, NYPL, box 14A, folder 1, 7–9–56, p. 98A.

25. Montgomery Clift papers, NYPL, box 14, folder 5, p. 143. Other notes give the reader a glimpse into Clift's way of thinking as he works out a performance. For instance, he compares moments in the script of *Raintree County* to specific pages in the book. In the margins of the March 26, 1956, script, he writes "BUS" to indicate business, things the actor should do, or "pantomime" (box 14A, folder 1). For the scene in which he cracks a whip at men pursuing his friend the professor, he writes on the facing page, "coils whip earlier" (box 14A, folder 1, facing p. 72).

26. When John first meets Susanna (Elizabeth Taylor), he is supposed to continue his conversation with a photographer. Instead, when she says, "You're John Shawnessy," Clift has his character interrupt his conversation and stare in amazement at Taylor. "Say it again," he writes. Then he revises his rewrite: "Say that again."

27. Bosworth, *Montgomery Clift*, 313.

28. Bosworth, *Montgomery Clift*, 313.

29. Bosworth, *Montgomery Clift*, 327.

30. Bosworth, *Montgomery Clift*, 319.

31. Quoted in Bosworth, *Montgomery Clift*, 319–20.

32. Hoskyns, *Montgomery Clift*, 138.

33. Clift interviewed by Roderick Mann for *The Sunday Express,* August 16, 1959, quoted in Doug Tomlinson, ed., *Actors on Acting for the Screen: Roles and Collaborations* (New York: Garland, 1994), 99. See also Bosworth, *Montgomery Clift*, 315; LaGuardia, *Monty,* 120.

34. Quoted in Tomlinson, *Actors on Acting,* 99.

35. Quoted in Tomlinson, *Actors on Acting,* 99.

36. Hoskyns, *Montgomery Clift*, 8.

37. Quoted in Bosworth, *Montgomery Clift*, 319.

38. Bosworth, *Montgomery Clift*, 315.

39. Bosworth, *Montgomery Clift*, 328.

40. Bosworth, *Montgomery Clift*, 332.

41. Bosworth, *Montgomery Clift*, 333.

42. Stefan Kanfer, *A Journal of the Plague Years* (New York: Atheneum, 1973), 77–78.

43. Victor S. Navasky, *Naming Names* (New York: Viking Press, 1980), 180.

44. Bosworth, *Montgomery Clift*, 125–26.

45. Navasky, *Naming Names*, 201.

46. Navasky, *Naming Names*, 200–201. Witness the controversy (and audience reaction) fifty years later when Kazan received a lifetime achievement award from the Academy of Motion Picture Arts and Sciences.

47. Edward Dmytryk, *Odd Man Out: A Memoir of the Hollywood Ten* (Carbondale: Southern Illinois University Press, 1996), 191. According to Bosworth, Clift's drinking on the set of *Raintree* had been a problem well before the accident (*Montgomery Clift*, 294).

48. Elia Kazan, *Elia Kazan: A Life* (New York: Alfred A. Knopf, 1988), 574.

49. Kazan, *Elia Kazan*, 597.

50. Kazan, *Elia Kazan*, 598, 600.

51. Quoted in Richard Schickel, *Elia Kazan: A Biography* (New York: Harper-Collins Publishers, 2005), 369.

52. Quoted in Schickel, *Elia Kazan*, 368.

53. There is a suggestion that Clift's Chuck Glover is Jewish. The implied Klansman (Albert Salmi) repeatedly calls him by "Jewish" names like "Mr. Goldberg" and "Mr. Goldwyn." In its studied lack of ethnicity, "Chuck Glover" could well be an anglicized version of something else. Schickel, *Elia Kazan*, 365–70.

54. Kazan, *Elia Kazan*, 596–97.

55. David K. Johnson, *The Lavender Scare* (Chicago: University of Chicago Press, 2004), 17, 2.

56. Johnson *Lavender Scare*, 26, 7. In what was described as the "purge of perverts," gay men were denounced on the floor of the House of Representatives by Arthur Miller (no relation to the playwright), the Republican from Nebraska who authored the 1948 Miller Sexual Psychopath Law (2, 58). The assumption that gays and lesbians posed a security threat was "standard government policy until the 1970s" (4).

57. Johnson, *Lavender Scare*, 2.

58. See Kanfer, *Journal of the Plague Years*, 199.

59. Kanfer, *Journal of the Plague Years*, 199, 198. Robert J. Corber has discussed the equating of homosexuality with political subversion in films of this period; *In the Name of National Security: Hitchcock, Homophobia, and the Political Construction of Gender in Postwar America* (Durham, NC: Duke University Press, 1993).

60. Navasky, *Naming Names*, 75.

61. Navasky, *Naming Names*, 304. Robbins testified May 5, 1953.

62. Bosworth, *Montgomery Clift*, 155. LaGuardia also conceals Robbins's identity, referring only to "a famous homosexual choreographer" (*Monty*, 56).

63. Deborah Jowitt, *Jerome Robbins: His Life, His Times, His Dance* (Simon and Schuster, 2004); Greg Lawrence, *Dance with Demons: The Life of Jerome Robbins* (New York: G. P. Putnam's Sons, 2004).

64. Jowitt, *Jerome Robbins*, 146–47.

65. The quote is in Bosworth, *Montgomery Clift*, 154. This account confuses different periods, as Robbins testified in 1953 and he and Clift parted around 1948 or 1949. According to Kanfer, members of Robbins's own family wouldn't speak to Robbins after he testified (*Journal of the Plague Years*, 199, 204). Greg Lawrence captures the way anticommunism and homophobia overlapped by titling his chapter on this period, "Are You Now or Have You Ever Been?" (*Dance with Demons*, 119–28). Jowitt and Lawrence both mention that Robbins credited Clift with the idea for *West Side Story* (though both authors ultimately find the matter indeterminable).

66. Bosworth, *Montgomery Clift*, 241.

67. Bosworth, *Montgomery Clift*, 242.

68. Bosworth: "He gives a lively provocative performance, which also was perhaps his most sexual one" (*Montgomery Clift*, 246).

69. This was true not only in the fifties: examples from the 1980s and 1990s include Pee-wee Herman and George Michael.

70. Hoskyns, *Montgomery Clift*, 145.

71. Conversation with Mother Dolores Hart, June 2007.

72. Hart rebelled against Hollywood after having major roles in *King Creole* with Elvis Presley, directed by Michael Curtiz (1958); *Lonelyhearts* (1959) and *Where the Boys Are* (1960). When she left, it was to become a Benedictine nun in a cloistered order in Connecticut (the Abbey of Regina Laudis, Bethlehem).

73. Stapleton said of Clift in this scene, "He was so *there* half my work was done when I acted with him" (Bosworth, *Montgomery Clift*, 335).

74. Montgomery Clift papers, NYPL, box 12, folder 7, "Final Revised June 30, 1958"; box 12, folder 8, "Revised 7–16–58," p. 89.

75. Quoted in Bosworth, *Montgomery Clift*, 333.

76. In one version of the script of *The Misfits* Clift's character does not show up until p. 56, and in another version, p. 68 (Montgomery Clift papers, NYPL, box 13, folder 4 [p. 57 missing]; undated script, box 13, folder 6).

77. Arthur Miller, *The Misfits* (London: Penguin, 1961), 59. This is Miller's novelization of his screenplay.

78. Bosworth, *Montgomery Clift*, 334.

79. Dmytryk, *Odd Man Out*, 192.

80. Kazan, *Elia Kazan*, 600.

81. Quoted in Bosworth, *Montgomery Clift*, 347; my italics.

82. Bosworth, *Montgomery Clift*, 347.

83. Bosworth, *Montgomery Clift*, 215.

84. Bosworth, *Montgomery Clift*, 352.

85. LaGuardia prints the outrage, citing one critic who calls Miller "ghoulish and cold-blooded" (*Monty*, 217). Bosworth misdescribes the scene, saying Perce

is calling to tell his mother "she won't recognize his badly beaten face" (*Montgomery Clift*, 352)—just the opposite of what he says.

86. Cohan, *Masked Men*, 233.

87. Cohan, *Masked Men*, 233.

88. James Elkins, *Pictures of the Body: Pain and Metamorphosis* (Stanford, CA: Stanford University Press, 1999), 155; original italics.

89. Friedrich Kittler, "Gramophone, Film, Typewriter," trans. Dorothea von Mücke and Philippe Similon, *October* 41 (Summer 87): 110–11.

90. Naremore, *Acting in the Cinema* (see chap. 1, n. 7), 20.

91. Naremore, *Acting in the Cinema*, 20.

92. Bosworth, *Montgomery Clift*, 359.

93. These comments are on the November 1, 1960, revised version of the script, p. 65 (Montgomery Clift papers, NYPL, box 12, folder 2). There are several versions of the script: October 26, 1960; November 1, 1960; January 9, 1961; January 20, 1961; and February 27, 1961.

94. Montgomery Clift papers, NYPL, box 12, folder 2, script of November 1, 1960, p. 66.

95. Montgomery Clift papers, NYPL, box 12, folder 2, script of November 1, 1960, p. 72.

96. Montgomery Clift papers, NYPL, box 12, folder 2, script of November 1, 1960, p. 75.

97. Montgomery Clift papers, NYPL, box 12, folder 2, script of January 20, 1961, p. 75b.

98. Montgomery Clift papers, NYPL, box 12, folder 2, script of January 20, 1961, p. 75b.

99. Montgomery Clift papers, NYPL, box 12, folder 2, script of January 20, 1961, p. 75b.

100. Montgomery Clift papers, NYPL, box 12, folder 2, script of January 20, 1961, p. 75b.

101. Hoskyns, *Montgomery Clift*, 169.

102. Quoted in LaGuardia, *Monty*, 226.

103. Leitch, *Find the Director*, 160–61.

SIX. A GAY MARTYR

1. See Farmer, *Spectacular Passions* (see chap. 2, n. 32), 234–35.

2. Brill, *Hitchcock Romance* (see chap. 3, n. 129), 103.

3. Hoskyns, *Montgomery Clift* (see intro., n. 1), 158.

4. Hoskyns reports that it was Hepburn who felt "nauseated" and that Williams responded with "drunken laughter . . . when [producer] Sam Spiegel gave him a private screening" of the final cut (*Montgomery Clift*, 152).

5. Richard A. Kaye, "Losing His Religion: Saint Sebastian as Contemporary Gay Martyr," in *Outlooks: Lesbian and Gay Sexualities and Visual Culture,* ed. Peter Horne and Reina Lewis (New York: Routledge, 1996), 96.

6. D. A. Miller, "Visual Pleasure in 1959," *October* 81 (Summer 1997): 35–58; Kevin Ohi, "Devouring Creation: Cannibalism, Sodomy, and the Scene of Analysis in *Suddenly, Last Summer," Cinema Journal* 38, no. 3 (Spring 1999): 27–49.

7. Evidently, times had changed. The Legion of Decency, some of whose members had insisted on changes to the script of *I Confess,* did not condemn *Suddenly, Last Summer* (Gregory Black, *The Catholic Crusade against the Movies, 1940–1975* [London: Cambridge University Press, 1997], 186–91).

8. Foucault, *History of Sexuality* (see chap. 3, n. 61), 124.

9. LaGuardia, *Monty* (see intro., n. 2), 102.

10. Miller, "Visual Pleasure," 35.

11. Miller, "Visual Pleasure," 36.

12. Ohi, "Devouring Creation," 37.

13. Miller, "Visual Pleasure," 42. "The genie of homosexual desire . . . expands to such vaporously protean dimensions as enable [Sebastian] to envelop and saturate the very body that is, visually speaking, his appointed censor" (41).

14. Miller, "Visual Pleasure," 41.

15. Miller, "Visual Pleasure," 43.

16. Miller, "Visual Pleasure," 43.

17. Miller, "Visual Pleasure," 48.

18. Miller, "Visual Pleasure," 39.

19. Miller, "Visual Pleasure," 51.

20. Miller, "Visual Pleasure," 52.

21. Miller, "Visual Pleasure," 52, 53.

22. Ohi, "Devouring Creation," 44.

23. Ohi, "Devouring Creation," 39.

24. Ohi, "Devouring Creation," 39.

25. Miller, "Visual Pleasure," 47. Montgomery Clift papers, NYPL, box 5, folder 15, "First Draft Screenplay," *Suddenly Last Summer,* p. 37.

26. Ohi, "Devouring Creation," 41.

27. Ohi, "Devouring Creation," 44.

28. As transcribed in Ohi, "Devouring Creation," 44.

29. Ohi, "Devouring Creation," 44.

30. Ohi, "Devouring Creation," 39.

31. Ohi, "Devouring Creation," 37.

32. Ohi, "Devouring Creation," 37.

33. Ohi, "Devouring Creation," 37.

34. Ohi, "Devouring Creation," 48 n. 13.

35. Ohi, "Devouring Creation," 48 n. 13. The review is in *Time* (January 11, 1960): 66.

36. LaGuardia, *Monty*, 192. LaGuardia refers memorably to Clift as a "garbage-head," someone who would take anything. He might be better described as a pharmacological autodidact—someone who thinks he knows how to manage the correct dosage, and is aware of possible drug interactions and which drugs can be mixed with vodka or bourbon without being fatal.

37. Kaye, "Losing His Religion," 88.

38. The best source for images is the Web site The Iconography of Saint Sebastian.

39. Kaye, "Losing His Religion," 90. "Erotization" *[sic]*.

40. The Reni is surprisingly small. The film may prefer the Botticelli because it is full-length (head to toe).

41. Kaye, "Losing His Religion," 91. Kaye describes how Sebastian became an "embodiment of the transition whereby homosexual desire, once a theologically construed sin, was increasingly understood in the late-Victorian epoch as medical illness" (89).

42. Mishima re-created the pose from Reni's Sebastian, having himself photographed by Kishin Shinoyama in 1966 in a loincloth with his arms bound over his head as he hangs from a tree. According to Kaye, Sebastian "became a trope for artists linked to the aestheticist movement such as Gustave Moreau, Odilon Redon, Wilde and Beardsley" ("Losing His Religion," 88). Moreau did seven Sebastians between 1870 and 1875; Redon did four (1910–12). Many of these artists did self-portraits as Sebastian. Egon Schiele's 1915 self-portrait as Sebastian shows the artist in a striking red dressing gown, defiantly not dead, not suffering but swooning, sans arrows. Lastly, F. Holland Day took photographs of young boys as Sebastian; in blurry images in the pictorialist manner, a boy poses out in the woods, a single, soft-focus arrow barely visible (see Kaye, "Losing His Religion," 91–93).

43. Kaye, "Losing His Religion," 89.

44. Kaye, "Losing His Religion," 90.

45. Kaye, "Losing His Religion," 95. A cartoon by Sipress deals with the comic possibilities of playing the martyr. It shows a balding husband in loincloth, with four arrows sticking out of him and his eyes cast to the heavens as he enters a suburban living room. His wife, reading on the sofa, says, "O.K., Howard. What is it *this* time?" *The New Yorker* (October 7, 2002): 82.

46. Kaye, "Losing His Religion," 90.

47. Kaye, "Losing His Religion," 89; my italics.

48. This production was banned by the archbishop in Paris. In addition to the overall "tone," the bishop objected to the saint being played by a woman (dancer Ida Rubinstein), and furthermore, a woman who was not wearing tights but appeared bare-legged. She was also Jewish (Richard Shead, *Ballets Russes* [New York: Knickerbocker Press, 1998], 70; Kaye, "Losing His Religion," 88). A century later, representing religious figures in dance was still raising hackles. In April 2005 it

was reported that a "new ballet called 'Rasputin'" was picketed by Orthodox activists in Moscow who were "offended by the idea of a dancing tsar, of Nicholas II in ballet tights. The Tsar's family, after all, has just been canonized" (Marsha Lipman, "A Night at the Opera," *The New Yorker* [April 4, 2005]: 42).

49. Kaye, "Losing His Religion," 87.

50. Kaye, "Losing His Religion," 89.

51. William Faulkner, *Light in August* (New York: Modern Library/Random House, 1950), 429.

52. Kaye, "Losing His Religion," 87; italics original.

53. Richard Howard, "Concerning K," in *No Traveler: Poems* (New York: Knopf, 1989).

54. Kaye, "Losing His Religion," 101.

55. Kaye, "Losing His Religion," 87.

56. Bosworth, *Montgomery Clift* (see intro., n. 2), 386.

57. Bosworth, *Montgomery Clift*, 383. One of the consequences of Jerome Robbins refusing to let himself be identified by name in Bosworth's book is that the reader may infer Robbins's identity where it may not be. One example relates to this scene; Clift tells his friend that "long ago he'd been involved with a famous male dancer, 'a cold cruel man' who introduced him to the gay orgy scene" (383).

58. LaGuardia, *Monty*, 272. Tornabene also notes Clift's tendency to hunch "his shoulders . . . as though he were expecting to be hit" in "Montgomery Clift: Film's Fall Guy," 77 (see intro., n. 17).

59. Tornabene cites Clift's "penchant for emotional torment" and calls him the "high priest" of a "cult of torment" ("Montgomery Clift: Film's Fall Guy," 78, 80).

60. Arthur Laurents, *Original Story By: A Memoir of Broadway and Hollywood* (New York: Applause, 2000), 114. Laurents's memoir gives a vivid account of gay life in the postwar period. He also writes about working with Jerome Robbins and Elia Kazan before and after the HUAC period.

61. Laurents, *Original Story By*, 131.

62. Isherwood, *The Lost Years* (see chap. 1, n. 21), 174. This "reconstructed diary" was written as a draft of a memoir begun by Isherwood in 1971 (Bucknell, "Introduction," vii).

63. Isherwood, *The Lost Years*, 174. He adds, "They had met several times already—Clift having been introduced into the Viertel circle by Fred Zinnemann."

64. Christopher Isherwood, *Diaries*, vol. 1: *1939–1960*, ed. Katherine Bucknell (London: Methuen, 1996), 518.

65. Isherwood, *Diaries*, 1.649.

66. Isherwood, *Diaries*, 1.648.

67. Isherwood, *Diaries*, 1.727.

68. LaGuardia, *Monty*, 271.

69. Farmer, *Spectacular Passions*, 238.

70. Quoted in Farmer, *Spectacular Passions,* 239–40.

71. Farmer, *Spectacular Passions,* 240, quoting Richard Lippe, "Montgomery Clift: A Critical Disturbance," *CineAction!* 17 (Summer 1989): 37. Despite his sympathy for the actor, Richard Dyer links Clift explicitly to the pre-Stonewall figure of the homosexual as "sad young man" (*The Matter of Images,* 2nd ed. [New York: Routledge, 2002], 42).

72. Bosworth, *Montgomery Clift,* 341–42; LaGuardia, *Monty,* 205–10.

73. Lawrence Grobel, *The Hustons* (New York: Charles Scribner's Sons, 1989), 403–04.

74. The photo is between pages 428 and 429 in Grobel, *Hustons.*

75. Peters, *Design for Living* (see chap. 1, n. 9), 187.

76. Quoted in Bosworth, *Montgomery Clift,* 113.

77. Quoted in Bosworth, *Montgomery Clift,* 355. On the flyleaf of the book's cover, Rex Reed writes that Clark Gable "was reduced to being an insecure bigot in [Clift's] presence."

78. LaGuardia, *Monty,* 233.

79. LaGuardia, *Monty,* 233–34; Bosworth, *Montgomery Clift,* 363–64. "Early the next morning, Huston opened the door of the guest bedroom without knocking" (LaGuardia, *Monty,* 233). Bosworth and LaGuardia differ on Huston's relation to Clift. Bosworth says Huston fought Universal to have Clift cast as Freud (362), while LaGuardia quotes *Freud* screenwriter Walter Reinhardt's opinion: "I really think John would have fired Monty on the spot if Universal's backing hadn't depended so much on John's casting a major star like Monty in the role, and who else could John have found at that late date?" (234). Of course, Huston's passion to have Clift in the part could just as easily have fueled his horror.

80. Quoted in Grobel, *Hustons,* 506.

81. Grobel, *Hustons,* 506; italics original.

82. Grobel, *Hustons,* 506. This kind of reaction evokes Baty's description of the grotesque body ("open, protruding . . . secreting") as opposed to the "monumental, static, closed and sleek" classical body reminiscent of the bare-chested Clift in *From Here to Eternity* (Baty, *American Monroe* [see intro., n. 7], 150).

83. Grobel, *Hustons,* 506; my italics.

84. Grobel, *Hustons,* 512.

85. Hoskyns, *Montgomery Clift,* 176. It is also implied (though never stated) that Chuck Glover in *Wild River* is Jewish.

86. Bosworth, *Montgomery Clift,* 359.

87. Grobel also reports that, as on the set of *Beat the Devil,* Huston enjoyed raising and then denying rumors about himself, growling at the *Freud* crew, "I know you all think I'm a repressed fucking fag" (*Hustons,* 513).

88. Quoted from a 1957 interview with Pati Hill in *The Paris Review,* in turn quoted in Grobel, *Hustons,* 403.

89. Montgomery Clift papers, NYPL, box 9, folder 2, "Call Sheet."

90. Grobel, *Hustons,* 515.

91. LaGuardia, *Monty,* 242–43.

92. Bosworth, *Montgomery Clift,* 369.

93. Rosalie Crutchley, who worked mostly in British television, was born in January 1920, Clift in October.

94. Parks made only one film in the United States in the fifties and two in England (in 1950 and 1952). *Freud* was not only his last film; he did no television work after this either, working instead on stage with his wife, Betty Garrett.

95. Kaye, "Losing His Religion," 89.

96. Foucault, *History of Sexuality,* 124.

97. Foucault, *History of Sexuality,* 124.

98. LaGuardia, *Monty,* 202–04. LaGuardia reports that Clift's own agent, Lew Wasserman, was telling people not to hire Clift after *Lonelyhearts.*

99. Hoskyns, *Montgomery Clift,* 172.

SEVEN. NOTHING SACRED

1. Louella O. Parsons, "Offer Priest Role to Montgomery Clift," syndicated newspaper column, March 17, 1954.

2. LaGuardia, *Monty* (see intro., n. 2), 203.

3. LaGuardia, *Monty,* 202–03.

4. He also said no to the washed-up theatrical has-been (never-was) played by Gene Kelly in *Marjorie Morningstar.*

5. Clift files at the Margaret Herrick Library at the Academy of Motion Picture Arts and Sciences, Beverly Hills, CA.

6. Mary C. Kalfatovic, *Montgomery Clift: A Bio-Bibliography* (Westport, CT: Greenwood Press, 1994), 266. She also lists, as roles Clift turned down, James Mason's role in *A Star Is Born* (265) and Bobby Darin's in *Too Late Blues* in 1962 (266). Hoskyns states that "George Stevens short-listed [Clift] for the role of Jesus" but does not list his sources (*Montgomery Clift* [see intro., n. 1], 98).

7. *Screen Parade* in 1960 is still looking to assign blame, calling Clift "The Man Who Gave away His Soul."

8. Waugh, *Fruit Machine* (see chap. 4, n. 4), 95.

9. Bosworth, *Montgomery Clift* (see intro., n. 2), 211. Evidently threats of legal action were sufficient for Anger's publishers, but it seems as if Clift would not have had a good case. Anger couched his allegations carefully, saying that some people referred to Clift in a derogatory way. Anger would not have to prove that the accusation was true; he would just have to find someone who had used or heard it used in reference to Clift.

10. Originally reported in the *New York Post,* July 29, 1983, quoted in Kalfatovic, *Montgomery Clift,* 261.

11. According to Hoskyns, "The *New York Post* reported the story with a pre-

dictable mixture of indignation and glee" (*Montgomery Clift*, 188). The West Coast "coroner to the stars" Thomas Noguchi also found himself in trouble "for leaking to the press information about the deaths of stars" (Baty, *American Monroe* [see intro., n. 7], 165–66). Baty discusses Noguchi's capitalizing on his autopsy of Marilyn Monroe ("his gateway to mass-mediated life") at 163–71.

12. Richard Kaye notes that "the American rock group R.E.M. chose Saint Sebastian as the unifying figure in their 1991 award-winning video for the group's song 'Losing My Religion' in which the lead singer Michael Stipe sings and performs a solitary dance amid an array of Saint Sebastians modeled on pop images vaguely adopted from Renaissance painting. This lyrically emotive video, shot by the Indian director Tarsem, was at once a mournful meditation on the difficulties of revealing an illness, a lament on the results of announcing one's homosexuality, and a coyly knowing autobiographical confession of gay self-identification at the heart of rock-music culture" ("Losing His Religion" [see chap. 6, n. 5], 99).

13. Richard Howard, "Concerning K" (see chap. 6, n. 53), 62.

14. Like Rock Hudson, Clift liked to watch his old films and show them to his friends. A legal memo from 1960, documenting Clift's request to borrow a print of *The Heiress* from Paramount, was offered on eBay in 2006.

15. LaGuardia's discussion of the 1964 *Menagerie* is one sentence long: "It is difficult to believe that any actor could outdo Monty's seemingly casual, but subtle reading of Tom's introductory narration" (*Monty*, 273).

16. Jeffrey Sconce, *Haunted Media* (Durham, NC: Duke University Press, 2000), 59–91.

17. Judith Kass reports that Clift took money from his parents "rather than act in radio, which he detested" (*Films of Montgomery Clift* [see chap. 4, n. 51], 34).

18. "Wuthering Heights," *Ford Theater*, April 1, 1949.

19. These radio plays are now available on CD. The "high voice" effect may in fact be due to the sound being played at the wrong speed. While the speed can be altered, this is the condition in which the text currently exists.

20. Albert J. LaValley, discussion with author.

21. "Producers' Choice," production folio, *Tennessee Williams The Glass Menagerie*, produced by Caedmon Records for the Theatre Recording Society, 1964.

22. "Producers' Choice."

23. Hoskyns, *Montgomery Clift*, 188. Hoskyns explicitly compares them: "An interfering old Helen Hayes is probably as close as we will get to imagining what the ageing Sunny Clift was like" (180).

24. Hoskyns, *Montgomery Clift*, 23.

25. Quoted in Adam Goldman, "Cooke's End Didn't Dim His Memory," *Valley News*, June 12, 2006, A2.

26. Roland Barthes, *Image-Music-Text,* trans. and ed. Stephen Heath (New York: Hill and Wang, 1977), 182–83.

27. Barthes, *Image-Music-Text,* 188. "The climactic pleasure hoped for," he insists, is the loss of "the psychological 'subject' in me who is listening" (188).

28. Mladen Dolar, *A Voice and Nothing More* (Cambridge, MA: MIT Press, 2006), 148.

29. Dolar, *A Voice,* 71.

30. What we see is "a world beyond representation which only shimmers through in certain moments of the film" (Willemen, "Through a Glass Darkly" [see chap. 1, n. 25], 241); Dolar, *A Voice,* 71.

31. Klinger, *Beyond the Multiplex* (see chap. 1, n. 53), 175, 177.

32. Dolar, *A Voice,* 81; italics original.

33. *Montgomery Clift: The Hidden Star* (1996), written and directed by John Griffin, A&E Television Networks.

34. Dolar, *A Voice,* 80.

35. Carson McCullers, who wrote *Reflections in a Golden Eye,* had been the original screenwriter of *Indiscretion of an American Wife* (Bosworth, *Montgomery Clift,* 243). Only a couple of lines in the novel evoke Clift, mostly negatively. His character's face is described as "habitually tense and a tic had developed in the muscles of his left eye. This spasmodic twitching of the eyelid gave to his drawn face a strangely paralyzed expression" ([Cambridge, MA: Houghton Mifflin/ Riverside Press, 1941], 155). We are told that in the captain's fantasies "he saw himself as a youth, a twin almost of the soldier whom he hated—with a young, easy body that even the cheap uniform of a common soldier could not make ungraceful, with thick glossy hair and round eyes unshadowed by study and strain" (157). On the last page, having murdered the object of his obsession, the captain is described this way: "In his queer, coarse wrapper, he resembled a broken and dissipated monk" (183).

36. Hoskyns quotes Andrew Sarris's assessment of Clift in the film, which replaces his acting with his body: "Clift is dreadful, a hollow, ravaged, trembling hulk of the actor he'd once been" (*Montgomery Clift,* 184).

37. Clift quoted in Tornabene, "Montgomery Clift: Film's Fall Guy" (see intro., n. 17), 80.

38. Bosworth says Clift and Rostova hadn't worked together since 1955, but Kazan remembers her being on the set of *Wild River* (Kazan, *Elia Kazan* [see chap. 5, n. 48], 600).

39. Bosworth, *Montgomery Clift,* 243, 245.

40. Hoskyns quotes this line as proof that Giovanni is "an archetypal Italian chauvinist," but that is not at all the way Clift reads the line (*Montgomery Clift,* 104).

41. Adrienne L. McLean, "The Cinderella Princess and the Instrument of Evil:

Surveying the Limits of Female Transgression in Two Postwar Hollywood Scandals," *Cinema Journal* 34, no. 3 (Spring 1995): 36–56 at 50.

42. Bosworth, *Montgomery Clift*, 246.

43. Bogdanovich, *Who the Hell's in It?* (see chap. 1, n. 3), 93.

44. Bogdanovich, *Who the Hell's in It?* 92–96.

45. This mirrored absorption may be what Barish means when he refers to "the twin roles of actor and spectator" (*Antitheatrical Prejudice* [see chap. 1, n. 50], 167).

46. Quoted in LaGuardia, *Monty,* 179; quoted in Kass, *Films of Montgomery Clift,* 213.

47. Hoskyns, *Montgomery Clift,* 189. Hoskyns adds about the obituary, "One wonders how much Monty's portrayal of Father Logan in *I Confess* influenced the writer." Brooks Clift reads the same obituary in the documentary *The Rebels: Montgomery Clift* (1986), directed by Claudio Masenza.

INDEX

Page numbers in italics indicate photographs.

broadcast), 263; in *The Misfits*, 205–08, 279, 312n85; in *A Place in the Sun*, 70, 208–10, 284; in *Raintree County*, 181–84; in *Red River*, 37–46, 220, 284; in *The Search*, 15–19, 28; in *Suddenly, Last Summer*, 223–24, 228–31, 244, 251, 285; in *Terminal Station*, 278–81; in *Wild River*, 190–92, 285; in *Wuthering Heights* (radio), 58–59, 263; in *The Young Lions*, 186–89, 268–69, 285

as actor, 2, 3, 5, 6, 7, 8, 9, 12, 13, 14, 16–20, 46–49, 56, 61, 65, 81, 86, 89, 103, 118, 142, 158, 167–68, 174, 175, 180, 208, 212, 213, 217, 239, 252, 256, 259, 260, 263, 275, 283, 284–86, 298nn50,1, 305n1

and alcohol, 2, 7, 141, 148–52, 178–80, 182, 190–91, 193, 202–03, 212, 218, 235–38, 241, 243, 255, 257, 264, 285, 305n1, 306n24, 311n47, 315n36

assumed to be Jewish, 241–42, 305n11, 311n53 (*see also* anti-Semitism)

beauty of, 1, 2, 9, 12, 25, 36, 40, 53, 180–81, 184, 216, 234, 237, 252, 259, 272, 280, 283, 298n49

body of, 156–59, 163–64, 168, 175, 181, 183, 186–87, 199–200, 208, 211, 212, 215–16, 231, 235, 240–43, 252, 256, 257, 259, 260, 274–75, 283, 284, 285, 307nn35,39, 317n82, 318n9, 320nn35–36

car accident of, 2, 6, 7, 8, 9, 174, 177–81, 184, 186–87, 189, 208, 211, 232, 234, 235, 237, 238, 257, 260, 261, 285, 292n62, 309n5, 311n47

death of, 2, 3, 8, 28, 142, 179, 237, 253, 259–60, 273, 284–86, 318n11

disappearance of, 184

drugs and, 2, 141, 149, 151, 180–81, 190, 193, 197–98, 203, 215, 218, 231, 235, 238, 241, 243, 257, 260, 285, 305n1, 309n5, 315n36

injuries of, 8, 40, 68, 144, 149, 178–81, 186, 187, 189, 205, 207–08, 211–12, 216, 237, 274, 285, 297n43, 309n5, 312n85

military service, disqualified, 62, 178

notes on scripts, revising, 19–20, 21, 123–24, 149, 170, 182–83, 186, 194, 201, 205, 213–15, 226, 229, 242, 301n57, 310n25

political views of, 8, 194–95, 197, 234

radio work of, 58–59, 261–70, 319n17

as rebel, 2, 46, 255

as religious figure: as martyr, 2, 3, 5, 7, 8, 217, 218, 234, 235–38, 253, 259, 260, 271, 284; as saint, 1, 2, 4–7, 20, 27, 34, 53, 86, 94, 138, 174, 177, 234, 236, 259, 271, 283, 285, 316n58

sexuality of, 2, 7, 141–52, 190, 193–97, 217–20, 224, 231, 234–41, 257, 259, 276–77, 285, 305nn1,11, 316n57

suffering of, 2, 5, 7, 55–56, 61, 177, 179, 180, 183, 186, 190, 205, 207–08, 211–12, 234, 237, 238, 259, 296n36, 316n59

theater work of, 12–14, 38, 59–60, 177, 193, 261, 263

as "tragic" victim, 2, 6, 141, 143, 212, 217, 236, 237, 252–53, 259, 308n2

voice of, 4, 7, 17, 18–19, 43, 58, 66, 84, 96–97, 125, 170, 184, 199, 200, 206–07, 222, 226, 244, 249, 251, 261–73, 278, 280, 283, 284, 285, 298n1, 319n19

Clift, Sunny (mother), 267, 289n15, 319n23

Clift, William (father), 195

Cohan, Steve, 6, 56, 75, 157–58, 179, 209–10, 239, 294n91, 298nn48–49, 309n16

Cohn, Harry, 149, 164

Columbia, 149

Compact: The Young People's Digest, 147, 306n15

confession. *See* religion, ritual and confession

Confessional, Le (1995), 111, 304n122

Confessions of a Mask, 233

Cooke, Alistair, 270

Coquelin, Constant, 110, 302n83

Corber, Robert J., 311n59

Corey, Wendell, 16, *17*

Cosmopolitan (magazine), 257

Text: 11.25/13.5 Adobe Garamond
Display: Adobe Garamond, Perpetua
Compositor: Integrated Composition Systems
Printer and Binder: Thomson-Shore, Inc.